Treasury of Christmas Recipes

From Your Favorite Brand Name Companies

JELL-O®

HERSHEY'S®

Velveeta

Dole®

Baker's®

EAGLE®BRAND

Miracle Whip

Plus Many More

Treasury of Christmas Recipes

From Your Favorite Brand Name Companies

PUBLICATIONS INTERNATIONAL, LTD.

Manufactured in USA.
h g f e d c b a

ISBN 0-88176-713-1

Library of Congress Catalog Card Number: 89-62188

Pictured on the front cover (*clockwise from top left*): Double-
Decker Fudge (*page 71*), Turkey with Apple Citrus Stuffing
(*page 44*), Cream Cheese Cutout Cookies (*page 68*),
Chocolate Pixies (*page 71*), Fruit-Filled Thumbprints
(*page 75*), Holiday Egg Nog (*page 10*), Christmas Tree Cake
(*page 66*).

Pictured on the back cover (*top to bottom*): Classic Christmas
Cake (*page 57*), Turkey Cranberry Croissant (*page 51*), Hot
Broccoli Dip (*page 4*), Cinnamon-Raisin Swirl Loaf (*page 21*),
Cherry Waldorf Gelatin (*page 33*).

This holiday collection of recipes is a compilation of
many of your favorite brand name recipes previously
published in Favorite Recipes™ magazine. Gathered into
this one convenient source are not only those most
requested favorites but also tempting new holiday recipes
from these same brand name companies.

Contents

Appetizers, Soups & Beverages

■ Hot Broccoli Dip

6 to 8 servings

- 1 1½-lb. round sourdough bread loaf
- ½ cup finely chopped celery
- ½ cup chopped red pepper
- ¼ cup finely chopped onion
- 2 tablespoons PARKAY Margarine
- 1 lb. VELVEETA Pasteurized Process Cheese Spread, cubed
- 1 10-oz. pkg. frozen chopped broccoli, thawed, drained
- ¼ teaspoon dried rosemary leaves, crushed

Cut slice from top of bread loaf; remove center leaving 1-inch shell. Cut removed bread into bite-size pieces. Cover shell with top. Place on cookie sheet with bread pieces. Bake at 350°, 15 minutes or until hot. In large skillet, saute celery, peppers and onions in margarine. Reduce heat to low. Add process cheese spread; stir until melted. Stir in remaining ingredients; heat thoroughly, stirring constantly. Spoon into bread loaf. Serve hot with toasted bread pieces and vegetable dippers.

Preparation time: 15 minutes

Baking time: 15 minutes

Microwave: Prepare bread loaf as directed. Combine celery, peppers, onions and margarine in 2-quart microwave-safe bowl. Microwave on High 1 minute. Add remaining ingredients; microwave on High 5 to 6 minutes or until hot, stirring after 3 minutes. Spoon into bread loaf. Serve hot with toasted bread pieces and vegetable dippers.

■ Country Italian Soup

Makes about 8 (1-cup) servings

- 1 tablespoon oil
- ½ pound boneless beef, cut into 1-inch cubes
- 1 can (14½ ounces) whole peeled tomatoes, undrained and chopped
- 1 envelope LIPTON® Onion or Beefy Mushroom Recipe Soup Mix
- 3 cups water
- 1 medium onion, cut into chunks
- 1 large stalk celery, cut into 1-inch pieces
- ½ cup sliced carrot
- 1 cup cut green beans
- 1 can (16 ounces) chick peas or garbanzos, rinsed and drained
- ½ cup sliced zucchini
- ¼ cup uncooked elbow macaroni
- ¼ teaspoon oregano

In large saucepan or stockpot, heat oil and brown beef over medium-high heat. Add tomatoes, then onion recipe soup mix blended with water. Simmer uncovered, stirring occasionally, 30 minutes. Add onion, celery, carrot and green beans. Simmer uncovered, stirring occasionally, 30 minutes. Stir in remaining ingredients and simmer uncovered, stirring occasionally, an additional 15 minutes or until vegetables and macaroni are tender. Serve, if desired, with grated Parmesan cheese.

Hot Broccoli Dip

■ Wisconsin Cheese 'n Beer Soup

Makes about 4 (1-cup) servings

2 tablespoons butter or margarine
2 tablespoons all-purpose flour
1 envelope LIPTON® Golden Onion Recipe
    Soup Mix
3 cups milk
1 teaspoon Worcestershire sauce
1 cup shredded Cheddar cheese (about
    4 ounces)
½ cup beer
1 teaspoon prepared mustard

In medium saucepan, melt butter and cook flour over medium heat, stirring constantly, 3 minutes or until bubbling. Stir in golden onion recipe soup mix thoroughly blended with milk and Worcestershire sauce. Bring just to the boiling point, then simmer, stirring occasionally, 10 minutes. Stir in remaining ingredients and simmer, stirring constantly, 5 minutes or until cheese is melted. Garnish, if desired, with additional cheese, chopped red pepper and parsley.

Wisconsin Cheese 'n Beer Soup

■ Baked Artichoke Squares

Makes 24 appetizers

½ cup plus 3 tablespoons CRISCO® Oil,
    divided
1 cup chopped mushrooms
¼ cup thinly sliced celery
1 clove garlic, minced
1 can (13¾ ounces) artichoke hearts,
    drained, chopped
⅓ cup chopped green onions
½ teaspoon dried marjoram, crushed
¼ teaspoon dried oregano, crushed
¼ teaspoon ground red pepper
1 cup (4 ounces) shredded Cheddar cheese
1 cup (4 ounces) shredded Monterey Jack
    cheese
2 eggs, slightly beaten
1½ cups all-purpose flour
½ teaspoon salt
¼ cup milk

Heat 3 tablespoons of the CRISCO oil in medium skillet over medium-high heat. Cook and stir mushrooms, celery and garlic in hot oil until celery is tender. Remove from heat. Stir in artichoke hearts, onions, marjoram, oregano and ground red pepper. Add cheeses and eggs; mix well. Set aside.

Combine flour and salt in medium bowl. Blend remaining ½ cup CRISCO oil and the milk in small bowl. Add to flour mixture. Stir with fork until mixture forms a ball. Press dough in bottom and 1½ inches up sides of 13×9×2-inch pan. Bake in preheated 350°F oven 10 minutes. Spread artichoke mixture on baked crust. Continue baking about 20 minutes more or until center is set. Cool slightly. Cut into 24 squares. Serve warm.

■ Kahlúa® Hot Spiced Apple Cider

Makes 1 serving

1½ ounces KAHLÚA®
1 cup hot apple cider or apple juice
1 cinnamon stick

Pour KAHLÚA® into hot cider. Stir with cinnamon stick.

Traditional Party Mix

■ Traditional Party Mix

Makes 9 cups

¼ cup (½ stick) margarine
1¼ teaspoons seasoned salt
4½ teaspoons worcestershire sauce
2⅔ cups CORN CHEX® Brand Cereal
2⅔ cups RICE CHEX® Brand Cereal
2⅔ cups WHEAT CHEX® Brand Cereal
1 cup salted mixed nuts
1 cup pretzel sticks

Preheat oven to 250°. In open roasting pan melt margarine in oven. Remove. Stir in seasoned salt and worcestershire sauce. Gradually add cereals, nuts and pretzels, stirring until all pieces are evenly coated. Bake 1 hour, stirring every 15 minutes. Spread on absorbent paper to cool. Store in airtight container.

*Microwave Directions:** In a 4-quart bowl or 13×9×2-inch microwave-safe dish melt margarine on HIGH 1 minute. Stir in seasoned salt and worcestershire sauce. Gradually add cereals, nuts and pretzels, stirring until all pieces are evenly coated. Microwave on HIGH 5 to 6 minutes, stirring every 2 minutes. Spread on absorbent paper to cool. Store in airtight container.

Due to differences in microwave ovens, cooking time may need adjustment. These directions were developed using 625 to 700 watt ovens.

Christmas Punch

■ Christmas Punch

Makes 8 to 9 cups

    5 cups DOLE® Pineapple Juice
    1 bottle (24 oz.) sparkling apple juice or
       champagne
ICE MOLD
    1 can (20 oz.) DOLE® Pineapple Chunks
    1 orange, sliced, quartered
    1 pint strawberries or bottled maraschino
       cherries
    Mint sprigs

Chill punch ingredients. Combine in punch bowl.
Float ice mold when ready to serve.

Ice mold: Combine undrained pineapple, fruit
and mint in 6-cup mold. Add enough water or
juice to fill. Freeze.

■ Stuffed Mushrooms Italiano

Makes about 24 appetizers

    1 pound large mushrooms
    ¼ cup WISH-BONE® Italian or Caesar
       Dressing
    1 cup fresh bread crumbs
    ¼ cup grated Parmesan cheese
    1 tablespoon finely chopped parsley

Remove and finely chop mushroom stems.
Combine dressing, bread crumbs, cheese, parsley
and chopped mushroom stems in medium bowl.
Fill each mushroom cap with bread crumb
mixture; arrange in shallow baking dish. Add
water to barely cover bottom of dish. Bake in
preheated 350°F oven 20 minutes.

■ Port Cheddar Cheese Spread

Makes about 3 cups

   4 cups (1 pound) shredded sharp Cheddar
      cheese
   ¼ cup butter or margarine, softened
   ¼ cup dairy sour cream
   2 tablespoons port wine
   ¼ teaspoon ground mace
   ⅛ teaspoon ground red pepper
   1 cup chopped toasted walnuts
      Assorted vegetables for dippers
      Assorted crackers

Combine cheese, butter, sour cream, wine, mace
and ground red pepper in food processor. Cover
and process until smooth. Mix in walnuts.
Refrigerate, covered, several days to allow flavors
to mellow. Soften slightly at room temperature
before serving. Serve with assorted vegetables and
crackers.

Favorite Recipe from **Walnut Marketing Board**

■ Kahlúa® Parisian Coffee

Makes 1 serving

   1 ounce cognac or brandy
   ½ ounce KAHLÚA®
   ½ ounce Grand Marnier
      Hot coffee
      Whipped cream
      Orange peel (optional)

Pour cognac, KAHLÚA® and Grand Marnier into
steaming cup of coffee. Top with whipped cream.
Garnish with orange peel.

■ Hot Spiced Wine

Makes about 2½ quarts, about 16 (5-ounce) servings

   1 quart water
   2 cups sugar
   25 whole cloves
   3 cinnamon sticks
   ½ lemon, peeled
   1 bottle (1.5 L) CRIBARI® Zinfandel

Combine water, sugar, spices and lemon in
medium saucepan. Boil over medium-high heat
until mixture is syrupy. Reduce heat to low. Add
wine; simmer 5 minutes. Do not let wine boil.

■ Easy Vegetable Squares

Makes 32 appetizer servings

   2 8-ounce packages refrigerated crescent
      rolls (16 rolls)
   1 8-ounce package cream cheese, softened
   1 3-ounce package cream cheese, softened
   ⅓ cup mayonnaise *or* salad dressing
   1 teaspoon dried dillweed
   1 teaspoon buttermilk salad dressing mix
      (¼ of a 0.4-ounce package)
   3 cups desired toppings (see below)
   1 cup shredded Wisconsin Cheddar,
      Mozzarella, *or* Monterey Jack cheese

For crust, unroll crescent rolls and pat into a
15½×10½×2-inch baking pan. Bake according to
package directions. Cool.

Meanwhile, in a small mixing bowl stir together
the cream cheese, mayonnaise, dillweed, and
salad dressing mix. Spread evenly over cooled
crust. Sprinkle with desired toppings, then the
shredded Cheddar, Mozzarella, or Monterey Jack
cheese.

Topping options: finely chopped broccoli,
cauliflower, *or* green pepper; seeded and
chopped tomato; thinly sliced green onion, black
olives, *or* celery; *or* shredded carrots.

Preparation time: 20 minutes

Favorite Recipe from **Wisconsin Milk Marketing Board** © 1989

Easy Vegetable Squares

■ Party Chicken Sandwiches

Makes 3 dozen

1½ cups finely chopped cooked chicken
1 cup MIRACLE WHIP Salad Dressing
1 4-oz. can chopped green chilies, drained
¾ cup (3 ozs.) 100% Natural KRAFT Shredded
   Sharp Cheddar Cheese
¼ cup finely chopped onion
36 party rye or pumpernickel bread slices

Combine chicken, salad dressing, chilies, cheese
and onions; mix lightly. Cover bread with chicken
mixture. Broil 5 minutes or until lightly browned.
Serve hot. Garnish as desired.

Preparation time: 15 minutes

Broiling time: 5 minutes

Variation: Substitute MIRACLE WHIP Light
Reduced Calorie Salad Dressing for Regular Salad
Dressing.

■ Coffee Egg Nog Punch

Makes about 1½ quarts

3 cups BORDEN® or MEADOW GOLD® Milk
1 (14-ounce) can EAGLE® Brand Sweetened
   Condensed Milk (NOT evaporated milk)
4 eggs*
3 to 4 teaspoons instant coffee
⅓ cup bourbon
⅓ cup coffee-flavored liqueur
1 cup (½ pint) BORDEN® or MEADOW GOLD®
   Whipping Cream, whipped
Dash ground cinnamon
Dash ground nutmeg

In large mixer bowl, combine milk, sweetened
condensed milk, eggs and coffee; beat on low
speed until coffee dissolves. Stir in bourbon and
liqueur; chill. Before serving, top with whipped
cream, cinnamon and nutmeg. Refrigerate
leftovers.

Holiday Egg Nog: Omit instant coffee and coffee-
flavored liqueur. Increase bourbon to ½ cup; add
1 teaspoon vanilla extract. Proceed as above.

Use only Grade A clean, uncracked eggs.

■ Creamy Broccoli Soup

Five 1-cup servings

¼ cup chopped onion
1 tablespoon PARKAY Margarine
2 cups milk
1 8-oz. pkg. PHILADELPHIA BRAND Cream
   Cheese, cubed
¾ lb. VELVEETA Pasteurized Process Cheese
   Spread, cubed
1 10-oz. pkg. frozen chopped broccoli,
   cooked, drained
¼ teaspoon ground nutmeg
   Dash of pepper

In 2-quart saucepan, saute onions in margarine
until tender. Reduce heat to medium. Add milk
and cream cheese; stir until cream cheese is
melted. Add remaining ingredients; heat
thoroughly, stirring occasionally.

Preparation time: 15 minutes

Cooking time: 15 minutes

Variations: Substitute frozen chopped spinach
for broccoli.

Substitute frozen cauliflower, chopped, for
broccoli.

Substitute frozen asparagus spears, chopped, for
broccoli.

Microwave: Microwave onions and margarine in
2-quart microwave-safe bowl on High 30 seconds
or until onions are tender. Add milk; microwave
on High 4 minutes, stirring after 2 minutes. Stir in
cream cheese; microwave on High 4 to 6 minutes
or until cream cheese is melted, stirring every 2
minutes. Stir in remaining ingredients; microwave
on High 30 seconds or until thoroughly heated.

Party Chicken Sandwiches

■ Shrimp Spread

Makes 2 cups

- 1 8-oz. pkg. PHILADELPHIA BRAND Cream Cheese, softened
- ½ cup MIRACLE WHIP Salad Dressing
- 1 4¼-oz. can tiny cocktail shrimp, drained, rinsed
- ⅓ cup finely chopped onion
- ⅛ teaspoon garlic salt

Combine cream cheese and salad dressing, mixing until well blended. Stir in remaining ingredients. Cover; chill. Serve with assorted crackers.

Preparation time: 10 minutes plus chilling

Shrimp Spread

■ Mexi-Beef Bites

Makes 36 appetizers

- 1 pound ground beef
- 1 cup (4 ounces) shredded Cheddar cheese
- 1 cup (4 ounces) shredded Monterey Jack cheese
- 1 can (4 ounces) chopped green chilies, drained
- ½ cup bottled green taco or enchilada sauce
- 2 large eggs, beaten
  Tortilla chips (optional)

Cook and stir beef in large skillet over medium-high heat until beef loses pink color. Pour off drippings. Stir in cheeses, chilies, taco sauce and eggs. Transfer mixture to 8×8-inch baking pan. Bake at 350°F 35 to 40 minutes or until knife inserted in center comes out clean and top is golden brown. Cool in pan 15 minutes. Cut into 36 squares. Serve with tortilla chips.

Favorite Recipe from **National Live Stock and Meat Board**

■ Hot Holiday Punch

Makes 8 (8-ounce) servings

- 1 cup granulated sugar
- ½ cup packed brown sugar
- 4 cups apple cider
- 1 cinnamon stick
- 12 whole cloves
- 2 cups Florida Grapefruit Juice
- 2 cups Florida Orange Juice
  Orange slices
  Maraschino cherry halves (optional)
  Whole cloves (optional)

Combine sugars and apple cider in large saucepan. Heat over medium heat, stirring until sugars dissolve. Add cinnamon stick and cloves. Bring to a boil over medium heat. Reduce heat to low; simmer 5 minutes. Add grapefruit and orange juices. Heat, but do not boil. Strain into heatproof punch bowl. Garnish with orange slices decorated with maraschino cherry halves and whole cloves. Serve in heatproof punch cups.

Vegetable Meat Stew

■ Vegetable Meat Stew

Makes 6 servings

   2 tablespoons all-purpose flour
1½ teaspoons salt
   1 teaspoon AC'CENT® Flavor Enhancer
⅛ teaspoon pepper
   1 pound beef stew meat
   3 tablespoons vegetable oil
¼ cup chopped onion
   3 cups water
   1 clove garlic, minced
   1 bay leaf
   1 teaspoon dried thyme, crushed
   4 small potatoes, pared, cubed
   4 carrots, chopped, or 12 mini-carrots, pared
   1 cup frozen peas, thawed
½ cup PET® Evaporated Milk

Combine flour, salt, AC'CENT Flavor Enhancer and pepper in shallow dish. Dredge meat in flour mixture; reserve excess flour mixture. Brown meat in hot oil in Dutch oven over medium-high heat. Sprinkle any remaining flour mixture over meat. Toss to coat meat. Add onion; cook until onion is limp. Add water, garlic, bay leaf and thyme. Bring to a boil over high heat. Reduce heat to low. Cover and simmer 1 hour. Add potatoes, carrots and additional water if needed. Simmer, covered, 15 minutes. Add peas; simmer, covered, 10 minutes or until vegetables are tender. Stir in evaporated milk; heat through. *Do not boil.* Remove bay leaf before serving.

Apple Spice Egg Nog

■ Apple Spice Egg Nog

Makes about 3½ quarts

   3 (32-ounce) cans BORDEN® Egg Nog, chilled
   3 cups apple cider, chilled
   ½ teaspoon ground cinnamon

In large bowl, combine ingredients; mix well.
Chill. Garnish as desired. Refrigerate leftovers.

■ Easy Tomato-Cheese Bisque

Makes 5 servings

   1 can (11 oz.) condensed cheddar cheese
      soup
   2 cups water
   1 cup tomato juice
   1 tablespoon butter or margarine
   1 tablespoon chopped chives (optional)
   ½ teaspoon salt
   ½ teaspoon sugar
   ½ teaspoon dry mustard
   ½ teaspoon Worcestershire sauce
   1 cup MINUTE® Rice
   ¾ cup milk, light cream or evaporated milk

Mix soup with water and tomato juice in large
saucepan. Add butter, chives and seasonings.
Bring to a full boil. Stir in rice and milk. Reduce
heat; cover and simmer 10 minutes, stirring
occasionally. Garnish with additional chopped
chives or popcorn, if desired.

■ Appetizer Ham Logs

Makes about 24 appetizers

   2 cups ground ham
   1 egg, beaten
   ¼ teaspoon pepper
   ¼ cup seasoned fine dry bread crumbs
   ½ cup horseradish sauce
   1 tablespoon prepared mustard
   ⅛ teaspoon celery salt
      Vegetable oil for frying
      Pimiento strips

Combine ham, egg and pepper in medium bowl;
mix well. Shape into 1-inch logs or balls. Roll in
bread crumbs. Refrigerate, covered, 1 hour.

To make mustard sauce, combine horseradish
sauce, mustard and celery salt in small bowl until
well blended. Refrigerate, covered, until serving
time.

Heat 3 inches oil in heavy, large saucepan over
medium-high heat until oil is 365°F; adjust heat to
maintain temperature. Fry ham logs, a few at a
time, 2 to 3 minutes or until golden. Drain on
paper towels. Garnish with pimiento strips. Serve
with mustard sauce.

Favorite Recipe from **National Pork Producers Council**

■ Miniature Teriyaki Pork Kabobs

Makes about 24 appetizers

   1 pound boneless pork, cut into
      4×1×½-inch strips
   1 can (11 ounces) mandarin oranges
   1 small green bell pepper, cut into
      1×¼×¼-inch strips
   ¼ cup teriyaki sauce
   1 tablespoon honey
   1 tablespoon vinegar
   ⅛ teaspoon garlic powder

Soak 24 (8-inch) bamboo skewers in water 10
minutes. Thread pork strips accordion-style with
mandarin oranges on skewers. Place 1 pepper
strip on end of each skewer. Arrange skewers on
broiler pan.

For sauce, combine teriyaki sauce, honey, vinegar
and garlic powder in small bowl; mix well. Brush
sauce over kabobs. Broil, 6 inches from heat,
about 15 minutes or until pork is done, turning
and basting with sauce occasionally.

Favorite Recipe from **National Pork Producers Council**

■ Rumaki

Makes about 32 appetizers

    16 slices bacon
     1 pound chicken livers, cut into quarters
     1 can (8 ounces) sliced water chestnuts,
        drained
    ⅓ cup soy sauce
     2 tablespoons packed brown sugar
     1 tablespoon Dijon-style mustard

Cut bacon slices in half crosswise. Wrap ½ slice bacon around piece of chicken liver and water chestnut slice. Secure with wooden pick. (Reserve any remaining water chestnut slices for another use.) Arrange on broiler pan. Combine soy sauce, brown sugar and mustard in small bowl. Brush over bacon rolls. Broil, 6 inches from heat, 15 to 20 minutes or until bacon is crisp and chicken livers are done, turning and brushing with soy sauce mixture occasionally.

Favorite Recipe from **National Pork Producers Council**

■ Ham-Wrapped Oysters

Makes 24 appetizers

     3 tablespoons prepared horseradish
    ½ pound ham, cut into 3×1×¼-inch strips
     2 dozen fresh oysters, shucked
     3 tablespoons butter or margarine, melted
     1 tablespoon lemon juice
    ¼ teaspoon garlic powder

Spread horseradish on 1 side of each ham strip. Place 1 oyster on each ham strip; roll up and secure with wooden pick. Arrange on broiler pan. Combine butter, lemon juice and garlic powder in small cup. Brush each ham roll with some of the lemon-butter. Broil, 5 inches from heat, 10 to 15 minutes or until edges of oysters curl, brushing occasionally with the remaining lemon-butter.

Favorite Recipe from **National Pork Producers Council**

Top: Appetizer Ham Logs, Miniature Teriyaki Pork Kabobs; bottom: Ham-Wrapped Oysters, Rumaki

■ South-of-the-Border Dip

3 cups

½ cup chopped onion
2 tablespoons PARKAY Margarine
1 lb. VELVEETA Mexican Pasteurized Process Cheese Spread with Jalapeño Pepper, cubed
1 14½-oz. can tomatoes, chopped, drained

In large skillet, saute onions in margarine; reduce heat to low. Add remaining ingredients; stir until process cheese spread is melted. Serve hot with tortilla chips or vegetable dippers.

Preparation time: 10 minutes

Cooking time: 10 minutes

Microwave: Microwave onions and margarine in 1½-quart microwave-safe bowl on High 1½ minutes or until tender. Add remaining ingredients; mix well. Microwave on High 5 minutes or until thoroughly heated, stirring after 3 minutes. Serve hot with tortilla chips or vegetable dippers.

■ Mulled Cider

Makes about 2 quarts

2 quarts apple cider
¾ to 1 cup REALEMON® Lemon Juice from Concentrate
1 cup firmly packed light brown sugar
8 whole cloves
2 cinnamon sticks
¾ cup rum, optional
Additional cinnamon sticks, optional

In large saucepan, combine all ingredients except rum and additional cinnamon sticks; bring to a boil. Reduce heat; simmer uncovered 10 minutes. Remove spices; add rum just before serving if desired. Serve hot with cinnamon sticks if desired.

Tip: Can be served cold.

Microwave: In deep 3-quart round baking dish, combine ingredients as above. Heat on 100% power (high) 13 to 14 minutes or until hot. Serve as above.

South-of-the-Border Dip

■ Chili Soup Jarlsberg

Makes 6 servings

- 1 pound beef round steak, diced
- 2 tablespoons vegetable oil
- 2 cans (14½ ounces each) ready-to-serve beef broth
- 1 can (15 ounces) dark red kidney beans
- 1 can (14½ ounces) tomatoes, chopped, undrained
- 1 medium green bell pepper, chopped
- 1 medium red bell pepper, chopped
- 1 large onion, chopped
- 1 large clove garlic, minced
- 3¼ teaspoons chili powder, divided
- ¼ teaspoon ground cumin
- 1½ cups (6 ounces) shredded Jarlsberg cheese, divided
- ¼ cup butter or margarine, softened
- 1 small clove garlic, minced
- 12 KAVLI Norwegian Crispbreads

Brown beef in hot oil in large, deep saucepan over medium-high heat. Add broth. Bring to a boil over high heat. Reduce heat to low. Cover and simmer 1 hour. Add beans, tomatoes, peppers, onion, large garlic clove, 3 teaspoons of the chili powder and the cumin. Simmer, covered, 30 minutes. Gradually blend in ½ cup of the Jarlsberg cheese. Heat just until cheese melts.

Blend butter, small garlic clove and remaining ¼ teaspoon chili powder in small bowl. Spread on crispbreads; arrange on cookie sheet. Bake in preheated 375°F oven several minutes or until butter is melted. Sprinkle with ½ cup of the Jarlsberg. Bake just until cheese is melted.

Ladle soup into bowls. Garnish with remaining ½ cup Jarlsberg. Serve with crispbreads.

Favorite Recipe from **Norseland Foods, Inc.**

■ Kahlúa® & Coffee

Makes 1 serving

- 1½ ounces KAHLÚA®
  - Hot coffee
  - Whipped cream (optional)

Pour KAHLÚA® into steaming cup of coffee. Top with whipped cream.

Sweet 'n' Sour Meatballs

■ Sweet 'n' Sour Meatballs

Makes about 5 dozen

- 1½ pounds lean ground beef
- 1 (8-ounce) can water chestnuts, drained and chopped
- 2 eggs
- ⅓ cup dry bread crumbs
- 1 tablespoon Worcestershire sauce
- 4 teaspoons WYLER'S® or STEERO® Beef-Flavor Instant Bouillon
- 1 cup water
- ½ cup firmly packed light brown sugar
- ½ cup REALEMON® Lemon Juice from Concentrate
- ¼ cup catsup
- 2 tablespoons cornstarch
- ¼ teaspoon salt
- 1 large red or green pepper, cut into squares
  Chopped parsley, optional

In large bowl, combine meat, water chestnuts, eggs, bread crumbs, Worcestershire and bouillon; mix well. Shape into 1¼-inch meatballs. In large skillet, brown meatballs. Remove from pan; pour off fat. In skillet, combine remaining ingredients except pepper and parsley; mix well. Over medium heat, cook and stir until sauce thickens. Reduce heat. Add meatballs; simmer uncovered 10 minutes. Add pepper; heat through. Garnish with parsley if desired. Refrigerate leftovers.

Breads & Coffee Cakes

■ Cream Cheese Swirl Coffee Cake

Makes one 10-inch cake

2 (3-ounce) packages cream cheese, softened
2 tablespoons confectioners' sugar
2 tablespoons REALEMON® Lemon Juice from Concentrate
2 cups unsifted flour
1 teaspoon baking powder
1 teaspoon baking soda
¼ teaspoon salt
1 cup granulated sugar
½ cup margarine or butter, softened
3 eggs
1 teaspoon vanilla extract
1 (8-ounce) container BORDEN® or MEADOW GOLD® Sour Cream
Cinnamon-Nut Topping (recipe follows)

Preheat oven to 350°. In small bowl, beat cheese, confectioners' sugar and ReaLemon® brand until smooth; set aside. Stir together flour, baking powder, baking soda and salt; set aside. In large mixer bowl, beat granulated sugar and margarine until fluffy. Add eggs and vanilla; mix well. Add dry ingredients alternately with sour cream; mix well. Pour half of batter into greased and floured 10-inch tube pan. Spoon cheese mixture on top of batter to within ½ inch of pan edge. Spoon remaining batter over filling, spreading to pan edge. Sprinkle with Cinnamon-Nut Topping. Bake 40 to 45 minutes or until wooden pick inserted near center comes out clean. Cool 10 minutes; remove from pan. Serve warm.

Cinnamon-Nut Topping: Combine ¼ cup finely chopped nuts, 2 tablespoons granulated sugar and ½ teaspoon ground cinnamon.

■ Streusel Lemon Bread

Makes one 9×5-inch loaf

½ cup finely chopped nuts
¼ cup firmly packed light brown sugar
½ teaspoon ground nutmeg
2 cups unsifted flour
1 teaspoon baking powder
½ teaspoon baking soda
1¼ cups granulated sugar
½ cup margarine or butter, softened
3 eggs
½ cup REALEMON® Lemon Juice from Concentrate
½ cup BORDEN® or MEADOW GOLD® Milk

Preheat oven to 350°. In small bowl, combine nuts, brown sugar and nutmeg; set aside. Stir together flour, baking powder and baking soda; set aside. In large mixer bowl, beat granulated sugar and margarine until fluffy. Add eggs, 1 at a time; beat well. Gradually beat in ReaLemon® brand. Add milk alternately with flour mixture; stir well. Spoon half of batter into greased and floured 9×5-inch loaf pan. Sprinkle half of nut mixture over batter; top with remaining batter, spreading to pan edge. Top with remaining nut mixture. Bake 50 to 55 minutes or until wooden pick inserted near center comes out clean. Cool 15 minutes; remove from pan. Cool completely. Store tightly wrapped.

Cream Cheese Swirl Coffee Cake

Pineapple Citrus Muffins

■ Pineapple Citrus Muffins

Makes 12 muffins

⅓ cup honey
¼ cup butter or margarine, softened
1 egg
1 can (8 ounces) DOLE® Crushed Pineapple
1 tablespoon grated orange peel
1 cup all-purpose flour
1 cup whole wheat flour
1½ teaspoons baking powder
¼ teaspoon salt
¼ teaspoon ground nutmeg
1 cup DOLE® Chopped Dates
½ cup chopped walnuts, optional

Preheat oven to 375°F. In large mixer bowl, beat together honey and butter 1 minute. Beat in egg, then undrained pineapple and orange peel. In medium bowl, combine remaining ingredients; stir into pineapple mixture until just blended. Spoon batter into 12 greased muffin cups. Bake in preheated oven 25 minutes or until wooden pick inserted in center comes out clean. Cool slightly in pan before turning out onto wire rack. Serve warm.

■ Golden Pumpkin Bread

Makes 1 loaf

1½ cups all-purpose flour
1 cup packed brown sugar
1 cup solid pack pumpkin
½ cup LAND O LAKES® Sweet Cream Butter, softened
2 eggs
1 teaspoon baking powder
1 teaspoon baking soda
½ teaspoon salt
1½ teaspoons ground cinnamon
½ teaspoon ground cloves
½ teaspoon ground ginger

In large bowl, combine all ingredients; beat until well mixed. Pour into greased 9×5×3-inch loaf pan. Bake in preheated 350° oven 45 to 55 minutes or until wooden pick inserted into center comes out clean. Let cool in pan on wire rack 10 minutes. Loosen edges; remove from pan. Cool completely on wire rack.

■ Banana Nut Bread

Makes 1 loaf

2 extra-ripe, large DOLE® Bananas, peeled
⅓ cup butter
⅔ cup sugar
2 eggs
2 cups all-purpose flour
2 teaspoons baking powder
½ teaspoon baking soda
½ cup buttermilk
¾ cup chopped nuts

Puree bananas in blender (1¼ cups). Cream butter with sugar, until light and fluffy. Beat in bananas and eggs. Combine flour, baking powder and baking soda. Add dry ingredients to banana mixture alternately in thirds with buttermilk, blending well after each addition. Stir in nuts. Pour into greased 9×5-inch loaf pan. Bake in 350°F oven 50 to 60 minutes until tests done. Cool in pan on a rack 10 minutes. Turn out onto rack to complete cooling.

Cinnamon-Raisin Swirl Loaf

Makes 2 loaves

2 cups SUN-MAID® Raisins
   Water
6¾ to 7¼ cups all-purpose flour
2 packages active dry yeast
2 cups milk
¾ cup granulated sugar
¼ cup butter or margarine
2 teaspoons salt
3 eggs
2 teaspoons ground cinnamon
   Powdered Sugar Icing (recipe follows)

In small bowl, combine raisins with enough hot tap water to cover. Plump 5 minutes; drain well. Set aside. In large bowl, combine 3 cups of the flour and the yeast. In medium saucepan, heat milk, ¼ cup of the granulated sugar, the butter and salt over low heat just until warm (115° to 120°F) and until butter is almost melted, stirring constantly. Add to flour mixture; add eggs. Beat at low speed of electric mixer for ½ minute, scraping sides of bowl constantly. Beat 3 minutes at high speed, scraping bowl occasionally. Stir in plumped raisins. Stir in as much remaining flour as can be mixed in with a spoon. Turn out onto lightly floured board. Knead in enough remaining flour to make a moderately stiff dough that is smooth and elastic (6 to 8 minutes total). Shape into a ball. Place dough in lightly greased bowl; turn once to grease surface. Cover; let rise in warm place (85°F) until doubled, about 1¼ hours.

Punch dough down; divide in half. Cover; let rest 10 minutes. Roll each half into 15×7-inch rectangle. Brush entire surface lightly with water. Combine remaining ½ cup granulated sugar and cinnamon; sprinkle ½ of the sugar mixture over each rectangle. Roll up, jelly-roll fashion, starting from a 7-inch side; pinch edges and ends to seal. Place, sealed edges down, in 2 greased 9×5×3-inch loaf pans. Cover; let rise in warm place until nearly doubled, 35 to 45 minutes. Bake in preheated 375°F oven 35 to 40 minutes or until bread sounds hollow when tapped, covering bread with foil the last 15 minutes to prevent overbrowning. Remove bread from pans; cool completely on wire racks. Drizzle with Powdered Sugar Icing.

Powdered Sugar Icing: In medium bowl, combine 1 cup sifted powdered sugar, ¼ teaspoon vanilla and enough milk (about 1½ tablespoons) to make of drizzling consistency.

Cinnamon-Raisin Swirl Loaf

■ Ladder Coffee Cakes

Makes 2 pastries

½ cup butter
½ cup dairy sour cream
1 cup all-purpose flour
1 cup canned cherry pie filling
¼ cup chopped walnuts (optional)
½ cup sifted powdered sugar
2 teaspoons milk

In a large mixer bowl beat butter on high speed of electric mixer for 30 seconds. Add sour cream; beat until fluffy. Add flour and mix well. Cover and chill dough about 1 hour or until firm enough to handle.

Divide the dough in half. Working with half of the dough at a time, roll to a 10×8-inch rectangle. Place rectangle on a greased baking sheet. Spread *half* of the pie filling lengthwise down the center third of the rectangle. If desired, sprinkle *half* of the chopped walnuts over the pie filling. Make cuts 2½ inches deep at 1-inch intervals along both long sides. Fold strips over filling, pinching into narrow points at center. Repeat with remaining dough. Bake in a 350° oven for 30 minutes or until golden. Remove to wire rack. Sprinkle with additional chopped walnuts, if desired. In a small mixing bowl stir together the powdered sugar and milk. Drizzle over baked pastries. Cut into slices to serve.

Preparation time: 1 hour

Favorite Recipe from **Wisconsin Milk Marketing Board** © 1989

■ Braided Sesame Ring

Makes 1 loaf

7 to 8 cups all-purpose flour
2 packages active dry yeast
¼ cup sugar
1 teaspoon salt
1½ cups hot water (120° to 130°)
½ cup **HELLMAN'S®** or **BEST FOODS®** Real Mayonnaise
4 eggs
2 tablespoons sesame seeds

In large bowl, combine 2 cups of the flour, the yeast, sugar and salt. Gradually beat in water until smooth. Add 2 more cups flour, the real mayonnaise and 3 of the eggs; beat well. Stir in enough of the remaining flour to make dough easy to handle. Turn out onto lightly floured surface. Knead 10 minutes or until dough is smooth and elastic, adding as much remaining flour as needed to prevent sticking. Shape dough into ball. Place in large, greased bowl; turn dough once to grease surface. Cover with towel; let rise in warm place (85°) until doubled, about 1 hour.

Punch dough down; divide into 3 equal pieces. Cover; let rest 10 minutes. Roll each piece into 24-inch rope. Place side-by-side on large greased baking sheet; loosely braid ropes. Shape braid into circle, pinching ends together to seal. Cover; let rise in warm place until doubled, about 1½ hours. In small bowl, beat remaining egg; brush over surface of dough. Sprinkle with sesame seeds. Bake in preheated 375° oven 40 minutes or until loaf is browned and sounds hollow when tapped. Remove to wire rack to cool.

■ Onion-Herb Baked Bread

Makes 1 loaf

1 envelope **LIPTON®** Golden Onion Recipe Soup Mix
1 medium clove garlic, finely chopped
1 teaspoon basil leaves
1 teaspoon oregano
⅛ teaspoon pepper
½ cup butter or margarine, softened
1 loaf Italian or French bread (about 16 inches long), halved lengthwise

Preheat oven to 375°.

In small bowl, thoroughly blend all ingredients except bread; generously spread on bread halves. On baking sheet, arrange bread, cut side up, and bake 15 minutes or until golden. Serve warm.

Note: Store any remaining spread, covered, in refrigerator for future use.

Ladder Coffee Cake

Chocolate Streusel Coffee Cake

■ Chocolate Streusel Coffee Cake

Makes 12 to 16 servings

Chocolate Streusel (recipe follows)
½ cup butter or margarine, softened
1 cup sugar
3 eggs
1 cup dairy sour cream
1 teaspoon vanilla extract
2 cups all-purpose flour
1 teaspoon baking powder
1 teaspoon baking soda
¼ teaspoon salt

Prepare Chocolate Streusel; set aside. Cream butter and sugar in large mixer bowl until light and fluffy. Add eggs; blend well on low speed. Stir in sour cream and vanilla. Combine flour, baking powder, baking soda and salt; add to batter. Blend well.

Sprinkle 1 cup of the Chocolate Streusel into greased and floured 12-cup Bundt® pan. Spread one-third of the batter (about 1⅓ cups) in pan; sprinkle with half the remaining streusel (about 1 cup). Repeat layers, ending with batter on top. Bake at 350° for 50 to 55 minutes or until cake tester comes out clean. Cool 10 minutes; invert onto serving plate. Cool completely.

Chocolate Streusel

¾ cup packed light brown sugar
¼ cup all-purpose flour
¼ cup butter or margarine, softened
¾ cup chopped nuts
¾ cup HERSHEY'S MINI CHIPS Semi-Sweet Chocolate

Combine brown sugar, flour and butter in medium bowl until crumbly. Stir in nuts and MINI CHIPS Chocolate.

■ Golden Apple Boston Brown Bread

Makes 2 loaves

¼ cup butter or margarine, softened
⅓ cup honey
⅓ cup light molasses
1 cup whole wheat flour
1 cup rye flour
1 cup yellow cornmeal
2 teaspoons baking soda
½ teaspoon salt
2 cups buttermilk
2 cups (2 medium) coarsely chopped Golden Delicious apples

In large bowl, cream butter, honey and molasses. In medium bowl, combine flours, cornmeal, baking soda and salt. Add flour mixture to butter mixture alternately with buttermilk, mixing well after each addition. Stir in apples. Pour batter into 2 greased 8½×4½×2½-inch loaf pans. Bake in preheated 350°F oven 1 hour or until wooden pick inserted near center comes out clean. Let cool in pans on wire racks 10 minutes. Loosen edges; remove from pans. Cool slightly on wire racks; serve warm.

Variation: To steam brown bread, divide batter evenly between 2 greased 1-pound coffee cans, filling cans about three fourths full. Cover tops of cans with aluminum foil; tie foil to cans with string. Place rack in large kettle; add boiling water to depth of 1 inch. Place cans on rack; cover kettle. Steam over low heat 3 hours or until wooden pick inserted near center comes out clean. If necessary, add more boiling water to kettle during steaming. Cool as above.

Favorite Recipe from **Washington Apple Commission**

■ Oatmeal Dinner Rolls

Makes 3 dozen rolls

> 2 cups old-fashioned oats, uncooked
> 1½ cups boiling water
> ¼ cup LAND O LAKES® Sweet Cream Butter
> 2 packages active dry yeast
> ½ cup warm water (105° to 115°)
> 6¼ to 7¼ cups all-purpose flour
> 1 cup packed brown sugar
> ⅓ cup light molasses
> 2 eggs
> 1½ teaspoons salt

In medium heatproof bowl, combine oats, boiling water and butter; stir until butter is melted. Cool until warm (105° to 115°). In large bowl, combine yeast and water; stir to dissolve yeast. Stir in oat mixture, 2 cups of the flour, the sugar, molasses, eggs and salt; beat until smooth. Stir in enough of the remaining flour to make dough easy to handle. Turn out onto lightly floured surface. Knead 10 minutes or until dough is smooth and elastic, adding as much remaining flour as needed to prevent sticking. Shape dough into ball. Place in large, greased bowl; turn dough once to grease surface. Cover with towel; let rise in warm place (85°) until doubled, about 1½ hours.

Punch dough down; divide in half. With floured hands, shape each half into 18 smooth balls. Place balls in 2 greased 13×9×2-inch pans. Cover; let rise in warm place until doubled, about 1 hour. Bake in preheated 375° oven 20 to 25 minutes or until golden brown. Remove from pans to wire racks. If desired, brush tops of hot rolls with melted butter; serve warm.

Oatmeal Dinner Rolls

French Breakfast Puffs

■ French Breakfast Puffs

32 puffs

> 1½ cups unsifted all-purpose flour
> ½ cup confectioners sugar
> 1 teaspoon baking powder
> 1 teaspoon salt
> ¾ teaspoon ground nutmeg
> ½ cup milk
> ½ cup water
> ¼ cup CRISCO® Oil
> 1½ teaspoons grated lemon peel
> 3 eggs
> CRISCO® Oil for frying
> Confectioners sugar

Mix flour, ½ cup confectioners sugar, baking powder, salt and nutmeg in small mixing bowl. Set aside. Combine milk, water, CRISCO Oil and lemon peel in medium saucepan. Heat to rolling boil over medium-high heat. Add flour mixture all at once. Beat with wooden spoon until mixture pulls away from sides of pan into a ball. Remove from heat; cool slightly. Add eggs, one at a time, beating after each addition.

Heat 2 to 3 inches CRISCO Oil in deep-fryer or large saucepan to 350°F.

Drop dough by tablespoonfuls into hot CRISCO Oil. Fry 3 or 4 puffs at a time, 4 to 6 minutes, or until golden brown, turning over several times. Drain on paper towels. Sprinkle top of each puff with confectioners sugar.

■ Almond Citrus Muffins

Makes 1 dozen muffins

½ cup whole natural almonds
1¼ cups all-purpose flour
2 teaspoons baking powder
¼ teaspoon salt
1 cup shreds of wheat bran cereal
¼ cup packed brown sugar
¾ cup milk
¼ cup orange juice
1 teaspoon grated orange peel
1 egg
¼ cup vegetable or almond oil

Spread almonds in single layer on baking sheet. Bake at 350°F, 12 to 15 minutes, stirring occasionally, until lightly toasted. Cool and chop. Increase oven to 400°F. In large bowl, combine flour, baking powder and salt. In medium bowl, combine cereal, sugar, milk, orange juice and peel. Let stand 2 minutes or until cereal is softened. Add egg and oil; beat well. Stir in almonds. Add liquid mixture to flour mixture; stir just until moistened. Batter will be lumpy; do not over mix. Spoon batter evenly into 12 greased 2½-inch muffin cups. Bake in preheated 400°F oven 20 minutes or until lightly browned. Remove to wire rack to cool.

Favorite Recipe from **Almond Board of California**

■ Peanut Butter and Jam Swirl Coffee Cake

Makes 1 coffee cake

½ cup milk
⅓ cup packed brown sugar
½ teaspoon salt
1 package active dry yeast
¼ cup warm water (105° to 115°)
1½ to 2½ cups all-purpose flour
¼ cup peanut butter
1 egg
⅓ cup raspberry or strawberry jam

In small saucepan over medium heat, scald milk. In medium heatproof bowl, combine sugar and salt. Add hot milk; stir to dissolve sugar. Cool until warm (105° to 115°). Add yeast to water; stir to dissolve yeast. Add 1 cup of the flour and the peanut butter to milk mixture; beat until smooth. Stir in yeast mixture and egg; beat well. Stir in

enough of the remaining flour to make thick batter; beat well. Cover with waxed paper; let rise in warm place (85°) until bubbly and doubled, about 1 hour. Stir down batter. Spread in well-greased 9-inch round pan. With floured fingers, press spiral-shaped indentation in top of batter, starting at center and working toward outside. Fill indentation with jam. Cover; let rise in warm place until doubled, about 45 minutes. Bake in preheated 350° oven 30 to 35 minutes or until golden brown. Remove to wire rack to cool.

Favorite Recipe from **Oklahoma Peanut Commission**

■ Cranberry Apple Streusel Coffee Cake

Makes 12 servings

CAKE
2 cups Any AUNT JEMIMA Pancake & Waffle Mix (see Note)
½ cup sugar
1 8-oz. carton sour cream
¾ cup milk
1 egg, beaten
¾ cup chopped cranberries
¾ cup peeled, coarsely chopped apple

STREUSEL
½ cup chopped nuts
¼ cup firmly packed brown sugar
½ teaspoon cinnamon
2 tablespoons margarine, melted

GLAZE
¾ cup powdered sugar
1 tablespoon milk
½ teaspoon vanilla

Heat oven to 350°F. Grease 13×9-inch baking pan. Combine pancake mix and sugar. Add sour cream, milk, and egg; mix just until dry ingredients are moistened. Spread into pan; top with cranberries and apple. Combine streusel ingredients; mix until crumbly. Sprinkle over fruit. Bake 30 to 35 minutes or until wooden pick inserted in center comes out clean. Combine glaze ingredients; drizzle over warm cake. Serve warm. (To reheat cooled cake, microwave each serving at high about 20 seconds.)

Note: AUNT JEMIMA Buttermilk Complete, Complete, Original, Whole Wheat or Lite Buttermilk Complete mixes may be used.

Apricot Date Coffee Cake

■ Apricot Date Coffee Cake

Makes 3 coffee cakes

1 cup warm milk (105° to 115°)
2 packages active dry yeast
1 cup butter, softened
½ cup granulated sugar
2 eggs, slightly beaten
1 teaspoon salt
1 teaspoon ground cardamom
5 to 5½ cups all-purpose flour
1 cup prepared apricot filling
½ cup chopped dates
2 cups sifted powdered sugar
3 tablespoons light cream or half-and-half
½ teaspoon vanilla
¼ teaspoon almond extract

In large bowl, combine milk and yeast; stir to dissolve yeast. Stir in butter, granulated sugar, eggs, salt, cardamom and 2 cups of the flour; beat until smooth. Stir in enough of the remaining flour to make dough easy to handle. Turn out onto lightly floured surface. Knead 10 minutes or until dough is smooth and elastic, adding as much remaining flour as needed to prevent sticking. Shape dough into ball. Place in large, buttered bowl; turn dough once to butter surface. Cover with waxed paper; let rise in warm place (85°) until doubled, about 1½ hours. Meanwhile, in small bowl, combine apricot filling and dates; set aside.

Punch dough down; divide into 3 equal pieces. Roll out one third of dough on lightly floured surface into 12×10-inch rectangle. Spoon one third of apricot mixture down center third of dough. Fold all 4 sides over so they meet at center of filling; pinch to seal. Place dough seam side down on buttered baking sheet. With scissors, snip 1-inch wide strips almost to center on both long sides of coffee cake. Turn each strip on its side to expose filling. Repeat with remaining dough and filling. Cover; let rise in warm place until doubled, about 30 minutes. Bake in preheated 375° oven about 18 minutes or until golden brown. Remove to wire racks to cool completely. In small bowl, combine powdered sugar, cream, vanilla and almond extract; mix well. Drizzle over coffee cakes.

Favorite Recipe from **American Dairy Association**

Lemon Pecan Sticky Rolls

■ Lemon Pecan Sticky Rolls

Makes 16 rolls

- ½ cup granulated sugar
- ½ cup firmly packed light brown sugar
- ¼ cup margarine or butter
- ¼ cup REALEMON® Lemon Juice from Concentrate
- ½ teaspoon ground cinnamon
- ½ cup chopped pecans
- 2 (8-ounce) packages refrigerated crescent rolls

Preheat oven to 375°. In small saucepan, combine sugars, margarine, ReaLemon® brand and cinnamon. Bring to a boil; boil 1 minute. Reserving *¼ cup,* pour remaining lemon mixture into 9-inch round layer cake pan. Sprinkle with nuts. Separate rolls into 8 rectangles; spread with reserved lemon mixture. Roll up jellyroll-fashion, beginning with short side; seal edges. Cut in half. Place rolls, cut-side down, in prepared pan. Bake 30 to 35 minutes or until dark golden brown. Loosen sides. Immediately turn onto serving plate; do not remove pan. Let stand 5 minutes; remove pan. Serve warm.

■ Savory Bubble Cheese Bread

Makes one 10-inch round loaf

- 6 to 7 cups flour, divided
- 2 tablespoons sugar
- 4 teaspoons instant minced onion
- 2 teaspoons salt
- 2 packages active dry yeast
- ½ teaspoon caraway seeds
- 1¾ cups milk
- ½ cup water
- 3 tablespoons butter or margarine
- 1 teaspoon TABASCO® pepper sauce
- 2 cups (8 ounces) shredded sharp Cheddar cheese, divided
- 1 egg, lightly beaten

In large bowl of electric mixer combine 2½ cups flour, sugar, onion, salt, yeast and caraway seeds. In small saucepan combine milk, water and butter. Heat milk mixture until very warm (120°F. to 130°F.); stir in TABASCO sauce.

With mixer at medium speed gradually add milk mixture to dry ingredients; beat 2 minutes. Add 1 cup flour. Beat at high speed 2 minutes. With wooden spoon stir in 1½ cups cheese and enough flour to make a stiff dough. Turn dough out onto lightly floured surface. Knead 8 to 10 minutes or until dough is smooth and elastic, adding as much remaining flour as needed to prevent sticking. Place in large greased bowl and invert dough to bring greased side up. Cover with towel; let rise in warm place (90°F. to 100°F.) 1 hour or until doubled in bulk.

Punch dough down. Divide dough into 16 equal pieces; shape each piece into a ball. Place ½ the balls in well-greased 10-inch tube pan. Sprinkle with remaining ½ cup cheese. Arrange remaining balls on top. Cover with towel; let rise in warm place 45 minutes or until doubled in bulk. Preheat oven to 375°F. Brush dough with egg. Bake 40 to 50 minutes or until golden brown. Remove from pan. Cool completely on wire rack.

■ Cheese Casserole Bread

Makes 1 loaf

- 2 cups warm milk (105° to 115°)
- 2 packages active dry yeast
- 3 tablespoons sugar
- 1 tablespoon butter
- ½ teaspoon salt
- 4½ cups all-purpose flour
- 6 ounces Cheddar cheese, cut into ½-inch cubes

In large bowl, combine milk and yeast; stir to dissolve yeast. Add sugar, butter and salt; stir until butter is melted. Stir in 3 cups of the flour; beat until smooth. Stir in remaining flour and cheese; mix well. Pour batter into well-buttered 1½-quart round casserole. Cover with waxed paper; let rise in warm place (85°) until doubled, about 1 hour. Remove waxed paper. Bake in preheated 350° oven 50 to 55 minutes or until wooden pick inserted into center comes out clean. Let cool in dish on wire rack 10 minutes. Loosen edge; remove from dish. Cool slightly on wire rack; serve warm with butter.

Favorite Recipe from **American Dairy Association**

■ Apple-Cranberry Muffins

Makes 1 dozen muffins

- 1¾ cups plus 2 tablespoons all-purpose flour
- ½ cup sugar
- 1½ teaspoons baking powder
- ½ teaspoon baking soda
- ½ teaspoon salt
- 1 egg
- ¾ cup milk
- ¾ cup sweetened applesauce
- ¼ cup butter or margarine, melted
- 1 cup fresh cranberries, coarsely chopped
- ½ teaspoon ground cinnamon

In medium bowl, combine 1¾ cups of the flour, ¼ cup of the sugar, the baking powder, baking soda and salt. In small bowl, combine egg, milk, applesauce and butter; mix well. Add egg mixture to flour mixture; stir just until moistened. Batter will be lumpy; do not over mix. In small bowl, toss cranberries with remaining 2 tablespoons flour; fold into batter. Spoon batter evenly into 12 greased 2¾-inch muffin cups. In measuring cup, combine remaining ¼ cup sugar and the cinnamon. Sprinkle over tops of muffins. Bake in preheated 400° oven 20 to 25 minutes or until golden brown. Remove to wire rack to cool.

Favorite Recipe from **Western New York Apple Growers Association, Inc.**

Cheese Casserole Bread

Salads & Side Dishes

■ Swiss Vegetable Medley

Makes 6 servings

1 bag (16 ounces) frozen vegetable combination (broccoli, carrots, cauliflower), thawed and drained
1 can (10¾ ounces) condensed cream of mushroom soup
1 cup (4 ounces) shredded Swiss cheese
⅓ cup sour cream
¼ teaspoon DURKEE Ground Black Pepper
1 jar (4 ounces) diced pimiento, drained (optional)
1 can (2.8 ounces) DURKEE French Fried Onions

Preheat oven to 350°. In large bowl, combine vegetables, soup, *½ cup* cheese, the sour cream, pepper, pimiento and *½ can* French Fried Onions. Pour into shallow 1-quart casserole. Bake, covered, at 350° for 30 minutes or until vegetables are done. Sprinkle remaining cheese and onions in diagonal rows across top; bake, uncovered, 5 minutes or until onions are golden brown.

Preparation time: **5** minutes

Microwave Directions: Prepare vegetable mixture as above; pour into shallow 1-quart microwave-safe casserole. Cook, covered, on HIGH 8 to 10 minutes or until vegetables are done. Stir vegetables halfway through cooking time. Top with remaining cheese and onions as above; cook, uncovered, 1 minute or until cheese melts. Let stand 5 minutes.

■ Original Green Bean Casserole

Makes 6 servings

2 cans (16 ounces *each*) cut green beans, drained, or 2 packages (9 ounces *each*) frozen cut green beans, cooked and drained
¾ cup milk
1 can (10¾ ounces) condensed cream of mushroom soup
⅛ teaspoon DURKEE Ground Black Pepper
1 can (2.8 ounces) DURKEE French Fried Onions

Preheat oven to 350°. In medium bowl, combine beans, milk, soup, pepper and *½ can* French Fried Onions; pour into 1½-quart casserole. Bake, uncovered, at 350° for 30 minutes or until heated through. Top with remaining onions; bake, uncovered, 5 minutes or until onions are golden brown.

Preparation time: **5** minutes

Microwave Directions: Prepare green bean mixture as above; pour into 1½-quart microwave-safe casserole. Cook, covered, on HIGH 8 to 10 minutes or until heated through. Stir beans halfway through cooking time. Top with remaining onions; cook, uncovered, 1 minute. Let stand 5 minutes.

Top: ***Original Green Bean Casserole;*** *bottom:* ***Swiss Vegetable Medley***

■ Savory Sausage Dressing

Makes 6 to 8 servings

>   1 package (12 ounces) seasoned bulk pork
>   sausage
>   ¼ cup CRISCO® Oil
>   ½ cup chopped onion
>   ½ cup chopped celery
>   1 clove garlic, minced
>   1½ cups sliced fresh mushrooms
>   ½ teaspoon Worcestershire sauce
>   ¼ teaspoon dried rosemary leaves
>   ⅛ teaspoon pepper
>   2 cups herb-seasoned stuffing mix
>   1 egg, slightly beaten
>   ½ cup hot water
>   1½ teaspoons instant chicken bouillon
>   granules

Preheat oven to 325°F. Place sausage in large
skillet. Cook over medium-high heat until no
longer pink. Drain. Transfer to medium mixing
bowl.

Heat CRISCO Oil in large skillet. Add onion,
celery and garlic. Sauté over moderate heat until
celery is tender-crisp. Add mushrooms,
Worcestershire sauce, rosemary and pepper.
Cook, stirring constantly, 1 minute. Add to
sausage. Mix well. Stir in stuffing mix and egg.
Mix hot water and bouillon granules in small
bowl. Stir into stuffing mixture. Place in 1½-quart
casserole. Bake at 325°F, 30 to 35 minutes, or
until heated through.

Savory Sausage Dressing

■ Cherry Cheese Mold

Makes 4 cups or 8 servings

>   1 can (8 ounces) dark sweet pitted cherries
>   1 package (4-serving size) JELL-O® Brand
>   Cherry Flavor Gelatin
>   1½ cups crushed ice
>   2 packages (3 ounces each) cream cheese,
>   softened and cut up

Drain cherries, reserving syrup. Add water to
syrup to make ¾ cup. Pour into small saucepan.
Bring to a boil over high heat. Pour boiling liquid
into blender. Add gelatin. Cover and blend at low
speed until gelatin is completely dissolved, about
30 seconds. Add crushed ice and cream cheese.
Blend at high speed for 1 minute. Pour into 4-cup
mold or bowl or individual dessert dishes. Drop
cherries into gelatin mixture, one at a time. Chill
until firm, about 1 hour. Unmold.

■ Golden Mashed Potatoes

Makes 4 to 6 servings

>   2½ cups cubed cooked potatoes, mashed
>   3 tablespoons milk
>   2 tablespoons PARKAY Margarine
>   1 tablespoon chopped fresh chives
>   ½ lb. VELVEETA Pasteurized Process Cheese
>   Spread, cubed
>   ¼ cup (1 oz.) KRAFT 100% Grated Parmesan
>   Cheese

Combine potatoes, milk, margarine and chives;
beat until fluffy. Stir in half of the process cheese
spread. Spoon into 1-quart casserole; sprinkle
with parmesan cheese. Bake at 350°, 20 to 25
minutes or until thoroughly heated. Top with
remaining process cheese spread; continue baking
until process cheese spread begins to melt.

Preparation time: 20 minutes

Baking time: 30 minutes

Cherry Waldorf Gelatin

■ Cherry Waldorf Gelatin

Makes 8 to 10 servings

2 cups boiling water
1 (6-ounce) package cherry flavor gelatin
1 cup cold water
¼ cup REALEMON® Lemon Juice from
    Concentrate
1½ cups chopped apples
1 cup chopped celery
½ cup chopped walnuts or pecans
    Lettuce leaves
    Apple slices and celery leaves, optional

In medium bowl, pour boiling water over gelatin;
stir until dissolved. Add cold water and ReaLemon®
brand; chill until partially set. Fold in apples,
celery and nuts. Pour into lightly oiled 6-cup
mold or 9-inch square baking pan. Chill until set,
4 to 6 hours or overnight. Serve on lettuce.
Garnish with apple and celery leaves if desired.

■ Ambrosia

Makes 4 servings

1 can (20 ounces) DOLE® Pineapple Chunks
1 can (11 ounces) DOLE® Mandarin Orange
    Segments
1 firm, large DOLE® Banana, sliced, optional
1½ cups DOLE® Seedless Grapes
1 cup miniature marshmallows
1 cup flaked coconut
½ cup pecan halves or coarsely chopped nuts
1 cup dairy sour cream or plain yogurt
1 tablespoon brown sugar

Drain pineapple and orange segments. In large
bowl, combine pineapple, orange segments,
banana, grapes, marshmallows, coconut and nuts.
In 1-quart measure, combine sour cream and
brown sugar. Stir into fruit mixture. Refrigerate,
covered, 1 hour or overnight.

■ Vegetables in Cheese Sauce

Makes about 5½ cups or 8 servings

    1 can (11 ounces) CAMPBELL'S Condensed
        Cheddar Cheese Soup/Sauce
    ⅓ cup milk
    ½ teaspoon dried basil leaves, crushed
    1 clove garlic, minced
    2 cups cauliflowerets
    1 small onion, cut into thin wedges
    1½ cups diagonally sliced carrots
    1 package (10 ounces) frozen peas

1. In 3-quart microwave-safe casserole, stir soup
until smooth. Stir in milk, basil and garlic; mix
well.

2. Add vegetables; stir to coat well. Cover with
lid; microwave on HIGH 15 minutes or until
vegetables are tender, stirring twice during
cooking. Let stand, covered, 5 minutes.

■ Winter Fruit Bowl

Makes about 6½ cups or 12 servings

    2 packages (4-serving size) or 1 package
        (8-serving size) JELL-O® Brand Lemon
        Flavor Gelatin
    1½ cups boiling water
    1 can (12 fluid ounces) lemon-lime
        carbonated beverage, chilled
        Ice cubes
    3 cups diced or sliced fresh fruits* (bananas,
        oranges, apples, pears, grapes)

Dissolve gelatin in boiling water. Combine
beverage and ice cubes to make 2½ cups. Add to
gelatin, stirring until slightly thickened. Remove
any unmelted ice. Chill until thickened, about 10
minutes. Fold in fruits. Pour into 8-cup serving
bowl. Chill until set, about 3 hours. Garnish with
whipped topping and orange sections, if desired.

*Do not use fresh pineapple, kiwifruit, mango,
papaya or figs.*

■ Christmas Ribbon

Makes about 6 cups or 12 servings

    2 packages (4-serving size) or 1 package
        (8-serving size) JELL-O® Brand
        Strawberry Flavor Gelatin
    5 cups boiling water
    ⅔ cup sour cream or vanilla yogurt
    2 packages (4-serving size) or 1 package
        (8-serving size) JELL-O® Brand Lime
        Flavor Gelatin

Dissolve strawberry flavor gelatin in 2½ cups of
the boiling water. Pour 1½ cups of the strawberry
flavor gelatin into 6-cup ring mold. Chill until set
but not firm, about 30 minutes. Chill remaining
strawberry flavor gelatin in bowl until slightly
thickened. Gradually blend in ⅓ cup of the sour
cream. Spoon over gelatin in mold. Chill until set
but not firm, about 15 minutes.

Dissolve lime flavor gelatin in remaining boiling
water. Chill until slightly thickened. Pour 1½
cups of the lime flavor gelatin over creamy layer
in mold. Chill until set but not firm, about 15
minutes. Chill remaining lime flavor gelatin in
bowl until slightly thickened. Gradually blend in
remaining sour cream. Spoon over gelatin in
mold. Chill about 2 hours. Unmold.

■ Home-Style Creamed Corn Casserole

Makes 6 servings

    2 cans (17 oz. each) cream-style corn
    1 cup MINUTE® Rice
    1 egg, slightly beaten
    ½ teaspoon salt
    ⅛ teaspoon pepper
    ⅛ teaspoon ground nutmeg

Combine all ingredients in large bowl; mix well.
Pour into greased 9-inch square baking dish. Bake
at 375° for 25 minutes or until liquid is absorbed.
Garnish as desired. Makes 6 servings.

Microwave Directions: Combine all ingredients
in large bowl; mix well. Pour into greased 9-inch
square microwavable dish. Cover with plastic
wrap and cook at HIGH 15 minutes or until liquid
is absorbed. Garnish as desired.

Vegetables in Cheese Sauce

■ Holiday Stuffing & Potato Bake

Makes 4 to 6 servings

1½ cups water
¼ cup butter or margarine
1 package (6 ounces) corn bread stuffing mix*
1 cup chopped apple
½ cup chopped celery
1 egg, beaten
1 can (2.8 ounces) DURKEE French Fried Onions
3 cups hot mashed potatoes
1 cup (4 ounces) shredded Cheddar cheese

Preheat oven to 350°. In large saucepan, heat water and butter until butter melts; remove from heat. Stir in both pouches of stuffing mix, apple, celery, egg and *½ can* French Fried Onions; mix well. Set aside. To hot mashed potatoes, add *½ cup* Cheddar cheese; stir. In greased 8×12-inch baking dish, make 4 alternating rows of potatoes and stuffing. Bake, covered, at 350° for 30 minutes or until heated through. Sprinkle remaining cheese and onions between each row of stuffing and potatoes; bake, uncovered, 5 minutes or until onions are golden brown.

3 cups corn bread stuffing crumbs may be substituted for stuffing mix. Substitute 1 cup chicken broth for the water.

Preparation time: 15 minutes

Microwave Directions: In medium microwave-safe bowl, place water and butter. Cook, covered, on HIGH 3 minutes or until butter melts. Stir in stuffing ingredients as above. Prepare potato mixture as above. In 8×12-inch microwave-safe dish, arrange stuffing and potatoes as above. Cook, covered, 8 to 10 minutes or until heated through. Rotate dish halfway through cooking time. Top with remaining cheese and onions as above; cook, uncovered, 1 minute or until cheese melts. Let stand 5 minutes.

■ Broccoli and Rice with Walnuts

Makes 4 servings

¼ cup coarsely chopped walnuts or slivered almonds
1 tablespoon oil
½ package (2¼ cups) BIRDS EYE® Broccoli Cuts*
2 tablespoons sliced scallions
1 garlic clove, minced
1 cup chicken broth or water
2 tablespoons dry sherry (optional)
1½ tablespoons soy sauce
1 cup MINUTE® Rice

Cook and stir walnuts in hot oil in large skillet until lightly browned; remove from skillet. Add broccoli, scallions and garlic to oil remaining in skillet. Cook and stir 2 to 3 minutes. Add broth, sherry and soy sauce. Bring to a full boil. Stir in rice. Cover; remove from heat. Let stand 5 minutes. Fluff with fork and sprinkle with walnuts.

You may use 1 package (9 oz.) BIRDS EYE® Cut Green Beans for the broccoli.

■ Easy Oyster Dressing

Makes 6 to 8 servings

1 teaspoon WYLER'S® or STEERO® Chicken-Flavor Instant Bouillon
½ cup boiling water
½ cup chopped celery
½ cup margarine or butter
1 (8-ounce) package herb-seasoned stuffing mix
1 (8-ounce) can ORLEANS® Whole Oysters, undrained

Preheat oven to 350°. Dissolve bouillon in water; set aside. In small skillet, cook celery in margarine until tender. In large bowl, combine all ingredients; mix well. Turn into buttered 1½-quart baking dish. Cover; bake 35 minutes or until hot. Refrigerate leftovers.

Ginger Pineapple Mold

■ Ginger Pineapple Mold

Makes 5 cups or 10 servings

 1 can (20 ounces) pineapple slices in juice
 2 packages (4-serving size) or 1 package
      (8-serving size) JELL-O® Brand Lime or
      Apricot Flavor Gelatin
1½ cups boiling water
 1 cup ginger ale or cold water
 ¼ teaspoon ginger

Drain pineapple, reserving juice. Cut 4 pineapple slices in half; set aside. Cut remaining pineapple slices into chunks. Dissolve gelatin in boiling water. Add reserved juice, ginger ale and ginger. Chill until slightly thickened. Measure 1 cup of the gelatin. Arrange some of the pineapple chunks in 6-cup ring mold; top with measured gelatin. Chill until set but not firm, about 10 minutes. Fold remaining pineapple chunks into remaining gelatin; spoon over gelatin in mold. Chill until firm, about 4 hours. Unmold. Garnish with halved pineapple slices, halved cherry tomatoes and crisp greens, if desired.

■ Cranberry Waldorf Fluff

Makes 6 servings

1½ cups cranberries, finely chopped
 1 cup KRAFT Miniature Marshmallows
 ¼ cup sugar
1½ cups finely chopped apple
 ½ cup MIRACLE WHIP Salad Dressing
 ¼ cup chopped walnuts
 ⅛ teaspoon ground cinnamon

Combine cranberries, miniature marshmallows and sugar; mix lightly. Cover; chill. Add remaining ingredients; mix lightly.

Preparation time: 20 minutes plus chilling

■ Holiday Waldorf Salad

Makes about 7 cups or 14 servings

> 2 packages (4-serving size) or 1 package
>   (8-serving size) JELL-O® Brand
>   Strawberry Flavor Gelatin
> 1½ cups boiling water
>   1 tablespoon lemon juice
>   1 cup cold water
>   Ice cubes
>   1 medium red apple, diced
>   ½ cup halved seedless grapes
>   ½ cup thinly sliced celery
>   ½ cup chopped walnuts
>   1 cup mayonnaise

Completely dissolve gelatin in boiling water; add lemon juice. Combine cold water and ice cubes to make 2½ cups. Add to gelatin, stirring until slightly thickened. Remove any unmelted ice. Chill until thickened, about 10 minutes. Fold in apple, grapes, celery and nuts. Measure 1 cup of the gelatin and set aside. Pour remaining gelatin into 8-cup bowl. Chill until set but not firm.

Blend mayonnaise into measured gelatin. Spoon over fruited layer in bowl. Chill until set, about 3 hours. Garnish with fresh fruit and crisp greens, if desired.

■ Pineapple Cranberry Relish

Makes 4 cups

> 1 can (8¼ oz.) DOLE® Crushed Pineapple in
>   Syrup
> 1 large thin-skinned navel orange, unpeeled
> 1 package (12 oz.) fresh cranberries, washed
> 1 cup sugar

Drain syrup from pineapple into blender. Cut orange into about 1-inch pieces; add to blender. Whir until pieces are coarse. Stop and stir as needed. Pour half of mixture from blender into a bowl. Add half of cranberries to blender; whir until coarsely chopped. Repeat with remaining cranberries and orange mixture. Pour all into a bowl; add pineapple and sugar. Cover with plastic wrap. Stand at room temperature overnight. Store in tightly covered jars in refrigerator.

Tip: Ripens and mellows when left on counter overnight.

■ Broccoli Casserole

Makes 6 to 8 servings

> 2 10-oz. pkgs. frozen chopped broccoli,
>   thawed, drained
> 1½ cups cooked rice
>   1 10¾-oz. can condensed cream of
>   mushroom soup
>   ¾ lb. VELVEETA Pasteurized Process Cheese
>   Spread, cubed
>   1 2.8-oz. can French fried onions

In large bowl, combine broccoli, rice, soup, process cheese spread and 1 cup onions; mix well. Spoon into 1½-quart casserole. Bake at 350°, 35 minutes. Top with remaining onions; continue baking 5 minutes.

Preparation time: 10 minutes

Baking time: 40 minutes

■ Apple-Cinnamon Sweet Potatoes

Serves 6

> 1 lb sweet potatoes, peeled (about
>   2 medium)
> 2 large apples, cored and sliced
> ¾ cup orange juice
> ¼ cup firmly packed brown sugar
> 1 Tbs lemon juice
> ½ tsp salt
> ½ tsp cinnamon
> 1 Tbs butter
> ½ cup chopped pecans

Grease a 1½ quart glass casserole. Thinly slice sweet potatoes and layer alternately with apples in prepared casserole. Mix orange juice, brown sugar, lemon juice, salt, and cinnamon. Pour over potatoes and apples. Cover and microwave on high power 5 minutes. Spoon sauce over, re-cover and microwave 5 minutes. Spoon sauce over again. Re-cover and continue microwaving on high power 5 to 6 minutes or until potatoes and apples are tender. Dot with butter and sprinkle with nuts. Microwave on high power, uncovered, 2 to 3 minutes. Let stand 5 minutes before serving.

Favorite Recipe from **Western New York Apple Growers Association, Inc.**

■ Wild Rice & Pepper Salad

Makes 6 servings

- 1 6-oz. pkg. long-grain & wild rice
- ½ cup MIRACLE WHIP Salad Dressing
- 2 tablespoons olive oil
- ½ teaspoon black pepper
- ¼ teaspoon grated lemon peel
- 1 cup chopped red pepper
- 1 cup chopped yellow pepper
- ¼ cup 1-inch green onion pieces

Prepare rice as directed on package, omitting margarine. Cool. Combine salad dressing, oil, black pepper and peel; mix well. Add remaining ingredients; mix lightly. Serve at room temperature or chilled.

Preparation time: 35 minutes

Variation: Substitute MIRACLE WHIP Light Reduced Calorie Salad Dressing for Regular Salad Dressing.

■ Applesauce Cranberry Mold

Serves 6 to 8

- 2 envelopes plain gelatin
- ½ cup orange or cranberry juice
- ½ cup boiling water
- 1 can or jar (16 oz) cranberry sauce
- 1 cup applesauce
- 1 apple, cored and cut up
- 1 cup diced celery
- ½ cup chopped walnuts
- 1 orange, peeled and diced
- 2 Tbs grated orange rind

Soften gelatin in juice. Add boiling water; cool. Mix all other ingredients; add to gelatin mixture. Pour into a greased mold (at least 2 quarts) and refrigerate several hours.

Favorite Recipe from **Western New York Apple Growers Association, Inc.**

Wild Rice & Pepper Salad

■ Sherried Mushroom Rice

Makes 4 servings

 1 garlic clove, minced
 2 tablespoons butter or margarine
 2 cups sliced mushrooms
 ¼ cup chopped red pepper
1¼ cups chicken broth
 ¼ cup dry sherry or chicken broth
 2 teaspoons onion flakes
 ½ teaspoon salt
1½ cups MINUTE® Rice
 2 tablespoons grated Parmesan cheese
 1 tablespoon chopped parsley

Cook and stir garlic in hot butter in large skillet 1 minute. Add mushrooms and red pepper; cook, stirring occasionally, 2 minutes.

Add broth, sherry, onion flakes and salt. Bring to a full boil. Stir in rice. Cover; remove from heat. Let stand 5 minutes. Fluff with fork and sprinkle with grated cheese and parsley. Serve with steak or your favorite main dish. Garnish as desired.

Microwave Directions: Cut butter into pieces. Cook garlic, butter and mushrooms in microwavable dish at HIGH 2 to 3 minutes. Stir in remaining ingredients except Parmesan cheese and parsley. Cover and cook at HIGH 4 minutes. Stir; cover and cook at HIGH 2 to 3 minutes longer. Let stand 5 minutes. Fluff with fork and sprinkle with Parmesan cheese and parsley. Serve with steak or your favorite main dish.

■ Cranberry Holiday Ring

Makes 12 servings

2¼ cups cold water
 1 3-oz. pkg. strawberry flavored gelatin
 1 10½-oz. can frozen cranberry-orange relish, thawed
 1 8-oz. can crushed pineapple
 1 3-oz. pkg. lemon flavored gelatin
 2 cups KRAFT Miniature Marshmallows
 ½ cup MIRACLE WHIP Salad Dressing
 1 cup whipping cream, whipped

Bring 1 cup water to boil. Gradually add to strawberry gelatin, stirring until dissolved. Add cranberry-orange relish; mix well. Pour into lightly oiled 6½-cup ring mold; cover. Chill until almost set. Drain pineapple, reserving liquid. Bring remaining water to boil. Gradually add to lemon gelatin, stirring until dissolved. Add marshmallows; stir until melted. Add reserved pineapple liquid; cover. Chill until partially set. Add salad dressing and pineapple to marshmallow mixture. Fold in whipped cream; pour over strawberry layer. Cover; chill until firm. Unmold. Garnish as desired.

Preparation time: 1½ hours plus final chilling

Variation: Substitute 12×8-inch baking dish for ring mold. Do not unmold.

Sherried Mushroom Rice

■ Spinach Bake

Makes 8 servings

2 eggs, beaten
¾ cup MIRACLE WHIP Salad Dressing
**2 10-oz. pkgs. frozen chopped spinach,
  thawed, well drained**
**1 14-oz. can artichoke hearts, drained, cut
  into quarters**
½ cup sour cream
**¼ cup (1 oz.) KRAFT 100% Grated Parmesan
  Cheese**
6 crisply cooked bacon slices, crumbled

Combine eggs and ½ cup salad dressing, mixing
until well blended. Add spinach and artichokes;
mix lightly. Spoon mixture into lightly greased
10×6-inch baking dish. Combine remaining salad
dressing, sour cream and cheese; mix well. Spoon
over spinach mixture. Bake at 350°, 30 minutes or
until set. Sprinkle with bacon.

Preparation time: 10 minutes

Baking time: 30 minutes

Microwave: Substitute 1½-quart microwave-safe
casserole for 10×6-inch baking dish. Combine
eggs and ½ cup salad dressing in casserole, mixing
until well blended. Add spinach and artichokes;
mix lightly. Microwave on High 8 to 9 minutes or
until thoroughly heated, stirring every 3 minutes.
Combine remaining salad dressing, sour cream
and cheese; mix well. Spoon over spinach
mixture. Microwave on High 1½ to 2 minutes or
until sour cream mixture is warmed. (Do not over
cook.) Sprinkle with bacon. Let stand 5 minutes.

Microwave tip: To thaw spinach, place frozen
spinach in 1½-quart microwave-safe casserole;
cover. Microwave on High 5 minutes. Break apart
with fork; drain well.

■ Rich Turkey Gravy

Makes about 1½ cups

¼ to ⅓ cup unsifted flour
¼ cup turkey pan drippings *or* margarine
2 cups hot water
**2 teaspoons WYLER'S® or STEERO® Chicken-
  Flavor Instant Bouillon *or* 2 Chicken-
  Flavor Bouillon Cubes**

In medium skillet, stir flour into drippings until
smooth; cook and stir until dark brown. Add water
and bouillon; cook and stir until thickened and
bouillon is dissolved. Refrigerate leftovers.

Holiday Fruit Salad

A colorful addition to a holiday buffet dinner.

■ Holiday Fruit Salad

Makes 12 servings

**3 packages (3 ounces each) strawberry
  flavor gelatin**
3 cups boiling water
2 ripe DOLE® Bananas
1 package (16 ounces) frozen strawberries
1 can (20 ounces) DOLE® Crushed Pineapple
1 package (8 ounces) cream cheese, softened
1 cup dairy sour cream or plain yogurt
¼ cup sugar
** Crisp DOLE® Lettuce leaves**

In large bowl, dissolve gelatin in boiling water.
Slice bananas into gelatin mixture. Add frozen
strawberries and undrained pineapple. Pour half
the mixture into 13×9-inch pan. Refrigerate 1
hour or until firm. In mixer bowl, beat cream
cheese with sour cream and sugar; spread over
chilled layer. Gently spoon remaining gelatin
mixture on top. Refrigerate until firm, about 2
hours. Cut into squares; serve on lettuce-lined
salad plates. Garnish with additional pineapple, if
desired.

Fresh Vegetable Ring

■ Fresh Vegetable Ring

Makes 6 servings

2 cups broccoli flowerets
2 cups cauliflowerets
1 small zucchini, cut into ¼-inch slices
1 small yellow squash, cut into ¼-inch slices
1 can (10¾ ounces) CAMPBELL'S® Condensed Chicken Broth
6 medium CAMPBELL'S® Fresh Mushrooms, halved
  Sweet red pepper strips for garnish
2 teaspoons cornstarch
1 teaspoon chopped fresh basil leaves or ½ teaspoon dried basil leaves, crushed
1 teaspoon wine vinegar

1. Arrange broccoli in a circle around rim of a 12-inch round microwave-safe platter. Arrange cauliflower next to broccoli. Arrange alternate slices of zucchini and yellow squash next to cauliflower, leaving space in center of platter. Pour ¼ cup of the broth over vegetables. Cover with vented plastic wrap; microwave on HIGH 5 minutes.

2. Place mushrooms in center of platter. Garnish with red pepper strips. Cover; microwave on HIGH 2 minutes or until vegetables are tender-crisp. Let stand, covered, while preparing sauce.

3. In small microwave-safe bowl, blend remaining broth, cornstarch, basil and vinegar until smooth. Cover with vented plastic wrap; microwave on HIGH 2 minutes or until mixture boils, stirring twice during cooking. Spoon over vegetables.

■ Parmesan Potato Crisp

Makes 6 servings

½ cup MIRACLE WHIP Salad Dressing
5 cups thin unpeeled potato slices
¾ cup (3 ozs.) KRAFT 100% Grated Parmesan
    Cheese
Pepper (optional)

Generously brush 9-inch pie plate with salad
dressing. Dry potato slices on paper towel.
Arrange one layer of potatoes, edges slightly
overlapping, on bottom of pie plate. Brush
generously with salad dressing; sprinkle
generously with cheese. Repeat layers, sprinkling
occasionally with pepper. Bake at 400°, 30
minutes. Cover with foil; continue baking 30
minutes or until potatoes are tender. Immediately
invert onto serving plate. Cut into wedges to
serve.

Preparation time: 10 minutes

Baking time: 1 hour

Variation: Substitute MIRACLE WHIP Light
Reduced Calorie Salad Dressing for Regular Salad
Dressing.

*If desired, leave the peels on the potatoes for a
more homey casserole.*

■ Potato and Cheese Casserole

Makes 6 servings

1 can (10¾ ounces) CAMPBELL'S® Condensed
    Cream of Celery Soup
1 cup shredded Cheddar cheese (4 ounces)
½ cup milk
Generous dash pepper
1 large clove garlic, minced
4 cups thinly sliced potatoes
1 cup thinly sliced onions

1. In medium bowl, stir soup until smooth. Add
cheese, milk, pepper and garlic; stir until well
blended.

2. In 2-quart microwave-safe casserole, arrange ½
of the potatoes, ½ of the onions and ½ of the soup
mixture. Repeat layers.

3. Cover with lid; microwave on HIGH 23 minutes
or until potatoes are tender, rotating dish 3 times
during cooking. Let stand, covered, 5 minutes.

■ Festive Rice

Makes 6 servings

2¼ cups MINUTE® Rice
1 medium green pepper, chopped*
¼ cup oil
1 envelope GOOD SEASONS® Italian or Mild
    Italian Salad Dressing Mix
2¼ cups water
2 tablespoons chopped pimiento or parsley

Cook and stir rice and green pepper in hot oil in
large skillet about 2 minutes. Sprinkle with salad
dressing mix. Stir in water. Cover and bring to a
boil. Remove from heat. Let stand 5 minutes. Stir
in pimiento.

*You may use ½ medium green pepper, chopped,
and ½ cup grated carrot for the green pepper.*

■ Raspberry-Lemon Gelatin Salad

Makes 8 to 10 servings

1 10-oz. pkg. frozen raspberries, thawed
Cold water
1 3-oz. pkg. raspberry flavored gelatin
1 envelope unflavored gelatin
½ cup lemon juice
1 3½-oz. pkg. lemon instant pudding and pie
    filling mix
2 cups cold milk
1 cup MIRACLE WHIP Salad Dressing

Drain raspberries, reserving liquid. Add enough
water to reserved liquid to measure ¾ cup; set
aside. Bring 1 cup water to boil. Gradually add to
raspberry flavored gelatin, stirring until dissolved.
Stir in reserved raspberry liquid. Cover; chill until
thickened but not set. Fold in raspberries. Pour
into 1½-quart clear serving bowl. Cover; chill
until almost set. Combine unflavored gelatin and
juice in small saucepan; let stand 1 minute. Stir
over low heat until gelatin is dissolved. Cool.
Combine pudding mix and milk; mix as directed
on package for pudding. Stir in salad dressing.
Gradually add gelatin mixture, mixing until well
blended. Pour over raspberry layer; cover. Chill
until firm.

Preparation time: 1½ hours plus final chilling

Main Dishes

■ Turkey with Apple Citrus Stuffing

Makes 10 to 12 servings (8 cups stuffing)

12- to 14-pound BUTTERBALL® Turkey, thawed
    if frozen
 1 cup chopped celery
½ cup chopped onion
 6 tablespoons margarine or butter
 2 teaspoons poultry seasoning
 8 cups slightly dried bread cubes
    (10 to 12 bread slices, cubed and dried
    overnight)
 2 cups chopped red apple
¼ cup chopped fresh parsley
1½ teaspoons shredded orange peel
    Juice from orange plus water to make
      ¾ cup

Cook and stir celery and onion in margarine in medium saucepan over medium heat until crisp-tender. Stir in poultry seasoning. Combine bread cubes, apple, parsley and orange peel in large bowl. Add celery mixture and orange juice mixture; toss to mix. Preheat oven to 325°F. Prepare turkey for roasting; stuff neck and body cavities lightly. Roast immediately according to package directions.

■ Holiday Baked Ham

Makes 8 to 10 servings

 1 bone-in smoked ham (8½ pounds)
 1 can (20 ounces) DOLE® Sliced Pineapple in
    Syrup
 1 cup apricot preserves
 1 teaspoon dry mustard
½ teaspoon ground allspice
    Whole cloves
    Maraschino cherries

Preheat oven to 325°F. Remove rind from ham. Place ham on rack in open roasting pan, fat side up. Insert meat thermometer with bulb in thickest part away from fat or bone. Roast ham in oven about 3 hours.

Drain pineapple; reserve syrup. In small saucepan, combine syrup, preserves, mustard and allspice. Bring to boil; boil, stirring occasionally, 10 minutes. Remove ham from oven, but keep oven hot. Stud ham with cloves; brush with glaze. Using wooden picks, secure pineapple and cherries to ham. Brush again with glaze. Return ham to oven. Roast 30 minutes longer or until thermometer registers 160°F (about 25 minutes per pound total cooking time). Brush with glaze 15 minutes before done. Let ham stand 20 minutes before slicing.

Turkey with Apple Citrus Stuffing

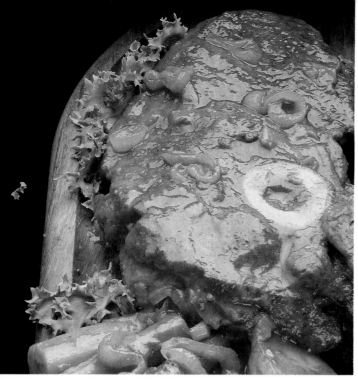

Savory Pot Roast

■ Savory Pot Roast

Makes 4 servings

6 tablespoons all-purpose flour, divided
1 teaspoon celery salt
1 teaspoon dried marjoram leaves
½ teaspoon dried summer savory leaves
⅛ teaspoon pepper
3½- to 4-pound beef chuck roast
¼ cup CRISCO® Oil
1 medium onion, thinly sliced
½ cup water
1 can (8 ounces) tomato sauce
2 teaspoons instant beef bouillon granules
4 medium carrots, cut into 3-inch pieces
4 medium potatoes, quartered
¼ cup cold water

Mix 4 tablespoons flour, celery salt, marjoram,
summer savory and pepper in shallow baking dish.
Coat roast evenly with flour mixture. Heat
CRISCO Oil in Dutch oven. Add roast and any
remaining flour mixture. Brown over medium-
high heat. Add onion, ½ cup water, tomato sauce
and bouillon granules. Cover. Reduce heat.
Simmer about 2 hours. Add carrots and potatoes;
re-cover. Simmer about 1 hour, or until vegetables
are tender. Transfer roast and vegetables to serving
platter, reserving cooking liquid in Dutch oven.

Place ¼ cup cold water in 1-cup measure or small
bowl. Mix in remaining 2 tablespoons flour. Stir
into reserved cooking liquid. Cook over medium-
high heat, stirring constantly, until thickened and
bubbly. Serve with beef and vegetables.

■ Turkey Tetrazzini

Makes 6 servings

⅔ cup MIRACLE WHIP Salad Dressing
⅓ cup flour
½ teaspoon celery salt
   Dash of pepper
2 cups milk
7 ozs. spaghetti, broken into thirds, cooked,
   drained
2 cups chopped cooked turkey or chicken
¾ cup (3 ozs.) KRAFT 100% Grated Parmesan
   Cheese
1 4-oz. can mushrooms drained
2 tablespoons chopped pimento (optional)
2 cups fresh bread cubes
3 tablespoons PARKAY Margarine, melted

Combine salad dressing, flour and seasonings in
medium saucepan. Gradually add milk. Cook,
stirring constantly, over low heat until thickened.
Add spaghetti, turkey, ½ cup cheese, mushrooms
and pimento; mix lightly. Spoon into 2-quart
casserole. Toss bread cubes with margarine and
remaining cheese; top casserole. Bake at 350°, 30
minutes or until lightly browned.

Preparation time: 30 minutes

Baking time: 30 minutes

Make ahead: Prepare as directed except for
topping with bread cubes and baking. Cover;
chill. When ready to bake, toss bread cubes with
margarine and remaining cheese. Top casserole;
cover with foil. Bake at 350°, 25 minutes.
Uncover; continue baking 30 minutes or until
lightly browned.

Microwave: Reduce margarine to 2 tablespoons.
Microwave margarine in 2-quart microwave-safe
casserole on High 30 seconds or until melted. Add
bread cubes; toss. Microwave on High 3½ to 4½
minutes or until crisp, stirring after 2 minutes.
Remove from casserole; set aside. Combine salad
dressing, flour and seasonings in same casserole;
gradually add milk. Microwave on High 5 to 6
minutes or until thickened, stirring after each
minute. Stir in spaghetti, turkey, ½ cup cheese,
mushrooms and pimento; mix lightly. Cover;
microwave on High 8 to 10 minutes or until
thoroughly heated, stirring after 5 minutes. Stir;
top with bread cubes. Sprinkle with remaining
cheese. Let stand 5 minutes.

■ Fried Chicken

4 servings

- ⅓ cup all-purpose flour
- ½ teaspoon salt
- ½ teaspoon paprika
- ¼ teaspoon garlic powder
- ¼ teaspoon pepper
- 1 can (5.3 ounces) evaporated milk
- 1 broiler-fryer chicken (2½ to 3 pounds), cut up
- ¼ cup CRISCO® Oil

Mix flour, salt, paprika, garlic powder and pepper in large plastic food storage bag. Set aside. Pour evaporated milk into bowl. Dip chicken in evaporated milk. Add a few chicken pieces to food storage bag. Shake to coat. Remove chicken from bag. Repeat with remaining chicken.

Heat CRISCO Oil in large skillet. Add chicken. Brown over medium-high heat. Cook over moderate heat about 25 minutes, or until meat near bone is no longer pink and juices run clear, turning pieces over frequently.

■ Simple Shrimp Creole

Makes about 5 cups or 4 servings

- 1 tablespoon butter or margarine
- ½ cup chopped onion
- 1 medium green pepper, cut into matchstick-thin strips
- ½ cup thinly sliced celery
- 1 jar (15 ounces) PREGO® al Fresco Spaghetti Sauce
- ¾ pound medium shrimp, shelled and deveined
- 1 bay leaf
- ⅛ teaspoon pepper
  Generous dash hot pepper sauce
  Hot cooked rice

1. In 2-quart microwave-safe casserole, combine butter, onion, green pepper and celery. Cover with lid; microwave on HIGH 4 minutes or until vegetables are tender, stirring once during cooking.

2. Stir in spaghetti sauce, shrimp, bay leaf, pepper and hot pepper sauce. Cover; microwave on HIGH 6 minutes or until shrimp are opaque, stirring once during cooking. Remove bay leaf. Serve over rice.

Fried Chicken

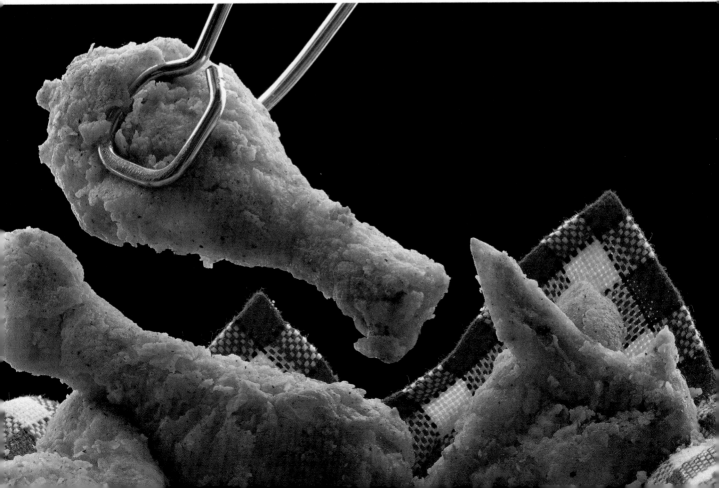

■ Tasty Turkey Pot Pie

Makes 4 to 6 servings

- ½ cup MIRACLE WHIP Salad Dressing
- 2 tablespoons flour
- 1 teaspoon instant chicken bouillon
- ⅛ teaspoon pepper
- ¾ cup milk
- 1½ cups chopped cooked turkey or chicken
- 1 10-oz. pkg. frozen mixed vegetables, thawed, drained
- 1 4-oz. can refrigerated quick crescent dinner rolls

Combine salad dressing, flour, bouillon and pepper in medium saucepan. Gradually add milk. Cook, stirring constantly, over low heat until thickened. Add turkey and vegetables; heat thoroughly, stirring occasionally. Spoon into 8-inch square baking dish. Unroll dough into two rectangles. Press perforations together to seal. Place rectangles side-by-side to form square; press edges together to form seam. Cover turkey mixture with dough. Bake at 375°, 15 to 20 minutes or until browned.

Preparation time: 15 minutes

Baking time: 20 minutes

Variations: Combine 1 egg, beaten, and 1 tablespoon cold water, mixing until well blended. Brush dough with egg mixture just before baking.

Substitute one chicken bouillon cube for instant chicken bouillon.

Substitute 10×6-inch baking dish for 8-inch square baking dish.

Substitute 12×8-inch baking dish for 8-inch square dish. Double all ingredients. Assemble recipe as directed, using three dough rectangles to form top crust. Decorate crust with cut-outs from remaining rectangle. Bake as directed.

Microwave tip: To prepare sauce, combine salad dressing, flour, bouillon and pepper in 1-quart microwave-safe measure or bowl; gradually add milk. Microwave on High 4 to 5 minutes or until thickened, stirring after each minute.

■ Oven-Baked Bourguignonne

Makes about 8 servings

- 2 pounds boneless beef chuck, cut into 1-inch cubes
- ¼ cup all-purpose flour
- 1⅓ cups sliced carrots
- 1 can (14½ ounces) whole peeled tomatoes, undrained and chopped
- 1 bay leaf
- 1 envelope LIPTON® Beefy Onion or Onion Recipe Soup Mix
- ½ cup dry red wine
- 1 cup fresh or canned sliced mushrooms
- 1 package (8 ounces) medium or broad egg noodles

Preheat oven to 400°.

In 2-quart casserole, toss beef with flour, then bake uncovered 20 minutes. Add carrots, tomatoes and bay leaf, then beefy onion recipe soup mix blended with wine. Bake covered 1½ hours or until beef is tender. Add mushrooms and bake covered an additional 10 minutes. Remove bay leaf.

Meanwhile, cook noodles according to package directions. To serve, arrange bourguignonne over noodles.

Microwave Directions: Toss beef with flour; set aside. In 2-quart casserole, combine tomatoes, bay leaf and beefy onion recipe soup mix blended with wine. Heat covered at HIGH (Full Power) 7 minutes, stirring once. Add beef and carrots. Heat covered at DEFROST (30% Full Power), stirring occasionally, 1¼ hours. Add mushrooms and heat covered at DEFROST 30 minutes or until beef is tender. Remove bay leaf. Let stand covered 5 minutes. Cook noodles and serve as above.

Freezing/Reheating Directions: Bourguignonne can be baked, then frozen. Simply wrap covered casserole in heavy-duty aluminum foil; freeze. To reheat, unwrap and bake covered at 400°, stirring occasionally to separate beef and vegetables, 1 hour. OR, microwave at HIGH (Full Power), stirring occasionally, 20 minutes or until heated through. Let stand covered 5 minutes.

Curried Turkey Dinner

■ Curried Turkey Dinner

Serves 4

  1 Package (10 oz.) frozen broccoli spears,
     cooked and drained
  2 Cups COOKED TURKEY, cubed
  1 Can (10½ oz.) reduced-sodium cream of
     mushroom soup
  ¼ Cup reduced-calorie mayonnaise
1½ Teaspoons lemon juice
  1 Teaspoon curry powder
  1 Cup seasoned croutons

1. Preheat oven to 350 degrees F.

2. In an 8-inch square baking dish layer broccoli;
   top with turkey.

3. In a small bowl combine soup, mayonnaise,
   lemon juice, and curry powder. Pour over
   turkey and top with croutons.

4. Bake 20 to 25 minutes or until bubbly.

APPROXIMATE NUTRIENT CONTENT PER SERVING: 321 KCAL; 24 gm
protein; 16 gm fat; 21 gm carbohydrate; 720 mg sodium; 63 mg
cholesterol.

Favorite Recipe from **National Turkey Federation**

■ Meat Loaf Italiano

Makes 6 servings

  1 egg, beaten
1½ lbs. ground beef
  1 8-oz. can pizza sauce
  ¾ cup (3 ozs.) VELVEETA Shredded
     Pasteurized Process Cheese Food
  ¾ cup old fashioned or quick oats, uncooked
  ¼ cup cold water
  ½ teaspoon dried oregano leaves, crushed

In large bowl, combine all ingredients except ¼
cup sauce; mix lightly. Shape into loaf in 10×6-
inch baking dish. Bake at 350°, 1 hour. Top with
remaining sauce. Let stand 10 minutes before
serving.

Preparation time: 10 minutes

Baking time: 60 minutes plus standing

■ Standing Rib Roast with Madeira Sauce

Makes about 6 servings

2 large cloves garlic, finely chopped
1 teaspoon marjoram leaves (optional)
1 teaspoon thyme leaves
1 teaspoon salt
¼ teaspoon pepper
5- pound standing rib roast (about 3 ribs)
¼ cup butter or margarine
2 cups thinly sliced mushrooms
¼ cup Madeira or dry red wine
1 tablespoon tomato paste
1 envelope LIPTON® Onion, Onion-Mushroom or Beefy Mushroom Recipe Soup Mix
1 tablespoon all-purpose flour
1½ cups water
1 tablespoon finely chopped parsley
Pepper to taste

Preheat oven to 500°. In small bowl, combine garlic, marjoram, thyme, salt and pepper; set aside.

Trim fat from roast. In roasting pan, on rack, place roast; rub with garlic mixture. Roast 10 minutes, then decrease heat to 350° and continue roasting 1½ hours or until meat thermometer reaches 130° (rare) or 150° (medium).

Remove roast to serving platter and keep warm. Skim fat from pan drippings. In medium saucepan, combine pan juices with butter; stir in mushrooms. Cook 5 minutes or until mushrooms are tender. Stir in wine and tomato paste, then onion recipe soup mix and flour blended with water. Bring to a boil, then simmer, stirring frequently, 5 minutes or until sauce is thickened. Stir in parsley and pepper. Serve sauce with roast.

■ Roasted Duckling with Orange & Plum Sauce

Makes about 2 servings

1 (3-pound) duckling
1 medium orange, halved
1 medium onion, halved
½ cup WISH-BONE® Deluxe French or Lite French-Style Dressing
½ cup orange juice
2 tablespoons brown sugar
1 teaspoon grated orange peel (optional)
¼ teaspoon ground cinnamon
⅛ teaspoon ground cloves
⅛ teaspoon ground nutmeg
1 tablespoon butter or margarine
½ cup chopped onion
1 teaspoon finely chopped garlic
2 tablespoons brandy
2 medium plums, pitted and cut into wedges
2 small oranges, peeled, sectioned and seeded

Preheat oven to 400°.

Stuff duckling with orange and onion halves. Close cavity with skewers or wooden toothpicks; tie legs together with string. With pin or fork, pierce skin. In roasting pan, on rack, place duckling breast side up. Roast 40 minutes, turning duckling every 10 minutes.

Meanwhile, in small bowl, blend deluxe French dressing, orange juice, sugar, orange peel, cinnamon, cloves and nutmeg. Pour ½ of the dressing mixture over duckling; loosely cover with heavy-duty aluminum foil. Continue roasting, basting occasionally, 30 minutes or until meat thermometer reaches 185°. Remove to serving platter and keep warm.

Meanwhile, in medium saucepan, melt butter and cook onion with garlic over medium heat, stirring occasionally, 5 minutes or until onion is tender. Add brandy, then plums and orange sections and cook, stirring occasionally, 5 minutes. Stir in remaining dressing mixture and heat through. Serve with duckling.

Turkey Cranberry Croissant

■ Turkey Cranberry Croissant

Yield: 6 sandwiches

> Thin-sliced cooked BUTTERBALL® turkey
>   (1 pound)
> 1 package (8 ounces) cream cheese, softened
> ¼ cup orange marmalade
> ½ cup chopped pecans
> 6 croissants or rolls, split
> ¾ cup whole berry cranberry sauce
>   Lettuce leaves

Combine cream cheese, marmalade and pecans in small bowl. Spread top and bottom halves of croissants with cream cheese mixture. Layer turkey on bottom halves. Spoon 2 tablespoons cranberry sauce over turkey. Add lettuce and croissant top.

■ Lemon Broiled Fish

Makes 4 servings

> ½ cup margarine or butter, melted
> ¼ cup REALEMON® Lemon Juice from
>   Concentrate
> 2 cups fresh bread crumbs (about 4 slices)
> 1 tablespoon chopped parsley
> ½ teaspoon paprika
> 1 pound fish fillets, fresh or frozen, thawed

Combine margarine and ReaLemon® brand. In medium bowl, combine bread crumbs, parsley and ¼ *cup* of the lemon mixture. Add paprika to remaining lemon mixture. Dip fish into paprika mixture; broil until fish flakes with fork. Top with bread crumb mixture. Return to broiler; heat through. Refrigerate leftovers.

Lasagna Italiano

■ Lasagna Italiano

Makes 6 to 8 servings

1½ lbs. ground beef
½ cup chopped onion
1 14½-oz. can tomatoes, cut up
1 6-oz. can tomato paste
⅓ cup cold water
1 garlic clove, minced
1 teaspoon dried oregano leaves, crushed
¼ teaspoon pepper
6 ozs. lasagna noodles, cooked, drained
2 6-oz. pkgs. 100% Natural KRAFT Low
 Moisture Part-Skim Mozzarella Cheese
 Slices
½ lb. VELVEETA Pasteurized Process Cheese
 Spread, thinly sliced
½ cup (2 ozs.) KRAFT 100% Grated Parmesan
 Cheese

In large skillet, brown meat; drain. Add onions; cook until tender. Stir in tomatoes, tomato paste, water, garlic and seasonings. Cover; simmer 30 minutes. In 12×8-inch baking dish, layer half of noodles, meat sauce, mozzarella cheese, process cheese spread and parmesan cheese; repeat layers. Bake at 350°, 30 minutes. Let stand 10 minutes before serving.

Preparation time: 40 minutes

Baking time: 30 minutes plus standing

■ Cajun Baked Fish

Makes 3 to 4 servings

⅓ cup MIRACLE WHIP Salad Dressing
½ teaspoon ground cumin
½ teaspoon onion powder
¼ teaspoon ground red pepper
¼ teaspoon garlic powder
1 lb. fish fillets
½ cup crushed sesame crackers

Combine salad dressing and seasonings; mix well. Brush fish with salad dressing mixture; coat with crumbs. Place in greased shallow baking dish. Bake at 350°, 30 minutes or until fish begins to flake when tested with a fork. Serve with your favorite accompaniments.

Preparation time: 15 minutes

Baking time: 30 minutes

Microwave: Combine salad dressing and seasonings; mix well. Brush fish with salad dressing mixture; coat with crumbs. Arrange fish in shallow microwave-safe baking dish, placing thickest portions toward outside of dish. Cover with plastic wrap; vent. Microwave on High 5 minutes, turning dish after 3 minutes. Let stand, covered, 2 to 3 minutes or until fish begins to flake when tested with a fork. Serve with your favorite accompaniments.

■ Fettuccine with Shrimp and Creamy Herb Sauce

Makes about 2 servings

1 envelope LIPTON® Creamy Herb Recipe
　　Soup Mix
1¾ cups milk
8 ounces frozen cleaned shrimp, partially
　　thawed*
½ cup frozen peas, partially thawed
6 ounces fettuccine or medium egg noodles,
　　cooked and drained
¼ cup grated Parmesan cheese

In 2-quart saucepan, with wire whip or fork, thoroughly blend creamy herb recipe soup mix with milk. Bring just to the boiling point, stirring frequently. Add shrimp and peas and simmer 3 minutes or until shrimp are tender. Toss shrimp sauce with hot noodles and cheese.

Substitution: Use 8 ounces uncooked fresh shrimp, cleaned.

Microwave Directions: Decrease milk to 1¼ cups. In 2-quart casserole, with wire whip or fork, thoroughly blend creamy herb recipe soup mix with milk. Heat uncovered at HIGH (Full Power), stirring occasionally, 5 minutes. Add shrimp and peas and heat uncovered, stirring occasionally, 6 minutes or until shrimp are tender. Toss as above.

■ Italian Stuffed Shells

Makes 6 to 8 servings

24 CREAMETTE® Jumbo Macaroni Shells,
　　cooked and drained
1 pound lean ground beef
⅔ cup chopped onion
1 clove garlic, chopped
2 cups boiling water
1 (12-ounce) can tomato paste
1 tablespoon WYLER'S® Beef-Flavor Instant
　　Bouillon *or* 3 Beef-Flavor Bouillon Cubes
1½ teaspoons oregano leaves
1 (16-ounce) container BORDEN® or
　　MEADOW GOLD® Cottage Cheese
2 cups (8 ounces) shredded Mozzarella
　　cheese
½ cup grated Parmesan cheese
1 egg

In large skillet, brown beef, onion and garlic; pour off fat. Stir in water, tomato paste, bouillon and oregano; simmer 30 minutes. In medium bowl, combine cottage cheese, *1 cup* Mozzarella, grated Parmesan and egg; mix well. Stuff shells with cheese mixture; arrange in individual ramekins or 13×9-inch baking dish. Pour sauce over shells; cover. Bake in preheated 350° oven 30 minutes. Uncover; sprinkle with remaining *1 cup* Mozzarella. Bake 3 minutes longer. Refrigerate leftovers.

■ Glazed Stuffed Cornish Hens

Makes 4 servings

2 (1½-pound) Cornish hens
¼ cup butter or margarine
½ cup chopped onion
½ cup sweet red pepper cut into julienne
　　strips
½ cup green pepper cut into julienne strips
4 cups herb-flavored stuffing mix
½ cup CAMPBELL'S® Condensed Chicken
　　Broth
½ cup water
½ cup apricot jam

1. Remove giblets and neck from inside hens (reserve for another use if desired). Rinse hens; pat dry. Split hens along backbone and breastbone; set aside.

2. In 3-quart microwave-safe casserole, combine butter, onion and peppers. Cover with vented plastic wrap; microwave on HIGH 3 minutes or until vegetables are tender, stirring once during cooking. Add stuffing, broth and water; toss to mix well.

3. Pat stuffing mixture into bottom of 12- by 8-inch microwave-safe baking dish. Arrange hen halves, skin-side up, over stuffing; set aside.

4. Place jam in small microwave-safe bowl. Microwave, uncovered, on HIGH 45 seconds or until melted. Brush jam over hens. Cover with waxed paper; microwave on HIGH 17 minutes or until hens are no longer pink in center, rotating dish twice and rearranging hens once during cooking. Let stand, covered, 5 minutes.

Desserts

■ Pumpkin Nut Pound Cake

Makes one 9×5-inch loaf

1¾ cups all-purpose flour
½ cup pecans, finely chopped or ground
1½ teaspoons ground cinnamon
 1 teaspoon baking soda
½ teaspoon salt
½ teaspoon ground allspice
¼ teaspoon ground nutmeg
¾ cup butter or margarine, softened
¾ cup granulated sugar
½ cup packed light brown sugar
 2 eggs
 1 cup LIBBY'S® Solid Pack Pumpkin
  Glaze (recipe follows)
  Sliced almonds, toasted (optional)

In medium bowl, combine flour, pecans, cinnamon, baking soda, salt, allspice, and nutmeg; set aside. In large mixer bowl, cream butter and sugars. Add eggs; beat until light and fluffy. Mix in pumpkin. Add liquid ingredients to dry ingredients; mix well. Spread into greased and floured 9×5-inch loaf pan. Bake in 325°F. oven for approximately 1 hour 15 minutes, or until toothpick comes out clean. Cool in pan for 10 minutes. Remove from pan; cool on wire rack. Drizzle glaze over cake; garnish with almonds, if desired.

Glaze: In small bowl, combine 1 cup sifted powdered sugar and 3 to 4 teaspoons water.

■ Old-Fashioned Rice Pudding

Makes 10 servings

4 cups cold milk
1 cup MINUTE® Rice
1 package (4-serving size) JELL-O® Vanilla or
 Coconut Cream Flavor Pudding and Pie
 Filling
¼ cup raisins (optional)
1 egg, well beaten
¼ teaspoon ground cinnamon
⅛ teaspoon ground nutmeg

Combine milk, rice, pudding mix, raisins and egg in medium saucepan. Bring to a full boil over medium heat, stirring constantly. Remove from heat. Cool 5 minutes, stirring twice. Pour into individual dessert dishes or serving bowl. Sprinkle with cinnamon and nutmeg; serve warm. (For chilled pudding, place plastic wrap directly on hot pudding. Cool slightly; chill about 1 hour. Stir before serving; sprinkle with cinnamon and nutmeg.)

Old-Fashioned Fruited Rice Pudding: Add 1 can (17½ oz.) drained fruit cocktail to pudding after cooling 5 minutes. Garnish as desired.

Top: Old-Fashioned Fruited Rice Pudding;
bottom: Old-Fashioned Rice Pudding

■ Brandied Fruit Pie

Makes 8 servings

1 KEEBLER® Ready-Crust® Graham Cracker
   Pie Crust
2 packages (8 ounces each) mixed, pitted
   dried fruit
¾ cup plus 1 tablespoon water
¼ cup plus 1 tablespoon brandy or cognac
5 thin lemon slices
¾ cup packed brown sugar
1 teaspoon ground cinnamon
¼ teaspoon ground nutmeg
¼ teaspoon ground cloves
¼ teaspoon salt
½ cup graham cracker crumbs
¼ cup butter or margarine, melted
   Hard sauce or whipped cream (optional)
   Lemon slices for garnish

In medium saucepan, combine dried fruit, ¾ cup
of the water, ¼ cup of the brandy and the 5 lemon
slices. Simmer over low heat 10 minutes or until
liquid is absorbed. Remove and discard lemon
slices. Stir in sugar, spices, salt, remaining 1
tablespoon water and remaining 1 tablespoon
brandy; pour into pie crust. Sprinkle graham
cracker crumbs evenly over top of pie. Drizzle
melted butter over crumbs. Bake in preheated
350° oven 30 minutes. Cool on wire rack. Serve
warm or at room temperature. If desired, serve
with hard sauce or whipped cream; garnish with
lemon slices.

Brandied Fruit Pie

■ Chilled Chocolate Rum Souffle

Makes 6 to 8 servings

1 envelope unflavored gelatin
¼ cup cold water
4 squares BAKER'S® Unsweetened Chocolate
¼ cup dark rum*
6 eggs, separated**
⅔ cup sugar
¼ teaspoon salt
1 cup heavy cream***
2 tablespoons sugar***
½ teaspoon vanilla***

Soften gelatin in water. Melt chocolate in
saucepan over very low heat, stirring constantly
until smooth. Stir in rum and softened gelatin; stir
until gelatin is dissolved. Remove from heat.
Combine egg yolks and ⅔ cup sugar in top of
double boiler. Place over hot water and beat with
hand or electric mixer until thick and light in
color. Remove from hot water. Blend in chocolate
mixture; pour into a bowl.

Beat egg whites with salt until stiff peaks form;
fold into chocolate mixture. Whip cream with 2
tablespoons sugar and the vanilla until soft peaks
form. Fold into chocolate mixture. Pour into
buttered 1½-quart serving dish or 1-quart souffle
dish fitted with paper collar (see Note). Chill at
least 3 hours. Garnish with additional sweetened
whipped cream and chocolate curls, if desired.

Or use ¼ cup milk and 1 teaspoon rum extract.

**Use clean eggs with no cracks in shells.*

***Or use 2 cups thawed COOL WHIP® Whipped
Topping.*

Note: To make paper collar, cut a piece of waxed
paper long enough to wrap around dish and
overlap slightly. Fold in half lengthwise; grease
one side lightly with shortening. Wrap the
doubled paper around dish, greased side toward
dish, extending it 2 inches above rim. Secure with
string or tape. Remove paper collar before
serving.

Classic Christmas Cake

■ Classic Christmas Cake

Makes one 10-inch cake

  1 package (8 ounces) cream cheese, softened
  1 cup butter or margarine, softened
1½ cups granulated sugar
1½ teaspoons vanilla
1½ teaspoons ground cinnamon
  ¼ teaspoon ground nutmeg
  4 eggs
2¼ cups sifted cake flour
1½ teaspoons baking powder
  1 jar (8 ounces) maraschino cherries,
      drained and chopped
  1 cup finely chopped pecans
1½ cups powdered sugar
  2 tablespoons milk
    Pecan halves and red and green candied
      cherries for garnish

In large bowl, beat cream cheese, butter, granulated sugar, vanilla and spices. Add eggs, 1 at a time, mixing well after each addition. In small bowl, combine flour with baking powder; gradually add 2 cups of the flour mixture to butter mixture. To remaining flour mixture, add maraschino cherries and ½ cup of the chopped pecans; fold into batter. Grease 10-inch Bundt® or tube pan; sprinkle with remaining ½ cup chopped pecans. Pour batter into prepared pan. Bake in preheated 325° oven 1 hour and 15 minutes or until toothpick inserted into center of cake comes out clean. Let cool in pan on wire rack 5 minutes. Loosen edge; remove from pan. Cool completely on wire rack. In small bowl, beat powdered sugar and milk until smooth. Spoon icing over cake. Garnish with pecan halves and candied cherries.

Favorite Recipe from **National Pecan Marketing Council, Inc.**

■ Apple Streusel Mince Pie

Makes one 9-inch pie

   3 all-purpose apples, pared and thinly sliced
   ½ cup plus 3 tablespoons unsifted flour
   2 tablespoons margarine or butter, melted
   1 (9-inch) unbaked pastry shell
   1 jar NONE SUCH® Ready-to-Use Mincemeat
      (Regular *or* Brandy & Rum)
   ¼ cup firmly packed light brown sugar
   1 teaspoon ground cinnamon
   ⅓ cup cold margarine or butter
   ¼ cup chopped nuts

In large bowl, toss apples with *3 tablespoons* flour and melted margarine; arrange in pastry shell. Top with mincemeat. In medium bowl, combine remaining *½ cup* flour, sugar and cinnamon; cut in cold margarine until crumbly. Add nuts; sprinkle over mincemeat. Bake in lower half of 425° oven 10 minutes. Reduce oven temperature to 375°; bake 25 minutes longer or until golden. Cool. Garnish as desired.

■ Old-Fashioned Bread Pudding

Makes about 4 cups or 6 servings

   1 package (4-serving size) JELL-O® Vanilla
      Flavor Pudding and Pie Filling
   ¼ cup sugar
   3 cups milk
   ¼ cup raisins
   2 tablespoons grated lemon rind (optional)
   1 tablespoon butter or margarine
   ½ teaspoon vanilla
   6 slices dry white bread, cut into cubes
   ¼ teaspoon cinnamon
   ⅛ teaspoon nutmeg

Combine pudding mix and 2 tablespoons of the sugar in medium saucepan. Add 2 cups of the milk; blend well. Add raisins and lemon rind. Cook and stir over medium heat until mixture comes to a full boil. Remove from heat; stir in butter and vanilla.

Pour remaining milk over bread cubes in bowl to moisten; stir into pudding mixture. Pour into 1-quart baking dish. Combine remaining sugar with spices. Sprinkle over pudding. Broil until sugar is lightly browned and bubbly, 4 to 5 minutes. Serve warm or chilled. Garnish with lemon slice, if desired.

Apple Streusel Mince Pie

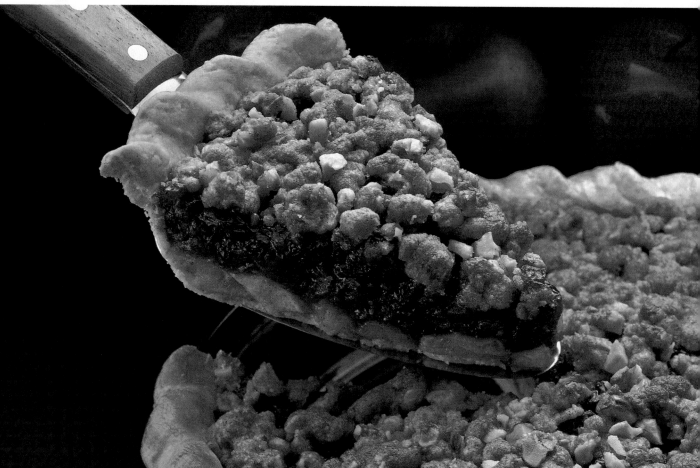

■ Eggnog Pie

Makes one 9-inch pie

1 cup cold dairy or canned eggnog
1 package (6-serving size) JELL-O® Vanilla
    Flavor Instant Pudding and Pie Filling
1 tablespoon rum or ¼ teaspoon rum extract
¼ teaspoon nutmeg
3½ cups (8 ounces) COOL WHIP® Non-Dairy
    Whipped Topping, thawed
1 prepared 8- to 9-inch graham cracker
    crumb crust, cooled

Pour cold eggnog into bowl. Add pie filling mix,
rum and nutmeg. With electric mixer at low
speed, beat until blended, about 1 minute. Let
stand 5 minutes. Fold in 2 cups of the whipped
topping. Spoon into pie crust. Chill until firm,
about 2 hours. Garnish with remaining whipped
topping. Sprinkle with additional nutmeg, if
desired.

■ Linzer Bars

Makes 2 dozen small bars

¾ cup butter or margarine, softened
½ cup sugar
1 egg
½ teaspoon grated lemon peel
¼ teaspoon salt
½ teaspoon ground cinnamon
⅛ teaspoon ground cloves
2 cups all-purpose flour
1 cup DIAMOND® Walnuts, finely chopped or
    ground
1 cup raspberry or apricot jam

In large bowl, cream butter, sugar, egg, lemon
peel, salt and spices. Blend in flour and walnuts.
Set aside about ¼ of the dough for lattice top. Pat
remaining dough into bottom and about ½ inch
up sides of greased 9-inch square pan. Spread with
jam. Make pencil-shaped strips of remaining
dough, rolling against floured board with palms of
hands. Arrange in lattice pattern over top, pressing
ends against dough on sides. Bake in preheated
325°F oven about 45 minutes or until lightly
browned. Cool in pan, then cut into bars.

Cherry-Topped Icebox Cake

■ Cherry-Topped Icebox Cake

Makes 12 servings

20 whole graham crackers
2 cups cold milk
1 package (6-serving size) JELL-O® Vanilla or
    Chocolate Flavor Instant Pudding and
    Pie Filling
1¾ cups thawed COOL WHIP® Non-Dairy
    Whipped Topping
2 cans (21 ounces each) cherry pie filling

Line 13×9-inch pan with some of the graham
crackers, breaking crackers, if necessary. Pour
cold milk into bowl. Add pudding mix. With
electric mixer at low speed, beat until well
blended, 1 to 2 minutes. Let stand 5 minutes; then
blend in whipped topping. Spread half of the
pudding mixture over crackers. Add another layer
of crackers. Top with remaining pudding mixture
and remaining crackers. Spread cherry pie filling
over crackers. Chill about 3 hours.

Chocolate-Frosted Icebox Cake: Prepare Cherry-
Topped Icebox Cake as directed, substituting ¾
cup ready-to-spread chocolate fudge frosting for
the cherry pie filling. Carefully spread frosting
over top layer of graham crackers.

■ Scrumptious Chocolate Layer Bars

About 3 dozen bars

 2 cups (12-ounce package) HERSHEY'S Semi-Sweet Chocolate Chips
 1 package (8 ounces) cream cheese
 ½ cup plus 2 tablespoons (5-ounce can) evaporated milk
 1 cup chopped walnuts
 ¼ cup sesame seeds (optional)
 ½ teaspoon almond extract
 3 cups all-purpose flour
 1½ cups sugar
 1 teaspoon baking powder
 ½ teaspoon salt
 1 cup butter or margarine
 2 eggs
 ½ teaspoon almond extract

Combine chocolate chips, cream cheese and evaporated milk in medium saucepan. Cook over low heat, stirring constantly, until chips are melted and mixture is smooth. Remove from heat; stir in walnuts, sesame seeds and ½ teaspoon almond extract. Blend well; set aside.

Combine remaining ingredients in large mixer bowl; blend well on low speed until mixture resembles coarse crumbs. Press half the crumb mixture in greased 13×9-inch pan; spread with chocolate mixture. Sprinkle rest of crumb mixture over filling. (If crumb mixture softens and forms a stiff dough, pinch off small pieces to use as topping.) Bake at 375°for 35 to 40 minutes or until golden brown. Cool; cut into bars.

■ Peanut Butter Paisley Brownies

About 3 dozen brownies

 ½ cup butter or margarine, softened
 ¼ cup peanut butter
 1 cup granulated sugar
 1 cup packed light brown sugar
 3 eggs
 1 teaspoon vanilla extract
 2 cups all-purpose flour
 2 teaspoons baking powder
 ¼ teaspoon salt
 ½ cup (5.5-ounce can) HERSHEY'S Syrup

Blend butter and peanut butter in large mixer bowl. Add granulated sugar and brown sugar; beat well. Add eggs, one at a time, beating well after each addition. Blend in vanilla. Combine flour, baking powder and salt; add to peanut butter mixture.

Spread half the batter in greased 13×9-inch pan. Spoon syrup over top. Carefully spread with remaining batter. Swirl with spatula or knife for marbled effect. Bake at 350° for 35 to 40 minutes or until lightly browned. Cool; cut into squares.

■ Best Brownies

About 16 brownies

 ½ cup butter or margarine, melted
 1 cup sugar
 1 teaspoon vanilla extract
 2 eggs
 ½ cup all-purpose flour
 ⅓ cup HERSHEY'S Cocoa
 ¼ teaspoon baking powder
 ¼ teaspoon salt
 ½ cup chopped nuts (optional)
    Creamy Brownie Frosting (recipe follows)

Blend butter, sugar and vanilla in large bowl. Add eggs; using a wooden spoon, beat well. Combine flour, cocoa, baking powder and salt; gradually blend into egg mixture. Stir in nuts.

Spread in greased 9-inch square pan. Bake at 350° for 20 to 25 minutes or until brownie begins to pull away from edges of pan. Cool; frost with Creamy Brownie Frosting. Cut into squares.

Creamy Brownie Frosting

About 1 cup frosting

 3 tablespoons butter or margarine, softened
 3 tablespoons HERSHEY'S Cocoa
 1 tablespoon light corn syrup or honey
 ½ teaspoon vanilla extract
 1 cup confectioners' sugar
 1 to 2 tablespoons milk

Cream butter, cocoa, corn syrup and vanilla in small mixer bowl. Add confectioners' sugar and milk; beat to spreading consistency.

Clockwise from top left: Peanut Butter Paisley Brownies, Scrumptious Chocolate Layer Bars and Best Brownies

Rosettes

■ Rosettes

Makes 3 dozen rosettes

> CRISCO® Oil for frying
> 1 cup unsifted all-purpose flour
> 2 tablespoons confectioners sugar
> ¼ teaspoon salt
> 1 cup milk
> 2 eggs
> 1 teaspoon vanilla
> 1 teaspoon almond extract
> Confectioners sugar

Heat 2 to 3 inches CRISCO Oil in deep-fryer or large saucepan to 365°F. Meanwhile, mix flour, 2 tablespoons confectioners sugar and salt in small mixing bowl. Add milk, eggs, vanilla and almond extract. Stir until smooth.

Place rosette iron in hot CRISCO Oil 1 minute. Tap excess oil from iron onto paper towel. Dip hot iron into batter, making sure batter does not cover top of iron. Place back into hot oil. Fry about 30 seconds, or until rosette is golden brown. Immediately remove rosette. Drain on paper towels. Reheat iron in hot oil 1 minute before frying each rosette. Sprinkle rosettes with confectioners sugar.

■ Cherry Cheese Pie

Makes one 9-inch pie

> 1 (9-inch) graham cracker crumb crust *or* baked pastry shell
> 1 (8-ounce) package cream cheese, softened
> 1 (14-ounce) can EAGLE® Brand Sweetened Condensed Milk (NOT evaporated milk)
> ⅓ cup REALEMON® Lemon Juice from Concentrate
> 1 teaspoon vanilla extract
> 1 (21-ounce) can cherry pie filling, chilled

In large bowl, beat cheese until fluffy. Gradually beat in sweetened condensed milk until smooth. Stir in ReaLemon® brand and vanilla. Pour into prepared crust. Chill 3 hours or until set. Top with desired amount of pie filling before serving. Refrigerate leftovers.

TOPPING VARIATIONS

Fresh Fruit: Omit cherry pie filling. Arrange well-drained fresh strawberries, banana slices (dipped in ReaLemon® brand and well-drained) and blueberries on top of chilled pie. Just before serving, brush fruit with light corn syrup if desired.

Ambrosia: Omit cherry pie filling. In small saucepan, combine ½ cup peach *or* apricot preserves, ¼ cup flaked coconut, 2 tablespoons orange juice *or* orange-flavored liqueur and 2 teaspoons cornstarch; cook and stir until thickened. Remove from heat. Arrange fresh orange sections over top of pie; top with coconut mixture. Chill.

Blueberry: Omit cherry pie filling. In medium saucepan, combine ¼ cup sugar and 1 tablespoon cornstarch; mix well. Add ½ cup water, 2 tablespoons ReaLemon® brand then 2 cups fresh or dry-pack frozen blueberries; mix well. Bring to a boil; reduce heat and simmer 3 minutes or until thickened and clear. Cool 10 minutes. Spread over pie. Chill.

Cranberry: Omit cherry pie filling. In medium saucepan, combine ⅓ cup sugar and 1 tablespoon cornstarch. Add ½ cup plus 2 tablespoons cold water and 2 cups fresh or dry-pack frozen cranberries; mix well. Bring to a boil; reduce heat and simmer 10 minutes, stirring constantly. Cool 15 minutes. Spread over pie. Chill.

Banana Cream Cheese Pie: Omit cherry pie filling. Prepare filling as above. Slice 2 bananas; dip in ReaLemon® brand and drain. Line crust with bananas. Pour filling over bananas; cover. Chill. Before serving, slice 2 bananas; dip in ReaLemon® brand and drain. Garnish top of pie with bananas.

■ Colonial Apple Cake

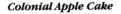

1 ring cake

2¾ cups unsifted all-purpose flour
1 teaspoon baking powder
1 teaspoon ground cinnamon
¾ teaspoon salt
½ teaspoon baking soda
1¾ cups granulated sugar
1¼ cups CRISCO® Oil
2 eggs
¼ cup milk
1 teaspoon vanilla
2 cups chopped, peeled apple
½ cup chopped dates
1 teaspoon grated lemon peel
1 to 2 tablespoons confectioners sugar

Preheat oven to 350°F. Grease and flour 12-cup fluted ring pan. Set aside.

Mix flour, baking powder, cinnamon, salt and baking soda in medium mixing bowl. Set aside. Combine granulated sugar, CRISCO Oil, eggs, milk and vanilla in large mixing bowl. Beat with electric mixer at medium speed until blended, scraping bowl constantly. Add dry ingredients. Beat at medium speed 2 minutes longer, scraping bowl frequently. Stir in apple, dates and lemon peel. Pour into prepared pan.

Bake at 350°F, 1 hour to 1 hour 15 minutes, or until wooden pick inserted in center comes out clean. Let stand 10 minutes. Invert onto serving plate. Cool slightly. Sift confectioners sugar onto cake. Serve warm. Top with *whipped cream*, if desired.

Colonial Apple Cake

■ Swirl of Chocolate Cheesecake Squares

Makes sixteen, 2-inch squares

CRUST
  1 cup graham cracker crumbs
  ¼ cup butter or margarine, melted
  3 tablespoons sugar

FILLING
  1 package (8 ounces) cream cheese, softened
  ¾ cup *undiluted* CARNATION® Evaporated Milk
  ½ cup sugar
  1 egg, lightly beaten
  2 tablespoons all-purpose flour
  2 teaspoons vanilla extract
  ½ cup (3 ounces) semi-sweet chocolate chips or pieces, melted

For Crust: In small bowl, combine crumbs, butter, and sugar. Firmly press mixture into bottom of buttered 8×8-inch baking pan.

For Filling: In blender container, place cream cheese, evaporated milk, sugar, egg, flour, and vanilla; process until smooth. Gradually stir ½ *cup* cheese mixture into melted chocolate. Pour *remaining* cheese mixture into crust. Pour chocolate mixture over cheese mixture. Swirl mixtures together with knife or spoon to create marbled effect. Bake in preheated 300°F. oven for 40 to 45 minutes, or until set. Cool in pan on wire rack before cutting. Store, covered, in refrigerator.

■ Simply Superb Pecan Pie

Makes one 9-inch pie

  3 eggs, beaten
  1 cup sugar
  ½ cup dark corn syrup
  1 teaspoon vanilla
  6 tablespoons butter or margarine, melted, cooled
  1 cup pecan pieces or halves
  1 (9-inch) unbaked pie shell

In large bowl, beat eggs, sugar, corn syrup, vanilla and butter. Stir in pecans. Pour into unbaked pie shell. Bake in preheated 350° oven 45 to 60 minutes or until knife inserted halfway between outside and center comes out clean. Cool on wire rack.

Favorite Recipe from **National Pecan Marketing Council, Inc.**

Simply Superb Pecan Pie

■ Sweet Potato Custard Pie

Makes one 9-inch pie

Pecan Crust (recipe follows)*
3 eggs
1 can (16 ounces) vacuum-packed sweet
    potatoes, drained, mashed
½ cup packed brown sugar
1½ teaspoons ground cinnamon
1 teaspoon ground allspice
½ teaspoon salt
1 can (13 ounces) evaporated milk
    Whipped cream (optional)
    Pecan halves (optional)

Prepare Pecan Crust. In large bowl, beat eggs, sweet potatoes, sugar, spices and salt. In small saucepan, heat evaporated milk over medium heat until hot; gradually stir into sweet potato mixture. Pour into unbaked pie shell. Bake in lower third of preheated 400° oven 40 to 45 minutes or until knife inserted near center comes out clean. Cool completely on wire rack. If desired, garnish with whipped cream and pecan halves.

A thawed frozen 9-inch deep-dish-style pie shell may be substituted.

Pecan Crust

1½ cups all-purpose flour
¼ cup ground pecans
½ teaspoon salt
½ cup shortening
1 egg yolk
4 to 5 tablespoons ice water
2 teaspoons lemon juice

In large bowl, combine flour, ground pecans and salt. Cut in shortening until mixture resembles coarse crumbs. In small bowl, blend egg yolk, 4 tablespoons of the water and the lemon juice. Add to flour mixture, mixing lightly with fork until dough just sticks together. Add more water, if necessary. Press into ball. Roll out on lightly floured surface into 10-inch circle. Carefully fit into 9-inch pie plate. Trim edge; flute as desired. Prick bottom and side of pastry with fork.

Favorite Recipe from **American Egg Board**

Applesauce Fruitcake Bars

■ Applesauce Fruitcake Bars

Makes 48 bars

1 (14-ounce) can EAGLE® Brand Sweetened
    Condensed Milk (NOT evaporated milk)
2 eggs
¼ cup margarine or butter, melted
2 teaspoons vanilla extract
3 cups biscuit baking mix
1 (15-ounce) jar applesauce
1 cup chopped dates
1 (6-ounce) container green candied
    cherries, chopped
1 (6-ounce) container red candied cherries,
    chopped
1 cup chopped nuts
1 cup raisins
    Confectioners' sugar

Preheat oven to 325°. In large mixer bowl, beat sweetened condensed milk, eggs, margarine and vanilla. Stir in remaining ingredients except confectioners' sugar. Spread evenly into well-greased and floured 15×10-inch jellyroll pan. Bake 35 to 40 minutes or until wooden pick inserted in center comes out clean. Cool thoroughly. Sprinkle with confectioners' sugar. Cut into bars. Store tightly covered at room temperature.

◼ Christmas Tree Cake

Makes 12 to 16 servings

> 1 two-layer cake mix (any flavor)
> Ingredients for cake mix
> Decorator Frosting (recipe follows)
> Assorted decorative candies

Preheat oven to 350°F. Prepare batter as directed on box. Pour into well-greased and floured Christmas tree cake pan. Bake 45 to 55 minutes or until wooden pick inserted in cake in widest part of pan comes out clean. Cool cake in pan 10 minutes on wire rack. Carefully run straight-edged knife or spatula around edge of cake to loosen; gently remove cake from pan. Cool cake completely. Meanwhile, prepare Decorator Frosting. Carefully transfer cake to large serving tray or board. Spread with frosting. Decorate with candies as desired to resemble decorated Christmas tree.

Decorator Frosting

Makes about 1½ cups

> 3 cups sifted powdered sugar
> ⅓ cup shortening
> 3 tablespoons water
> 1 tablespoon light corn syrup
> ½ teaspoon vanilla
> Green food coloring

Combine ingredients in large bowl of electric mixer. Beat at medium speed until well blended. Beat at high speed 5 minutes. Tint with food coloring to desired color.

◼ Pumpkin Trifle

Makes 12 servings

> 1 pound cake (16 ounces), cut into 12 slices
> 6 tablespoons orange juice
> 1 cup (14-ounce jar) cranberry-orange relish
> 3 cups whipping cream
> ¾ cup sifted powdered sugar
> 2 cups LIBBY'S Pumpkin Pie Mix
> 1 cup sliced almonds, toasted

Drizzle cake slices with orange juice. Spread with relish; set aside. In large bowl, beat whipping cream and powdered sugar until stiff peaks form; fold in pumpkin pie mix.

To Assemble: In trifle bowl, arrange 4 cake slices on bottom. Layer with 3 cups pumpkin mixture, and ⅓ cup almonds; repeat layers two more times. Cover; chill several hours or overnight. Garnish as desired.

Note: Sherry or orange liqueur may be substituted for orange juice.

◼ Easy Carrot Cake

Makes 10 to 12 servings

> 1 two-layer yellow cake mix
> 1¼ cups MIRACLE WHIP Salad Dressing
> 4 eggs
> ¼ cup cold water
> 2 teaspoons ground cinnamon
> 2 cups finely shredded carrots
> ½ cup chopped walnuts
> Vanilla "Philly" Frosting (recipe follows)

In large bowl of electric mixer, combine cake mix, salad dressing, eggs, water and cinnamon, mixing at medium speed until well blended. Stir in carrots and walnuts. Pour into greased 13×9-inch baking pan. Bake at 350°, 35 minutes or until wooden pick inserted in center comes out clean. Cool. Frost with Vanilla "Philly" Frosting.

Preparation time: 25 minutes

Baking time: 35 minutes plus cooling

Vanilla "Philly" Frosting

> 1 3-oz. pkg. PHILADELPHIA BRAND Cream Cheese, softened
> 1 tablespoon milk
> ½ teaspoon vanilla
> 3 cups sifted powdered sugar

Combine cream cheese, milk and vanilla, mixing until well blended. Gradually add sugar, beating until light and fluffy.

Marble Cheesecake

■ Marble Cheesecake

10 to 12 servings

    Graham Crust (recipe follows)
3 packages (8 ounces each) cream cheese, softened
¾ cup sugar
½ cup dairy sour cream
2 teaspoons vanilla extract
3 tablespoons all-purpose flour
3 eggs
¼ cup HERSHEY'S Cocoa
¼ cup sugar
1 tablespoon vegetable oil
½ teaspoon vanilla extract

Prepare Graham Crust; set aside. Combine cream cheese, ¾ cup sugar, the sour cream and 2 teaspoons vanilla in large mixer bowl; beat on medium speed until smooth. Add flour, 1 tablespoon at a time, blending well. Add eggs; beat well. Combine cocoa and ¼ cup sugar in small bowl. Add oil, ½ teaspoon vanilla and 1½ cups of the cream cheese mixture; mix until well blended.

Spoon plain and chocolate mixtures alternately into prepared crust, ending with dollops of chocolate on top; gently swirl with knife or spatula for marbled effect. Bake at 450° for 10 minutes; without opening oven door, decrease temperature to 250° and continue to bake for 30 minutes. Turn off oven; let cheesecake remain in oven 30 minutes without opening door. Remove from oven; loosen cake from side of pan. Cool completely; chill thoroughly.

Graham Crust

1 cup graham cracker crumbs
2 tablespoons sugar
¼ cup butter or margarine, melted

Combine graham cracker crumbs, sugar and melted butter. Press mixture onto bottom and ½ inch up side of 9-inch springform pan. Bake at 350° for 8 to 10 minutes; cool.

Cookies & Candies

■ Cream Cheese Cutout Cookies

Makes about 90 cookies

1 cup butter, softened
1 8-ounce package cream cheese, softened
1½ cups sugar
1 egg
1 teaspoon vanilla
½ teaspoon almond extract
3½ cups all-purpose flour
1 teaspoon baking powder
Almond Frosting (recipe follows)

In a large mixer bowl combine butter and cream cheese. Beat until well combined. Add sugar; beat until fluffy. Add egg, vanilla, and almond extract and beat well.

In a medium bowl stir together flour and baking powder. Add flour mixture to cream cheese mixture; beat until well mixed. Divide dough in half. Cover and chill in the refrigerator about 1½ hours or until dough is easy to handle.

On a lightly floured surface roll dough to ⅛-inch thickness. Cut with desired cookie cutters. Place on an ungreased cookie sheet. Bake in a 375° oven for 8 to 10 minutes or until done. Remove to wire racks; cool. Pipe or spread Almond Frosting onto cooled cookies.

Almond Frosting: In a small mixer bowl beat 2 cups sifted *powdered sugar,* 2 tablespoons softened *butter,* and ¼ teaspoon *almond extract* until smooth. Beat in enough *milk* (4 to 5 teaspoons) until of piping consistency. For spreadable icing, add a little more milk. Stir in a few drops of *food coloring,* if desired. Garnish with colored sugar, dragées or nuts, if desired.

Favorite Recipe from **Wisconsin Milk Marketing Board** © 1989

■ Dutch St. Nicolas Cookies

Makes about 3½ dozen cookies

½ cup whole natural almonds
¾ cup butter or margarine, softened
½ cup packed brown sugar
2 tablespoons milk
1½ teaspoons ground cinnamon
¼ teaspoon ground nutmeg
¼ teaspoon ground ginger
¼ teaspoon ground cloves
2 cups sifted all-purpose flour
1½ teaspoons baking powder
½ teaspoon salt
¼ cup coarsely chopped citron

Spread almonds in single layer on baking sheet. Bake at 375°F, 10 to 12 minutes, stirring occasionally, until lightly toasted. Cool. Chop finely. In large bowl, cream butter, sugar, milk and spices. In small bowl, combine flour, baking powder and salt. Add flour mixture to creamed mixture; blend well. Stir in almonds and citron. Knead dough slightly to make ball. Cover; refrigerate until firm. Roll out dough ¼ inch thick on lightly floured surface. Cut out with cookie cutters. Place 2 inches apart on greased cookie sheets. Bake at 375°F, 7 to 10 minutes, until lightly browned. Remove to wire racks to cool.

Favorite Recipe from **Almond Board of California**

Cream Cheese Cutout Cookies

■ Rich Cocoa Fudge

About 3 dozen candies

   3 cups sugar
   ⅔ cup HERSHEY'S Cocoa
   ⅛ teaspoon salt
1½ cups milk
   ¼ cup butter or margarine
   1 teaspoon vanilla extract

Butter 8- or 9-inch square pan; set aside. Combine sugar, cocoa and salt in heavy 4-quart saucepan; stir in milk. Cook over medium heat, stirring constantly, until mixture comes to full rolling boil. Boil, without stirring, to soft-ball stage, 234°F on a candy thermometer (or until syrup, when dropped into very cold water, forms a soft ball that flattens when removed from water). Bulb of candy thermometer should not rest on bottom of saucepan.

Remove from heat. Add butter and vanilla; *do not stir.* Cool at room temperature to 110°F (lukewarm). Beat until fudge thickens and loses some of its gloss. Quickly spread in prepared pan; cool. Cut into 1- to 1½-inch squares.

VARIATIONS

Nutty Rich Cocoa Fudge: Beat cooked fudge as directed. *Immediately* stir in 1 cup broken almonds, pecans or walnuts and quickly spread in prepared pan.

Marshmallow-Nut Cocoa Fudge: Increase cocoa to ¾ cup. Cook fudge as directed. Add 1 cup marshmallow creme with butter and vanilla; *do not stir.* Cool to 110°F. (lukewarm). Beat 10 minutes; stir in 1 cup broken nuts and pour into prepared pan. (Fudge does not set until poured into pan.)

Top to bottom: Double-Decker Fudge, Chocolate-Almond Fudge and Nutty Rich Cocoa Fudge

■ Chocolate-Almond Fudge

About 5 dozen

  4 cups sugar
1¾ cups (7-ounce jar) marshmallow creme
1½ cups (12-ounce can) evaporated milk
  1 tablespoon butter or margarine
  2 cups (12-ounce package) HERSHEY'S MINI
     CHIPS Semi-Sweet Chocolate
  1 HERSHEY'S Milk Chocolate Bar with
     Almonds (8 ounces), chopped
  1 teaspoon vanilla extract
¾ cup chopped slivered almonds

Butter 9-inch square pan; set aside. Combine sugar, marshmallow creme, evaporated milk and butter in heavy 4-quart saucepan. Cook over medium heat, stirring constantly, until mixture comes to a full boil; boil and stir 7 minutes. Remove from heat; *immediately* add MINI CHIPS Chocolate and chocolate bar pieces, stirring until completely melted. Blend in vanilla; stir in almonds. Pour into prepared pan; cool completely. Cut into 1-inch squares.

■ Double-Decker Fudge

About 4 dozen candies

  1 cup REESE'S Peanut Butter Chips
  1 cup HERSHEY'S Semi-Sweet Chocolate
     Chips
2¼ cups sugar
1¾ cups (7-ounce jar) marshmallow creme
¾ cup evaporated milk
¼ cup butter or margarine
  1 teaspoon vanilla extract

Measure peanut butter chips into one bowl and chocolate chips into another; set aside. Butter 8-inch square pan; set aside. Combine sugar, marshmallow creme, evaporated milk and butter in heavy 3-quart saucepan. Cook over medium heat, stirring constantly, until mixture boils; continue cooking and stirring for 5 minutes.

Remove from heat; stir in vanilla. Immediately stir half the hot mixture into peanut butter chips until completely melted. Quickly pour into prepared pan. Stir remaining hot mixture into chocolate chips until completely melted. Quickly spread over top of peanut butter layer; cool. Cut into 1-inch squares.

Chocolate Pixies

■ Chocolate Pixies

Makes 4 dozen cookies

¼ cup LAND O LAKES® Sweet Cream Butter
  4 squares (1 ounce each) unsweetened
     chocolate
  2 cups all-purpose flour
  2 cups granulated sugar
  4 eggs
  2 teaspoons baking powder
½ teaspoon salt
½ cup chopped walnuts or pecans
     Powdered sugar

In small saucepan over low heat, melt butter and chocolate; stir to blend. Cool. In large bowl, beat chocolate mixture, 1 cup of the flour, the granulated sugar, eggs, baking powder and salt until well mixed. Stir in remaining 1 cup flour and the nuts. Cover; refrigerate until firm, 2 hours or overnight. Shape teaspoonfuls of dough into 1-inch balls; roll in powdered sugar. Place 2 inches apart on greased cookie sheets. Bake in preheated 300° oven 12 to 15 minutes or until firm to the touch. Remove to wire racks to cool.

■ Crisp Peanut Butter Cookies

Makes 6 dozen cookies

2½ cups all-purpose flour
  1 teaspoon baking powder
  1 teaspoon baking soda
  ¼ teaspoon salt
  1 cup MAZOLA® Margarine, softened
  1 cup SKIPPY® Creamy or SUPER CHUNK™
     Peanut Butter
  1 cup granulated sugar
  1 cup packed brown sugar
  2 eggs
  1 teaspoon vanilla
    Granulated sugar

In small bowl, combine flour, baking powder, baking soda and salt. In large bowl, beat margarine and peanut butter until well blended. Beat in sugars until blended. Beat in eggs and vanilla. Add flour mixture; beat until well blended. If dough is too soft to handle, cover and refrigerate until firm. Shape dough into 1-inch balls. Place 2 inches apart on ungreased cookie sheets. Using back of fork dipped in granulated sugar, flatten balls making crisscross pattern. Bake in preheated 350° oven 12 minutes or until lightly browned. Remove to wire racks to cool completely.

Cherry-Coconut Peanut Butter Cookies: Prepare cookie dough as directed; shape into 1-inch balls. Roll balls in 2 cans (3½ ounces each) flaked coconut. *Do not flatten.* Place red or green candied cherry half in center of each cookie. Bake as directed for 15 minutes. Makes 6 dozen cookies.

Cloverleaf Cookies: Prepare cookie dough as directed; divide into 3 parts. Stir ⅓ cup miniature semisweet chocolate chips into first part. Stir ⅔ cup miniature semisweet chocolate chips, melted, into second part. Leave third part plain. To form each cookie, shape ½ teaspoon of each dough into a ball. Place balls cloverleaf-style on ungreased cookie sheets, leaving 2 inches between clusters. Bake as directed. Let cookies cool 1 minute before carefully removing from cookie sheets to wire racks. Makes 5 dozen cookies.

Counterclockwise from top left: Peanut Butter Cutouts (page 74), Cherry-Coconut Peanut Butter Cookies, Peanut Butter Crackles, Santa Lollipop Cookies (page 74), Crisp Peanut Butter Cookies, Peanut Butter Gingerbread Men (page 74) and Peanut Butter Chocolate Chip Cookies

■ Peanut Butter Crackles

Makes about 5 dozen cookies

1½ cups all-purpose flour
  1 teaspoon baking soda
  ⅛ teaspoon salt
  ½ cup MAZOLA® Margarine, softened
  ½ cup SKIPPY® Creamy or SUPER CHUNK™
    Peanut Butter
  ½ cup granulated sugar
  ½ cup packed brown sugar
  1 egg
  1 teaspoon vanilla
    Granulated sugar
    Chocolate candy stars

In small bowl, combine flour, baking soda and salt. In large bowl, beat margarine and peanut butter until well blended. Beat in sugars until blended. Beat in egg and vanilla. Gradually beat in flour mixture until well mixed. Shape dough into 1-inch balls. Roll in granulated sugar. Place 2 inches apart on ungreased cookie sheets. Bake in preheated 375° oven 10 minutes or until lightly browned. Remove from oven and quickly press chocolate star firmly into top of each cookie (cookie will crack around edges). Remove to wire racks to cool completely.

■ Peanut Butter Chocolate Chip Cookies

Makes about 3½ dozen cookies

  1 cup sugar
  ½ cup SKIPPY® Creamy or SUPER CHUNK™
    Peanut Butter
  ½ cup *undiluted* evaporated milk
  1 package (6 ounces) semisweet chocolate
    chips
  1 cup coarsely chopped nuts

In medium bowl, mix sugar and peanut butter until well blended. Stir in evaporated milk, chips and nuts until well mixed. Drop batter by heaping teaspoonfuls 1½ inches apart onto foil-lined cookie sheets. Spread batter evenly into 2-inch rounds. Bake in preheated 325° oven 18 to 20 minutes or until golden. Cool completely on foil on wire racks. Peel foil from cookies.

■ Peanut Butter Cutouts

Makes about 4 dozen cookies

1½ cups all-purpose flour
¾ teaspoon baking soda
⅛ teaspoon salt
½ cup MAZOLA® Margarine, softened
½ cup SKIPPY® Creamy Peanut Butter
½ cup granulated sugar
½ cup packed brown sugar
1 egg
    Colored sugars (optional)

In small bowl, combine flour, baking soda and salt. In large bowl, beat margarine and peanut butter until well blended. Beat in granulated and brown sugars until blended. Beat in egg. Gradually beat in flour mixture until well mixed. Divide dough into thirds. Wrap each portion; refrigerate until firm, about 3 hours. Roll out dough, one third at a time, ¼ inch thick on lightly floured surface. Cut out with cookie cutters. Place 2 inches apart on ungreased cookie sheets. If desired, sprinkle cookies with colored sugars. Bake in preheated 350° oven 8 to 10 minutes or until lightly browned. Remove to wire racks to cool.

Santa Lollipop Cookies: Prepare cookie dough as above. Place lollipop sticks 3 inches apart on ungreased cookie sheets. Roll out dough ⅛ inch thick. Cut out with 4-inch Santa cookie cutter; place over 1 end of each lollipop stick. Bake as above. Decorate as desired. Makes 3 dozen cookies.

■ Peanut Butter Gingerbread Men

Makes about 2½ dozen cookies

5 cups all-purpose flour
1½ teaspoons ground cinnamon
1 teaspoon baking soda
½ teaspoon ground ginger
¼ teaspoon salt
¾ cup MAZOLA® Margarine, softened
¾ cup SKIPPY® Creamy Peanut Butter
1 cup packed brown sugar
1 cup KARO® Dark Corn Syrup
2 eggs
    Frosting for decorating (optional)

In large bowl, combine flour, cinnamon, baking soda, ginger and salt. In another large bowl, beat margarine and peanut butter until well blended. Add sugar, corn syrup and eggs; beat until smooth. Gradually beat in 2 cups of the dry ingredients. With wooden spoon, beat in remaining dry ingredients, 1 cup at a time, until well blended. Divide dough into thirds. Wrap each portion; refrigerate until firm, at least 1 hour. Roll out dough, one third at a time, ⅛ inch thick on lightly floured surface. Cut out with 5½-inch gingerbread cutter. Place 2 inches apart on ungreased cookie sheets. Bake in preheated 300° oven 10 to 12 minutes or until very lightly browned. Remove to wire racks to cool completely. If desired, pipe frosting on cookies to make eyes and buttons.

■ Lemony Spritz Sticks

Makes about 8½ dozen

1 cup butter or margarine, softened
1 cup confectioners' sugar
¼ cup REALEMON® Lemon Juice from Concentrate
2½ cups unsifted flour
¼ teaspoon salt
    Chocolate Glaze (recipe follows)
    Finely chopped nuts

Preheat oven to 375°. In large mixer bowl, beat butter and sugar until fluffy. Add ReaLemon® brand; beat well. Stir in flour and salt; mix well. Place dough in cookie press with star-shaped plate. Press dough onto greased baking sheets into 3-inch strips. Bake 5 to 6 minutes or until lightly browned on ends. Cool 1 to 2 minutes; remove from baking sheets. Cool completely. Dip ends of cookies in Chocolate Glaze then into nuts.

Chocolate Glaze: In small saucepan, melt 3 ounces sweet cooking chocolate and 2 tablespoons margarine or butter. Makes about ⅓ cup.

Tip: When using electric cookie gun, use decorator tip. Press dough onto greased baking sheets into ½×3-inch strips. Bake 8 to 10 minutes or until lightly browned on ends.

Chocolate-Dipped Morsels

■ Chocolate-Dipped Morsels

Makes 1 to 1½ dozen

> **4 squares BAKER'S® Semi-Sweet Chocolate**
> **Assorted morsel centers**

Melt chocolate in saucepan over very low heat,
stirring constantly until smooth. Insert wooden
picks or skewers into fruit and marshmallow
centers. Dip quickly, one at a time, into
chocolate. (To dip pretzels or nuts, stir into
chocolate; remove with fork.) Let stand or chill on
rack or waxed paper until chocolate is firm. For
best eating quality, chill dipped fresh or canned
fruits and serve the same day.

SUGGESTED MORSEL CENTERS

Fruits: Firm strawberries, ½-inch banana slices,
fresh pineapple wedges or drained canned
pineapple chunks, peeled orange slices, orange
wedges, well-drained stemmed maraschino
cherries, dried figs, dried dates or dried apricots.

Unsalted Pretzels and Large Marshmallows

Nuts: Walnut or pecan halves or whole almonds or
Brazil nuts.

■ Fruit-Filled Thumbprints

Makes 3 dozen cookies

> **2 cups all-purpose flour**
> **1 cup LAND O LAKES® Sweet Cream Butter,**
> **softened**
> **½ cup packed brown sugar**
> **2 eggs, separated**
> **1 teaspoon vanilla**
> **⅛ teaspoon salt**
> **1½ cups finely chopped pecans**
> **Fruit preserves**

In large bowl, combine flour, butter, sugar, egg
yolks, vanilla and salt; beat until well mixed.
Shape teaspoonfuls of dough into 1-inch balls. In
small bowl, beat egg whites with fork until foamy.
Dip each ball into egg whites; roll in chopped
pecans. Place 1 inch apart on greased cookie
sheets. Make a depression in center of each cookie
with back of a teaspoon. Bake in preheated 350°
oven 8 minutes; remove from oven. Fill centers
with preserves; continue baking 6 to 10 minutes
or until lightly browned. Remove to wire racks to
cool.

Jingle Jumbles

Makes about 2 dozen cookies

¾ cup butter or margarine, softened
1 cup packed brown sugar
¼ cup molasses
1 egg
2¼ cups all-purpose flour
2 teaspoons baking soda
1 teaspoon ground ginger
1 teaspoon ground cinnamon
½ teaspoon ground cloves
½ teaspoon salt
1¼ cups SUN-MAID® Raisins
Granulated sugar

In large bowl, cream butter and sugar. Add molasses and egg; beat until fluffy. In medium bowl, sift flour with soda, ginger, cinnamon, cloves and salt. Stir into molasses mixture. Stir in raisins. Cover and chill about 30 minutes. Form dough into 1½-inch balls; roll in granulated sugar, coating generously. Place 2 inches apart on greased baking sheet. Bake in preheated 375°F oven 12 to 14 minutes or until edges are firm and centers are still slightly soft. Remove to wire rack to cool.

Swiss Cinnamon Cookies

Makes about 3 dozen (3-inch) cookies

3 egg whites
3¼ cups powdered sugar (approximately)
3 cups DIAMOND® Walnuts, finely ground
1 tablespoon ground cinnamon
Chopped DIAMOND® Walnuts, colored sugars, candied cherries, dragées, for garnish

In medium bowl, beat egg whites until foamy. Gradually beat in 2 cups of the sugar. Beat until mixture holds soft peaks, 3 to 4 minutes; remove ¾ cup of the batter, cover and set aside. Mix the 3 cups walnuts, the cinnamon and ¾ cup more of the sugar into larger egg white-sugar portion. Working with a third of the dough at a time, roll out to ⅛-inch thickness on pastry cloth or board heavily dusted with powdered sugar. Cut into desired shapes with cookie cutters. Place on greased or parchment-lined baking sheets. With tip of knife, spread reserved egg white mixture ⅛

Swiss Cinnamon Cookies (top, center right, bottom right), Jingle Jumbles (center left) and Festive Cookie Bars (bottom left)

inch thick onto top of each cookie, spreading almost to edges. Decorate immediately, as desired, with chopped walnuts, colored sugars, candied cherries and dragées. Bake in preheated 300°F oven 12 to 14 minutes or until cookies are just set and very lightly browned. Remove to wire racks to cool completely. Store in airtight container. Cookies can be securely wrapped and frozen up to 2 months.

Festive Cookie Bars

Makes 3½ to 4 dozen bars

BOTTOM LAYER
1¼ cups all-purpose flour
1 teaspoon granulated sugar
1 teaspoon baking powder
Dash salt
⅔ cup butter or margarine
2 tablespoons cold coffee or water
1 egg yolk
1 package (12 ounces) real semisweet chocolate pieces

TOP LAYER
½ cup butter or margarine, softened
1 cup granulated sugar
1 tablespoon vanilla
2 eggs plus 1 egg white
1 cup SUN-MAID® Raisins
1 cup DIAMOND® Walnuts
Powdered sugar, for garnish

To prepare Bottom Layer: In large bowl, combine flour, granulated sugar, baking powder and salt. Cut in butter until mixture resembles coarse crumbs. In small bowl, mix coffee and egg yolk to blend; stir into flour mixture to moisten evenly. Form dough into a roll. With floured fingertips, press evenly onto bottom of greased 15×10-inch jelly-roll pan. (Layer will be thin.) Bake in preheated 350°F oven 10 minutes. Sprinkle chocolate pieces evenly over crust; return to oven 2 minutes to melt chocolate. Remove from oven; spread evenly with spatula. Let stand several minutes to set.

To prepare Top Layer: In large bowl, cream butter, granulated sugar and vanilla. Beat in eggs and egg white, one at a time, mixing well after each addition. (Mixture will appear slightly curdled.) Stir in raisins and walnuts. Spread evenly over chocolate layer. Return to oven; bake 20 to 25 minutes or until top is browned. Dust with powdered sugar. Cool in pan; cut into bars.

Note: Cookies freeze well.

Hershey's Great American Chocolate Chip Cookies

■ Hershey's Great American Chocolate Chip Cookies

About 6 dozen cookies

  1 cup butter, softened
  ¾ cup granulated sugar
  ¾ cup packed light brown sugar
  1 teaspoon vanilla extract
  2 eggs
2¼ cups all-purpose flour
  1 teaspoon baking soda
  ½ teaspoon salt
  2 cups (12-ounce package) HERSHEY'S Semi-Sweet Chocolate Chips
  1 cup chopped nuts (optional)

Cream butter, granulated sugar, brown sugar and vanilla in large mixer bowl until light and fluffy. Add eggs; beat well. Combine flour, baking soda and salt; gradually add to creamed mixture. Beat well. Stir in chocolate chips and nuts.

Drop by teaspoonfuls onto ungreased cookie sheet. Bake at 375° for 8 to 10 minutes or until lightly browned. Cool slightly. Remove from cookie sheet; cool completely on wire rack.

VARIATION
Milk Chocolate Chip Cookies: Substitute 2 cups (11.5-ounce package) HERSHEY'S Milk Chocolate Chips for the semi-sweet chocolate chips.

■ Chocolate Brittle Drops

Makes 2 dozen

  4 squares BAKER'S® Semi-Sweet Chocolate
1½ cups (½ lb.) coarsely crushed peanut brittle

Melt chocolate in saucepan over very low heat, stirring constantly. Remove from heat and stir in peanut brittle. Drop from teaspoon onto waxed paper. Let stand until chocolate is firm.

■ Peanut Butter Rice Snacks

Makes about 16 squares

  1 cup light corn syrup
  ½ cup granulated sugar
  ½ cup packed brown sugar
  1 cup crunchy peanut butter
  6 cups RICE CHEX® Brand Cereal

Line 9×9-inch pan with waxed paper. Combine corn syrup and sugars in large saucepan. Cook over medium heat just until mixture comes to a boil, stirring frequently. Remove from heat. Stir in peanut butter until well combined. Gradually add cereal, stirring until all pieces are evenly coated. Turn into prepared pan. Refrigerate 15 minutes or until firm. Cut into squares. Store covered.

Peanut Butter Rice Snacks

■ Magic Cookie Bars

Makes 24 to 36 bars

½ cup margarine or butter
1½ cups graham cracker *or* other crumbs
1 (14-ounce) can EAGLE® Brand Sweetened
    Condensed Milk (NOT evaporated milk)
1 cup semi-sweet chocolate chips
1 (3½-ounce) can flaked coconut (1⅓ cups)
1 cup chopped nuts

Preheat oven to 350° (325° for glass dish). In 13×9-inch baking pan, melt margarine in oven. Sprinkle crumbs over margarine; pour sweetened condensed milk evenly over crumbs. Top with remaining ingredients; press down firmly. Bake 25 to 30 minutes or until lightly browned. Cool. Chill if desired. Cut into bars. Store loosely covered at room temperature.

Seven Layer Magic Cookie Bars: Add 1 (6-ounce) package butterscotch flavored chips after chocolate chips.

Double Chocolate Magic Cookie Bars: Increase chocolate chips to 1 (12-ounce) package.

Rainbow Magic Cookie Bars: Add 1 cup plain candy-coated chocolate pieces after chocolate chips.

Magic Peanut Cookie Bars: Omit chocolate chips. Add 2 cups (about ¾ pound) chocolate-covered peanuts.

Mint: Combine ½ teaspoon peppermint extract and 4 drops green food coloring if desired with sweetened condensed milk. Proceed as above.

Mocha: Add 1 tablespoon instant coffee and 1 tablespoon chocolate-flavored syrup with sweetened condensed milk. Proceed as above.

Peanut Butter: Beat ⅓ cup peanut butter with sweetened condensed milk. Proceed as above.

Maple: Combine ½ to 1 teaspoon maple flavoring with sweetened condensed milk. Proceed as above.

Magic Cookie Bars

■ Spiced Apple-Raisin Cookies

Makes about 5 dozen cookies

¾ cup butter, softened
1 cup packed brown sugar
1 egg
1 teaspoon vanilla
1½ cups all-purpose flour
1 teaspoon baking powder
½ teaspoon baking soda
½ teaspoon salt
½ teaspoon ground cinnamon
½ teaspoon ground nutmeg
1½ cups quick-cooking oats, uncooked
1 cup finely chopped unpeeled apple
½ cup raisins
½ cup chopped nuts

In large bowl, cream butter. Gradually add sugar; beat until light and fluffy. Beat in egg and vanilla. In small bowl, combine flour, baking powder, baking soda, salt and spices. Gradually add flour mixture to creamed mixture; blend well. Stir in oats, apple, raisins and nuts. Drop dough by rounded teaspoonfuls 2 inches apart onto lightly greased cookie sheets. Bake in preheated 350° oven 10 to 12 minutes or until lightly browned. Remove to wire racks to cool completely.

Favorite Recipe from **American Dairy Association**

■ Old-Fashioned Molasses Cookies

Makes about 3 dozen cookies

4 cups sifted all-purpose flour
2 teaspoons ARM & HAMMER® Pure Baking Soda
1½ teaspoons ground ginger
½ teaspoon ground cinnamon
⅛ teaspoon salt
1½ cups molasses
½ cup shortening, melted
¼ cup butter or margarine, melted
⅓ cup boiling water
   Sugar

In medium bowl, combine flour, baking soda, spices and salt. In large bowl, mix molasses, shortening, butter and water. Add dry ingredients to molasses mixture; blend well. Cover; refrigerate until firm, about 2 hours. Roll out dough ¼ inch thick on well-floured surface. Cut out with 3½-inch cookie cutters; sprinkle with sugar. Place 2 inches apart on ungreased cookie sheets. Bake in preheated 375° oven about 12 minutes. Remove to wire racks to cool.

■ Oatmeal Macaroons

Makes 4½ dozen cookies

1¼ cups all-purpose flour
1 teaspoon baking soda
1 cup margarine, softened
1 cup packed brown sugar
2 eggs
½ teaspoon almond extract
3 cups QUAKER® Oats (quick or old-fashioned, uncooked)
1 package (4 ounces) flaked or shredded coconut

In medium bowl, combine flour and baking soda. In large bowl, cream margarine and sugar until light and fluffy. Blend in eggs and almond extract. Add flour mixture; mix well. Stir in oats and coconut. Drop dough by rounded teaspoonfuls onto greased cookie sheets. Bake in preheated 350° oven 10 minutes or until light golden brown. Let cookies cool 1 minute before removing them from cookie sheets to wire racks.

■ Pinwheels and Checkerboards

Makes about 5 dozen

2 cups flour
1 teaspoon CALUMET® Baking Powder
½ teaspoon salt
⅔ cup butter or margarine
1 cup sugar
1 egg
1 teaspoon vanilla
2 squares BAKER'S® Unsweetened Chocolate, melted

Mix flour, baking powder and salt; set aside. Cream butter. Gradually add sugar and continue beating until light and fluffy. Add egg and vanilla; beat well. Gradually add flour mixture, mixing well after each addition. Divide dough in half; blend chocolate into one half. Use prepared doughs to make Pinwheels or Checkerboards.

Pinwheels: Roll chocolate and vanilla doughs separately between sheets of waxed paper into 12×8-inch rectangles. Remove top sheets of paper and invert vanilla dough onto chocolate dough. Remove remaining papers. Roll up as for jelly roll; then wrap in waxed paper. Chill until firm, at least 3 hours (or freeze 1 hour). Cut into ¼-inch slices and place on baking sheets. Bake at 375° about 10 minutes, or until cookies just begin to brown around edges. Cool on racks.

Checkerboards: Set out small amount of milk. Roll chocolate and vanilla doughs separately on lightly floured board into 9×4½-inch rectangles. Brush chocolate dough lightly with milk and top with vanilla dough. Using a long sharp knife, cut lengthwise into 3 strips, 1½ inches wide. Stack strips, alternating colors and brushing each layer with milk. Cut lengthwise again into 3 strips, ½ inch wide. Invert middle section so that colors are alternated; brush sides with milk. Press strips together lightly to form a rectangle. Wrap in waxed paper. Chill overnight. Cut into ⅛-inch slices, using a very sharp knife. Place on baking sheets. Bake at 375° for about 8 minutes, or just until white portions begin to brown. Cool on racks.

Top: Checkerboards; bottom: Pinwheels

Gifts From the Kitchen

■ Walnut Christmas Balls

Makes about 1½ dozen sandwich cookies

  1 cup California walnuts
⅔ cup powdered sugar
  1 cup butter or margarine, softened
  1 teaspoon vanilla
1¾ cups all-purpose flour
    Chocolate Filling (recipe follows)

In food processor or blender, process walnuts with 2 tablespoons of the sugar until finely ground; set aside. In large bowl, cream butter and remaining sugar. Beat in vanilla. Add flour and ¾ cup of the walnuts; mix until blended. Roll dough into about 3 dozen walnut-size balls. Place 2 inches apart on ungreased cookie sheets. Bake in preheated 350° oven 10 to 12 minutes or until just golden around edges. Remove to wire racks to cool completely. Prepare Chocolate Filling. Place generous teaspoonful of filling on flat side of half the cookies. Top with remaining cookies, flat side down, forming sandwiches. Roll chocolate edges of cookies in remaining ground walnuts.

Chocolate Filling: Chop 3 squares (1 ounce each) semisweet chocolate into small pieces; place in food processor or blender with ½ teaspoon vanilla. In small saucepan, heat 2 tablespoons *each* butter or margarine and whipping cream over medium heat until hot; pour over chocolate. Process until chocolate is melted, turning machine off and scraping sides as needed. With machine running, gradually add 1 cup powdered sugar; process until smooth.

Favorite Recipe from **Walnut Marketing Board**

■ Cherry Fruit Cake

Makes 1 cake

¾ cup flour
½ teaspoon baking powder
½ teaspoon salt
  1 (16 oz.) jar Maraschino cherries, whole, drained
  8 ounces diced pitted dates
  8 ounces glace pineapple
  9 ounces pecan halves
  3 eggs
1½ ounces rum
¼ cup light corn syrup

Combine flour, baking powder and salt in large mixing bowl; mix well. Add well-drained cherries, dates, pineapple and pecans. Toss together until fruits and nuts are coated with flour mixture. Beat eggs and rum until blended. Pour over coated fruit and mix thoroughly. Grease one 9×5×3-inch loaf pan; line with parchment paper and grease again. Turn cake mixture into pan, pressing with spatula to pack tightly. Bake at 300°F. 1 hour 45 minutes or until wooden pick inserted near center comes out clean. Cool cake in pan 15 minutes. Remove paper from cake; brush with corn syrup while still warm. Cool completely before serving or storing.

Favorite Recipe from **National Cherry Foundation**

Walnut Christmas Balls

■ Creamy White Fudge

Makes about 2¼ pounds

1½ pounds white confectioners' coating*
1 (14-ounce) can EAGLE® Brand Sweetened Condensed Milk (NOT evaporated milk)
⅛ teaspoon salt
¾ to 1 cup chopped nuts
1½ teaspoons vanilla extract

In heavy saucepan, over low heat, melt confectioners' coating with sweetened condensed milk and salt. Remove from heat; stir in nuts and vanilla. Spread evenly into wax paper-lined 8- or 9-inch square pan. Chill 2 hours or until firm. Turn fudge onto cutting board; peel off paper and cut into squares. Store tightly covered at room temperature.

Microwave: In 2-quart glass measure, combine coating, sweetened condensed milk and salt. Microwave on full power (high) 3 to 5 minutes or until coating melts, stirring after 3 minutes. Stir in nuts and vanilla. Proceed as above.

Praline Fudge: Omit vanilla. Add 1 teaspoon maple flavoring and 1 cup chopped pecans. Proceed as above.

Confetti Fudge: Omit nuts. Add 1 cup chopped mixed candied fruit. Proceed as above.

Rum Raisin Fudge: Omit vanilla. Add 1½ teaspoons white vinegar, 1 teaspoon rum flavoring and ¾ cup raisins. Proceed as above.

Cherry Fudge: Omit nuts. Add 1 cup chopped candied cherries.

White confectioners' coating can be purchased in candy specialty stores.

■ Chocolate Pecan Critters

Makes about 5 dozen

1 (11½-ounce) package milk chocolate chips
1 (6-ounce) package semi-sweet chocolate chips
¼ cup margarine or butter
1 (14-ounce) can EAGLE® Brand Sweetened Condensed Milk (NOT evaporated milk)
⅛ teaspoon salt
2 cups coarsely chopped pecans
2 teaspoons vanilla extract
Pecan halves

In heavy saucepan, over medium heat, melt chips and margarine with sweetened condensed milk and salt. Remove from heat; stir in chopped nuts and vanilla. Drop by teaspoonfuls onto wax paper-lined baking sheets. Top with pecan halves. Chill. Store tightly covered.

Microwave: In 2-quart glass measure, microwave chips, margarine, sweetened condensed milk and salt on full power (high) 3 minutes, stirring after 1½ minutes. Stir to melt chips; stir in chopped nuts and vanilla. Proceed as above.

■ Layered Mint Chocolate Candy

Makes about 1¾ pounds

1 (12-ounce) package semi-sweet chocolate chips
1 (14-ounce) can EAGLE® Brand Sweetened Condensed Milk (NOT evaporated milk)
2 teaspoons vanilla extract
6 ounces white confectioners' coating*
1 tablespoon peppermint extract
Few drops green or red food coloring, optional

In heavy saucepan, over low heat, melt chips with *1 cup* sweetened condensed milk. Stir in vanilla. Spread half the mixture into wax paper-lined 8- or 9-inch square pan; chill 10 minutes or until firm. Hold remaining chocolate mixture at room temperature. In heavy saucepan, over low heat, melt confectioners' coating with remaining sweetened condensed milk. Stir in peppermint extract and food coloring if desired. Spread on chilled chocolate layer; chill 10 minutes longer or until firm. Spread reserved chocolate mixture on mint layer. Chill 2 hours or until firm. Turn onto cutting board; peel off paper and cut into squares. Store loosely covered at room temperature.

White confectioners' coating can be purchased in candy specialty stores.

Clockwise from top: Coconut Rum Balls, Chocolate Pecan Critters, Fruit Bon Bons (page 86), Milk Chocolate Bourbon Balls, Buckeyes (page 87), Foolproof Dark Chocolate Fudge (page 86), Peanut Butter Logs (page 86), Layered Mint Chocolate Candy and Cherry Fudge

■ Coconut Rum Balls

Makes about 8 dozen

> 1 (12-ounce) package vanilla wafer cookies, finely crushed (about 3 cups crumbs)
> 1 (3½-ounce) can flaked coconut (1⅓ cups)
> 1 cup finely chopped nuts
> 1 (14-ounce) can EAGLE® Brand Sweetened Condensed Milk (NOT evaporated milk)
> ¼ cup rum
> Additional flaked coconut or confectioners' sugar

In large mixing bowl, combine crumbs, coconut and nuts. Add sweetened condensed milk and rum; mix well. Chill 4 hours. Shape into 1-inch balls. Roll in coconut. Store tightly covered in refrigerator.

Tip: Flavor of these candies improves after 24 hours. They can be made ahead and stored in refrigerator for several weeks.

■ Milk Chocolate Bourbon Balls

Makes about 5½ dozen

> 1 (12-ounce) package vanilla wafer cookies, finely crushed (about 3 cups crumbs)
> 5 tablespoons bourbon or brandy
> 1 (11½-ounce) package milk chocolate chips
> 1 (14-ounce) can EAGLE® Brand Sweetened Condensed Milk (NOT evaporated milk)
> Finely chopped nuts

In medium mixing bowl, combine crumbs and bourbon. In heavy saucepan, over low heat, melt chips. Remove from heat; add sweetened condensed milk. Gradually add crumb mixture; mix well. Let stand at room temperature 30 minutes or chill. Shape into 1-inch balls; roll in nuts. Store tightly covered.

Tip: Flavor of these candies improves after 24 hours. They can be made ahead and stored in freezer. Thaw before serving.

■ Foolproof Dark Chocolate Fudge

Makes about 2 pounds

3 (6-ounce) packages semi-sweet chocolate chips
1 (14-ounce) can EAGLE® Brand Sweetened Condensed Milk (NOT evaporated milk)
Dash salt
½ to 1 cup chopped nuts
1½ teaspoons vanilla extract

In heavy saucepan, over low heat, melt chips with sweetened condensed milk and salt. Remove from heat; stir in nuts and vanilla. Spread evenly into wax paper-lined 8- or 9-inch square pan. Chill 2 hours or until firm. Turn fudge onto cutting board; peel off paper and cut into squares. Store loosely covered at room temperature.

Microwave: In 1-quart glass measure, combine chips with sweetened condensed milk. Microwave on full power (high) 3 minutes. Stir until chips melt and mixture is smooth. Stir in remaining ingredients. Proceed as above.

Creamy Dark Chocolate Fudge: Melt 2 cups CAMPFIRE® Miniature Marshmallows with chips and sweetened condensed milk. Proceed as above.

Milk Chocolate Fudge: Omit 1 (6-ounce) package semi-sweet chocolate chips. Add 1 cup milk chocolate chips. Proceed as above.

Creamy Milk Chocolate Fudge: Omit 1 (6-ounce) package semi-sweet chocolate chips. Add 1 cup milk chocolate chips and 2 cups CAMPFIRE® Miniature Marshmallows. Proceed as above.

Mexican Chocolate Fudge: Reduce vanilla to 1 teaspoon. Add 1 tablespoon instant coffee and 1 teaspoon ground cinnamon to sweetened condensed milk. Proceed as above.

Butterscotch Fudge: Omit chocolate chips and vanilla. In heavy saucepan, melt 2 (12-ounce) packages butterscotch flavored chips with sweetened condensed milk. Remove from heat; stir in 2 tablespoons white vinegar, ⅛ teaspoon salt, ½ teaspoon maple flavoring and 1 cup chopped nuts. Proceed as above.

■ Peanut Butter Logs

Makes two 12-inch logs

1 (12-ounce) package peanut butter flavored chips
1 (14-ounce) can EAGLE® Brand Sweetened Condensed Milk (NOT evaporated milk)
1 cup CAMPFIRE® Miniature Marshmallows
1 cup chopped peanuts

In heavy saucepan, over low heat, melt chips with sweetened condensed milk. Add marshmallows; stir until melted. Remove from heat; cool 20 minutes. Divide in half; place each portion on a 20-inch piece of wax paper. Shape each into 12-inch log. Roll in nuts. Wrap tightly; chill 2 hours or until firm. Remove paper; cut into ¼-inch slices.

Microwave: In 2-quart glass measure, microwave chips, sweetened condensed milk and marshmallows on full power (high) 4 minutes or until melted, stirring after 2 minutes. Let stand at room temperature 1 hour. Proceed as above.

Peanut Butter Fudge: Stir peanuts into mixture. Spread into wax paper-lined 8- or 9-inch square pan. Chill 2 hours or until firm. Turn fudge onto cutting board; peel off paper and cut into squares.

■ Fruit Bon Bons

Makes about 5 dozen

1 (14-ounce) can EAGLE® Brand Sweetened Condensed Milk (NOT evaporated milk)
2 (7-ounce) packages flaked coconut (5⅓ cups)
1 (6-ounce) package fruit flavor gelatin, any flavor
1 cup ground blanched almonds
1 teaspoon almond extract
Food coloring, optional

In large mixing bowl, combine sweetened condensed milk, coconut, ⅓ *cup* gelatin, almonds, extract and enough food coloring to tint mixture desired shade. Chill 1 hour or until firm enough to handle. Using about ½ tablespoon mixture for each, shape into 1-inch balls. Sprinkle remaining gelatin onto wax paper; roll each ball in gelatin to coat. Place on wax paper-lined baking sheets; chill. Store covered at room temperature or in refrigerator.

■ Buckeyes

Makes about 7 dozen

2 (3-ounce) packages cream cheese, softened
1 (14-ounce) can EAGLE® Brand Sweetened
   Condensed Milk (NOT evaporated milk)
2 (12-ounce) packages peanut butter
   flavored chips
1 cup finely chopped peanuts
½ pound chocolate confectioners' coating*

In large mixer bowl, beat cheese until fluffy.
Gradually beat in sweetened condensed milk until
smooth. In heavy saucepan, over low heat, melt
peanut butter chips; stir into cheese mixture. Add
nuts. Chill 2 to 3 hours; shape into 1-inch balls. In
small heavy saucepan, over low heat, melt
confectioners' coating. With wooden pick, dip
each peanut ball into melted coating, not covering
completely. Place on wax paper-lined baking
sheets until firm. Store covered at room
temperature or in refrigerator.

*Chocolate confectioners' coating can be
purchased in candy specialty stores.*

■ Pumpkin Nut Bread

Makes two 9×5-inch loaves

3½ cups unsifted flour
2 teaspoons baking soda
1½ teaspoons ground cinnamon
½ teaspoon baking powder
2 cups sugar
⅔ cup shortening
4 eggs
1 (16-ounce) can pumpkin (about 2 cups)
½ cup water
1 (9-ounce) package NONE SUCH®
   Condensed Mincemeat, crumbled
1 cup chopped nuts

Preheat oven to 350°. Stir together flour, baking
soda, cinnamon and baking powder; set aside. In
large mixer bowl, beat sugar and shortening until
fluffy. Add eggs, pumpkin and water; mix well.
Stir in flour mixture, mincemeat and nuts. Turn
into 2 greased 9×5-inch loaf pans. Bake 55 to 60
minutes or until wooden pick inserted near center
comes out clean. Cool 10 minutes; remove from
pan. Cool completely.

■ Glazed Popcorn

Makes 2 quarts

8 cups popped popcorn
¼ cup butter or margarine
3 tablespoons light corn syrup
½ cup packed light brown sugar or
   granulated sugar
1 package (4-serving size) JELL-O® Brand
   Gelatin, any flavor

Place popcorn in large bowl. Heat butter and
syrup in small saucepan over low heat. Stir in
brown sugar and gelatin; bring to a boil over
medium heat. Reduce heat to low and gently
simmer for 5 minutes. Pour syrup immediately
over popcorn, tossing to coat well. Spread
popcorn on aluminum-foil-lined 15×10×1-inch
pan, using two forks to spread evenly. Bake in
preheated 300° oven for 10 minutes. Cool.
Remove from pan and break into small pieces.

Rainbow Popcorn: Prepare Glazed Popcorn 3
times, using 3 different gelatin colors, such as
strawberry, lemon and lime. Bake as directed and
break into pieces. Layer 3 cups of each variety in
3-quart bowl. Serve remaining popcorn at another
time. Makes 6 quarts.

Glazed Popcorn

NEW
Treasury of
Christmas
Recipes

From Your Favorite Brand Name Companies

JELL-O®

PHILADELPHIA
BRAND
CREAM CHEESE
PASTEURIZED
KRAFT

Campbell's.

BORDEN®

®Baker's®

LAND O LAKES®

Kellogg's.

Plus Many More

■ Golden Carrot Cake

Makes one 10-inch cake

1 (9-ounce) package NONE SUCH®
    Condensed Mincemeat, crumbled
2 cups finely shredded carrots
½ cup chopped nuts
2 teaspoons grated orange rind
2 cups unsifted flour
1 cup firmly packed light brown sugar
¾ cup vegetable oil
4 eggs
2 teaspoons baking powder
1 teaspoon baking soda
1 teaspoon salt
    Orange Glaze (recipe follows)

Preheat oven to 325°. In large bowl, combine mincemeat, carrots, nuts and rind; toss with *½ cup* flour and set aside. In large mixer bowl, combine sugar and oil; mix well. Add eggs, 1 at a time, beating well after each addition. Stir together remaining *1½ cups* flour, baking powder, baking soda and salt; gradually add to batter, beating until smooth. Stir in mincemeat mixture. Turn into well-greased and floured 10-inch Bundt® or tube pan. Bake 50 to 60 minutes or until wooden pick comes out clean. Cool 10 minutes; remove from pan. Cool completely. Drizzle with Orange Glaze.

Orange Glaze: In small saucepan, melt 2 tablespoons margarine with 4 teaspoons orange juice. Stir in 1 cup confectioners' sugar and 1 teaspoon grated orange rind; mix well. Makes about ½ cup.

■ Hot Fudge Sauce

Makes about 2 cups

1 (6-ounce) package semi-sweet chocolate
    chips *or* 4 (1-ounce) squares semi-sweet
    chocolate
2 tablespoons margarine or butter
1 (14-ounce) can EAGLE® Brand Sweetened
    Condensed Milk (NOT evaporated milk)
2 tablespoons water
1 teaspoon vanilla extract

In heavy saucepan, over medium heat, melt chips and margarine with sweetened condensed milk and water. Cook and stir constantly until thickened, about 5 minutes. Add vanilla. Serve warm over ice cream or as a fruit dipping sauce. Refrigerate leftovers.

To Reheat: In small heavy saucepan, combine desired amount of sauce with small amount of water. Over low heat, stir constantly until heated through.

*Microwave:** In 1-quart glass measure, combine ingredients. Cook on 100% power (high) 3 to 3½ minutes, stirring after each minute. Proceed as above.

VARIATIONS:

Mocha: Add 1 teaspoon instant coffee. Proceed as above.

Toasted Almond: Omit vanilla extract. Add ½ teaspoon almond extract. When sauce is thickened, stir in ½ cup chopped toasted almonds.

Choco-Mint: Omit vanilla extract. Add ½ to 1 teaspoon peppermint extract. Proceed as above.

Spirited: Add ⅓ cup almond, coffee, mint *or* orange-flavored liqueur after mixture has thickened.

Mexican: Omit water. Add 2 tablespoons coffee-flavored liqueur *or* 1 teaspoon instant coffee dissolved in 2 tablespoons water and 1 teaspoon ground cinnamon after mixture has thickened.

*Microwave ovens vary in wattage and power output; cooking times may need to be adjusted.

Golden Carrot Cake

Almond Lemon Pound Cake

■ Almond Lemon Pound Cake

Makes 1 loaf

  2 cups cake flour
  ½ teaspoon cream of tartar
  ½ teaspoon salt
  1 cup butter or margarine, softened
  1 cup granulated sugar
  4 eggs
  5 tablespoons lemon juice
  1¼ cups BLUE DIAMOND® Chopped Natural
      Almonds, toasted
  ½ cup powdered sugar
  ½ teaspoon vanilla

In small bowl, combine flour, cream of tartar and salt. In large bowl, cream butter and granulated sugar. Add eggs, 1 at a time, beating well after each addition. Beat in 2 tablespoons of the lemon juice. Gradually add flour mixture; mix thoroughly. Fold in 1 cup of the almonds. Pour batter into greased 9×5×3-inch loaf pan. Sprinkle top with remaining ¼ cup almonds. Bake in preheated 325° oven 1 hour or until toothpick inserted into center comes out clean. Meanwhile, in small saucepan, combine powdered sugar, remaining 3 tablespoons lemon juice and the vanilla. Stir over medium heat until sugar is dissolved. Remove cake from oven. Drizzle hot glaze over top. Let cool in pan on wire rack 15 minutes. Loosen edges; remove from pan. Cool completely on wire rack.

Favorite Recipe from **Blue Diamond Growers**

■ Toasted Pecan Toffee Bars

Makes 3 dozen bars

  2 cups all-purpose flour
  1 cup packed brown sugar
  1 cup LAND O LAKES® Sweet Cream Butter,
      softened
  1 teaspoon vanilla
  ½ teaspoon ground cinnamon
  1 cup chopped pecans, toasted
  1 cup milk chocolate chips

In large bowl, combine flour, sugar, butter, vanilla and cinnamon; beat until crumbly. Stir in ¾ cup of the pecans and ½ cup of the chips. Press into greased 13×9×2-inch pan. Bake in preheated 350° oven 25 to 30 minutes or until edges are lightly browned. Remove from oven. Immediately sprinkle with remaining ½ cup chips; let stand 5 minutes. Slightly swirl chips as they melt; leave some whole for a marbled effect. *Do not spread chips.* Sprinkle with remaining ¼ cup pecans. Cool completely in pan on wire rack. Cut into bars.

■ Chocolate Truffles

Makes about 6 dozen

> 3 (6-ounce) packages semi-sweet chocolate
> chips
> 1 (14-ounce) can EAGLE® Brand Sweetened
> Condensed Milk (NOT evaporated milk)
> 1 tablespoon vanilla extract
> Finely chopped nuts, flaked coconut,
> chocolate sprinkles, colored sprinkles,
> unsweetened cocoa *or* colored sugar

In heavy saucepan, over low heat, melt chips with
sweetened condensed milk. Remove from heat;
stir in vanilla. Chill 2 hours or until firm. Shape
into 1-inch balls; roll in any of the above coatings.
Chill 1 hour or until firm. Store covered at room
temperature.

Microwave: In 1-quart glass measure, combine
chips and sweetened condensed milk. Microwave
on full power (high) 3 minutes, stirring after 1½
minutes. Stir until smooth. Proceed as above.

Amaretto: Omit vanilla. Add 3 tablespoons
amaretto or other almond-flavored liqueur and ½
teaspoon almond extract. Roll in finely chopped
toasted almonds.

Orange: Omit vanilla. Add 3 tablespoons orange-
flavored liqueur. Roll in finely chopped toasted
almonds mixed with finely grated orange rind.

Rum: Omit vanilla. Add ¼ cup dark rum. Roll in
flaked coconut.

Bourbon: Omit vanilla. Add 3 tablespoons
bourbon. Roll in finely chopped toasted nuts.

■ Mint Cream Liqueur

Makes about 1 quart

> 1 (14-ounce) can EAGLE® Brand Sweetened
> Condensed Milk (NOT evaporated milk)
> 1¼ cups mint-flavored liqueur
> 1 cup (½ pint) BORDEN® or MEADOW GOLD®
> Whipping *or* Coffee Cream

In blender container, combine ingredients; blend
until smooth. Serve over ice if desired. Store
tightly covered in refrigerator. Stir before serving.
Refrigerate leftovers.

Chocolate Truffles

■ Chewy Chocolate Candies

Makes 2 dozen

- ½ pound soft caramels
- 2 tablespoons heavy cream
- 1 cup (about) pecan halves
- 4 squares BAKER'S® Semi-Sweet Chocolate, melted and cooled

Heat caramels with cream in saucepan over very low heat, stirring constantly. Cool 10 minutes. Set pecans on lightly buttered baking sheets in clusters of 3. Spoon caramel mixture over nuts, leaving outer ends of nuts showing. Let stand to set, about 30 minutes. Spread melted chocolate over caramel mixture.

■ Cherry Pecan Pound Cake

Makes 1 loaf

- 1 cup butter or margarine, softened
- 1 cup sugar
- 4 eggs
- 1 teaspoon vanilla
- ½ teaspoon almond extract
- ½ teaspoon salt
- ⅛ teaspoon ground nutmeg or mace
- 1½ cups all-purpose flour
- 1 jar (6 ounces) maraschino cherries, drained and chopped
- ¼ cup chopped pecans

In large bowl, beat butter and sugar until light and fluffy. Add eggs, vanilla, almond extract, salt and nutmeg; beat until thoroughly blended. Stir in flour, ½ cup at a time, mixing just until blended. Stir in cherries and pecans. Spread batter evenly in greased and floured 9×5×3-inch loaf pan. Bake in preheated 325°oven 60 to 70 minutes or until toothpick inserted near center comes out clean. Let cool in pan on wire rack 10 minutes. Loosen edges; remove from pan. Cool completely on wire rack.

Favorite Recipe from **American Egg Board**

■ Hot Cocoa Mix

Makes about 3 cups

- 1 cup CREMORA® Non-Dairy Creamer*
- 1 cup nonfat dry milk
- ¼ to 1 cup sugar
- ½ cup unsweetened cocoa

In medium bowl, combine ingredients; mix well. Store in airtight container. To serve, spoon 3 heaping tablespoons mix into mug; add ¾ cup boiling water. Stir.

Mocha: Add ¼ cup instant coffee.

Mexican: Add 1 teaspoon ground cinnamon.

Low-calorie: Omit sugar. Add 15 envelopes low-calorie sweetener with NutraSweet® *or* 2 teaspoons (5 envelopes) low-calorie granulated sugar substitute. To serve, spoon 2 heaping tablespoons into mug; add ¾ cup boiling water. Stir.

Cremora is a coffee whitener and should not be used as a milk replacement.

■ Pineapple-Almond Cheese Spread

Makes 4 cups

- 2 cans (8 ounces each) DOLE® Crushed Pineapple
- 1 package (8 ounces) cream cheese, softened
- 4 cups shredded sharp Cheddar cheese
- ½ cup mayonnaise
- 1 tablespoon soy sauce
- 1 cup DOLE® Chopped Natural Almonds, toasted
- ½ cup finely chopped DOLE® Green Bell Pepper
- ¼ cup minced green onion or chives
  DOLE® Celery stalks or assorted breads

Drain pineapple. In large bowl, beat cream cheese until smooth; beat in Cheddar cheese, mayonnaise and soy sauce until smooth. Stir in pineapple, almonds, green pepper and onion. Refrigerate, covered. Use to stuff celery stalks or serve as dip with assorted breads. Serve at room temperature.

Homemade Cream Liqueurs

■ Homemade Cream Liqueurs

Makes about 1 quart

> 1 (14-ounce) can EAGLE® Brand Sweetened
> Condensed Milk (NOT evaporated milk)
> 1¼ cups flavored liqueur (almond, coffee,
> orange *or* mint)
> 1 cup (½ pint) BORDEN® or MEADOW GOLD®
> Whipping or Coffee Cream

In blender container, combine all ingredients; blend until smooth. Serve over ice and garnish if desired. Store tightly covered in refrigerator. Stir before serving.

■ Peppered Pecans

Makes 3 cups

> 3 tablespoons butter or margarine
> 3 cloves garlic, minced
> 1½ teaspoons TABASCO® pepper sauce
> ½ teaspoon salt
> 3 cups pecan halves

Preheat oven to 250°F. In small skillet melt butter. Add garlic, Tabasco® sauce and salt; cook 1 minute. Toss pecans with butter mixture; spread in single layer on baking sheet. Bake 1 hour or until pecans are crisp; stir occasionally.

■ Classic Fudge

Makes 1 pound or about 1½ dozen pieces

> 2 squares BAKER'S® Unsweetened Chocolate
> ¾ cup milk
> 2 cups sugar
> Dash of salt
> 2 tablespoons butter or margarine
> 1 teaspoon vanilla

Place chocolate and milk in heavy saucepan. Stir constantly over very low heat until smooth and slightly thickened, about 5 minutes. Add sugar and salt; stir over medium heat until sugar is dissolved and mixture boils. Continue boiling, without stirring, until small amount of mixture forms a soft ball in cold water (or to a temperature of 234°).

Remove from heat; add butter and vanilla. *Do not stir.* Cool to lukewarm (110°). Beat until mixture begins to lose its gloss and holds its shape. Pour at once into buttered 8×4-inch loaf pan. Cool until set; then cut into squares. Let stand in pan until firm.

Acknowledgments

The publishers would like to thank the companies and organizations listed below for the use of their recipes in this book.

Almond Board of California
American Dairy Association
American Egg Board
Best Foods, a Division of CPC International Inc.
Blue Diamond Growers
Borden Kitchens, Borden, Inc.
Campbell Soup Company
Carnation Evaporated Milk
Checkerboard Kitchens, Ralston Purina Company
Church & Dwight Co., Inc.
Cribari & Sons Winery
The Dole Food Company
Durkee-French Foods, Division of Reckitt Colman Inc.
Florida Department of Citrus
General Foods Corporation
Hershey Foods Corporation
Keebler Company
Kraft, Inc.
Land O' Lakes, Inc.

Libby's Pumpkin, Division of Carnation Company
Maidstone Wine & Spirits, Inc.
McIlhenny Company
National Cherry Foundation
National Live Stock and Meat Board
National Pecan Marketing Council, Inc.
National Pork Producers Council
National Turkey Federation
Norseland Foods, Inc.
Oklahoma Peanut Commission
Pet Incorporated
Procter & Gamble
The Quaker Oats Company
Sun-Diamond Growers of California
Swift-Eckrich, Inc.
Thomas J. Lipton, Inc.
Walnut Marketing Board
Washington Apple Commission
Western New York Apple Growers Association, Inc.
Wisconsin Milk Marketing Board

Photo Credits

The publishers would like to thank the companies and organizations listed below for the use of their photographs in this book.

American Dairy Association
Best Foods, a Division of CPC International Inc.
Blue Diamond Growers
Borden Kitchens, Borden, Inc.
Campbell Soup Company
Checkerboard Kitchens, Ralston Purina Company
The Dole Food Company
Durkee-French Foods, Division of Reckitt Colman Inc.
General Foods Corporation
Hershey Foods Corporation
Keebler Company

Kraft, Inc.
Land O' Lakes, Inc.
National Pecan Marketing Council, Inc.
National Pork Producers Council
National Turkey Federation
Pet Incorporated
Procter & Gamble
Sun-Diamond Growers of California
Swift-Eckrich, Inc.
Thomas J. Lipton, Inc.
Walnut Marketing Board
Wisconsin Milk Marketing Board

Index

NEW
Treasury of
Christmas
Recipes

From Your Favorite Brand Name Companies

PUBLICATIONS INTERNATIONAL, LTD.

Louis Weber, C.E.O.
Publications International, Ltd.
7373 North Cicero Avenue
Lincolnwood, Illinois 60646

Permission is never granted for commercial purposes.

Manufactured in U.S.A.

8 7 6 5 4 3 2 1

ISBN: 0-88176-009-9

Library of Congress Catalog Card Number: 90-61499

Pictured on the front cover (*clockwise from top left*): Roasted Turkey with Savory Cranberry Stuffing (*page 48*), Festive Eggnog Cake (*page 85*), Fireside Punch (*page 15*), Triple Chocolate Squares (*page 68*), Fruit Burst Cookies (*page 69*), Lemon Cut-Out Cookies (*page 65*) and Snowballs (*page 65*).

Pictured on the back cover (*clockwise from left*): Christmas Ribbon (*page 41*), Merry Cranberry Bread (*page 31*) and Scandinavian Smörgåsbord (*page 4*).

Microwave ovens vary in wattage and power output; cooking times given with microwave directions in this book may need to be adjusted.

NEW
Treasury of Christmas Recipes

From Your Favorite Brand Name Companies

Appetizers & Beverages

Scandinavian Smörgåsbord

Makes 36 appetizers

36 slices party bread, crackers or flat bread
    Reduced-calorie mayonnaise or salad dressing
    Mustard
36 small lettuce leaves or Belgian endive leaves
 1 can (6½ ounces) STARKIST® Tuna, drained
    and flaked or broken into chunks
 2 hard-cooked eggs, sliced
¼ pound frozen cooked bay shrimp, thawed
½ medium cucumber, thinly sliced
36 pieces steamed asparagus tips or pea pods
    Capers, plain yogurt, dill sprigs, pimiento
    strips, red or black caviar, sliced green
    onion for garnish

Arrange party bread on a tray; spread each with 1
teaspoon mayonnaise and/or mustard. Top with a
small lettuce leaf. Top with tuna, egg slices, shrimp,
cucumber or steamed vegetables. Garnish as desired.

Preparation time: 20 minutes

Calorie count: 47 calories per appetizer. Garnishes are extra.

Hot Maple Toddy

Makes about 3 cups

1 to 1¼ cups whiskey
1 cup CARY'S®, VERMONT MAPLE
    ORCHARDS or MACDONALD'S Pure
    Maple Syrup
¾ cup REALEMON® Lemon Juice from
    Concentrate
    Butter and cinnamon sticks, optional

In medium saucepan, combine all ingredients except
butter and cinnamon sticks. Over low heat, simmer
to blend flavors. Serve hot with butter and cinnamon
sticks if desired.

Microwave: In 1-quart glass measure, combine
ingredients as above. Microwave on 100% power
(high) 4 to 5 minutes or until heated through. Serve
as above.

Kahlúa® & Eggnog

Makes about 8 servings

1 quart dairy eggnog
¾ cup KAHLÚA®
    Whipped cream
    Ground nutmeg

Combine eggnog and KAHLÚA® in 1½-quart
pitcher. Pour into punch cups. Top with whipped
cream. Sprinkle with nutmeg.

Microwave Hot Chocolate

Makes about 4 cups or 4 servings

4 cups milk
1 package (4-serving size) **JELL-O® Pudding
    and Pie Filling, Chocolate or Chocolate
    Fudge Flavor**
    COOL WHIP® Whipped Topping, thawed
    (optional)
    Chocolate curls (optional)

Pour milk into 2-quart microwavable bowl. Add
pudding mix. Beat with wire whisk until well
blended. Microwave on HIGH 5 minutes; whisk
again. Pour into mugs. Top with whipped topping
and garnish with chocolate curls, if desired.

Preparation time: 5 minutes
Cooking time: 5 minutes

"Glogg"

Makes about 3 cups or 4 to 6 servings

1 package (4-serving size) **JELL-O® Brand
    Gelatin, any flavor**
3 cups boiling water
1 cinnamon stick
6 whole cloves
3 orange slices

Dissolve gelatin in boiling water in 4-cup measuring
cup. Add cinnamon stick, cloves and orange slices.
Cover; let stand 5 minutes. Remove spices and
oranges. Pour gelatin mixture into mugs; serve
warm. Garnish with additional cinnamon sticks and
clove-studded orange slices, if desired.

Preparation time: 5 minutes

"Glogg" (left), Microwave Hot Chocolate (right)

Deviled Shrimp

Makes 4 to 6 appetizer servings

Devil Sauce (recipe follows)
2 eggs, lightly beaten
¼ teaspoon salt
¼ teaspoon **TABASCO® pepper sauce**
1 quart vegetable oil
1 pound shrimp, peeled and cleaned
1 cup dry bread crumbs

Prepare Devil Sauce; set aside. In shallow dish stir
together eggs, salt and TABASCO® pepper sauce
until well blended. Pour oil into heavy 3-quart
saucepan or deep-fat fryer, filling no more than ⅓
full. Heat over medium heat to 375°F. Dip shrimp
into egg mixture, then into bread crumbs; shake off
excess. Carefully add to oil, a few at a time. Cook 1
to 2 minutes or until golden. Drain on paper towels.
Just before serving, drizzle Devil Sauce over shrimp.

Devil Sauce

2 tablespoons butter or margarine
1 small onion, finely chopped
1 clove garlic, minced
1½ teaspoons dry mustard
½ cup beef consomme
2 tablespoons Worcestershire sauce
2 tablespoons dry white wine
¼ teaspoon **TABASCO® pepper sauce**
¼ cup lemon juice

In 1-quart saucepan melt butter over medium heat;
add onion and garlic. Stirring frequently, cook 3
minutes or until tender. Blend in mustard. Gradually
stir in consomme, Worcestershire sauce, wine and
TABASCO® pepper sauce until well blended. Bring
to a boil and simmer 5 minutes. Stir in lemon juice.
Serve warm over shrimp or use as a dip. Makes
about 1¼ cups.

Celebration Punch

Makes 16 (6-ounce) servings

1 bottle (48 fl. oz.) **DEL MONTE® Pineapple
    Orange Blended Juice Drink, chilled**
1 can (46 fl. oz.) **DEL MONTE® Apricot
    Nectar, chilled**
1 cup orange juice
¼ cup fresh lime juice
2 tablespoons grenadine
1 cup rum (optional)
    Ice cubes

In punch bowl, combine all ingredients. Garnish
with pineapple wedges and lime slices, if desired.

Torta California

Torta California

Makes 3 cups

2 8-oz. pkgs. **PHILADELPHIA BRAND**®
   Cream Cheese, softened
1 8-oz. pkg. goat cheese
1 to 2 garlic cloves
2 tablespoons olive oil
1 teaspoon dried thyme leaves, crushed
3 tablespoons pesto, well drained
1/3 cup roasted red peppers, drained, chopped

Line 1-quart souffle dish or loaf pan with plastic wrap. Place cream cheese, goat cheese and garlic in food processor or blender container; process until well blended. Add oil and thyme; blend well. Place one-third of cheese mixture in souffle dish; cover with pesto, half of remaining cheese mixture and peppers. Top with remaining cheese mixture. Cover; chill.

Unmold; remove plastic wrap. Smooth sides. Garnish with fresh herbs and additional red peppers, if desired. Serve with assorted crackers or·French bread.

Preparation time: 15 minutes plus chilling

Fancy Ham-Wrapped Fruit

Makes 32 appetizers

1 (3-ounce) package cream cheese, softened
1 tablespoon orange marmalade
1/3 pound thinly sliced fully-cooked ham, cut into
   1×4-inch strips
2 papayas, peeled and cut into eighths
2 kiwifruit, peeled and sliced
1 orange (optional)

In a small bowl combine cream cheese and orange marmalade; mix well. Spread cream cheese mixture on one side of each ham strip. Place a piece of fruit on each ham strip and wrap ham around fruit. Cover and chill. To make orange peel garnish, peel orange in a long continuous strip about 1-inch wide. Roll into flower shape.

Preparation time: 20 minutes

Favorite Recipe from **National Pork Producers Council**

Oven-Fried Mushrooms

Oven-Fried Mushrooms

Makes about 24 appetizers

1/2 cup all-purpose flour
1/2 teaspoon paprika
1 cup soft bread crumbs
1/2 cup grated Parmesan cheese
2 teaspoons dried basil or oregano leaves, crushed
2 eggs, slightly beaten
2 tablespoons milk
1 package (16 ounces) CAMPBELL'S FRESH® mushrooms
1/4 cup butter or margarine, melted
Dipping Sauce (recipe follows)

Preheat oven to 450°F. Lightly grease 15×10-inch jelly-roll pan. In plastic bag, combine flour and paprika. In another plastic bag, combine crumbs, cheese and basil. In small bowl, combine eggs and milk. Shake mushrooms in flour mixture and dip in egg mixture. Shake in crumb mixture, pressing crumb mixture to mushrooms to coat. Arrange mushrooms cap-side down on prepared jelly-roll pan. Drizzle with butter. Bake 10 minutes or until golden brown. Serve with Dipping Sauce.

Dipping Sauce: In small bowl, combine 1/4 cup mayonnaise, 1 tablespoon Dijon-style mustard or prepared horseradish and 1 tablespoon chopped fresh parsley. Makes 1/4 cup.

Tip: To prepare ahead, coated mushrooms can be covered and refrigerated until baking time.

Florentine Crescents

Makes 32 appetizers

1 10-oz. pkg. frozen chopped spinach, thawed, well drained
1/2 lb. VELVEETA® Pasteurized Process Cheese Spread, cubed
1/4 cup dry bread crumbs
3 crisply cooked bacon slices, crumbled
2 8-oz. cans refrigerated crescent dinner rolls

In 2-quart saucepan, combine spinach, process cheese spread, crumbs and bacon. Stir over low heat until process cheese spread is melted. Unroll dough; separate into sixteen triangles. Cut each in half lengthwise, forming thirty-two triangles. Spread each triangle with rounded teaspoonful spinach mixture. Roll up, starting at wide end. Place on greased cookie sheet. Brush dough with beaten egg, if desired. Bake at 375°F, 11 to 13 minutes or until golden brown.

Preparation time: 20 minutes
Baking time: 13 minutes per batch

Microwave: Combine spinach, process cheese spread, crumbs and bacon in 1½-quart microwave-safe bowl. Microwave on High 2½ to 4½ minutes or until process cheese spread is melted, stirring every 1½ minutes. Continue as directed.

Monterey Dipping Sauce

Makes about 3 cups

1 can (14½ oz.) DEL MONTE® Stewed Tomatoes
1 can (8 oz.) DEL MONTE® Tomato Sauce
1/4 cup chopped onion
1 clove garlic, minced
2 tablespoons chopped fresh cilantro
2 teaspoons fresh lemon juice
1/2 teaspoon crushed oregano
1/4 teaspoon hot pepper sauce

Place stewed tomatoes in blender container. Cover and blend on medium 2 seconds. Combine remaining ingredients; stir in stewed tomatoes. Chill several hours. Serve as dip with shrimp or tortilla chips.

Carolers' Orange Cocoa

Makes 1 serving

1 envelope **ALBA®** Milk Chocolate Hot Cocoa
¾ cup boiling water
1 tablespoon orange-flavored liqueur
1 tablespoon frozen whipped topping, thawed
¼ teaspoon grated orange peel

Empty **ALBA®** Hot Cocoa into mug or cup. Add water; stir until completely dissolved. Stir in liqueur. Top with whipped topping and orange peel.

Only 123 calories per serving.

Easy Sausage Empanadas

Makes 12 appetizer servings

1 (15-ounce) package refrigerated pie crusts
  (2 crusts)
¼ pound bulk pork sausage
2 tablespoons finely chopped onion
⅛ teaspoon garlic powder
⅛ teaspoon ground cumin
⅛ teaspoon dried oregano, crushed
1 tablespoon chopped pimiento-stuffed olives
1 tablespoon chopped raisins
1 egg, separated

Let pie crusts stand at room temperature for 20 minutes or according to package directions. Crumble sausage into a medium skillet. Add onion, garlic powder, cumin and oregano; cook over medium-high heat until sausage is no longer pink. Drain drippings. Stir in olives and raisins. Beat the egg yolk slightly; stir into sausage mixture, mixing well. Carefully unfold crusts. Cut into desired shapes using 3-inch cookie cutters. Place about 2 teaspoons of the sausage filling on half the cutouts. Top with remaining cutouts. Moisten fingers with water and pinch dough to seal edges. Slightly beat the egg white; gently brush over tops of empanadas. Bake in a 425°F oven 15 to 18 minutes or until golden brown.

Preparation time: 25 minutes
Cooking time: 15 minutes

Favorite Recipe from **National Pork Producers Council**

Apple Cinnamon Cream Liqueur

Makes about 1 quart

1 (14-ounce) can **EAGLE®** Brand Sweetened
  Condensed Milk (NOT evaporated milk)
1 cup apple schnapps
2 cups (1 pint) **BORDEN®** or **MEADOW
  GOLD®** Whipping Cream *or* Half-and-Half
½ teaspoon ground cinnamon

In blender container, combine ingredients; blend until smooth. Serve over ice. Garnish as desired. Store tightly covered in refrigerator. Stir before serving.

Fuzzy Navel Cream Liqueur: Omit apple schnapps and cinnamon. Add 1 cup peach schnapps and ¼ cup frozen orange juice concentrate, thawed. Proceed as above.

Apple Cinnamon Cream Liqueur

Tangy Wisconsin Blue Cheese Whip

Makes about 2 cups

1 cup whipping cream
½ cup finely crumbled Wisconsin Blue cheese (2 ounces)
1 teaspoon dried basil, crushed
¼ teaspoon garlic salt
½ cup almonds, toasted and chopped
Assorted vegetable or fruit dippers

In a small mixer bowl combine whipping cream, Blue cheese, basil, and garlic salt. Beat with an electric mixer on medium speed until slightly thickened. Gently fold in chopped almonds. Serve with vegetable or fruit dippers. (Dip can be made ahead and chilled, covered, up to 2 hours.)

Preparation time: 15 minutes

Favorite Recipe from **Wisconsin Milk Marketing Board**©1990

Fresh Cranberry Frost

Makes 4 servings

1 cup ice water
2 envelopes ALBA® Vanilla Shake
1 cup fresh cranberries
½ teaspoon grated orange peel
12 large ice cubes

Pour water into blender container; add ALBA® Shake, cranberries and orange peel. Cover; process at low speed, adding ice cubes one at a time. Process at highest speed 60 seconds or until ALBA® mixture is thickened and ice cubes are completely processed. Spoon into stemmed dessert glasses. Serve immediately with spoons and straws.

Only 47 calories per serving.

Fresh Cranberry Frost

Curried Popcorn Mix

Makes about 2 quarts

6 cups unseasoned popped corn
2 cups pretzel sticks
1½ cups DIAMOND® Walnut pieces
¼ cup butter or margarine, melted
2 teaspoons curry powder
¼ teaspoon hot pepper sauce
Salt to taste
1½ cups SUN-MAID® Golden Raisins

In large, deep baking or roasting pan, combine popped corn, pretzels and walnuts. In small bowl, mix butter, curry powder and pepper sauce; drizzle over popcorn mixture and toss to coat evenly. Bake in 300°F oven about 30 minutes, tossing twice. Remove from oven. Mix in salt. Cool completely. Store in airtight container. Mix in raisins before serving.

Teriyaki Scallop Roll-Ups

Makes about 2 dozen appetizers

12 slices bacon, partially cooked and cut in half crosswise
⅓ cup REALIME® Lime Juice from Concentrate
¼ cup soy sauce
¼ cup vegetable oil
1 tablespoon light brown sugar
2 cloves garlic, finely chopped
½ teaspoon pepper
½ pound sea scallops, cut in half
24 fresh pea pods
12 water chestnuts, cut in half

To make teriyaki marinade, combine REALIME® brand, soy sauce, oil, sugar, garlic and pepper; mix well. Wrap 1 scallop half, 1 pea pod and 1 water chestnut half in each bacon slice; secure with wooden pick. Place in shallow baking dish; pour marinade over. Cover; refrigerate 4 hours or overnight, turning occasionally. Preheat oven to 450°F. Place roll-ups on rack in aluminum foil-lined shallow baking pan, bake 6 minutes. Turn; continue baking 6 minutes or until bacon is crisp. Serve hot. Refrigerate leftovers.

Mariachi Drumsticks (top), Potato Wraps (bottom)

Mariachi Drumsticks

Makes about 20 drummettes

1¼ cups crushed plain tortilla chips
1 package (1.25 ounces) **LAWRY'S**® Taco
   Seasoning Mix
18 to 20 chicken drummettes
   Salsa

Preheat oven to 350°F. In large plastic bag, combine tortilla chips with taco seasoning mix. Dampen chicken with water and shake off excess. Place a few pieces at a time in plastic bag; shake thoroughly to coat with chips. Arrange chicken in greased shallow baking pan; bake uncovered 30 minutes or until chicken is crispy. Serve with salsa for dipping.

Potato Wraps

Makes 16 appetizers

4 small new potatoes (1½-inch diameter each)
½ teaspoon **LAWRY'S**® Seasoned Salt
½ teaspoon **LAWRY'S**® Seasoned Pepper
¼ teaspoon crushed bay leaves
8 slices bacon, cut in half crosswise

Preheat oven to 400°F. Wash potatoes and cut into quarters. Sprinkle each with a mixture of seasoned salt, seasoned pepper and bay leaves. Wrap 1 bacon piece around each potato piece. Sprinkle with any remaining seasonings. Place in baking dish and bake uncovered 20 minutes or until bacon is crispy and potatoes are cooked through. Drain on paper towels. Serve, if desired, with sour cream and chives.

Pineapple Raspberry Punch

Spinach Dip

Makes about 3 cups

1 package (10 ounces) frozen chopped spinach,
   thawed and drained
1½ cups sour cream
1 cup **HELLMANN'S®** or **BEST FOODS®** Real,
   Light or Cholesterol Free Reduced Calorie
   Mayonnaise
1 package (1.4 ounces) **KNORR®** vegetable soup
   and recipe mix
1 can (8 ounces) water chestnuts, drained and
   chopped (optional)
3 green onions, chopped

In medium bowl combine spinach, sour cream,
mayonnaise, soup mix, water chestnuts and green
onions. Cover; chill. Serve with fresh vegetables,
crackers or chips. Garnish as desired.

Cucumber Dill Dip

Makes about 2½ cups

1 package (8 ounces) light cream cheese,
   softened
1 cup **HELLMANN'S®** or **BEST FOODS®** Real,
   Light or Cholesterol Free Reduced Calorie
   Mayonnaise
2 medium cucumbers, peeled, seeded and
   chopped
2 tablespoons sliced green onions
1 tablespoon lemon juice
2 teaspoons snipped fresh dill *or* ½ teaspoon
   dried dillweed
½ teaspoon hot pepper sauce

In medium bowl beat cream cheese until smooth.
Stir in mayonnaise, cucumbers, green onions, lemon
juice, dill and hot pepper sauce. Cover; chill. Serve
with fresh vegetables, crackers or chips. Garnish as
desired.

Pineapple Raspberry Punch

Makes 9 cups

5 cups **DOLE®** Pineapple Juice
1 quart raspberry cranberry drink
1 pint fresh or frozen raspberries
1 lemon, thinly sliced
   Ice

Chill ingredients. Combine in punch bowl.

French Onion Dip

Makes about 2½ cups

2 cups sour cream
½ cup **HELLMANN'S®** or **BEST FOODS®** Real,
   Light or Cholesterol Free Reduced Calorie
   Mayonnaise
1 package (1.9 ounces) **KNORR®** French onion
   soup and recipe mix

In medium bowl combine sour cream, mayonnaise
and soup mix. Cover; chill. Serve with fresh
vegetables or potato chips. Garnish as desired.

Left to right: French Onion Dip,
Cucumber Dill Dip, Spinach Dip

Tangy Holiday Meatballs (left), Peanut Butter-Cheese Triangles (right)

Tangy Holiday Meatballs

Makes 3 dozen meatballs (12 appetizer servings)

Meatballs
  1 cup **KELLOGG'S® RICE KRISPIES®**
    cereal
  2/3 cup nonfat dry milk powder
  1/4 cup finely chopped onion
  2 tablespoons ketchup
  1 egg
  1 teaspoon salt
  1/8 teaspoon pepper
  1 pound lean ground beef

Sauce
  1 can (15 oz.) tomato sauce
  1/2 cup ketchup
  1/4 cup firmly packed brown sugar
  1/4 cup finely chopped onion
  1/4 cup sweet pickle relish
  2 tablespoons Worcestershire sauce
  1 tablespoon vinegar
  1/4 teaspoon pepper

For meatballs, combine KELLOGG'S® RICE KRISPIES® cereal, dry milk, onion, ketchup, egg, salt and pepper. Add beef, mixing only until combined. Using level measuring-tablespoon, portion meat mixture. Roll into balls and place in foil-lined shallow baking pan. Bake in 400°F oven about 12 minutes or until browned.

In 4-quart saucepan, combine sauce ingredients. Simmer over low heat 15 minutes, stirring frequently. Add meatballs to sauce and continue simmering 10 minutes longer. Serve hot.

Per Serving (3 meatballs): 130 Calories

Note: *Tangy Holiday Meatballs may be served as an entree over hot rice.*

Peanut Butter-Cheese Triangles

Makes 24 triangles

  2 tablespoons nonfat dry milk powder
  1/2 cup corn syrup
  1/2 cup crunchy peanut butter
  3 cups **KELLOGG'S® RICE KRISPIES®** cereal
  2 packages (3 oz. each) cream cheese, softened
  2 cups shredded cheddar cheese
  2 tablespoons margarine or butter, softened

In 2-quart saucepan, combine dry milk and corn syrup, mixing until smooth. Cook over medium heat, stirring constantly, until mixture starts to boil. Remove from heat. Stir in peanut butter. Add KELLOGG'S® RICE KRISPIES® cereal, stirring until cereal is coated. Spread mixture evenly in wax paper-lined 13×9×2-inch pan. Chill until firm.

In food processor or electric mixer bowl, combine cream cheese, cheddar cheese and margarine. Process until cheese is smooth. Cut cereal mixture in half crosswise to form 2 (9×6-inch) rectangles. Set aside 1/3 cup cheese mixture and spread remaining cheese on 1 of the cereal rectangles. Place second cereal rectangle on top of cheese, pressing to form a sandwich. Chill until firm, about 2 hours.

To serve, cut cereal into 2-inch squares. Cut squares diagonally into 2 pieces to form triangles. Garnish each triangle with remaining cheese and small parsley leaf. Serve cold.

Per Serving (2 triangles): 270 Calories

Fireside Punch

Makes about 5 servings

1½ cups cranberry juice cocktail
1½ cups cold water
  4 bags **LIPTON®** Cinnamon Apple or Gentle
      Orange Herbal Flo-Thru Tea Bags
  2 tablespoons brown sugar
    Cinnamon sticks (optional)
    Fresh cranberries (optional)

In medium saucepan, bring cranberry juice and
water to a boil. Add cinnamon apple herbal tea bags;
cover and brew 5 minutes. Remove tea bags; stir in
sugar. Pour into mugs and garnish with cinnamon
sticks and fresh cranberries.

Stuffed Mushrooms

Makes 12 appetizer servings

  1 package (6 oz.) **STOVE TOP®** Chicken Flavor
      Stuffing Mix
24 large mushrooms (about 1½ lbs.)
¼ cup (½ stick) butter or margarine
¼ cup *each* finely chopped red and green pepper
  3 tablespoons butter or margarine, melted

Prepare stuffing mix as directed on package,
omitting butter. Remove stems from mushrooms;
chop stems. Melt ¼ cup butter in skillet. Add
mushroom caps; cook and stir until lightly browned.
Arrange in shallow baking dish. Cook and stir
chopped mushroom stems and the peppers in the
skillet until tender; stir into prepared stuffing. Spoon
onto mushroom caps; drizzle with 3 tablespoons
butter. Place under preheated broiler for 5 minutes
to heat through.

Pina Colada Punch

Makes 15 servings

  5 cups **DOLE®** Pineapple Juice
  1 can (15 oz.) real cream of coconut
  1 liter lemon-lime soda
  2 limes
1½ cups light rum, optional
    Ice cubes
    Mint sprigs

Chill all ingredients. Whir 2 cups pineapple juice
with cream of coconut in blender. Combine pureed
mixture with remaining pineapple juice, soda, juice
of 1 lime, rum (if desired) and ice. Garnish with 1
sliced lime and mint.

Hot Mulled Cider

Makes 8 servings

  1 quart apple cider
⅔ cup firmly packed **DOMINO®** Light Brown
      Sugar
  2 small sticks cinnamon
  8 whole cloves
¼ teaspoon ground nutmeg
¼ teaspoon ground ginger
    Lemon slices

Combine all ingredients except lemon slices in
saucepan. Bring to a boil, stirring constantly. Reduce
heat; simmer 10 minutes. Remove cinnamon sticks
and cloves. Garnish with lemon slices. Serve at once.

Hot Buttered Rum

Makes 4 cups (16 servings)

  1 cup granulated sugar
  1 cup firmly packed brown sugar
  1 cup **LAND O LAKES®** Sweet Cream Butter
  2 cups vanilla ice cream, softened
    Rum or rum extract
    Boiling water
    Nutmeg

In 2-quart saucepan combine granulated sugar,
brown sugar and butter. Cook over low heat, stirring
occasionally, until butter is melted and sugar is
dissolved (6 to 8 minutes). In large mixer bowl
combine cooked mixture with ice cream; beat at
medium speed, scraping bowl often, until smooth
(1 to 2 minutes). Store refrigerated up to 2 weeks.
For each serving, fill mug with ¼ cup mixture, 1
ounce rum or ¼ teaspoon rum extract and ¾ cup
boiling water; sprinkle with nutmeg.

Tip: Mixture can be frozen up to 1 month.

Hot Buttered Rum

Continental Cheese Mold

Continental Cheese Mold

Makes 4 cups

1 package (4-serving size) **JELL-O**® **Brand Gelatin, Orange or Lemon Flavor**
³/₄ cup boiling water
1 container (16 ounces) cottage cheese
2 ounces Roquefort or bleu cheese, crumbled
¹/₂ cup sour cream
1 teaspoon seasoned salt
1 teaspoon lemon juice
1 teaspoon Worcestershire sauce
2 tablespoons chopped parsley
  Sliced carrots (optional)
  Watercress (optional)
  Assorted crackers and vegetables

Dissolve gelatin in boiling water. Combine cheeses, sour cream, seasoned salt, lemon juice and Worcestershire sauce in large bowl; beat until smooth. (Or, combine in blender and blend until smooth.) Gradually blend in gelatin. Add parsley. Pour into 4-cup mold or bowl. Chill until set, about 3 hours. Unmold. Garnish with carrot slices and watercress, if desired. Serve with assorted crackers and vegetables.

Preparation time: 15 minutes
Chill time: 3 hours

Steamed Stuffed Zucchini Rounds

Makes 6 to 8 appetizer servings

4 zucchini, 6 to 7 inches long, about 1½ inches in diameter
½ cup **KIKKOMAN**® Teriyaki Sauce
½ pound ground beef
½ cup dry bread crumbs
¼ cup minced green onions and tops

Trim off and discard ends of zucchini; cut crosswise into ¾-inch lengths. Scoop out flesh, leaving about ⅛-inch shell on sides and bottoms; reserve flesh. Place zucchini rounds in large plastic bag; pour in teriyaki sauce. Press air out of bag; tie top securely. Marinate 30 minutes, turning bag over occasionally. Meanwhile, coarsely chop zucchini flesh; reserve ½ cup. Remove zucchini rounds from marinade; reserve ¼ cup marinade. Combine reserved marinade with beef, bread crumbs, green onions and ½ cup reserved zucchini flesh. Fill each round with about 2 teaspoonfuls beef mixture. Place rounds, filled side up, on steamer rack. Set rack in large pot or wok of boiling water. (Do not allow water level to reach zucchini.) Cover and steam 6 minutes, or until zucchini rounds are tender-crisp when pierced with fork. Serve immediately.

Waikiki Appetizers

Makes 6 to 8 appetizer servings

1½ pounds bulk pork sausage
1 can (20 oz.) pineapple chunks in syrup
½ cup brown sugar, packed
¼ cup lemon juice
2 tablespoons cornstarch
2 tablespoons **KIKKOMAN**® Soy Sauce
½ cup chopped green pepper
½ cup drained maraschino cherries

Shape sausage into ½- to ¾-inch balls. Place in single layer in baking pan. Bake in 400°F oven 25 minutes, or until cooked; drain on paper towels. Meanwhile, drain pineapple; reserve syrup. Add enough water to syrup to measure 1 cup; combine with brown sugar, lemon juice, cornstarch and soy sauce in large saucepan. Cook and stir until sauce boils and thickens. Fold in green pepper, cherries, pineapple chunks and drained cooked sausage. To serve, turn into chafing dish.

Toasted Almond Party Spread

Makes 2⅓ cups

1 8-oz. pkg. **PHILADELPHIA BRAND**® Cream Cheese, softened
1½ cups (6 ozs.) shredded **CASINO**® Brand Natural Swiss Cheese
⅓ cup **MIRACLE WHIP**® Salad Dressing
2 tablespoons chopped green onions
⅛ teaspoon ground nutmeg
⅛ teaspoon pepper
⅓ cup sliced almonds, toasted

Preheat oven to 350°F. Combine all ingredients; mix well. Spread mixture into 9-inch pie plate or quiche dish. Bake for 15 minutes, stirring after 8 minutes. Garnish with additional toasted sliced almonds, if desired. Serve with assorted crackers or toasted bread cut-outs.

Preparation time: 10 minutes
Baking time: 15 minutes

***Steamed Stuffed Zucchini Rounds (top),
Waikiki Appetizers (bottom)***

Christmas Carol Punch

Makes about 2 quarts

2 medium red apples
2 quarts clear apple cider
8 cinnamon sticks
2 teaspoons whole cloves
½ cup SUN-MAID® Raisins
 Orange slices
 Lemon slices
¼ cup lemon juice

Core apples; slice into ½-inch rings. In Dutch oven, combine cider, cinnamon, cloves, apple rings and raisins. Bring to boil over high heat; reduce heat to low and simmer 5 to 8 minutes or until apples are just tender. Remove cloves; add orange and lemon slices and lemon juice. Pour into punch bowl. Ladle into large mugs, including an apple ring, some raisins and citrus slices in each serving. Serve with spoons.

Holiday Eggnog

Makes 8 servings

½ cup ice water
½ cup brandy
2 envelopes ALBA® Vanilla Shake
6 large ice cubes
2 egg whites
 Nutmeg

Pour water and brandy into blender container; add ALBA® Shake. Cover; process at low speed, adding ice cubes one at a time. Process at highest speed 60 seconds or until ALBA® mixture is thickened and ice cubes are completely processed. Beat egg whites to form soft peaks; fold into ALBA® mixture. Pour into small cups. Dust with nutmeg.

Only 58 calories per serving.

Holiday Eggnog

Double Berry Coco Punch

Makes about 4 quarts

 Ice Ring, optional, or block of ice
2 (10-ounce) packages frozen strawberries in syrup, thawed
1 (15-ounce) can COCO LOPEZ® Cream of Coconut
1 (48-ounce) bottle cranberry juice cocktail, chilled
2 cups light rum, optional
1 (32-ounce) bottle club soda, chilled

Prepare ice ring in advance if desired. In blender container, puree strawberries with cream of coconut until smooth. In large punch bowl, combine strawberry mixture, cranberry juice and rum if desired. Just before serving, add club soda and ice ring or block of ice.

Ice Ring: Fill ring mold with water to within 1 inch of top rim; freeze. Arrange strawberries, cranberries, mint leaves, lime slices or other fruits on top of ice. Gradually pour small amount of cold water over fruits; freeze.

Beef Kushisashi

Makes 10 to 12 appetizer servings

½ cup KIKKOMAN® Soy Sauce
¼ cup chopped green onions and tops
2 tablespoons sugar
1 tablespoon vegetable oil
1½ teaspoons cornstarch
1 clove garlic, pressed
1 teaspoon grated fresh ginger root
2½ pounds boneless beef sirloin steak

Blend soy sauce, green onions, sugar, oil, cornstarch, garlic and ginger in small saucepan. Simmer, stirring constantly, until thickened, about 1 minute; cool. Cover and set aside. Slice beef into ⅛-inch-thick strips about 4 inches long and 1-inch wide. Thread onto bamboo or metal skewers keeping meat as flat as possible; brush both sides of beef with sauce. Place skewers on rack of broiler pan; broil to desired degree of doneness.

Bacon Appetizer Crescents

Preheat oven to 375°F. Beat cream cheese, bacon, parmesan cheese, onion, parsley and milk in small mixing bowl at medium speed with electric mixer until well blended. Separate dough into eight rectangles; firmly press perforations together to seal. Spread each rectangle with 2 rounded measuring tablespoonfuls cream cheese mixture.

Cut each rectangle in half diagonally; repeat with opposite corners. Cut in half crosswise to form six triangles. Roll up triangles, starting at short ends. Place on greased cookie sheet; brush with combined egg and water. Sprinkle with poppy seed, if desired. Bake 12 to 15 minutes or until golden brown. Serve immediately.

Preparation time: 30 minutes
Cooking time: 15 minutes

Fruity Cheese Spread

Makes about 1 1/2 cups

      8 ounces cream cheese, softened
      1 teaspoon grated orange peel
   3/4 teaspoon almond extract
   1/2 teaspoon ground ginger
1 1/2 cups RALSTON® brand Fruit Muesli with
          Cranberries, crushed to 1 cup
      Apple and pear slices
      Crackers and cookies

In medium bowl combine cream cheese, orange peel, almond extract and ginger; beat until smooth. Place 1/2 cup cereal in serving dish; spoon cheese mixture on top. Refrigerate 2 to 3 hours. Just before serving, sprinkle remaining 1/2 cup cereal over cheese spread. Serve with apple and pear slices, crackers and cookies.

Bacon Appetizer Crescents

Makes about 4 dozen appetizers

   1 8-oz. pkg. PHILADELPHIA BRAND® Cream
        Cheese, softened
   8 OSCAR MAYER® Bacon Slices, crisply
        cooked, crumbled
1/3 cup (1 1/2 ozs.) KRAFT® 100% Grated
        Parmesan Cheese
1/4 cup finely chopped onion
   2 tablespoons chopped parsley
   1 tablespoon milk
   2 8-oz. cans refrigerated crescent dinner rolls
   1 egg, beaten
   1 teaspoon cold water

Festive Brunches

Egg & Asparagus Casserole

Makes about 4 servings

   1 package LIPTON® Rice & Sauce–Asparagus
      with Hollandaise Sauce
   1 medium red bell pepper, chopped
   1/2 cup sliced green onions
   8 eggs, beaten
   2 cups milk
   1 cup water
   2 tablespoons butter or margarine, cut into
      small pieces
   1 tablespoon Dijon-style mustard
   3/4 teaspoon salt
   1/4 teaspoon pepper
   2 cups shredded Swiss cheese (about 8 ounces)

In large bowl, combine all ingredients except 1/2 cup
cheese. Chill at least 6 hours or overnight.

Preheat oven to 350°F. Pour egg mixture into greased
11×7-inch baking pan. Sprinkle with remaining
1/2 cup cheese. Bake 45 minutes or until set.

Skillet Walnut Pumpkin Bread

Makes 6 to 8 servings

      Cornmeal
   1/3 cup butter or margarine, softened
   1 cup sugar
   2 eggs, slightly beaten
   1 cup canned pumpkin
   3/4 cup milk
   1 cup all-purpose flour
   3/4 cup cornmeal
   1 teaspoon ground allspice
   1 teaspoon baking soda
   1/2 teaspoon baking powder
   1 cup chopped DIAMOND® Walnuts
      DIAMOND® Walnut halves, for garnish

Grease 9-inch cast-iron skillet. Dust with cornmeal;
set aside. In large bowl, beat butter, sugar and eggs.
Add pumpkin and milk; mix to blend thoroughly. In
medium bowl, combine flour, the 3/4 cup cornmeal,
allspice, baking soda and baking powder. Add to wet
ingredients, stirring just until blended. Stir in
chopped walnuts. Pour into prepared skillet. Garnish
center with walnut halves. Bake in preheated 375°F
oven 45 minutes or until pick inserted into center
comes out clean. Serve warm.

*Note: Substitute a deep 9-inch round or square baking pan if
cast-iron skillet is unavailable.*

Spinach Cheese Torta

Makes about 8 servings

3 medium corn muffins, crumbled (about
2¹/₂ cups crumbs)
3 tablespoons butter or margarine, melted
3 teaspoons chopped fresh basil leaves*
Salt and pepper to taste
1 tablespoon olive or vegetable oil
2 teaspoons finely chopped garlic
1 package (10 ounces) frozen chopped spinach,
thawed and squeezed dry
1 cup ricotta cheese
¹/₄ cup grated Parmesan cheese
1 egg, slightly beaten
1 package LIPTON® Rice & Sauce–Cheddar
Broccoli
1¹/₂ cups shredded mozzarella cheese (about
6 ounces)

Preheat oven to 400°F. In medium bowl, thoroughly
combine corn muffin crumbs, butter, 2 teaspoons
basil, salt and pepper. Press into bottom and ¹/₂ inch
up sides of 9-inch springform or square baking pan.
Bake 12 minutes; cool on wire rack.

In medium saucepan, heat oil and cook garlic over
medium heat 30 seconds. Add spinach and cook over
medium heat, stirring constantly, 2 minutes or until
heated through; add salt and pepper. Stir in ricotta
cheese, Parmesan cheese, egg and remaining 1
teaspoon basil; set aside.

Prepare rice & Cheddar broccoli sauce according to
package directions. Into prepared pan, layer ³/₄ cup
mozzarella cheese, rice mixture, spinach mixture,
then remaining ³/₄ cup mozzarella cheese. Decrease
heat to 375°F and bake 30 minutes or until set.
Remove sides of springform pan. Garnish as desired.
Serve warm or cool.

*Substitution: Use ¹/₂ teaspoon dried basil leaves in crust and
1 teaspoon dried basil leaves in filling.*

Spinach Cheese Torta

Noel Bran Muffins

Makes 12 muffins

1¹/₄ cups whole bran cereal
1 cup milk
1¹/₂ cups flour
¹/₂ cup firmly packed brown sugar
¹/₂ cup shredded carrots
2 teaspoons baking powder
¹/₄ teaspoon salt
¹/₄ teaspoon nutmeg
¹/₄ cup butter or margarine, melted
2 eggs
1 cup chopped DEL MONTE®
Dried Apricots or Seedless Raisins

Soften bran in milk. In large bowl, blend together
flour, sugar, carrots, baking powder, salt and
nutmeg. Combine bran mixture, butter and eggs;
add to dry ingredients. Stir until flour is moistened.
Fold in chopped apricots or raisins. Fill 12 paper-
lined or greased 2¹/₂-inch muffin-pan cups. Bake at
375°F, 25 to 30 minutes or until golden. Serve warm.

Crab & Shrimp Quiche

Makes one 9-inch quiche

1 (9-inch) unbaked pastry shell
6 slices BORDEN® Process American Cheese
Food
2 tablespoons sliced green onion
2 tablespoons chopped pimiento
1 tablespoon flour
1 (6-ounce) can ORLEANS® or HARRIS®
Crabmeat, drained
1 (4¹/₄-ounce) can ORLEANS® Shrimp, drained
and soaked as label directs
1¹/₂ cups BORDEN® or MEADOW GOLD®
Half-and-Half
3 eggs, beaten

Place rack in lowest position in oven; preheat oven to
425°F. Cut *4 slices* cheese food into pieces. In large
bowl, toss cheese food pieces, onion and pimiento
with flour. Add remaining ingredients except pastry
shell and cheese food slices. Pour into pastry shell.
Bake 20 minutes. Reduce oven temperature to 325°F;
bake 20 minutes longer or until set. Arrange
remaining *2 slices* cheese food on top of quiche. Let
stand 10 minutes before serving. Garnish as desired.
Refrigerate leftovers.

Quiche Florentine

Makes 6 to 8 servings

1 15-oz. pkg. refrigerated pie crusts
2 cups (8 ozs.) VELVEETA® Shredded
    Pasteurized Process Cheese Food
1/3 cup (1½ ozs.) KRAFT® 100% Grated
    Parmesan Cheese
1 10-oz. pkg. frozen chopped spinach, thawed,
    well drained
4 crisply cooked bacon slices, crumbled
3/4 cup milk
3 eggs, beaten
1/4 teaspoon pepper

Prepare pie crust according to package directions for filled one-crust pie using 9-inch pie plate. (Refrigerate remaining crust for later use.) In large bowl, combine remaining ingredients; mix well. Pour into unbaked pie crust. Bake at 350°F, 35 to 40 minutes or until knife inserted in center comes out clean. Let stand 10 minutes before serving.

Preparation time: 15 minutes
Baking time: 40 minutes plus standing

Nutcracker Fruit Bread

Makes 6 mini loaves

2¼ cups all-purpose flour
1½ cups sugar
  1 cup LAND O LAKES® Sweet Cream Butter,
    softened
  1 (8-oz.) pkg. cream cheese, softened
  4 eggs
1½ teaspoons baking powder
1½ teaspoons vanilla
  1 cup candied red and green cherries, quartered
1/2 cup chopped dates
1/2 cup golden raisins
1/2 cup chopped walnuts

Heat oven to 325°F. In large mixer bowl combine 1¼ cups flour, the sugar, butter, cream cheese, eggs, baking powder and vanilla. Beat at medium speed, scraping bowl often, until well mixed (2 to 3 minutes). By hand, stir in remaining 1 cup flour, candied cherries, dates, raisins and walnuts. Pour into 6 greased 5½×3-inch mini-loaf pans. Bake for 45 to 55 minutes or until wooden pick inserted in center comes out clean. Cool 10 minutes; remove from pans. Cool completely.

Puffy Tuna Omelet

Puffy Tuna Omelet

Makes 1 serving

2 eggs, separated
1/4 teaspoon pepper
1 tablespoon water
1 tablespoon butter or margarine
2 tablespoons chicken broth
1/2 small red or green bell pepper, cut into strips
1 cup chopped spinach leaves
1 can (3¼ ounces) STARKIST® Tuna, drained
    and broken into chunks
1/4 teaspoon dried oregano, crushed
    Salt and pepper to taste
2 teaspoons grated Parmesan cheese

In a small bowl beat egg yolks and pepper on high speed of electric mixer about 5 minutes, or until thick and lemon-colored. In a medium bowl beat egg whites and water until stiff peaks form. Pour yolks over whites and gently fold in.

Preheat oven to 325°F. In a 7-inch nonstick skillet with ovenproof handle melt butter over low heat. Lift and tilt skillet to coat sides. Pour egg mixture into hot skillet, mounding it slightly higher around edges. Cook over low heat about 6 minutes, or until eggs are puffed and set and bottom is golden brown. Bake for 6 to 8 minutes, or until a knife inserted near center comes out clean.

Meanwhile, in a small skillet heat chicken broth. Cook and stir bell pepper and spinach in broth for 2 minutes. Stir in tuna and oregano; season to taste with salt and pepper. Drain; keep warm. Loosen sides of omelet with spatula. Make a shallow cut across omelet, cutting slightly off center; fill with tuna mixture. Fold smaller portion of omelet over larger portion. Sprinkle with cheese. Serve immediately.

Preparation time: 10 minutes

Calorie count: 422 calories per serving.

Caramel Pecan Sticky Buns

Caramel Pecan Sticky Buns

Makes 2 dozen

1 8-oz. pkg. PHILADELPHIA BRAND® Cream
    Cheese, cubed
3/4 cup cold water
1 16-oz. pkg. hot roll mix
1 egg
1/3 cup granulated sugar
1 teaspoon cinnamon
1 cup pecan halves
3/4 cup packed brown sugar
1/2 cup light corn syrup
1/4 cup PARKAY® Margarine, melted

Preheat oven to 350°F. Stir together 6 ounces cream
cheese and water in small saucepan. Cook over low
heat until mixture reaches 115° to 120°F, stirring
occasionally. Stir together hot roll mix and yeast
packet in large bowl. Add cream cheese mixture and
egg, mixing until dough pulls away from sides of
bowl. Knead dough on lightly floured surface 5
minutes or until smooth and elastic. Cover; let rise
in warm place 20 minutes.

Beat remaining cream cheese, granulated sugar and
cinnamon in small mixing bowl at medium speed
with electric mixer until well blended. Roll out
dough to 18×12-inch rectangle; spread cream cheese
mixture over dough to within 1 inch from outer
edges of dough. Roll up from long end; seal edges.
Cut into twenty-four 3/4-inch slices.

Stir together remaining ingredients in small bowl.
Spoon 2 teaspoonfuls mixture into bottoms of
greased medium-sized muffin pans. Place dough, cut
side up, in cups. Cover; let rise in warm place 30
minutes. Bake 20 to 25 minutes or until golden
brown. Invert onto serving platter immediately.

Preparation time: 30 minutes plus rising
Cooking time: 25 minutes

Cream Cheese and Pecan Danish

Makes 10 to 12 servings

1 sheet frozen puff pastry, thawed
2 3-oz. pkgs. PHILADELPHIA BRAND®
    Cream Cheese, softened
1/4 cup powdered sugar
1 egg
1 teaspoon vanilla
3/4 cup chopped pecans
    Creamy Glaze

Preheat oven to 375°F. Unfold pastry; roll to 15×10-
inch rectangle. Place in 15×10×1-inch jelly roll pan.
Beat 6 ounces cream cheese, 1/4 cup sugar, egg and
vanilla in small mixing bowl at medium speed with
electric mixer until well blended. Stir in 1/2 cup
pecans. Spread cream cheese mixture over pastry to
within 3 inches from outer edges. Make 2-inch cuts
at 1-inch intervals on long sides of pastry. Crisscross
strips over filling. Bake 25 to 30 minutes or until
golden brown. Cool. Drizzle with Creamy Glaze.
Sprinkle with remaining pecans.

Creamy Glaze

1 3-oz. pkg. PHILADELPHIA BRAND® Cream
    Cheese, softened
3/4 cup powdered sugar
1 tablespoon milk

Beat ingredients until smooth.

Preparation time: 20 minutes
Cooking time: 30 minutes

Cranberry Conserve

Makes 3 1/2 cups

1 (12-ounce) package fresh cranberries
1 1/2 large seedless oranges, cut into wedges
1 1/2 cups DOMINO® Granulated Sugar
1/3 cup cherry brandy

Place all ingredients into blender or food processor
container; blend until coarsely chopped. Store,
covered, in refrigerator.

Cream Cheese and Pecan Danish

Welsh Rarebit

Welsh Rarebit

Makes 4 servings

½ cup HELLMANN'S® or BEST FOODS® Real,
    Light or Cholesterol Free Reduced Calorie
    Mayonnaise
3 tablespoons flour
½ teaspoon dry mustard
½ teaspoon Worcestershire sauce
¾ cup beer
2 cups (8 ounces) shredded Cheddar cheese
8 slices white or whole wheat bread, toasted,
    halved diagonally
3 large tomatoes, cut into 16 slices

In 2-quart saucepan combine mayonnaise, flour, dry
mustard and Worcestershire sauce. Stirring
constantly, cook over low heat 1 minute. Gradually
stir in beer until thick and smooth (do not boil). Stir
in cheese until melted. Arrange 4 toast halves and 4
tomato slices alternately on each of 4 serving plates;
spoon on cheese sauce. Serve immediately.

Microwave Directions: In 2-quart microwavable bowl
combine mayonnaise, flour, dry mustard and
Worcestershire sauce. Gradually stir in beer and
cheese. Microwave on HIGH (100%), 4 minutes,
stirring vigorously after each minute. Serve as above.

Easy Spinach Soufflé

Makes 4 to 6 servings

½ cup HELLMANN'S® or BEST FOODS® Real,
    Light or Cholesterol Free Reduced Calorie
    Mayonnaise
¼ cup flour
2 tablespoons grated onion
¾ teaspoon salt
¼ teaspoon nutmeg
¼ teaspoon freshly ground pepper
1 cup milk
1 package (10 ounces) frozen chopped spinach,
    thawed and well drained on paper towels
4 eggs, separated
¼ teaspoon cream of tartar

Preheat oven to 400°F. Grease 2-quart soufflé dish.
In 3-quart saucepan combine mayonnaise, flour,
onion, salt, nutmeg and pepper. Stirring constantly,
cook over medium heat 1 minute. Gradually stir in
milk until smooth. Stirring constantly, cook until
thick. Remove from heat. Stir in spinach. Beat in
egg yolks. In small bowl with mixer at high speed,
beat egg whites with cream of tartar until stiff peaks
form. Gently fold into spinach mixture. Spoon into
prepared dish. Place on lowest rack of oven.
Immediately reduce oven temperature to 375°F. Bake
40 minutes or until top is puffed and golden brown.
Serve immediately.

Chocolate Spice Surprise Muffins

Makes about 1½ dozen

⅓ cup firmly packed light brown sugar
¼ cup margarine or butter, softened
1 egg
1 cup BORDEN® or MEADOW GOLD® Milk
2 cups biscuit baking mix
⅓ cup unsweetened cocoa
1 (9-ounce) package NONE SUCH® Condensed
    Mincemeat, crumbled
18 solid milk chocolate candy drops
½ cup confectioners' sugar
1 tablespoon water

Preheat oven to 375°F. In large mixer bowl, beat
brown sugar and margarine until fluffy. Add egg and
milk; mix well. Stir in biscuit mix, cocoa and
mincemeat until moistened. Fill greased or paper-
lined muffin cups ¾ full. Top with candy drop; press
into batter. Bake 15 to 20 minutes. Cool 5 minutes;
remove from pan. Meanwhile, mix confectioners'
sugar and water; drizzle over warm muffins.

Fruited Pain Perdu

Makes 6 to 8 servings

4 eggs, slightly beaten
1¼ cups milk
1 teaspoon vanilla extract
½ teaspoon ground cinnamon
⅛ teaspoon salt
1 large loaf Italian bread, cut diagonally into
   1-inch slices
2 to 3 tablespoons butter or margarine
1 cup shredded **GJETOST®** cheese
   Mixed Fruit Sauce (recipe follows)

In large, shallow baking dish, blend eggs, milk, vanilla, cinnamon and salt. Add bread, turning to moisten on both sides. Cover; refrigerate overnight.

In large skillet, melt 1 tablespoon butter. Add several slices of bread. Cook over low heat until browned. Turn slices; top with some of the cheese. Brown on second side. Repeat with remaining bread and cheese, adding additional butter to skillet as necessary. Serve with Mixed Fruit Sauce.

Mixed Fruit Sauce

1 can (16 ounces) pineapple chunks
1 cup orange juice
2 tablespoons lemon juice
2 teaspoons cornstarch
1 large banana, sliced
1 cup diced papaya
1 teaspoon grated orange peel

Drain pineapple, reserving juice. In large saucepan, combine pineapple juice, orange and lemon juices and cornstarch. Stir to dissolve cornstarch. Cook over medium heat, stirring until thickened and smooth. Add fruits and orange peel. Makes about 2½ cups.

Jeweled Coffee Cake

Makes 1 coffee cake

Coffee Cake
8 ounces cream cheese, softened
2 tablespoons granulated sugar
1 teaspoon ground cinnamon
1 cup grated apple
1 loaf frozen bread dough, thawed
2 cups **RALSTON®** brand Fruit Muesli with
   Cranberries

Glaze
¾ cup powdered sugar
4 teaspoons cranberry juice or milk

To prepare Coffee Cake: Lightly grease baking sheet. In medium bowl combine cream cheese, granulated sugar and cinnamon; stir in apple. Set aside. On floured surface roll dough into 18×9-inch rectangle. Spread cream cheese mixture evenly over dough. Sprinkle cereal over cheese mixture. Starting with long side, roll dough into cylinder. Place on prepared baking sheet seam side down; bring ends together to form circle. Pinch ends together to seal. Cut slits halfway through dough 1½ inches apart around entire circle. Cover with towel; let rise in warm place 1 hour or until doubled in size. Preheat oven to 350°F. Bake, uncovered, 20 to 22 minutes or until golden brown. Cool on wire rack 5 minutes; drizzle glaze over coffee cake.

To prepare Glaze: In small bowl beat powdered sugar with cranberry juice until smooth.

Jeweled Coffee Cake

Moist Orange Mince Muffins

Makes about 1½ dozen

2 cups unsifted flour
½ cup sugar
1 tablespoon baking powder
1 teaspoon salt
½ teaspoon baking soda
1 egg, slightly beaten
1 (8-ounce) container BORDEN® LITE-LINE®
    or VIVA® Orange Yogurt
⅓ cup BORDEN® or MEADOW GOLD® Milk
⅓ cup vegetable oil
1 (9-ounce) package NONE SUCH® Condensed
    Mincemeat, finely crumbled
⅓ cup BAMA® Orange Marmalade, melted,
    optional

Preheat oven to 400°F. In large bowl, combine dry ingredients. In medium bowl, combine egg, yogurt, milk, oil and mincemeat; mix well. Stir into flour mixture only until moistened. Fill greased or paper-lined muffin cups ¾ full. Bake 20 to 25 minutes or until golden. Immediately remove from pans. Brush warm muffins with marmalade if desired. Serve warm.

Moist Orange Mince Muffins

Cinnamon Apple Coffee Cake

Makes about 8 servings

1½ cups boiling water
5 LIPTON® Cinnamon Apple Herbal Tea Bags
½ cup confectioners sugar
1 cup all-purpose flour
½ cup sugar
6 tablespoons IMPERIAL® Margarine, melted
1 egg
1 teaspoon baking powder
¼ teaspoon salt
¼ cup golden raisins
1 cup chopped apples
½ cup chopped walnuts
½ teaspoon grated lemon peel

Preheat oven to 375°F. In teapot, pour boiling water over cinnamon apple herbal tea bags. Cover and brew 5 minutes. Remove tea bags. In 1-quart saucepan, combine ¾ cup tea with confectioners sugar. Chill remaining tea at least 10 minutes. Boil tea-sugar mixture over medium-high heat 7 minutes or until thick and syrupy.

In large bowl, combine chilled tea, flour, sugar, margarine, egg, baking powder and salt. With electric mixer or rotary beater, beat to moisten, then beat at medium speed 2 minutes. Fold in raisins and ½ cup apples. Spread into greased 8-inch round cake pan. Bake 25 minutes or until toothpick inserted in center comes out clean. On wire rack, cool 10 minutes. Garnish, if desired, with apple slices.

In small bowl, combine tea-sugar glaze with remaining ½ cup apples, walnuts and lemon peel. Spoon over warm cake and serve.

Apple-Cranberry Relish

Makes about 4½ cups

2 unpeeled oranges, quartered and seeded
2 unpeeled Empire apples, quartered and cored
1 pound fresh cranberries
1 cup sugar (or to taste)

Chop oranges, apples and cranberries in food processor into fine pieces. Add sugar and mix well. Store, covered, in refrigerator. This relish gets better as it seasons.

Favorite recipe from **Western New York Apple Growers Association, Inc.**

Layered Vegetable Pie

Layered Vegetable Pie

Makes 6 main-course or 12 appetizer servings

2 tablespoons vegetable or olive oil
1 package (16 ounces) **CAMPBELL'S FRESH®**
   mushrooms, sliced
¼ cup finely chopped shallots or onion
1 medium clove garlic, minced
1 package (10 ounces) frozen chopped spinach,
   cooked and well drained
1 tablespoon all-purpose flour
4 eggs, slightly beaten
1 container (15 ounces) ricotta cheese
¼ cup grated Parmesan cheese
¾ cup diced fontinella or mozzarella cheese
¼ teaspoon ground nutmeg
¼ teaspoon pepper
   Pastry for 2-crust 10-inch pie
1 egg, separated
1 jar (6 ounces) roasted red peppers, drained
   and cut into strips
1 tablespoon sour cream or heavy cream

In 10-inch skillet over medium heat, in hot oil, cook mushrooms and shallots with garlic until tender, stirring occasionally. Add spinach; cook 2 minutes or until liquid is evaporated, stirring constantly. Stir in flour; set aside.

Preheat oven to 375°F. In large bowl, beat together 4 eggs, cheeses, nutmeg and pepper. Stir 1 cup of the cheese mixture into mushroom mixture.

On lightly floured surface, roll half of the pastry into 13-inch round. Line 10-inch deep-dish pie plate with pastry; trim even with rim, saving scraps. Prick with a fork. Brush with beaten egg white. Bake 10 minutes.

In prebaked piecrust, layer: 2 cups of the mushroom mixture, 1 cup of the cheese mixture, remaining mushroom mixture, red peppers and remaining cheese mixture. Roll remaining pastry to 12-inch round. Cut slits. Place over filling; trim edge to ½ inch beyond rim of pie plate. Fold top crust under, forming a ridge. Flute edge. Reroll any pastry scraps and use to decorate top of pastry. In cup, combine egg yolk and sour cream; brush on pastry. Place pie plate on cookie sheet. Bake 1 hour or until golden brown. Let cool on wire rack 20 minutes. Cut into wedges.

Maple French Toast

Makes 4 to 6 servings

¼ cup **CARY'S®, VERMONT MAPLE ORCHARDS** or **MACDONALD'S** Pure Maple Syrup
¼ cup **BORDEN®** or **MEADOW GOLD®** Milk
2 eggs, beaten
12 (¾-inch) slices French or Italian bread
Butter

In medium bowl, combine all ingredients except bread and butter. Dip bread into egg mixture. In large greased skillet, cook bread in butter until golden. Serve warm with Maple Butter and pure maple syrup.

Maple Butter: In small mixer bowl, beat ½ cup softened unsalted butter and 2 tablespoons pure maple syrup until light and fluffy. Makes about ⅔ cup.

Sweet & Spicy Nuts

Makes 3½ cups

¼ cup **LAND O LAKES®** Sweet Cream Butter
2 cups (8 oz.) pecan halves
½ cup (2 oz.) blanched whole almonds
½ cup (2 oz.) filberts
½ cup plus 3 tablespoons sugar
2 teaspoons cumin
1½ teaspoons salt

In 10-inch skillet melt butter over medium heat. Stir in nuts and ½ cup sugar; continue cooking, stirring constantly, until sugar is melted and nuts are brown (10 to 12 minutes). Meanwhile, in large bowl stir together 3 tablespoons sugar, cumin and salt. Stir in caramelized nuts. Spread onto waxed paper; cool. Break clusters into individual nuts.

Maple French Toast with Maple Butter

Banana Spice Coffee Cake

Makes one 10-inch coffee cake

2 extra-ripe medium **DOLE®** Bananas, peeled
    and cut into chunks
1/2 cup packed brown sugar
1 teaspoon ground cinnamon
1/4 teaspoon ground nutmeg
1/2 cup margarine
3/4 cup chopped walnuts
1 cup all-purpose flour
1 cup whole wheat flour
1 teaspoon baking powder
1 teaspoon baking soda
1/2 teaspoon salt
1/2 cup granulated sugar
3 eggs
1 teaspoon vanilla
1 cup **DOLE®** Raisins

In food processor or blender, puree bananas (1 cup
puree). In small bowl, combine brown sugar,
cinnamon and nutmeg. Cut in 1/4 cup of the
margarine until mixture resembles coarse crumbs.
Stir in walnuts; set aside. In small bowl, combine
flours, baking powder, baking soda and salt. In large
bowl, beat remaining 1/4 cup margarine and the
granulated sugar until light and fluffy. Beat in eggs
and vanilla. Add flour mixture to egg mixture
alternately with bananas, ending with flour mixture
and beating well after each addition. Stir in raisins.
Spread half the batter in greased and floured 10-inch
tube pan. Sprinkle with half the brown sugar
mixture. Repeat layers. Bake in preheated 350°F
oven 45 to 50 minutes or until wooden pick inserted
into center of cake comes out clean. Let cool in pan
on wire rack 10 minutes. Loosen edge; remove from
pan. Cool completely on wire rack.

Merry Cranberry Bread

Merry Cranberry Bread

Makes 1 loaf

3/4 cup **MIRACLE WHIP®** Salad Dressing
2 cups flour
1 12-oz. pkg. (1 1/4 cups) cranberry orange sauce
3/4 cup sugar
1/2 cup chopped walnuts
2 eggs, beaten
1 teaspoon baking soda
1/2 teaspoon salt

Mix together all ingredients. Pour into greased 9×5-
inch loaf pan. Bake at 350°F, 45 to 50 minutes or
until edges pull away from sides of pan. Let stand 10
minutes; remove from pan.

Preparation time: 5 minutes
Cooking time: 50 minutes

Turkey and Caper Quiche

Makes 4 servings

³/₄ cup diced cooked **BUTTERBALL**® turkey
    Pastry for single 9-inch pie crust*
¹/₂ cup (2 ounces) shredded Swiss cheese
¹/₃ cup diced tomato
¹/₄ cup minced onion
 1 tablespoon capers, drained
 3 eggs, beaten
 1 teaspoon Dijon mustard
 1 teaspoon seasoned salt
 1 cup half and half

Preheat oven to 350°F. Line 9-inch quiche dish or pie pan with pastry. Trim edge and flute. Layer turkey, cheese, tomato, onion and capers in crust. Blend eggs, mustard, salt and half and half in small bowl. Pour mixture into pie crust. Bake 40 to 50 minutes or until knife inserted 1 inch from center comes out clean.

*Substitute frozen 9-inch deep dish pie crust, thawed, for pastry. Omit quiche dish; bake directly in foil pan.

Orange Marmalade Bread

Makes 1 loaf

 3 cups all-purpose flour
 4 teaspoons baking powder
 1 teaspoon salt
¹/₂ cup chopped walnuts
 2 eggs, lightly beaten
³/₄ cup **SMUCKER'S**® Simply Fruit Orange
    Marmalade
³/₄ cup milk
¹/₄ cup honey
 2 tablespoons vegetable oil

Preheat oven to 350°F. Grease 9×5×3-inch loaf pan. Into a large bowl, sift together flour, baking powder and salt. Stir in nuts. In small bowl, combine eggs, marmalade, milk, honey and oil; blend well. Add to flour mixture; stir only until flour is well moistened (batter will be lumpy). Turn batter into prepared pan. Bake 65 to 70 minutes or until lightly browned and a wooden toothpick inserted into center comes out clean. Cool in pan on rack 10 minutes. Remove from pan; cool completely on rack.

Turkey and Caper Quiche

Crab and Artichoke Crepe Towers

Makes 8 main-dish or 16 appetizer servings

20 ALMOND DELIGHT® Crepes (recipe follows)
 2 tablespoons margarine or butter
 1 cup sliced mushrooms
 ¼ cup chopped onion
 3 tablespoons all-purpose flour
2½ cups milk
 ½ cup grated Parmesan cheese
 1 package (9 oz.) frozen artichoke hearts,
    prepared according to package directions,
    coarsely chopped
 8 ounces frozen or canned crab, drained
 2 tablespoons chopped fresh parsley
   Salt and pepper to taste

Prepare crepes; set aside. In large saucepan over medium heat, melt margarine. Add mushrooms and onion; cook, stirring constantly, until onion is transparent. Stir in flour. Gradually add milk, stirring until sauce is smooth and has slightly thickened. Stir in cheese, artichokes, crab and parsley; add salt and pepper. Place 1 crepe on serving plate. Spread 2 tablespoons crab and artichoke filling on top. Repeat layers to form a stack with 10 layers, ending with filling. Use remaining crepes and filling to form a second stack. Cut into wedges to serve.

Almond Delight® Crepes

 3 cups ALMOND DELIGHT® brand cereal,
    crushed to 1½ cups
1¼ cups all-purpose flour
 3 eggs
 2 cups milk
 3 tablespoons margarine or butter, melted

In large bowl combine cereal, flour and eggs; gradually add milk and margarine, beating until smooth. Cover; refrigerate several hours or overnight to thicken. (Batter should be consistency of heavy cream. If too thick, add 2 to 3 tablespoons milk. If too thin, add 2 to 3 tablespoons flour.) Cook on crepe maker following manufacturer's instructions. Or, lightly grease 5- to 6-inch skillet. Heat skillet over medium heat; remove from heat. Pour 2 tablespoons batter into pan; tilt pan until batter is spread evenly over bottom. Return to heat, cooking until surface looks dry and bottom of crepe is slightly brown. Invert pan allowing crepe to fall onto plate. Repeat with remaining batter. To make ahead of time, stack crepes with waxed paper between, place in plastic bag and freeze. Let crepes thaw at room temperature 1 hour before using. Makes 22 to 24 crepes.

Crab and Artichoke Crepe Towers

Cranberry All-Bran® Muffins

Makes 12 muffins

1¼ cups all-purpose flour
 ½ cup sugar
 ¼ teaspoon salt
 1 tablespoon baking powder
 ½ teaspoon pumpkin pie spice
1½ cups KELLOGG'S® ALL-BRAN® cereal
1¼ cups skim milk
 2 egg whites
 ¼ cup vegetable oil
 1 cup coarsely chopped cranberries
 ½ cup raisins
 1 teaspoon grated orange peel

Stir together flour, sugar, salt, baking powder and pumpkin pie spice; set aside. Measure KELLOGG'S® ALL-BRAN® cereal and milk into large mixing bowl; stir to combine. Let stand 2 minutes or until cereal is softened. Add egg whites and oil; beat well. Stir in cranberries, raisins and orange peel. Add dry ingredients to cereal mixture, stirring only until combined. Divide batter evenly among 12 greased 2½-inch muffin-pan cups. Bake in 400°F oven about 22 minutes or until lightly browned; serve hot.

Per Serving (1 muffin): 180 calories, 5g dietary fiber, 6g fat

Salads & Side Dishes

Spiced Cranberry-Orange Mold

Makes 10 servings

1 bag (12 ounces) fresh cranberries*
½ cup sugar*
2 packages (4-serving size each) *or* 1 package
    (8-serving size) JELL-O® Brand Gelatin,
    Orange or Lemon Flavor
1½ cups boiling water
1 cup cold water*
1 tablespoon lemon juice
¼ teaspoon ground cinnamon
⅛ teaspoon ground cloves
1 orange, sectioned and diced
½ cup chopped walnuts
    Orange slices (optional)
    White kale or curly leaf lettuce (optional)

Chop cranberries finely in food processor. Mix with sugar; set aside. Dissolve gelatin in boiling water. Add cold water, lemon juice, cinnamon and cloves. Chill until thickened. Fold in cranberries, orange and nuts. Spoon into 5-cup mold. Chill until firm, about 4 hours. Unmold. Garnish with orange slices and kale, if desired.

Preparation time: 20 minutes
Chill time: 4 hours

You may substitute 1 can (16 ounces) whole berry cranberry sauce for fresh cranberries. Omit sugar and reduce cold water to ½ cup.

Crowd-Pleasing Vegetable Pilaf

Makes 8 to 10 servings

3 cups cooked unsalted regular rice (1 cup
    uncooked)
1 can (10¾ ounces) condensed cream of
    mushroom soup
1 can (10¾ ounces) condensed cream of celery
    soup
1 cup (4 ounces) shredded Cheddar cheese
1 jar (2 ounces) diced pimiento, drained
1 package (10 ounces) frozen chopped spinach,
    thawed and well drained
1 package (10 ounces) frozen chopped broccoli,
    thawed and drained
1 can (2.8 ounces) DURKEE® French Fried
    Onions

Preheat oven to 350°F. To hot rice in saucepan, add soups, cheese and pimiento; stir well and set aside. In medium bowl, combine spinach, broccoli and ½ *can* French Fried Onions. Spread *half* the rice mixture in 12×8-inch baking dish; top with vegetable mixture, then with remaining rice mixture. Bake, covered, for 40 minutes or until heated through. Top with remaining onions; bake, uncovered, 5 minutes or until onions are golden brown.

Microwave Directions: Prepare rice and vegetable mixtures and layer as above in 12×8-inch microwave-safe dish. Cook, covered, on HIGH 12 to 14 minutes or until heated through. Rotate dish halfway through cooking time. Top with remaining onions; cook, uncovered, 1 minute. Let stand 5 minutes.

Spiced Cranberry-Orange Mold

Raisin Almond Stuffing

Makes 3³/₄ cups

1 package (6 oz.) STOVE TOP® Stuffing Mix,
    any variety
1²/₃ cups water*
¹/₂ cup raisins
¹/₄ cup (¹/₂ stick) butter or margarine
¹/₂ cup (2 oz.) slivered almonds

Combine contents of vegetable/seasoning packet,
water and raisins in medium saucepan. Add butter.
Bring to a boil. Reduce heat; cover and simmer 5
minutes. Add stuffing crumbs and almonds; stir to
moisten. Cover; remove from heat and let stand 5
minutes. Fluff with fork.

**For moister stuffing, increase water by 2 tablespoons; for less
moist stuffing, decrease water by 2 tablespoons.*

Cheesy Broccoli 'n Mushroom Bake

Makes 6 to 8 servings

2 10-oz. pkgs. frozen broccoli spears, thawed
1 10³/₄-oz. can condensed cream of mushroom
    soup
¹/₂ cup MIRACLE WHIP® Salad Dressing
¹/₂ cup milk
1 cup (4 ozs.) 100% Natural KRAFT® Shredded
    Cheddar Cheese
¹/₂ cup coarsely crushed croutons

Preheat oven to 350°F. Arrange broccoli in 12×8-inch
baking dish. Whisk together soup, salad dressing and
milk. Pour over broccoli. Sprinkle with cheese and
croutons. Bake 30 to 35 minutes or until heated
through.

Preparation time: 10 minutes
Baking time: 30 to 35 minutes

Cheesy Broccoli 'n Mushroom Bake

Confetti Chicken Salad

Makes 6 servings

¹/₄ cup white vinegar
3 tablespoons Chef Paul Prudhomme's
    POULTRY MAGIC®
1 teaspoon ground allspice
¹/₂ teaspoon ground bay leaf
¹/₂ teaspoon salt
1 cup vegetable oil
4 cups cooked rice
12 ounces cooked chicken, cut into bite-size
    pieces
2 cups small broccoli florets
2 cups chopped fresh tomatoes
1 cup shredded carrots
¹/₂ cup chopped onion
¹/₂ cup chopped celery
Lettuce leaves

Make dressing by combining vinegar, POULTRY
MAGIC®, allspice, bay leaf and salt in food
processor. Process until well mixed. With motor
running, add oil in slow steady stream until
incorporated and dressing is thick and creamy.
Combine remaining measured ingredients in a large
mixing bowl. Mix well. Stir in dressing. To serve,
line 6 serving plates with lettuce leaves. Divide salad
into portions. Mound each portion of salad onto
center of lettuce leaf.

Turkey Waldorf Salad

Makes about 4 to 6 servings

²/₃ cup HELLMANN'S® or BEST FOODS® Real,
    Light or Cholesterol Free Reduced Calorie
    Mayonnaise
2 tablespoons lemon juice
¹/₂ teaspoon salt
¹/₄ teaspoon freshly ground pepper
2 cups diced cooked turkey or chicken
2 red apples, cored and diced
²/₃ cup sliced celery
¹/₂ cup chopped walnuts

In large bowl combine mayonnaise, lemon juice, salt
and pepper. Add turkey, apples and celery; toss to
coat well. Cover; chill. Just before serving, sprinkle
with walnuts.

Hot & Spicy Glazed Carrots

Hot & Spicy Glazed Carrots

Makes 4 servings

2 tablespoons vegetable oil
2 dried red chili peppers
1 pound carrots, peeled and cut diagonally into
    ⅛-inch slices
¼ cup **KIKKOMAN® Teriyaki Baste & Glaze**

Heat oil in hot wok or large skillet over high heat.
Add peppers and stir-fry until darkened; remove and
discard. Add carrots; reduce heat to medium. Stir-
fry 4 minutes, or until tender-crisp. Stir in teriyaki
baste & glaze and cook until carrots are glazed.
Serve immediately.

Scalloped Potatoes Nokkelost®

Makes 8 servings

1 cup chopped leeks
¼ cup (½ stick) butter or margarine
¼ cup all-purpose flour
1½ teaspoons salt
⅛ teaspoon pepper
2 cups milk
8 cups sliced red-skinned potatoes, unpeeled
2 cups shredded **NOKKELOST®** cheese
¾ cup bread crumbs
¼ melted butter or margarine

In saucepan, cook leeks in ¼ cup butter until tender.
Stir in flour, salt and pepper. Gradually stir in milk.
Cook, stirring until thickened. In 2-quart buttered
baking dish, layer half of the potatoes, half of the
leek sauce and half of the cheese. Repeat layering.
Bake, covered, at 375°F for 45 minutes. Uncover.
Blend bread crumbs and melted butter. Sprinkle
around edge of casserole. Bake 15 minutes longer.

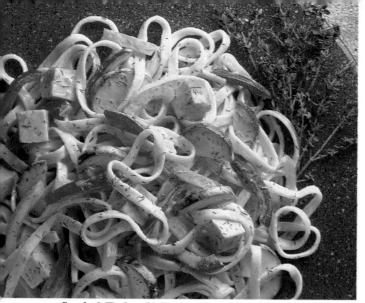

Smoked Turkey & Pepper Pasta Salad

Smoked Turkey & Pepper Pasta Salad

Makes about 6 servings

3/4 cup **MIRACLE WHIP**® Salad Dressing
1 tablespoon dijon mustard
1/2 teaspoon dried thyme leaves
8 ozs. fettucini, cooked, drained
1 cup (8 ozs.) diced **LOUIS RICH**® Smoked
    Boneless Turkey Breast
3/4 cup zucchini slices, cut into halves
1/2 cup red bell pepper strips
1/2 cup yellow bell pepper strips
    Salt and black pepper

Mix salad dressing, mustard and thyme until well blended. Add pasta, turkey and vegetables; mix lightly. Season with salt and pepper to taste. Chill. Add additional dressing before serving, if desired.

Preparation time: 15 minutes plus chilling

Pineapple Lime Mold

Makes 8 servings

1 can (20 oz.) **DOLE**® Pineapple Chunks
2 pkgs. (3 oz. each) lime gelatin
2 cups boiling water
1 cup dairy sour cream
1/2 cup chopped walnuts
1/2 cup chopped celery

Drain pineapple, reserve syrup. Dissolve gelatin in boiling water. Add sour cream and reserved syrup. Chill until slightly thickened. Stir in pineapple, walnuts and celery. Pour into 7-cup mold. Chill until set.

Sweet Potato Salad

Makes 6 servings

2 pounds sweet potatoes, peeled and cubed
2 tablespoons lemon juice
1 cup **HELLMANN'S**® or **BEST FOODS**® Real,
    Light or Cholesterol Free Reduced Calorie
    Mayonnaise
1 teaspoon grated orange peel
2 tablespoons orange juice
1 tablespoon honey
1 teaspoon chopped fresh ginger
1/4 teaspoon salt
1/8 teaspoon nutmeg
1 cup coarsely chopped pecans
1 cup sliced celery
1/3 cup chopped pitted dates
    Lettuce leaves
1 can (11 ounces) mandarin orange sections,
    drained

In medium saucepan cook potatoes 8 to 10 minutes in boiling, salted water just until tender. (Do not overcook.) Drain. Toss with lemon juice. In large bowl combine mayonnaise, orange peel, orange juice, honey, ginger, salt and nutmeg. Stir in warm potatoes, pecans, celery and dates. Cover; chill. To serve, spoon salad onto lettuce-lined platter. Arrange orange sections around salad. Garnish as desired.

Homestead Succotash

Makes 6 to 8 servings

1/4 lb. bacon, diced
1 cup chopped onion
1/2 teaspoon thyme
1 can (17 oz.) **DEL MONTE**® Whole Kernel
    Golden Sweet Corn, drained
1 can (17 oz.) **DEL MONTE**® Green Lima
    Beans, drained

In skillet, cook bacon until crisp; drain. Add onion and thyme; cook until tender. Stir in vegetables and heat through.

Microwave: In shallow 1-quart microwavable dish, cook bacon on high 6 minutes or until crisp; drain. Add onion and thyme; cover and cook on high 2 to 3 minutes or until tender. Add vegetables. Cover and cook on high 3 to 4 minutes or until heated through.

Total time for conventional method: 13 minutes

Sweet Potato Salad

Harvest Sausage Stuffing

Makes about 3 quarts

1 pound bulk sausage
2 cups chopped celery
8 ounces fresh mushrooms, sliced (about 2 cups)
1 1/2 cups chopped onion
4 teaspoons **WYLER'S®** or **STEERO®** Chicken-Flavor Instant Bouillon *or* 4 Chicken-Flavor Bouillon Cubes
1 to 1 1/2 cups boiling water
2 (7-ounce) packages herb-seasoned stuffing mix
1 1/3 cups (one-half jar) **NONE SUCH®** Ready-to-Use Mincemeat
1 (8-ounce) can sliced water chestnuts, coarsely chopped
2 teaspoons poultry seasoning

In large skillet, brown sausage; pour off fat. Add celery, mushrooms and onion; cook until onion is tender. Add bouillon and water to sausage mixture; bring to a boil. In large bowl, combine remaining ingredients with sausage mixture; mix well. Use to loosely stuff turkey just before roasting. Place remaining stuffing in 2-quart greased baking dish; cover. Bake at 350°F for 45 minutes or until hot. Refrigerate leftovers.

Gorgonzola Green Bean Salad

Makes 4 servings

1/3 cup Gorgonzola or blue cheese
3 tablespoons olive oil
2 tablespoons red wine vinegar
1 can (16 oz.) **DEL MONTE®** Blue Lake Cut Green Beans, drained
1 cup cherry tomatoes, halved
1/2 cup chopped walnuts
1/4 cup sliced green onions
    Romaine lettuce, optional
    Salt and pepper

In bowl, mash cheese with oil and vinegar. Toss with beans, tomatoes, nuts and onions. Serve on a bed of romaine lettuce, if desired. Add salt and pepper to taste.

Total time: 10 minutes

Harvest Sausage Stuffing

Sea Breeze Fish Salad

Makes 4 servings

1 pound firm white fish fillets (red snapper, sea bass or orange roughy), about 1 inch thick
1³/4 cups water
1 tablespoon grated lemon peel
6 tablespoons lemon juice, divided
3 tablespoons **KIKKOMAN®** Lite Soy Sauce, divided
6 ounces fresh snow peas, trimmed and cut diagonally into 1-inch pieces
2 tablespoons vegetable oil
1 tablespoon minced onion
¹/2 teaspoon thyme, crumbled
¹/4 teaspoon sugar
¹/2 medium cantaloupe, chunked
1 tablespoon minced fresh cilantro or parsley

Cut fish into 1-inch cubes. Combine water, lemon peel, 4 tablespoons lemon juice and 1 tablespoon lite soy sauce in large skillet. Heat only until mixture starts to simmer. Add fish; simmer, uncovered, 3 minutes, or until fish flakes easily when tested with fork. Remove fish with slotted spoon to plate. Cool slightly; cover and refrigerate 1 hour, or until thoroughly chilled. Meanwhile, cook snow peas in boiling water 2 minutes, or until tender-crisp; cool under cold water and drain thoroughly. Chill. Measure remaining 2 tablespoons lemon juice and 2 tablespoons lite soy sauce, oil, onion, thyme and sugar into jar with screw-top lid; cover and shake well. Combine peas, cantaloupe and cilantro in large bowl; add dressing and toss to coat all ingredients. Add fish and gently stir to combine. Serve immediately.

Christmas Ribbon

Christmas Ribbon

Makes 12 servings

2 packages (4-serving size each) *or* 1 package (8-serving size) JELL-O® Brand Gelatin, Strawberry Flavor
5 cups boiling water
²/3 cup sour cream *or* plain or vanilla yogurt
2 packages (4-serving size each) *or* 1 package (8-serving size) JELL-O® Brand Gelatin, Lime Flavor

Dissolve strawberry flavor gelatin in 2¹/2 cups of the boiling water. Pour 1¹/2 cups gelatin into 6-cup ring mold. Chill until set but not firm, about 30 minutes. Chill remaining gelatin in bowl until slightly thickened; gradually blend in ¹/3 cup of the sour cream. Spoon over gelatin in mold. Chill until set but not firm, about 15 minutes.

Repeat with lime flavor gelatin, remaining 2¹/2 cups boiling water and ¹/3 cup sour cream, chilling dissolved gelatin before measuring and pouring into mold. Chill at least 2 hours. Unmold.

Preparation time: 30 minutes
Chill time: 3 hours

Apple Praline Squash

Apple Praline Squash

Makes 4 servings

2 medium acorn squash, halved lengthwise,
  seeds removed
1/2 cup water
1/4 cup LAND O LAKES® Unsalted Butter
1 large cooking apple, cored, cut into 3/4-inch
  pieces
1/3 cup firmly packed brown sugar
1/4 teaspoon cinnamon
2 teaspoons vanilla
2 tablespoons chopped pecans

Heat oven to 400°F. In 13×9-inch baking pan place
squash cut side up; pour water into pan. Cover with
aluminum foil. Bake for 40 to 50 minutes or until
tender. In 8-inch skillet melt butter. Stir in apple,
brown sugar, cinnamon and vanilla. Cook over
medium heat, stirring constantly, until apples are
crisp-tender (3 to 4 minutes). Spoon an equal
amount into each baked squash half; sprinkle with
pecans.

Candied Sweet Potatoes

Makes 6 servings

1 cup DOMINO® BROWNULATED® Light
  Brown Sugar
  Grated rind and juice of 1 navel orange
2 tablespoons butter or margarine
6 medium sweet potatoes, parboiled, peeled and
  halved lengthwise

In large skillet, combine sugar, grated rind, orange
juice and butter. Heat, stirring occasionally, over
medium heat until blended and smooth. Add
potatoes and simmer, uncovered, for 20 minutes.
Baste and turn potatoes occasionally to glaze evenly.

Mandarin Orange and Red Onion Salad

Makes 4 to 6 servings

1 cup BLUE DIAMOND® Sliced Natural
  Almonds
1 tablespoon butter
2 tablespoons lemon juice
1 teaspoon Dijon mustard
1/2 teaspoon sugar
1/2 teaspoon salt
1/4 teaspoon white pepper
1/2 cup vegetable oil
1 head romaine lettuce, torn into pieces
1 can (11 ounces) mandarin orange segments,
  drained
1 small red onion, thinly sliced

Sauté almonds in butter until golden; reserve.
Combine next 5 ingredients. Whisk in oil. Combine
lettuce, oranges, onion, and almonds. Toss with
dressing.

Spinach Squares

Makes 8 to 10 servings

1 10-oz. pkg. frozen chopped spinach, cooked,
  well drained
1/3 cup chopped onion
1/3 cup chopped red pepper
1/2 lb. VELVEETA® Pasteurized Process Cheese
  Spread, cubed
2 cups cooked rice
3 eggs, beaten
1/8 teaspoon pepper

In large bowl, combine ingredients; spoon into
greased 10×6-inch baking dish. Bake at 350°F, 25
minutes. Let stand 5 minutes before serving. Cut
into squares.

Preparation time: 10 minutes
Baking time: 25 minutes plus standing

Mandarin Orange and Red Onion Salad

Mandarin Orange and Red Onion Salad

1 cup Blue Diamond
    Almonds
1 tablespoon butter
2 tablespoons lemon
  1 teaspoon &

Fruited Rice Pilaf

Fruited Rice Pilaf

Makes 4 servings

2 1/2 cups water
  1 cup uncooked rice
  2 tablespoons butter or margarine
  1 medium tomato, chopped
  1/3 cup minced dried apples
  1/4 cup minced dried apricots
  1/4 cup sliced green onions
  3/4 teaspoon LAWRY'S® Seasoned Salt
  1/4 teaspoon LAWRY'S® Garlic Powder with
      Parsley
  3 tablespoons sliced almonds

In 2-quart saucepan, bring water to a boil; add rice
and butter. Return to a boil. Reduce heat; cover and
simmer 15 minutes. Add remaining ingredients
except almonds; cook 5 to 10 minutes longer or until
rice is tender. Stir in almonds.

Presentation: Garnish with apple slices and celery leaves.
Serve with baked pork chops, roasted meats or poultry.
Hint: For variety and added flavor, try adding 1/4 teaspoon
curry powder to cooked rice.

Honey Mustard Peas

Makes 4 servings

1/2 cup coarsely chopped onion
1/4 cup julienne carrots
  1 tablespoon butter or margarine
  1 tablespoon honey
  1 tablespoon Dijon mustard
  1 can (17 oz.) DEL MONTE® Sweet Peas,
      drained

In saucepan, cook onion and carrots in butter until
tender. Blend in honey and mustard. Stir in peas;
heat through.

Microwave Directions: In 1-quart microwavable dish,
combine onion, carrots and butter. Cover and cook
on high 4 minutes or until tender. Stir in honey and
mustard. Stir in peas. Cook on high 1 minute.

Total time for conventional method: 10 minutes

Old-Fashioned Bread Stuffing

Makes 8 cups (enough for 12- to 14-pound turkey)

1½ cups chopped onion
1½ cups diced celery
  1 stick (½ cup) butter or margarine
  1 teaspoon poultry seasoning
  1 teaspoon rubbed sage
  1 teaspoon salt
    Dash ground black pepper
 ½ cup water or chicken broth
  8 cups dried bread cubes (10 to 12 bread slices,
    cubed and dried overnight)

Cook and stir onion and celery in butter in medium skillet over medium heat until tender. Stir in seasonings. Add onion mixture and water to bread cubes in large bowl. Toss to mix. Stuff neck and body cavities of BUTTERBALL® turkey. Roast immediately.

Cranberry-Sausage: Cut 1 cup fresh cranberries into halves. Cut 1 package (8 ounces) fully cooked sausage links into pieces. Add to bread cubes.

Bacon and Green Pepper: Substitute 1½ cups chopped green bell pepper for celery. Substitute 1 teaspoon dried thyme leaves, crushed, for poultry seasoning and sage. Reduce salt to ½ teaspoon. Add 12 slices cooked diced bacon to bread cubes.

Classic Waldorf Salad

Makes about 8 servings

 ½ cup HELLMANN'S® or BEST FOODS® Real,
    Light or Cholesterol Free Reduced Calorie
    Mayonnaise
  1 tablespoon sugar
  1 tablespoon lemon juice
 ⅛ teaspoon salt
  3 medium-size red apples, cored and diced
  1 cup sliced celery
 ½ cup chopped walnuts

In medium bowl combine mayonnaise, sugar, lemon juice and salt. Add apples and celery; toss to coat well. Cover; chill. Just before serving, sprinkle with walnuts.

Turkey Salad with Pita Bread

Makes 6 servings

  3 cups cubed cooked BUTTERBALL® turkey
    (1 pound)
  1 cup sour cream
  3 green onions, sliced
  1 tablespoon dried dill weed
  1 teaspoon seasoned salt
  1 medium cucumber, sliced thin
  1 small red onion, sliced thin
 12 small cherry tomatoes, cut into halves
 12 small fresh mushrooms, sliced thin
    Lettuce leaves
  6 pita breads, 6½-inch diameter, cut into halves

Blend sour cream, green onions, dill weed and salt in medium bowl. Add turkey and vegetables except lettuce; toss to combine. Serve on lettuce with pita bread. Or fill pita bread halves with turkey mixture and serve as sandwiches.

Turkey Salad with Pita Bread

Savory Lemon Vegetables

"Lite" Apricot Stuffing

Makes 8 servings

1 cup sliced celery
³/₄ cup chopped onion
1¹/₂ cups turkey broth or reduced-sodium chicken bouillon
16 slices reduced-calorie bread, cubed and dried
2 tablespoons parsley flakes
1¹/₂ teaspoons poultry seasoning
¹/₂ teaspoon salt
2 egg whites
¹/₄ cup dried apricots, chopped

In small saucepan, over medium-high heat, combine celery, onion and turkey broth; bring to a boil. Reduce heat to low; cover and simmer 5 minutes or until vegetables are tender. In large bowl, combine celery mixture, bread cubes, parsley, poultry seasoning, salt, egg whites and apricots. Spoon into lightly greased 2-quart casserole; cover. Bake at 350°F 30 minutes or until heated through.

Favorite Recipe from **National Turkey Federation**

Savory Lemon Vegetables

Makes 8 servings

6 slices bacon, cooked and crumbled, reserving ¹/₄ cup drippings
1 pound carrots, pared and sliced
1 medium head cauliflower, core removed
1 cup finely chopped onion
¹/₂ cup REALEMON® Lemon Juice from Concentrate
¹/₂ cup water
4 teaspoons sugar
1 teaspoon salt
1 teaspoon thyme leaves
Chopped parsley

In large saucepan, cook carrots and cauliflower in small amount of water until tender. Meanwhile, in medium skillet, cook onion in reserved drippings. Add ReaLemon® brand, ¹/₂ cup water, sugar, salt and thyme; bring to a boil. Drain vegetables; arrange on serving dish. Pour warm sauce over vegetables. Garnish with bacon and parsley.

Microwave: Cook bacon, reserving ¹/₄ cup drippings. On large microwavable platter with rim, arrange carrots and cauliflower. Cover with plastic wrap; cook on 100% power (high) 14 to 16 minutes. In 1-quart glass measure, cook reserved bacon drippings and onion on 100% power (high) 1 minute. Add ReaLemon® brand, water, sugar, salt and thyme. Cook on 100% power (high) 5¹/₂ to 6 minutes or until sauce boils. Proceed as above.

Creamy Italian Pasta Salad

Makes about 6 servings

1 cup HELLMANN'S® or BEST FOODS® Real, Light or Cholesterol Free Reduced Calorie Mayonnaise
2 tablespoons red wine vinegar
1 clove garlic, minced
1 tablespoon chopped fresh basil *or* 1 teaspoon dried basil
1 teaspoon salt
¹/₄ teaspoon freshly ground black pepper
1¹/₂ cups twist or spiral pasta, cooked, rinsed with cold water and drained
1 cup quartered cherry tomatoes
¹/₂ cup coarsely chopped green pepper
¹/₂ cup slivered pitted ripe olives

In large bowl combine mayonnaise, vinegar, garlic, basil, salt and pepper. Stir in pasta, cherry tomatoes, green pepper and olives. Cover; chill.

Beet and Pear Salad

Makes 4 to 6 servings

1 can (16 oz.) **DEL MONTE**® Bartlett Pear
    Halves
1 can (16 oz.) **DEL MONTE**® Sliced Beets,
    drained
½ cup thinly sliced red onion
2 tablespoons vegetable oil
1 tablespoon white wine vinegar
⅓ cup crumbled blue cheese
    Lettuce leaves, optional

Drain pears reserving 1 tablespoon syrup. Cut pears
in half lengthwise. Place pears, beets and onion in
medium bowl. Whisk together oil, vinegar and
reserved syrup. Pour over salad; toss gently. Just
before serving, add cheese and toss. Serve on bed of
lettuce leaves, if desired.

Total time: 10 minutes

Sweet Potato-Cranberry Bake

Makes 4 to 6 servings

1 can (40 ounces) whole sweet potatoes, drained
1 can (2.8 ounces) **DURKEE**® French Fried
    Onions
2 cups fresh cranberries
2 tablespoons packed brown sugar
⅓ cup honey

Preheat oven to 400°F. In 1½-quart casserole, layer
sweet potatoes, *½ can* French Fried Onions and *1 cup*
cranberries. Sprinkle with brown sugar; drizzle with
half the honey. Top with remaining cranberries and
honey. Bake, covered, for 35 minutes or until heated
through. Gently stir casserole. Top with remaining
onions; bake, uncovered, 1 to 3 minutes or until
onions are golden brown.

Beet and Pear Salad

Main Dishes

Roasted Turkey with Savory Cranberry Stuffing

Makes 10 to 12 servings

  1 cup chopped celery
  1 cup chopped onion
½ cup margarine or butter
  1 (16-ounce) can whole berry cranberry sauce
  2 tablespoons WYLER'S® or STEERO®
     Chicken-Flavor Instant Bouillon *or*
     6 Chicken-Flavor Bouillon Cubes
12 cups dry bread cubes (about 16 slices)
  1 cup chopped pecans
  2 teaspoons poultry seasoning
  1 teaspoon rubbed sage
  3 cups hot water
  1 (12- to 14-pound) turkey, thawed if frozen
     Vegetable oil

In large skillet, cook celery and onion in margarine until tender; add cranberry sauce and bouillon. Cook and stir until bouillon dissolves. In large bowl, combine bread cubes, pecans, seasonings and water; add cranberry mixture. Mix well.

Preheat oven to 325°F. Remove neck and giblets from turkey cavities. Rinse turkey; drain well. Stuff neck and body cavities lightly with stuffing. Place extra stuffing in greased baking dish. Cover; refrigerate. Turn wings back to hold neck skin in place. Place turkey, breast side up, on flat rack in open pan. Insert meat thermometer into thickest part of thigh next to body, not touching bone. Brush skin with oil. Place turkey in oven and roast about 4 hours. (Bake extra stuffing with turkey during last 40 minutes or until hot.) When skin is golden brown, shield breast loosely with foil to prevent overbrowning. Check for doneness; thigh temperature should be 180° to 185°F. Let turkey stand 15 to 20 minutes before carving. Refrigerate leftovers.

Rich Turkey Gravy: In medium skillet, stir ¼ to ⅓ cup flour into ¼ cup pan drippings; cook and stir until dark brown. Stir in 2 cups hot water and 2 teaspoons WYLER'S® or STEERO® Chicken-Flavor Instant Bouillon *or* 2 Chicken-Flavor Bouillon Cubes; cook and stir until thickened and bouillon is dissolved. Refrigerate leftovers. Makes about 1½ cups.

Ham in Peach Sauce

Makes 10 servings

  1 can (5 lbs.) fully-cooked ham
    Whole cloves
  2 cans (16 oz. each) DEL MONTE® Yellow
    Cling Sliced Peaches, drained
  1 jar (10 oz.) apricot preserves
  1 cup dry sherry
  1 teaspoon grated orange peel
¼ teaspoon allspice

Place ham in 13×9×2-inch baking dish. Score ham and insert cloves. In food processor or blender container, process remaining ingredients until smooth. Pour over ham. Bake at 325°F, 1 hour, basting occasionally. Remove ham to serving platter; serve with sauce. Garnish with lemon slices and parsley, if desired. Can be served hot or cold.

Roasted Turkey with Savory Cranberry Stuffing

Baked Salmon with Almonds and Lime-Parsley Sauce

Baked Salmon with Almonds and Lime-Parsley Sauce

Makes 4 to 6 servings

   1 large clove garlic, chopped finely
   1 egg yolk
   1 teaspoon lime juice
 ¹/₂ teaspoon cumin
     Salt
     White pepper
 ¹/₂ cup vegetable oil
4¹/₂ teaspoons olive oil, divided
   6 tablespoons chopped parsley
   4 salmon fillets, about 6 ounces each
 ³/₄ cup **BLUE DIAMOND**® Sliced Natural
     Almonds, lightly toasted

In food processor or blender, combine garlic, egg yolk, lime juice, cumin, ¹/₄ teaspoon salt, and a pinch pepper. With machine running, *slowly* pour in vegetable oil and 1¹/₂ teaspoons olive oil. (To prepare by hand, beat egg yolk until thick and lemon colored. Beat in garlic, lime juice, cumin, ¹/₄ teaspoon salt, and a pinch pepper. Combine vegetable oil and 1¹/₂ teaspoons olive oil. Whisking constantly, add oils *one drop at a time* until mixture begins to thicken. Pour remaining oil in a thin, steady stream, whisking constantly.) Mixture will resemble mayonnaise. Fold in chopped parsley. Brush salmon with remaining 3 teaspoons olive oil; season with salt and pepper. Spread parsley sauce down center of each fillet. Top with almonds. Bake at 400°F for 8 to 12 minutes or until fish is just firm.

Beef Burgundy

Makes 6³/₄ cups or 6 servings

   2 pounds beef for stew, cut into 1¹/₂-inch pieces
 ¹/₄ cup all-purpose flour
   4 slices bacon, diced
     Vegetable oil
   2 medium cloves garlic, minced
  12 ounces small whole white onions
   1 package (8 ounces) **CAMPBELL'S FRESH**®
     mushrooms
   1 tablespoon chopped fresh thyme leaves *or*
       1 teaspoon dried thyme leaves, crushed
   1 tablespoon tomato paste
   2 cups Burgundy or other dry red wine
   1 can (14¹/₂ ounces) **SWANSON**® clear ready to
     serve beef broth
   1 medium bay leaf
     Coarsely ground pepper
     Hot cooked noodles
     Chopped fresh parsley for garnish

On waxed paper, coat beef with flour; set aside. In 4-quart Dutch oven over medium heat, cook bacon until browned. With slotted spoon, remove bacon; set aside.

In drippings over medium-high heat, cook beef a few pieces at a time, until browned on all sides. Remove beef as it browns. Add vegetable oil if necessary. Add garlic, onions, mushrooms and thyme to hot drippings; cook until mushrooms and onions are lightly browned, stirring occasionally. Remove from Dutch oven; set aside.

Return beef and bacon to Dutch oven. Add tomato paste, wine, broth and bay leaf; heat to boiling. Reduce heat to low. Cover; simmer 1 hour. Add mushroom mixture; cover and cook 30 minutes more or until beef and onions are fork-tender. Simmer, uncovered, until slightly thickened, about 10 minutes. Remove bay leaf. Season with pepper. Serve over noodles; garnish with parsley.

Pinwheel Meat Loaf

Makes about 8 servings

¹/₂ cup milk
1¹/₂ cups crustless Italian or French bread cubes
1¹/₂ pounds ground beef
¹/₂ pound sweet Italian sausage, removed from
    casings and crumbled
2 eggs, slightly beaten
2 tablespoons finely chopped parsley
1 tablespoon finely chopped garlic
1 teaspoon salt
¹/₂ teaspoon pepper
2 cups water
1 tablespoon butter or margarine
1 package LIPTON® Rice & Sauce–
    Cajun-Style
2 packages (10 ounces each) frozen chopped
    spinach, thawed and squeezed dry

In large bowl, pour milk over bread cubes, then mash with fork until bread is soaked. Thoroughly combine bread mixture with ground beef, sausage, eggs, parsley, garlic, salt and pepper. Place on 12×12-inch sheet of aluminum foil moistened with water.

Cover with 12×14-inch sheet of waxed paper moistened with water. Using hands or rolling pin, press into 12×12-inch square. Refrigerate 2 hours or until well chilled.

In medium saucepan, bring water, butter and rice & Cajun-style sauce to a boil. Continue boiling over medium heat, stirring occasionally, 10 minutes or until rice is tender. Refrigerate 2 hours or until well chilled.

Preheat oven to 350°F. Remove waxed paper from ground beef mixture. If desired, season spinach with additional salt and pepper. Spread spinach over ground beef mixture leaving 1-inch border. Spread rice evenly over spinach. Roll, starting at long end and using foil as a guide, jelly-roll style, removing foil while rolling; seal edges tightly. In 13×9-inch baking pan, place meat loaf seam-side down. Bake 1 hour or until done. Let stand 15 minutes before serving. Cut into 1-inch slices.

Pinwheel Meat Loaf

Savory Lamb with Couscous

Savory Lamb with Couscous

Makes 6 servings

1½ pounds lean boneless lamb shoulder, cut into
    1-inch cubes
1 tablespoon vegetable oil
¾ cup chopped onions
2 cloves garlic, minced
1 tablespoon dried tarragon leaves, crushed
1½ cups tomato juice
1 medium green pepper, cut into strips
¾ cup dried apricots, halved
1 cup **NEAR EAST®** Couscous
1 tablespoon butter
    Dried apricots (optional)
    Fresh tarragon (optional)

In large skillet, brown lamb in oil. Add onions,
garlic and dried tarragon; cook until onions are
tender-crisp. Drain fat. Stir in tomato juice, green
pepper and the ¾ cup apricots. Cover; simmer 15
to 20 minutes or until lamb is cooked. Prepare
couscous according to package directions using only
1 tablespoon butter. Fluff couscous lightly with fork;
spoon onto platter. Top with lamb mixture. Garnish
with dried apricots and fresh tarragon.

Easy Paella

Makes 4 servings

1 medium onion, cut into halves and chopped
1 large red or green bell pepper, sliced
1 clove garlic, minced
2 tablespoons vegetable oil
1 can (16 ounces) tomatoes with juice, cut up
1 package (10 ounces) frozen artichoke hearts,
    cut into quarters
½ cup dry white wine
½ teaspoon dried thyme, crushed
¼ teaspoon salt
⅛ teaspoon saffron or turmeric
2 cups cooked rice
1 cup frozen peas
1 can (6½ ounces) **STARKIST®** Tuna, drained
    and broken into chunks
½ pound large shrimp, peeled and deveined

In a large skillet sauté onion, bell pepper and garlic
in oil for 3 minutes. Stir in tomatoes with juice,
artichoke hearts, wine and seasonings. Bring to a
boil; reduce heat. Simmer for 10 minutes. Stir in
rice, peas, tuna and shrimp. Cook for 3 to 5 minutes
more, or until shrimp turn pink and mixture is
heated.

Preparation time: 30 minutes

Calorie count: 382 calories per serving.

Strawberry Glazed Ham

Makes 8 to 10 servings

1 (5- to 7-pound) fully-cooked smoked butt or
    shank-half ham
1½ cups **SMUCKER'S®** Simply Fruit Strawberry
⅓ cup prepared mustard
¼ cup lemon juice

Trim skin from ham. With sharp knife, score fat
surface, making uniform diagonal cuts about ⅛-inch
deep and ¾-inch apart. Place ham fat side up on a
rack in a shallow roasting pan; bake in 325°F oven
1¾ to 2½ hours. Meanwhile, in a small saucepan,
combine fruit spread, mustard and lemon juice; cook
over low heat, stirring, until blended. During last 20
minutes of baking time, brush ham with about ½
cup strawberry glaze. Let ham stand 10 minutes for
easier slicing. Heat remaining glaze and serve as a
sauce for the ham.

Easy Paella

Turkey with Mushroom Stuffing and Mushroom Gravy

Turkey with Mushroom Stuffing

Makes 10 to 12 servings

¼ cup butter or margarine
1 package (8 ounces) CAMPBELL'S FRESH®
   mushrooms, coarsely chopped
1 package (8 ounces) PEPPERIDGE FARM®
   herb seasoned stuffing
1 cup SWANSON® clear ready to serve chicken
   broth
½ cup chopped fresh parsley
1 teaspoon grated lemon peel
⅛ teaspoon pepper
1 (10- to 12-pound) ready-to-stuff turkey
   Mushroom Gravy (recipe follows)

To prepare stuffing: In 10-inch skillet over medium heat, in hot butter, cook mushrooms until tender, stirring occasionally. In large bowl, toss together stuffing, mushrooms, broth, parsley, lemon peel and pepper. Remove giblets and neck from inside turkey. Rinse turkey with cold running water; drain well. Spoon stuffing mixture lightly into neck and body cavities. Fold skin over stuffing; skewer closed. Tie legs. On rack in roasting pan, place turkey breast-side up. Insert meat thermometer into thickest part

of meat between breast and thigh, not touching bone. Roast, uncovered, at 325°F for 3½ hours or until internal temperature reaches 180°F and drumstick moves easily. Baste occasionally with pan drippings. When skin turns golden, cover loosely with tent of foil. Serve with Mushroom Gravy.

Mushroom Gravy

3 to 4 tablespoons poultry drippings
1 package (8 ounces) CAMPBELL'S FRESH®
   mushrooms, sliced (about 3 cups)
¼ cup all-purpose flour
2 cups SWANSON® clear ready to serve chicken
   broth
1 cup milk
   Salt
   Pepper

In 10-inch skillet or roasting pan over medium heat, in hot drippings, cook mushrooms until tender and liquid is evaporated. Stir in flour until blended. Gradually stir in broth and milk. Cook until mixture boils and thickens, stirring often. Season with salt and pepper. Makes about 3 cups.

Sausage-Stuffed Cornish Hens

Makes 2 servings

1/2 pound bulk pork sausage
1/4 pound mushrooms, sliced
2 cups STOVE TOP® Chicken Flavor Flexible
    Serving Stuffing Mix
1/4 cup grated carrot
1 cup hot water
2 Cornish game hens (1 to 1 1/2 pounds each)
    Vegetable oil
2 tablespoons apple jelly

Brown sausage and mushrooms in skillet; drain fat. Mix in stuffing mix, carrot and water. Rinse hens with cold water; pat dry. Spoon stuffing into cavities. Skewer neck skin to back. Tie legs to tail and twist wing tips under. Place birds breast side up in shallow roasting pan. Brush with oil. Roast at 350°F for 1 hour. Spoon apple jelly over hens. Bake 10 minutes longer. Place any remaining stuffing in casserole dish. Cover; bake with hens during last 20 minutes of baking time.

Marvelous Marinated London Broil

Makes 6 to 8 servings

1/2 cup HELLMANN'S® or BEST FOODS® Real,
    Light or Cholesterol Free Reduced Calorie
    Mayonnaise
1/3 cup soy sauce
1/4 cup lemon juice
2 tablespoons prepared mustard
1 clove garlic, minced or pressed
1/2 teaspoon ground ginger
1/4 teaspoon freshly ground pepper
1 beef top round steak (3 pounds), 2 inches
    thick

In large shallow dish combine mayonnaise, soy sauce, lemon juice, mustard, garlic, ginger and pepper. Add steak, turning to coat. Cover; marinate in refrigerator several hours or overnight. Grill or broil about 6 inches from heat, turning once, 25 to 30 minutes or until desired doneness. To serve, slice diagonally across grain.

Pasta Roll-Ups

Makes 6 servings

1 package (1.5 ounces) LAWRY'S® Original-
    Style Spaghetti Sauce Spices & Seasonings
1 can (6 ounces) tomato paste
2 1/4 cups water
2 tablespoons butter or vegetable oil
2 cups cottage cheese or ricotta cheese
1 cup (4 ounces) grated mozzarella cheese
1/4 cup grated Parmesan cheese
2 eggs, lightly beaten
1/2 to 1 teaspoon LAWRY'S® Garlic Salt
1/2 teaspoon dried basil, crushed (optional)
8 ounces lasagna noodles, cooked and drained

In medium saucepan, prepare Spaghetti Sauce Spices & Seasonings according to package directions using tomato paste, water and butter. In large bowl, combine remaining ingredients except noodles; blend well. Spread 1/4 cup cheese mixture on entire length of each lasagna noodle; roll up. Place noodles, seam-side down, in microwave-safe baking dish. Cover with vented plastic wrap and microwave on HIGH 6 to 7 minutes or until cheese begins to melt. Pour sauce over rolls and microwave on HIGH 1 minute longer, if necessary, to heat sauce.

Presentation: *Sprinkle with additional grated Parmesan cheese. Garnish with fresh basil leaves.*

Hint: *For quick microwavable meals, wrap prepared rolls individually and freeze. Sauce may be frozen in 1/4 cup servings.*

Pasta Roll-Ups

Fiesta Potato Bake

Fiesta Potato Bake

Makes 4 servings

2 cups cubed cooked BUTTERBALL® turkey
   (³/4 pound)
6 medium (1¹/2 pounds) potatoes, pared, sliced
   thin
3 tablespoons all-purpose flour
2 teaspoons seasoned salt
¹/4 teaspoon ground black pepper
1 medium onion, sliced thin (about 1 cup)
1 cup diced green bell pepper
¹/2 cup diced red bell pepper
¹/2 cup milk
2 tablespoons butter or margarine

Preheat oven to 350°F. Place half of the turkey in
buttered, deep 2-quart casserole. Cover with half of
the potatoes. Sprinkle with 1 tablespoon flour and
half of the salt and pepper. Top with half of the
onion slices and half of the green and red peppers.
Combine remaining 2 tablespoons flour with milk;
pour half over layered ingredients. Repeat layers with
potatoes, onions, remaining turkey, green and red
peppers, salt and pepper. Pour remaining milk over
top; dot with butter. Cover and bake in oven 45
minutes. Remove cover; bake an additional 30
minutes or until potatoes are done.

Shrimp Milano

Makes 4 to 6 servings

1 lb. frozen cleaned shrimp, cooked, drained
2 cups mushroom slices
1 cup green or red pepper strips
1 garlic clove, minced
¹/4 cup PARKAY® Margarine
³/4 lb. VELVEETA® Pasteurized Process Cheese
   Spread, cubed
³/4 cup whipping cream
¹/2 teaspoon dill weed
¹/3 cup (1¹/2 ozs.) KRAFT® 100% Grated
   Parmesan Cheese
8 ozs. fettucini, cooked, drained

In large skillet, saute shrimp, vegetables and garlic in
margarine. Reduce heat to low. Add process cheese
spread, cream and dill. Stir until process cheese
spread is melted. Stir in parmesan cheese. Add
fettucini; toss lightly.

Preparation time: 20 minutes
Cooking time: 15 minutes

Braised Duckling and Pears

Makes 3 to 4 servings

1 (4- to 5-pound) frozen duckling, thawed and
   quartered
1 can (16 oz.) pear halves in heavy syrup
¹/3 cup KIKKOMAN® Stir-Fry Sauce
1 cinnamon stick, about 3 inches long

Wash duckling quarters; dry thoroughly with paper
towels. Heat large skillet or Dutch oven over medium
heat. Add duckling; brown slowly on both sides
about 15 minutes, or until golden. Meanwhile, drain
pears; reserve all syrup. Remove ¹/4 cup pear syrup
and combine with stir-fry sauce; set aside. Drain off
fat from pan. Pour syrup mixture over duckling; add
cinnamon stick. Cover and simmer 40 minutes, or
until tender, turning quarters over once. Remove
duckling to serving platter; keep warm. Remove and
discard cinnamon stick. Pour drippings into
measuring cup; skim off fat. Combine ¹/2 cup
drippings with 2 tablespoons reserved pear syrup;
return to pan with pears. Gently bring to boil and
cook until pears are heated through, stirring
occasionally. Serve duckling with pears and sauce.

Crown Roast of Pork

Makes 8 servings

1 (6-pound) pork crown roast (12 to 16 small
    ribs)
¼ cup butter or margarine
1 package (12 ounces) CAMPBELL'S FRESH®
    mushrooms, sliced
½ cup thinly sliced celery
½ cup water
1 package (8 ounces) PEPPERIDGE FARM®
    corn bread stuffing
1 cup coarsely chopped apple
⅛ teaspoon ground allspice
⅓ cup apricot preserves, melted

In roasting pan, place roast, bones pointing up.
Cover bone tips with small pieces of foil. Insert meat
thermometer into thickest part of meat, not touching
bone. Roast at 325°F for 1½ hours.

Meanwhile, to prepare stuffing: In 10-inch skillet
over medium heat, in hot butter, cook mushrooms
and celery until tender, stirring occasionally. Stir in
water; heat to boiling. In large bowl, combine
stuffing, apple and allspice. Pour mushroom mixture
over stuffing mixture; toss to mix well. Spoon
stuffing mixture into center of roast, mounding high.
Cover stuffing with foil. Roast 1 hour more. Remove
foil from stuffing. Brush melted preserves over roast.
Roast 30 minutes more or until internal temperature
reaches 170°F, brushing often with preserves. Let
roast stand 15 minutes for easier carving. Remove
foil from bones before serving.

Pecan Turkey Sauté with Warm Cranberry Sauce

Makes 4 servings

½ cup unseasoned dry bread crumbs
¼ cup ground pecans
½ teaspoon LAWRY'S® Garlic Powder with
    Parsley
½ teaspoon LAWRY'S® Seasoned Salt
1 pound turkey cutlets
3 eggs, beaten
3 tablespoons butter or margarine
1 can (8 ounces) jellied cranberry sauce or
    whole berry cranberry sauce
⅓ cup French salad dressing
3 tablespoons water
2 tablespoons chopped green onion

In pie plate, combine bread crumbs, pecans and
seasonings; blend well. Dip each turkey cutlet in
eggs, then coat both sides with crumb mixture. In
large skillet, melt butter and brown turkey cutlets 5
minutes on each side or until cooked through. In
small saucepan, combine cranberry sauce, salad
dressing, water and onion; blend well. Gently heat
until warmed through, about 5 minutes. Spoon warm
cranberry sauce over cutlets.

Presentation: *Serve with mashed potatoes or stuffing.*

Spicy Tomato Chicken

Makes 4 servings

½ cup QUAKER® Oat Bran hot cereal,
    uncooked
1½ teaspoons thyme leaves, crushed
1½ teaspoons garlic powder
⅛ to ¼ teaspoon ground red pepper
2 egg whites
2 chicken breasts, split, boned, skinned (about
    ¾ lb.)
2 tablespoons vegetable oil
¼ cup dry white wine
1 can (8 oz.) low sodium tomato sauce
½ cup sliced green onions

In shallow dish, combine oat bran, thyme, garlic
powder and red pepper. In another shallow dish,
lightly beat egg whites. Pound each chicken breast
between sheets of waxed paper to even thickness.
Coat with oat bran mixture; shake off excess. Dip
into egg whites, then coat again with oat bran
mixture. Saute chicken in oil over medium heat
about 6 minutes; turn. Cook an additional 6 to 8
minutes or until juices run clear when pierced with
fork. Remove to serving platter; keep warm.

Increase heat to high; add wine, mixing well with
drippings. Add tomato sauce and green onions; heat
through. Pour over chicken just before serving.
Garnish with sliced green onions, if desired.

Spicy Tomato Chicken

Pork Chops with Almond Plum Sauce

Pork Chops with Almond Plum Sauce

Makes 4 servings

   1 cup water
   6 tablespoons lemon juice
   6 tablespoons soy sauce
   4 cloves garlic, chopped finely
1½ teaspoons cornstarch
   ¼ teaspoon salt
   ½ teaspoon white pepper
      Pinch cayenne
   4 pork chops, about 1 inch thick
   1 tablespoon vegetable oil
   ⅔ cup plum jam
   ¼ cup **BLUE DIAMOND**® Sliced Natural
      Almonds, lightly toasted
   ¼ cup sliced green onion tops, for garnish

Combine first 8 ingredients. Marinate pork chops in mixture in refrigerator 1 hour or overnight. Remove pork chops, reserving marinade. Sauté pork chops in oil over high heat 2 to 3 minutes on each side or until golden brown. Remove and reserve. Add marinade and plum jam to pan. Cook over medium heat until mixture thickens and coats the back of a spoon, about 5 minutes. Return pork chops to pan in single layer. Simmer, covered, 5 to 7 minutes. Remove cover and continue cooking 3 to 4 minutes or until pork chops are just cooked through and tender. To serve, remove chops to serving plate; sprinkle 1 tablespoon almonds over each chop. Pour sauce over and sprinkle each chop with 1 tablespoon sliced green onion tops.

Zesty Zucchini Lasagna

Makes about 6 servings

   1 pound ground beef
   1 package (1.5 ounces) **LAWRY'S**® Original-
      Style Spaghetti Sauce Spices & Seasonings
   1 can (6 ounces) tomato paste
1¾ cups water
   2 tablespoons **IMPERIAL**® Margarine
   ½ teaspoon basil leaves
   ⅛ teaspoon thyme leaves
   2 cups ricotta cheese
   1 egg, slightly beaten
   4 medium zucchini, thinly sliced lengthwise
   1 cup shredded mozzarella cheese (about
      4 ounces)

Preheat oven to 350°F. In medium saucepan, brown ground beef until no longer pink; drain. Into saucepan, stir in Spaghetti Sauce Spices & Seasonings, tomato paste, water, margarine, basil and thyme. Bring to a boil, then simmer uncovered 10 minutes. In small bowl, combine ricotta cheese with egg; set aside. In medium saucepan, bring 1 quart water to a boil. Add zucchini and cook 2 minutes; remove and rinse under cold running water. In 12×8-inch casserole, layer ½ of the zucchini, ricotta mixture and meat sauce. Repeat layers. Top with mozzarella cheese and bake uncovered 30 minutes or until cheese is melted.

Louisiana Chicken

Makes 4 servings

   4 chicken breast halves, skinned and boned
   2 cans (14½ oz. each) **DEL MONTE**® Cajun
      Style Stewed Tomatoes
   2 tablespoons cornstarch
   4 slices Monterey Jack cheese
      Parsley

Place chicken in baking dish. Cover and bake at 375°F, 30 to 35 minutes; drain. Combine tomatoes and cornstarch in saucepan; stir to dissolve cornstarch. Cook, stirring constantly, until thickened. Remove chicken from baking dish. Pour all but 1 cup sauce into dish. Arrange chicken over sauce in dish; top with remaining sauce. Place 1 slice cheese on each piece of chicken. Bake until cheese melts. Garnish with parsley. Serve with hot cooked rice, if desired.

Zesty Zucchini Lasagna

Spicy Sichuan Pork Stew

Makes 6 servings

2 pounds boneless pork shoulder (Boston butt)
¼ cup all-purpose flour
2 tablespoons vegetable oil
1¾ cups water, divided
¼ cup **KIKKOMAN**® Soy Sauce
3 tablespoons dry sherry
2 cloves garlic, pressed
1 teaspoon minced fresh ginger root
½ teaspoon crushed red pepper
¼ teaspoon fennel seed, crushed
8 green onions and tops, cut into 1-inch lengths,
    separating whites from tops
2 large carrots, chunked
    Hot cooked rice

Cut pork into 1-inch cubes. Coat in flour; reserve 2 tablespoons flour. Heat oil in Dutch oven or large pan over medium-high heat; brown pork on all sides in hot oil. Add 1½ cups water, soy sauce, sherry, garlic, ginger, red pepper, fennel and white parts of green onions. Cover pan; bring to boil. Reduce heat and simmer 30 minutes. Add carrots; simmer, covered, 30 minutes longer, or until pork and carrots are tender. Meanwhile, combine reserved flour and remaining ¼ cup water; set aside. Stir green onion tops into pork mixture; simmer 1 minute. Add flour mixture; bring to boil. Cook and stir until mixture is slightly thickened. Serve over rice.

Spicy Sichuan Pork Stew

Seafood over Angel Hair Pasta

Makes about 4 servings

¼ cup **WISH-BONE**® Italian Dressing*
¼ cup chopped shallots or onions
1 cup thinly sliced carrots
4 ounces snow peas, thinly sliced (about 1 cup)
1 cup chicken broth
¼ cup sherry
½ pound uncooked medium shrimp, cleaned
    (keep tails on)
½ pound sea scallops
8 mussels, well scrubbed
¼ cup whipping or heavy cream
2 tablespoons all-purpose flour
    Salt and pepper to taste
8 ounces angel hair pasta or capellini, cooked
    and drained

In 12-inch skillet, heat Italian dressing and cook shallots over medium-high heat 2 minutes. Add carrots and snow peas and cook 2 minutes. Add broth, then sherry. Bring to a boil, then add shrimp, scallops and mussels. Simmer covered 3 minutes or until seafood is done and mussel shells open. (Discard any unopened shells.) Stir in cream blended with flour and cook over medium heat, stirring occasionally, 2 minutes or until sauce is slightly thickened. Stir in salt and pepper. Serve over hot pasta and sprinkle, if desired, with freshly ground pepper and grated Parmesan cheese.

Also terrific with WISH-BONE® Robusto Italian, Italian & Cheese, Herbal Italian, Blended Italian, Classic Dijon Vinaigrette, Olive Oil Vinaigrette or Lite Classic Dijon Vinaigrette Dressing.

Easy Beef Stroganoff

Makes about 2 servings

2 tablespoons oil
2 teaspoons finely chopped garlic
½ pound boneless sirloin steak, cut into thin
    strips
¼ cup dry red wine
2 teaspoons Worcestershire sauce
1¼ cups water
½ cup milk
2 tablespoons butter or margarine
1 package **LIPTON**® Noodles & Sauce–
    Stroganoff*
½ cup pearl onions

In large skillet, heat oil and cook garlic over medium heat 30 seconds. Add beef and cook over medium-high heat 1 minute or until almost done. Add wine and Worcestershire sauce and cook 30 seconds; remove beef. Into skillet, stir water, milk, butter and noodles & stroganoff sauce. Bring to the boiling point, then continue boiling, stirring occasionally, 7 minutes. Stir in onions and beef, then cook 2 minutes or until noodles are tender. Garnish, if desired, with chopped parsley and paprika.

Also terrific with LIPTON® Noodles & Sauce—Beef Flavor.

Land O Lakes® Chicken Kiev

Makes 4 servings

Filling
- ⅓ cup chopped fresh mushrooms
- ¼ cup LAND O LAKES® Unsalted Butter, softened
- 1 (2-oz.) jar diced pimiento, drained
- 1 tablespoon chopped green onion
- ¼ teaspoon salt
- ⅛ teaspoon pepper

Chicken
- 4 whole boneless chicken breasts, skinned
- ¼ cup LAND O LAKES® Unsalted Butter
- ½ cup fine, dry bread crumbs
- ¼ teaspoon dried thyme leaves
- ¼ teaspoon dried rubbed sage

Stir together all filling ingredients in medium bowl. Divide into 4 equal portions. Freeze portions for 30 minutes or longer. *Heat oven to 350°F.* Flatten each chicken breast to about ¼-inch thickness by pounding between sheets of waxed paper. Place portion of frozen filling onto each flattened chicken breast. Roll and tuck in edges of chicken breast; fasten with skewer or wooden picks. In 12×8-inch baking pan melt ¼ cup butter in oven (4 to 6 minutes). Combine bread crumbs, thyme and sage. Dip rolled chicken breasts in melted butter, then coat with crumbs. Place chicken breasts in same baking pan; sprinkle with remaining crumbs. Bake for 55 to 65 minutes or until chicken breasts are fork tender. Remove skewers before serving. To serve, spoon butter over chicken breasts.

Roast Stuffed Turkey

Roast Stuffed Turkey

Makes 8 to 10 servings

- 2 packages (6 oz. each) STOVE TOP® Stuffing Mix, any variety
- ½ cup (1 stick) butter or margarine, cut into pieces
- 3 cups hot water
- 1 (8- to 10-pound) turkey

Prepare stuffing by placing contents of vegetable/seasoning packets and butter in a large bowl. Add hot water; stir just to partially melt butter. Add stuffing crumbs. Stir just to moisten. *Do not stuff bird until ready to roast.*

Rinse turkey with cold water; pat dry. *Do not* rub cavity with salt. Lightly stuff neck and body cavities with prepared stuffing. Skewer neck skin to back. Tie legs to tail and twist wing tips under. Place turkey breast side up in roasting pan. Roast at 325°F for 3 to 4 hours or as directed on poultry wrapper. Bake any remaining stuffing at 325°F for 30 minutes. Cover the baking dish for moist stuffing. If drier stuffing is desired, bake uncovered.

Cookies & Candies

Lemon Nut Bars

Makes about 3 dozen

1 1/3 cups flour
1/2 cup packed brown sugar
1/4 cup granulated sugar
3/4 cup PARKAY® Margarine
1 cup old fashioned or quick oats, uncooked
1/2 cup chopped nuts
1 8-oz. pkg. PHILADELPHIA BRAND® Cream Cheese, softened
1 egg
3 tablespoons lemon juice
1 tablespoon grated lemon peel

Preheat oven to 350°F. Stir together flour and sugars in medium bowl. Cut in margarine until mixture resembles coarse crumbs. Stir in oats and nuts. Reserve 1 cup crumb mixture; press remaining crumb mixture onto bottom of greased 13×9-inch baking pan. Bake 15 minutes. Beat cream cheese, egg, juice and peel in small mixing bowl at medium speed with electric mixer until well blended. Pour over crust; sprinkle with reserved crumb mixture. Bake 25 minutes. Cool; cut into bars.

Preparation time: 30 minutes
Cooking time: 25 minutes

Chocolate Sugar Cookies

Makes about 3 1/2 dozen

3 squares BAKER'S® Unsweetened Chocolate
1 cup (2 sticks) butter or margarine
1 cup sugar
1 egg
1 teaspoon vanilla
2 cups all-purpose flour
1 teaspoon baking soda
1/4 teaspoon salt
Additional granulated sugar

Microwave chocolate and butter in large microwavable bowl at HIGH 2 minutes or until butter is melted. *Stir until chocolate is completely melted.* Stir 1 cup sugar into melted chocolate until well blended. Stir in egg and vanilla until completely mixed. Mix in flour, baking soda and salt until well blended. Chill dough until easy to handle, about 30 minutes. Shape into 1-inch balls; roll in sugar. Place on greased cookie sheet. (If a flatter, crisper cookie is desired, flatten with bottom of glass.) Bake at 375°F for 8 to 10 minutes or until set. Remove and cool on rack.

Range Top: Melt chocolate and butter in heavy saucepan over very low heat; stir constantly until just melted. Remove from heat; continue as directed above.

Kahlúa® Kisses (left), Kahlúa® Bonbons (right)

Kahlúa® Bonbons

Makes 4 dozen

  ¹/₄ cup KAHLÚA®
  4 teaspoons instant coffee powder
³/₄ cup unsalted butter, softened
  1 ounce cream cheese, softened
  2 egg yolks
1¹/₂ cups powdered sugar
  12 ounces semisweet chocolate, chopped
  ¹/₄ cup vegetable shortening
  10 ounces amaretti cookies*, crushed

In small bowl combine KAHLÚA® and coffee powder. Let stand 10 minutes. In medium bowl, cream butter with cream cheese until fluffy. Add egg yolks and sugar and beat until smooth. Stir KAHLÚA® and coffee powder until powder is completely dissolved. Gradually beat into butter mixture. Drop mixture by rounded teaspoonfuls onto baking sheets or trays lined with waxed paper or plastic wrap. Set in freezer 1 hour or overnight.

When ready to dip, remove from freezer 1 sheet at a time; roll between palms to shape into balls. Return to freezer.

Melt chocolate and shortening in top of double boiler over simmering water, stirring frequently. Cool to lukewarm, stirring occasionally. Place crushed amaretti in bowl.

Using wooden skewer or toothpick, dip bonbon balls, 1 at a time, into warm chocolate. Allow excess chocolate to drip off, then transfer to bowl of amaretti crumbs. Using small spoon, sprinkle crumbs over bonbon to cover completely. Transfer to baking sheets or trays lined with clean plastic wrap. Using second skewer, gently push bonbon off dipping skewer. If hole remains, cover with additional amaretti crumbs. If chocolate becomes too thick, reheat gently as needed. Store bonbons in refrigerator.

*Amaretti are Italian meringue cookies and can be purchased at Italian or specialty food shops. If desired, substitute an equal amount of finely chopped toasted hazelnuts or almonds.

Kahlúa® Kisses

Makes 2½ dozen

¾ teaspoon instant coffee powder
⅓ cup water
1 cup plus 2 tablespoons sugar
¼ cup KAHLÚA®
3 egg whites, room temperature
¼ teaspoon cream of tartar
    Dash salt

In heavy 2-quart saucepan, dissolve coffee powder in water. Add 1 cup sugar; stir over low heat until sugar dissolves. Do not allow to boil. Stir in KAHLÚA®. Brush down sides of pan with pastry brush dipped frequently into cold water. Bring mixture to a boil over medium heat. *Do not stir.* Boil until candy thermometer registers 240° to 242°F, about 15 minutes, adjusting heat if necessary to prevent boiling over. Mixture will be very thick. Remove from heat (temperature will continue to rise).

Immediately beat egg whites with cream of tartar and salt until soft peaks form. Add remaining 2 tablespoons sugar; continue beating until stiff peaks form. Gradually beat hot KAHLÚA® syrup into egg whites, beating after each addition to thoroughly mix. Continue beating 4 to 5 minutes or until meringue is very thick, firm and cooled to lukewarm.

Line baking sheet with foil, shiny side down. Using pastry bag fitted with large (#6) star tip, pipe meringue into kisses about 1½ inches wide at base and 1½ inches high onto baking sheet. Set on center rack of 200°F oven for 4 hours. Without opening door, turn heat off and let kisses dry in oven 2 more hours or until crisp. Remove from oven; cool completely on pan. Store in airtight container up to 1 week.

Snowballs

Makes 5 dozen cookies

½ cup DOMINO® Confectioners 10-X Sugar
¼ teaspoon salt
1 cup butter or margarine, softened
1 teaspoon vanilla extract
2¼ cups all-purpose flour
½ cup chopped pecans
    DOMINO® Confectioners 10-X Sugar

In large bowl, combine ½ cup sugar, salt and butter; mix well. Add extract. Gradually stir in flour. Work nuts into dough. Chill well. Form into 1-inch balls. Place on ungreased cookie sheets. Bake at 400°F for 8 to 10 minutes or until set but not brown. Roll in confectioners sugar immediately. Cool on rack. Roll in sugar again. Store in airtight container.

Lemon Cut-Out Cookies

Makes 4 to 5 dozen

2¾ cups unsifted flour
1 teaspoon baking powder
½ teaspoon baking soda
¼ teaspoon salt
½ cup margarine or butter, softened
1½ cups sugar
1 egg
⅓ cup REALEMON® Lemon Juice from
    Concentrate
    Lemon Icing, optional

Stir together flour, baking powder, baking soda and salt; set aside. In large mixer bowl, beat margarine and sugar until fluffy; beat in egg. Gradually add dry ingredients alternately with REALEMON® brand; mix well (dough will be soft). Chill overnight in refrigerator or 2 hours in freezer. Preheat oven to 375°F. On well-floured surface, roll out one-third of dough to ⅛-inch thickness; cut with floured cookie cutters. Place 1 inch apart on greased baking sheets; bake 8 to 10 minutes. Cool. Repeat with remaining dough. Ice and decorate as desired.

Lemon Icing: Mix 1¼ cups confectioners' sugar and 2 tablespoons REALEMON® brand until smooth. Add food coloring if desired. Makes about ½ cup.

Lemon Cut-Out Cookies

Chocolate Almond Buttons

Makes 6 dozen cookies

1 1/3 cups flour
1/3 cup unsweetened cocoa powder
1/4 teaspoon salt
1 cup **BLUE DIAMOND**® Blanched Almond Paste
1/2 cup plus 1 1/2 tablespoons softened butter, divided
1/4 cup corn syrup
1 teaspoon vanilla extract
3 squares (1 ounce each) semisweet chocolate
2/3 cup **BLUE DIAMOND**® Blanched Whole Almonds, toasted

Sift flour, cocoa powder, and salt; reserve. Cream almond paste and 1/2 cup butter until smooth. Beat in corn syrup and vanilla. Beat in flour mixture, scraping sides of bowl occasionally, until well-blended. Shape into 3/4-inch balls. Place on lightly greased cookie sheet; indent center of cookies with finger. Bake at 350°F for 8 to 10 minutes or until done. (Cookies will be soft but will become firm when cooled.) In top of double boiler, stir chocolate and remaining 1 1/2 tablespoons butter over simmering water until melted and smooth. With spoon, drizzle small amount of chocolate into center of each cookie. Press an almond into chocolate on each cookie.

Chocolate Almond Buttons

Peanut Butter Kisses

Makes 6 to 7 1/2 dozen cookies

1 cup **BUTTER FLAVOR CRISCO**®
1 cup **JIF**® Creamy Peanut Butter
1 cup firmly packed brown sugar
1 cup granulated sugar
2 eggs
1/4 cup milk
2 teaspoons vanilla
3 1/4 cups all-purpose flour
2 teaspoons baking soda
1 teaspoon salt
Granulated sugar for rolling
72 to 90 milk chocolate kisses or stars, unwrapped

Heat oven to 375°F. Combine BUTTER FLAVOR CRISCO®, JIF® Creamy Peanut Butter, brown sugar and 1 cup granulated sugar in large bowl. Beat at medium speed of electric mixer until well blended. Beat in eggs, milk and vanilla. Combine flour, baking soda and salt. Mix into creamed mixture at low speed until just blended. Dough will be stiff.

Form dough into 1-inch balls. Roll in granulated sugar. Place 2 inches apart on ungreased baking sheet. Bake for 8 minutes. Press milk chocolate kiss into center of each cookie. Return to oven. Bake 3 minutes. Cool 2 minutes on baking sheet. Remove to cooling rack.

Jam-Filled Peanut Butter Kisses: Omit milk chocolate kisses. Prepare recipe as directed through placing balls on baking sheet. Bake at 375°F for 8 minutes. Press handle of wooden spoon gently in center of each cookie. Return to oven. Bake 3 minutes. Finish as directed. Fill cooled cookies with favorite jam.

Austrian Tea Cookies

Makes 3 1/2 dozen

1 1/2 cups sugar, divided
1/2 cup butter, softened
1/2 cup vegetable shortening
1 egg, beaten
1/2 teaspoon vanilla extract
2 cups all-purpose flour
2 cups **ALMOND DELIGHT**® brand cereal, crushed to 1 cup
1/2 teaspoon baking powder
1/4 teaspoon ground cinnamon
14 ounces almond paste
2 egg whites
5 tablespoons raspberry or apricot jam, warmed

In large bowl beat 1 cup sugar, the butter and shortening. Add egg and vanilla; mix well. Stir in flour, cereal, baking powder and cinnamon until well combined. Chill 1 to 2 hours or until firm.

Preheat oven to 350°F. Roll dough on lightly floured surface to ¼-inch thickness; cut into 2-inch circles. Place on ungreased cookie sheet; set aside. In small bowl beat almond paste, egg whites and remaining ½ cup sugar until smooth. With pastry tube fitted with medium-sized star tip, pipe almond paste mixture ½-inch thick on top of each cookie along outside edge. Place ¼ teaspoon jam in center of cookie, spreading out to paste. Bake 8 to 10 minutes or until lightly browned. Let stand 1 minute before removing from sheet. Cool on wire rack.

Almond Butter Crunch

Disco Whirls

Makes about 3½ dozen cookies

½ cup butter or margarine, softened
¾ cup granulated sugar
1 egg
1 teaspoon vanilla
1½ cups all-purpose flour
¼ teaspoon baking powder
3 tablespoons packed brown sugar
1½ teaspoons unsweetened cocoa powder
2 teaspoons milk
¾ cup **DIAMOND®** Walnuts, finely chopped

In medium bowl, beat butter, granulated sugar, egg and vanilla. In small bowl, sift flour with baking powder. Blend into creamed mixture to make a stiff dough. Cover and chill dough about 1 hour for easier handling. In small bowl, mix brown sugar, cocoa and milk; set aside. Roll out dough on lightly floured pastry cloth or board into 10-inch square. Spread with cocoa mixture and sprinkle with walnuts, leaving about ½ inch uncovered at opposite sides of dough. Roll up tightly, jelly-roll fashion, starting at 1 side where dough is not spread with filling. Wrap in plastic wrap and freeze until firm, several hours or overnight. Cut into ¼-inch slices and arrange on lightly greased cookie sheets. Bake in preheated 375°F oven 14 to 15 minutes or until edges are lightly browned. Remove to wire racks to cool.

Almond Butter Crunch

Makes about ¾ pound

1 cup **BLUE DIAMOND®** Blanched Slivered Almonds
½ cup butter
½ cup sugar
1 tablespoon light corn syrup

Line bottom and sides of an 8- or 9-inch cake pan with aluminum foil (*not* plastic wrap or wax paper). Butter foil heavily; reserve. Combine almonds, butter, sugar, and corn syrup in 10-inch skillet. Bring to a boil over medium heat, stirring constantly. Boil, stirring constantly, until mixture turns golden brown, about 5 to 6 minutes. Working quickly, spread candy in prepared pan. Cool about 15 minutes or until firm. Remove candy from pan by lifting edges of foil. Peel off foil. Cool thoroughly. Break into pieces.

Triple Chocolate Squares

Triple Chocolate Squares

Makes 64 squares

1 1/2 cups **BLUE DIAMOND®** Blanched Almond
    Paste, divided
  8 ounces semisweet chocolate, melted
3/4 cup softened butter, divided
  8 ounces milk chocolate, melted
  8 ounces white chocolate, melted

Line bottom and sides of 8-inch square pan with
aluminum foil. Beat 1/2 cup almond paste with
semisweet chocolate. Beat in 1/4 cup butter. Spread
evenly in bottom of prepared pan. Chill to harden.
Beat 1/2 cup almond paste with milk chocolate. Beat
in 1/4 cup butter. Spread mixture evenly over chilled
semisweet chocolate layer. Chill to harden. Beat
remaining 1/2 cup almond paste with white chocolate.
Beat in remaining 1/4 cup butter. Spread mixture
evenly over milk chocolate layer. Chill. Remove
candy from pan by lifting edges of foil. Peel off foil
and cut candy into 1-inch squares.

Sparkly Cookie Stars

Makes about 6 1/2 dozen 3-inch cookies

3 1/2 cups unsifted flour
  1 tablespoon baking powder
1/2 teaspoon salt
  1 (14-ounce) can **EAGLE®** Brand Sweetened
    Condensed Milk (**NOT** evaporated milk)
3/4 cup margarine or butter, softened
  2 eggs
  1 tablespoon vanilla *or* 2 teaspoons almond or
    lemon extract
  1 egg white, slightly beaten
    Red and green colored sugars *or* colored
    sprinkles

Combine flour, baking powder and salt. In large
mixer bowl, beat sweetened condensed milk,
margarine, eggs and vanilla until well blended. Add
dry ingredients; mix well. Chill 2 hours. On floured
surface, knead dough to form a smooth ball. Divide
into thirds. On well-floured surface, roll out each
portion to 1/8-inch thickness. Cut with floured star
cookie cutter. Reroll as necessary to use all dough.
Place 1 inch apart on greased baking sheets. Brush
with egg white; sprinkle with sugar. Bake in
preheated 350°F oven 7 to 9 minutes or until lightly
browned around edges *(do not overbake)*. Cool. Store
loosely covered at room temperature.

Note: *If desired, cut small stars from dough and place on top
of larger stars. Proceed as above.*

Chocolate Mint Truffles

Makes about 6 dozen

  1 (10-ounce) package mint chocolate chips
  1 (6-ounce) package semi-sweet chocolate chips
    (1 cup)
  1 (14-ounce) can **EAGLE®** Brand Sweetened
    Condensed Milk (**NOT** evaporated milk)
    Finely chopped nuts, flaked coconut,
    chocolate sprinkles, colored sprinkles,
    unsweetened cocoa *or* colored sugar

In heavy saucepan, over low heat, melt chips with
sweetened condensed milk. Chill 2 hours or until
firm. Shape into 1-inch balls; roll in any of the above
coatings. Chill 1 hour or until firm. Store covered at
room temperature.

Microwave: In 1-quart glass measure, combine chips
and sweetened condensed milk. Cook on 100%
power (high) 3 minutes or until chips melt, stirring
after each 1 1/2 minutes. Stir until smooth. Proceed as
above.

Black Forest Brownies

Makes 24 to 36 brownies

1 (12-ounce) package semi-sweet chocolate chips
¼ cup margarine or butter
2 cups biscuit baking mix
1 (14-ounce) can **EAGLE**® Brand Sweetened
    Condensed Milk (**NOT** evaporated milk)
1 egg, beaten
1 teaspoon almond extract
½ cup chopped candied cherries
½ cup sliced almonds, toasted

Preheat oven to 350°F. In large saucepan, over low heat, melt *1 cup* chips with margarine; remove from heat. Add biscuit mix, sweetened condensed milk, egg and extract. Stir in remaining chips and cherries. Turn into well-greased 13×9-inch baking pan. Top with almonds. Bake 20 to 25 minutes or until brownies begin to pull away from sides of pan. Cool. Cut into bars. Store tightly covered at room temperature.

Sparkly Cookie Stars (top left), Black Forest Brownies (top right), Chocolate Mint Truffles (bottom)

Fruit Burst Cookies

Makes 2½ dozen

1 cup margarine or butter, softened
¼ cup sugar
1 teaspoon almond extract
2 cups all-purpose flour
½ teaspoon salt
1 cup finely chopped nuts
    SMUCKER'S® Simply Fruit

Cream margarine and sugar until light and fluffy. Blend in almond extract. Combine flour and salt; add to mixture and blend well. Shape level tablespoons of dough into balls; roll in nuts. Place 2 inches apart on ungreased cookie sheets; flatten slightly. Indent centers; fill with fruit spread. Bake at 400°F for 10 to 12 minutes or just until lightly browned. Cool.

Walnut Jam Crescents

Makes 2 dozen crescents

⅔ cup butter or margarine
1⅓ cups all-purpose flour
½ cup dairy sour cream
⅔ cup raspberry jam or orange marmalade
⅔ cup **DIAMOND**® Walnuts, finely chopped

In medium bowl, cut butter into flour until mixture resembles fine crumbs. Add sour cream and mix until stiff dough is formed. Divide evenly into 2 portions. Shape each into a ball, flatten slightly, wrap in waxed paper and chill well. Working with 1 portion of dough at a time, roll dough into 11-inch round on lightly floured pastry cloth or board. Spread with ⅓ cup of the jam and sprinkle with ⅓ cup of the walnuts. Cut into quarters, then cut each quarter into 3 wedges. Roll up, 1 at a time, starting from outer edge, and place on lightly greased cookie sheets. Repeat with second portion of dough. Bake in preheated 375°F oven 25 to 30 minutes or until lightly browned. Remove to wire racks to cool.

Apricot Almond Chewies

Makes about 6¹/₂ dozen

4 cups finely chopped dried apricots (about
   1 pound)
4 cups flaked coconut *or* coconut macaroon
   crumbs (about 21 macaroons)
2 cups slivered almonds, toasted and finely
   chopped
1 (14-ounce) can EAGLE® Brand Sweetened
   Condensed Milk (NOT evaporated milk)
   Whole almonds, optional

In large bowl, combine all ingredients except whole
almonds. Chill 2 hours. Shape into 1-inch balls. Top
each with whole almond if desired. Store tightly
covered in refrigerator.

Chipper Peanut Candy

Makes about 2 pounds

1 (6-ounce) package semi-sweet chocolate chips
   (1 cup) *or* butterscotch flavored chips
1 (14-ounce) can EAGLE® Brand Sweetened
   Condensed Milk (NOT evaporated milk)
1 cup peanut butter
2 cups crushed potato chips
1 cup coarsely chopped peanuts

In large heavy saucepan, over low heat, melt
chocolate chips with sweetened condensed milk and
peanut butter; stir until well blended. Remove from
heat. Add potato chips and peanuts; mix well. Press
into aluminum foil-lined 8- or 9-inch square pan.
Chill 2 hours or until firm. Turn onto cutting board;
peel off foil and cut into squares. Store loosely
covered at room temperature.

Microwave: In 2-quart glass measure, combine
chocolate chips, sweetened condensed milk and
peanut butter. Cook on 100% power (high) 4
minutes, stirring after each 2 minutes. Proceed as
above.

Caramel Peanut Balls

Makes about 4¹/₂ dozen

3 cups finely chopped dry roasted peanuts
1 (14-ounce) can EAGLE® Brand Sweetened
   Condensed Milk (NOT evaporated milk)
1 teaspoon vanilla extract
¹/₂ pound chocolate confectioners' coating*

In heavy saucepan, combine peanuts, sweetened
condensed milk and vanilla. Over medium heat, cook
and stir 8 to 10 minutes or until mixture forms ball
around spoon and pulls away from side of pan. Cool
10 minutes. Chill if desired. Shape into 1-inch balls.
In small heavy saucepan, over low heat, melt
confectioners' coating. With wooden pick, dip each
ball into melted coating, covering half of ball. Place
on wax paper-lined baking sheets until firm. Store
covered at room temperature or in refrigerator.

*Chocolate confectioners' coating can be purchased in candy
specialty stores.*

Crunchy Clusters

Makes about 3 dozen

1 (12-ounce) package semi-sweet chocolate chips
   or 3 (6-ounce) packages butterscotch
   flavored chips
1 (14-ounce) can EAGLE® Brand Sweetened
   Condensed Milk (NOT evaporated milk)
1 (3-ounce) can chow mein noodles *or* 2 cups
   pretzel sticks, broken into ¹/₂-inch pieces
1 cup dry roasted peanuts *or* whole roasted
   almonds

In heavy saucepan, over low heat, melt chips with
sweetened condensed milk. Remove from heat. In
large bowl, combine noodles and nuts; stir in
chocolate mixture. Drop by tablespoonfuls onto wax
paper-lined baking sheets; chill 2 hours or until firm.
Store loosely covered at room temperature.

Microwave: In 2-quart glass measure, combine chips
and sweetened condensed milk. Cook on 100%
power (high) 3 minutes, stirring after each 1¹/₂
minutes. Stir until smooth. Proceed as above.

*Top to bottom: Apricot Almond Chewies,
Chipper Peanut Candy, Caramel Peanut Balls,
Crunchy Clusters—Butterscotch and Chocolate,
Chipper Peanut Candy*

Jam-Up Oatmeal Cookies

Jam-Up Oatmeal Cookies

Makes about 2 dozen cookies

 1 cup **BUTTER FLAVOR CRISCO®**
1½ cups firmly packed brown sugar
 2 eggs
 2 teaspoons almond extract
 2 cups all-purpose flour
 1 teaspoon baking powder
 1 teaspoon salt
 ½ teaspoon baking soda
2½ cups quick oats (not instant or old fashioned)
 1 cup finely chopped pecans
 1 jar (12 ounces) pineapple jam
 Granulated sugar for sprinkling

Combine BUTTER FLAVOR CRISCO® and sugar in large bowl. Beat at medium speed of electric mixer until well blended. Beat in eggs and almond extract. Combine flour, baking powder, salt and baking soda. Mix into creamed mixture at low speed until just blended. Stir in oats and chopped nuts with spoon. Cover and refrigerate at least 1 hour.

Heat oven to 350°F. Grease baking sheet with BUTTER FLAVOR CRISCO®. Roll out ½ of the dough, at a time, to about ¼-inch thickness on floured surface. Cut out with 2½-inch round cookie cutter. Place 1 teaspoonful of jam in center of ½ of the rounds. Top with remaining rounds. Press edges to seal. Prick center. Sprinkle with sugar. Place 1 inch apart on baking sheet. Bake for 12 to 15 minutes, or until lightly browned. Cool 2 minutes on baking sheet. Remove to cooling rack.

Cut-Out Sugar Cookies

Makes about 3 dozen cookies

⅔ cup **BUTTER FLAVOR CRISCO®**
¾ cup sugar
 1 tablespoon plus 1 teaspoon milk
 1 teaspoon vanilla
 1 egg
 2 cups all-purpose flour
1½ teaspoons baking powder
 ¼ teaspoon salt

Combine BUTTER FLAVOR CRISCO®, sugar, milk and vanilla in large bowl. Beat at medium speed of electric mixer until well blended. Beat in egg. Combine flour, baking powder and salt. Mix into creamed mixture at low speed until well blended. Cover and refrigerate several hours or overnight.

Heat oven to 375°F. Roll out ½ of the dough, at a time, to about ⅛-inch thickness on floured surface. Cut out with cookie cutters. Place 2 inches apart on ungreased baking sheet. Sprinkle with colored sugars and decors or leave plain and frost* when cooled. Bake for 7 to 9 minutes, or until set. Remove immediately to cooling rack.

Lemon or Orange Cut-Out Sugar Cookies: Add 1 teaspoon grated lemon or orange peel and 1 teaspoon lemon or orange extract to dough before flour is added.

****Creamy Vanilla Frosting:*** Combine ½ cup BUTTER FLAVOR CRISCO®, 1 pound (4 cups) powdered sugar, ⅓ cup milk and 1 teaspoon vanilla in medium bowl. Beat at low speed of electric mixer until well blended. Scrape bowl. Beat at high speed for 2 minutes, or until smooth and creamy. One or two drops food color can be used to tint each cup of frosting, if desired. Frost cooled cookies. This frosting works well in decorating tube.

Lemon or Orange Creamy Frosting: Omit milk. Add ⅓ cup lemon or orange juice. Add 1 teaspoon orange peel with orange juice.

Walnut Shortbread Bars

Makes about 5 dozen

1 8-oz. pkg. PHILADELPHIA BRAND® Cream
    Cheese, softened
1 cup PARKAY® Margarine
³/₄ cup granulated sugar
³/₄ cup packed brown sugar
1 egg
1 teaspoon vanilla
2¹/₂ cups flour
1 teaspoon CALUMET® Baking Powder
¹/₂ teaspoon salt
³/₄ cup chopped walnuts

Preheat oven to 350°F. Beat cream cheese, margarine
and sugars in large mixing bowl at medium speed
with electric mixer until well blended. Blend in egg
and vanilla. Add combined dry ingredients; mix
well. Stir in walnuts. Spread into greased 15×10×1-
inch jelly roll pan. Bake 20 to 25 minutes or until
lightly browned. Cool. Sprinkle with powdered
sugar, if desired. Cut into bars.

Preparation time: 15 minutes
Cooking time: 25 minutes

Chocolate Peanut Butter Balls

Makes 4¹/₂ dozen

1 cup crunchy peanut butter
¹/₄ cup margarine or butter, softened
2 cups KELLOGG'S® RICE KRISPIES® cereal
1 cup confectioners sugar
1 package (14 oz.) chocolate candy coating
2 tablespoons shortening
    White candy coating, melted (optional)

In large bowl, combine peanut butter and margarine.
Add KELLOGG'S® RICE KRISPIES® cereal and
sugar, mixing until evenly combined. Portion cereal
mixture, using a rounded measuring-teaspoon. Roll
into balls; set aside.

In top of double boiler, over hot water, melt
chocolate coating and shortening. Dip each peanut
butter ball in coating and place on waxed paper-lined
baking sheet. Drizzle with melted white coating, if
desired. Refrigerate until firm. Place in small candy
paper cups to serve.

Note: *One package (12 oz.) semi-sweet chocolate morsels may
be used in place of chocolate candy coating.*

Per Serving (1 ball): 90 Calories

Crisp Chocolate Truffles

Makes 4¹/₂ dozen

1 jar (7 oz.) marshmallow creme
2 tablespoons margarine or butter
1 package (6 oz.) semi-sweet chocolate morsels
    (1 cup)
2 cups KELLOGG'S® RICE KRISPIES® cereal
1 package (14 oz.) white candy coating
2 tablespoons shortening
    Multicolored sprinkles (optional)

In heavy 2-quart saucepan, combine marshmallow
creme, margarine and chocolate morsels. Cook over
low heat, stirring constantly, until chocolate is melted
and mixture is smooth; remove from heat. Stir
KELLOGG'S® RICE KRISPIES® cereal into hot
chocolate mixture, mixing until thoroughly
combined. Drop by rounded measuring-teaspoonfuls
onto waxed paper-lined baking sheet. Refrigerate
until firm, about 1 hour.

In top of double boiler, over hot water, melt white
coating and shortening. Dip each chocolate ball in
coating and place on waxed paper-lined baking sheet.
Decorate with sprinkles, if desired. Refrigerate until
firm. Place in small candy paper cups to serve.

Per Serving (1 truffle): 80 Calories

Chocolate Peanut Butter Balls, Crisp Chocolate Truffles

Pecan Pie Bars

Makes 36 bars

2 cups unsifted flour
1/2 cup confectioners' sugar
1 cup cold margarine or butter
1 (14-ounce) can EAGLE® Brand Sweetened
    Condensed Milk (NOT evaporated milk)
1 egg
1 teaspoon vanilla extract
1 (6-ounce) package almond brickle chips
1 cup chopped pecans

Preheat oven to 350°F (325° for glass dish). In medium bowl, combine flour and sugar; cut in margarine until crumbly. Press firmly on bottom of 13×9-inch baking pan. Bake 15 minutes. Meanwhile, in medium bowl, beat sweetened condensed milk, egg and vanilla. Stir in chips and pecans. Spread evenly over crust. Bake 25 minutes or until golden brown. Cool. Cut into bars. Store covered in refrigerator.

Triple Layer Cookie Bars

Makes 24 to 36 bars

1/2 cup margarine or butter
1 1/2 cups graham cracker crumbs
1 (7-ounce) package flaked coconut (2 2/3 cups)
1 (14-ounce) can EAGLE® Brand Sweetened
    Condensed Milk (NOT evaporated milk)
1 (12-ounce) package semi-sweet chocolate chips
1/2 cup creamy peanut butter

Preheat oven to 350°F (325° for glass dish). In 13×9-inch baking pan, melt margarine in oven. Sprinkle crumbs evenly over margarine. Top evenly with coconut then sweetened condensed milk. Bake 25 minutes or until lightly browned. In small saucepan, over low heat, melt chips with peanut butter. Spread evenly over hot coconut layer. Cool 30 minutes. Chill thoroughly. Cut into bars. Garnish as desired. Store loosely covered at room temperature.

Meringue Kisses

Makes 4 to 5 dozen cookies

2 egg whites
1/4 teaspoon cream of tartar
1/2 cup sugar
    Variation Ingredients* (optional)

In small mixer bowl, beat egg whites with cream of tartar at high speed until foamy. Add sugar, 2 tablespoons at a time, beating constantly until sugar is dissolved and whites are glossy and stand in stiff peaks. If desired, beat or fold in Variation Ingredients. Drop meringue by rounded teaspoonfuls or pipe through pastry tube 1 inch apart onto greased or waxed-paper-lined cookie sheets. Bake in preheated 225°F oven until firm, about 1 hour. Turn off oven. Let cookies stand in oven with door closed until cool, dry and crisp, at least 1 additional hour. Store in tightly sealed container.

Variation Ingredients: Amounts listed are for one batch of cookies. To make two variations at a time, divide meringue mixture equally between two bowls. Beat or fold into each bowl half of the amounts listed for each variation.

Chocolate: Beat in 1/4 cup unsweetened cocoa and 1 teaspoon vanilla.

Citrus: Beat in 1 tablespoon grated orange peel, 1/4 teaspoon lemon extract and a few drops yellow food coloring.

Mint: Beat in 1/4 teaspoon mint extract and a few drops green food coloring.

Rocky Road: Beat in 1 teaspoon vanilla. Fold in 1/2 cup semisweet chocolate chips and 1/2 cup chopped nuts.

Cherry-Almond: Fold in 1/2 cup chopped, drained maraschino cherries and 1/2 cup chopped almonds.

Favorite recipe from **American Egg Board**

Pecan Pie Bars (left), Triple Layer Cookie Bars (right)

Simply Delicious Minty Cookies

Makes about 5 dozen cookies

1 cup **BUTTER FLAVOR CRISCO**®
1 package (8 ounces) cream cheese, softened
³/₄ cup granulated sugar
¹/₂ cup firmly packed brown sugar
1 teaspoon vanilla
2 cups all-purpose flour
1³/₄ cups mint chocolate chips

Heat oven to 350°F. Combine BUTTER FLAVOR CRISCO®, cream cheese, granulated sugar, brown sugar and vanilla in large bowl. Beat at medium speed of electric mixer until well blended. Mix flour into creamed mixture at low speed until just blended. Stir in mint chocolate chips. Drop rounded teaspoonfuls of dough 2 inches apart onto ungreased baking sheet. Bake for 8 minutes, or until lightly browned. Cool 2 minutes on baking sheet. Remove to cooling rack.

Kris Kringle Cookies (top), Lebkuchen Jewels (bottom)

Lebkuchen Jewels

Makes about 4 dozen cookies

³/₄ cup packed brown sugar
1 egg
1 cup honey
1 tablespoon grated lemon peel
1 teaspoon lemon juice
2³/₄ cups all-purpose flour
1 teaspoon *each* ground nutmeg, cinnamon and
    cloves
¹/₂ teaspoon *each* baking soda and salt
1 cup **SUN-MAID**® Golden Raisins
¹/₂ cup *each* mixed candied fruits and citron
1 cup chopped **DIAMOND**® Walnuts
    Lemon Glaze (recipe follows)
    Candied cherries and citron, for garnish

In large bowl, beat sugar and egg until smooth and fluffy. Add honey, lemon peel and juice; beat well. In medium bowl, sift flour with nutmeg, cinnamon, cloves, baking soda and salt; gradually mix into egg-sugar mixture on low speed. Stir in fruits and nuts. Spread batter into greased 15×10-inch jelly-roll pan. Bake in preheated 375°F oven 20 minutes or until lightly browned. Cool slightly in pan; brush with Lemon Glaze. Cool; cut into diamonds. Decorate with candied cherries and slivers of citron, if desired. Store in covered container up to 1 month.

Lemon Glaze: In small bowl, combine 1 cup sifted powdered sugar with enough lemon juice (1¹/₂ to 2 tablespoons) to make a thin glaze.

Kris Kringle Cookies

Makes 1¹/₂ to 2 dozen cookies

1¹/₃ cups butter or margarine, softened
1¹/₃ cups granulated sugar
2 eggs
2²/₃ cups all-purpose flour
¹/₄ teaspoon salt
1¹/₂ cups **SUN-MAID**® Raisins, chopped
¹/₂ cup chopped candied ginger*
1 egg white, beaten for glaze
    Colored sugars, dragées, candied fruits and
    DIAMOND® Walnuts, for garnish

In large bowl, cream butter, granulated sugar and eggs. Stir in flour and salt, mixing until blended. Stir in raisins and ginger. Cover and chill dough. Roll out dough on lightly floured board to ¹/₈-inch thickness; cut into desired shapes with sharp-edged cookie cutters. Space 2 inches apart on greased baking sheets. Brush with beaten white; sprinkle with additional granulated sugar, or decorate with colored sugars, dragées, candied fruits and walnuts, if desired. Bake in preheated 350°F oven 12 to 15 minutes or until golden. Cool 2 to 3 minutes on pan; remove to wire rack to cool completely.

An additional ¹/₂ cup of raisins may be substituted for candied ginger; add 1 tablespoon ground ginger.

One-Bowl Homemade Brownies from Baker's®

One-Bowl Homemade Brownies from Baker's®

Makes 24 brownies

 4 squares BAKER'S® Unsweetened Chocolate
³⁄4 cup (1¹⁄2 sticks) margarine or butter
 2 cups sugar
 3 eggs
 1 teaspoon vanilla
 1 cup all-purpose flour
 1 cup coarsely chopped nuts (optional)

Microwave chocolate and margarine in large microwavable bowl at HIGH 2 minutes or until margarine is melted. *Stir until chocolate is completely melted.* Stir in sugar until well blended. Stir in eggs and vanilla until completely mixed. Mix in flour until well blended. Stir in nuts. Spread in greased 13×9-inch pan. Bake at 350°F for 35 to 40 minutes or until wooden pick inserted into center comes out almost clean. *(Do not overbake.)* Cool in pan; cut into squares.

Range Top: Melt chocolate and margarine in 3-quart saucepan over very low heat; stir constantly until just melted. Remove from heat. Continue as above.

Brownie Options

Cakelike Brownies: Stir in ¹⁄2 cup milk with eggs and vanilla. Increase flour to 1¹⁄2 cups.

Double Chocolate Brownies: Add 1 cup BAKER'S® Real Semi-Sweet Chocolate Chips with the nuts.

Extra Thick Brownies: Bake in 9-inch square pan for 50 minutes.

Rocky Road Brownies: Prepare Brownies as directed. Bake 35 minutes. Immediately sprinkle 2 cups KRAFT® Miniature Marshmallows, 1 cup BAKER'S® Real Semi-Sweet Chocolate Chips and 1 cup coarsely chopped nuts over brownies. Continue baking 3 to 5 minutes or until topping begins to melt together. Cool.

Cream Cheese Brownies: Prepare Brownies as directed using 4 eggs; spread in prepared pan. In same bowl mix 2 (3 oz.) packages PHILADELPHIA BRAND® Cream Cheese, softened, ¹⁄4 cup sugar, 1 egg and 2 tablespoons flour. Spoon mixture over brownie batter; swirl with knife to marbelize. Bake 40 minutes.

Cranberry-Orange Muesli Bars

Makes 24 bars

Filling
 1 package (12 oz.) OCEAN SPRAY® cranberries, fresh or frozen
 1 cup granulated sugar
 1 teaspoon grated orange peel, optional
 1 cup orange juice

Base/Topping
 4 cups RALSTON® brand Fruit Muesli with Cranberries, crushed to 3 cups
1¹⁄2 cups all-purpose flour
 ³⁄4 cup packed brown sugar
1¹⁄2 teaspoons baking powder
 ¹⁄2 teaspoon salt
 ³⁄4 cup (1¹⁄2 sticks) margarine or butter, softened

To prepare Filling: In medium saucepan over medium heat combine cranberries, granulated sugar, orange peel, if desired, and orange juice. Cook, stirring frequently, until mixture comes to a boil. Reduce heat; simmer 15 to 18 minutes, stirring frequently. Cool.

To prepare Base/Topping: Preheat oven to 350°F. In large bowl combine cereal, flour, brown sugar, baking powder, salt and margarine. Reserve 1¹⁄2 cups cereal mixture for topping; set aside. Press remaining cereal mixture firmly and evenly into ungreased 13×9×2-inch baking pan. Bake 10 minutes. Spread cranberry filling evenly over base; sprinkle with reserved cereal mixture. Bake an additional 18 to 20 minutes or until lightly browned.

Frost on the Pumpkin Cookies

Makes about 48 cookies

2 cups all-purpose flour
1 teaspoon baking powder
1 teaspoon ground cinnamon
½ teaspoon baking soda
½ teaspoon ground nutmeg
1 cup butter, softened
¾ cup JACK FROST® granulated sugar
¾ cup JACK FROST® brown sugar (packed)
1 egg
1 cup canned pumpkin
2 teaspoons vanilla
½ cup raisins
½ cup chopped walnuts
Cream Cheese Frosting

In small mixing bowl combine flour, baking powder, cinnamon, baking soda and nutmeg. Set aside. In large mixer bowl beat butter for 1 minute. Add granulated sugar and brown sugar. Beat until fluffy. Add egg, pumpkin and vanilla; beat well. Add dry ingredients to beaten mixture; mix until well blended. Stir in raisins and walnuts. Drop by teaspoonfuls 2 inches apart onto greased cookie sheet. Bake in 350°F oven for 10 to 12 minutes. Cool on cookie sheet for 2 minutes, then transfer to wire rack to finish cooling. Frost with Cream Cheese Frosting. Garnish with chopped nuts, if desired.

Cream Cheese Frosting: In medium mixing bowl, beat 3 ounces softened cream cheese, ¼ cup softened butter and 1 teaspoon vanilla until light and fluffy. Gradually add 2 cups JACK FROST® powdered sugar, beating until smooth.

Chunky Chocolate Cookie Squares

Makes 2 dozen

2½ cups all-purpose flour
1 teaspoon baking soda
½ teaspoon salt
¾ cup butter or margarine, softened
1 cup firmly packed brown sugar
¾ cup light or dark corn syrup
1 egg
1 teaspoon vanilla
1 cup chopped pecans
1 package (8 oz.) BAKER'S® Semi-Sweet
    Chocolate *or* 2 packages (4 oz. each)
    BAKER'S® GERMAN'S® Sweet Chocolate,
    cut into large chunks

Mix flour, baking soda and salt; set aside. Beat butter and sugar in large bowl of electric mixer at medium speed until light and fluffy. Slowly beat in corn syrup, then egg and vanilla. Beat in flour mixture until blended. Stir in pecans and half of the chocolate. Spread evenly in ungreased 15½×10½×1-inch jelly roll pan. Sprinkle remaining chocolate on top. Bake at 350°F for 30 minutes, or until lightly browned. Cool on rack. Cut into 2½-inch squares.

Easy Peanut Butter Chocolate Fudge

Makes about 2 pounds

1 (12-ounce) package peanut butter flavored
    chips
¼ cup margarine or butter
1 (14-ounce) can EAGLE® Brand Sweetened
    Condensed Milk (**NOT** evaporated milk)
½ cup chopped peanuts, optional
1 (6-ounce) package semi-sweet chocolate chips
    (1 cup)

In heavy saucepan, melt peanut butter chips and *2 tablespoons* margarine with *1 cup* sweetened condensed milk. Remove from heat; stir in peanuts if desired. Spread into wax paper-lined 8-inch square pan. In small heavy saucepan, melt chocolate chips and remaining *2 tablespoons* margarine with remaining sweetened condensed milk. Spread chocolate mixture on top of peanut butter mixture. Chill 2 hours or until firm. Turn fudge onto cutting board; peel off paper and cut into squares. Store loosely covered at room temperature.

Easy Peanut Butter Chocolate Fudge

Desserts

Almond Chocolate Torte with Raspberry Sauce

Makes 10 to 12 servings

2¹/₂ cups **BLUE DIAMOND®** Blanched Whole
    Almonds, lightly toasted
 9 squares (1 ounce each) semisweet chocolate
¹/₄ cup butter
 6 eggs, beaten
³/₄ cup sugar
 2 tablespoons flour
¹/₄ cup brandy
    Fudge Glaze (recipe follows)
    Raspberry Sauce (recipe follows)

In food processor or blender, process 1 cup of the almonds until finely ground. Generously grease 9-inch round cake pan; sprinkle with 2 tablespoons ground almonds. In top of double boiler, melt chocolate and butter over simmering water, blending thoroughly; cool slightly. In large bowl, beat eggs and sugar. Gradually beat in chocolate mixture. Add flour, remaining ground almonds and brandy; mix well. Pour batter into prepared pan. Bake in preheated 350°F oven 25 minutes or until toothpick inserted into center comes out almost clean. Let cool in pan on wire rack 10 minutes. Loosen edge; remove from pan. Cool completely on wire rack. Prepare Fudge Glaze. Place torte on wire rack over sheet of waxed paper. Pour Fudge Glaze over torte, spreading over top and sides with spatula. Carefully transfer torte to serving plate; let glaze set. Prepare Raspberry Sauce; set aside. Arrange remaining 1¹/₂ cups whole almonds, points toward center, in circle around outer edge of torte. Working towards center, repeat circles, overlapping almonds slightly. To serve, pour small amount of Raspberry Sauce on each serving plate; top with slice of torte.

Fudge Glaze: In small saucepan, combine 6 tablespoons water and 3 tablespoons sugar. Simmer over low heat until sugar dissolves. Stir in 3 squares (1 ounce each) semisweet chocolate and 1 tablespoon brandy. Heat, stirring occasionally, until chocolate melts and glaze coats back of spoon.

Raspberry Sauce: In food processor or blender, puree 2 packages (10 ounces each) thawed frozen raspberries. Strain raspberry puree through a fine sieve to remove seeds. Stir in sugar to taste.

Quick Rumtopf

Makes 2 quarts

1 can (16 oz.) **DEL MONTE®** Yellow Cling
    Sliced Peaches
1 can (16 oz.) **DEL MONTE®** Bartlett Pear
    Halves
1 can (15¹/₂ oz.) **DEL MONTE®** Pineapple
    Chunks
1 can (11 oz.) **DEL MONTE®** Mandarin
    Oranges
1 cup rum
1 cinnamon stick
¹/₂ cup **DEL MONTE®** Seedless Raisins

Drain fruit reserving syrup in medium saucepan. Add rum and cinnamon stick to reserved syrup. Bring to a boil, stirring occasionally. Cool. Layer fruit and raisins in rumtopf pot or large jars. Pour syrup mixture over fruit. Refrigerate. Allow 1 week to mellow. Serve as fruit compote or on ice cream or pound cake.

Almond Chocolate Torte with Raspberry Sauce

Almond Chocolate Torte with
Raspberry Sauce

Torte:
1 cup Blue Diamond Blanched
Whole Almonds, toasted
semi-sweet chocolate

Charlotte Russe

Charlotte Russe

Makes 10 servings

> 2 packages (4-serving size each) *or* 1 package (8-serving size) JELL-O® Brand Gelatin, any red flavor
> 2 cups boiling water
> 1 quart vanilla ice cream, softened
> 12 ladyfingers, split
> COOL-WHIP® Whipped Topping, thawed (optional)
> Fresh raspberries (optional)
> Mint leaves (optional)

Dissolve gelatin in boiling water. Spoon in ice cream, stirring until melted and smooth. Chill until thickened.

Trim about 1 inch off one end of each ladyfinger; reserve trimmed ends for snacking or other use. Place ladyfingers, cut ends down, around side of 8-inch springform pan. Spoon gelatin mixture into pan. Chill until firm, about 3 hours. Remove side of pan. Garnish with whipped topping, raspberries and mint leaves, if desired.

Preparation time: 20 minutes
Chill time: 3 hours

New England Maple Apple Pie

Makes one 9-inch pie

> 1 (9-inch) unbaked pastry shell
> 2 pounds all-purpose apples, pared, cored and thinly sliced (about 6 cups)
> ½ cup plus 2 tablespoons unsifted flour
> ½ cup CARY'S®, VERMONT MAPLE ORCHARDS or MACDONALD'S Pure Maple Syrup
> 2 tablespoons margarine or butter, melted
> ¼ cup firmly packed light brown sugar
> 1 teaspoon ground cinnamon
> ⅓ cup cold margarine or butter
> ½ cup chopped nuts

Place rack in lowest position in oven; preheat oven to 400°F. In large bowl, combine apples and *2 tablespoons* flour. Combine syrup and melted margarine. Pour over apples; mix well. Turn into pastry shell. In medium bowl, combine remaining *½ cup* flour, sugar and cinnamon; cut in cold margarine until crumbly. Add nuts; sprinkle over apples. Bake 10 minutes. *Reduce oven temperature to 375°F;* bake 35 minutes longer or until golden brown. Cool slightly. Serve warm.

German Sweet Chocolate Cake

Makes about 10 servings

1 package (4 oz.) **BAKER'S® GERMAN'S®**
    Sweet Chocolate
1/2 cup boiling water
1 cup (2 sticks) butter or margarine
2 cups sugar
4 eggs, separated
1 teaspoon vanilla
2 cups all-purpose flour
1 teaspoon baking soda
1/2 teaspoon salt
1 cup buttermilk
    Coconut-Pecan Frosting (recipe follows)

Line bottoms of three 9-inch layer pans with waxed paper. Melt chocolate in water; cool. Beat butter and sugar. Beat in egg yolks. Stir in vanilla and chocolate. Mix flour, baking soda and salt. Beat into chocolate mixture alternately with buttermilk. Beat egg whites until stiff peaks form; fold into batter. Pour into prepared pans. Bake at 350°F for 30 minutes or until cake springs back when lightly pressed in center. Cool 15 minutes; remove and cool on racks. Spread Coconut-Pecan Frosting between layers and over top of cake.

Coconut-Pecan Frosting: Combine 1 1/2 cups (12 fl. oz.) evaporated milk, 1 1/2 cups sugar, 4 slightly beaten egg yolks, 3/4 cup butter and 1 1/2 teaspoons vanilla in saucepan. Cook and stir over medium heat until thickened. Remove from heat. Stir in 2 cups **BAKER'S® ANGEL FLAKE®** Coconut and 1 1/2 cups chopped pecans. Cool until thick enough to spread. Makes 4 1/4 cups.

Holiday Creme Chantilly

Makes about 8 servings

2 cups milk
1/2 cup sugar
1/3 cup all-purpose flour
1 envelope unflavored gelatin
1/4 teaspoon salt
2 eggs
2 egg yolks
1/4 to 1/3 cup dark rum
1 cup heavy whipping cream
1/2 cup finely chopped **DIAMOND®** Walnuts
    Orange Walnut Sauce (recipe follows)

In medium saucepan, scald milk over low heat. In medium bowl, combine sugar, flour, gelatin and salt. Add eggs and egg yolks; beat well. Stir in hot milk. Return to saucepan and cook over medium-low heat, stirring constantly, until mixture thickens and just reaches a boil. Remove from heat; stir in rum. Set pan in bowl of ice water; cool thoroughly, stirring occasionally. In medium bowl, beat cream until stiff peaks form. Fold cream and walnuts into the cooled custard mixture. Spoon into individual serving dishes or individual oiled molds. Chill thoroughly. At serving time, spoon Orange Walnut Sauce over Chantilly.

Orange Walnut Sauce

2 to 3 oranges
1/2 cup sugar
1/2 teaspoon cornstarch
1 tablespoon lemon juice
1/4 cup coarsely chopped **DIAMOND®** Walnuts

With vegetable peeler, remove the outer colored layer of oranges. Cut enough of orange peel into slivers with sharp knife to measure 3 tablespoons. Squeeze juice from oranges to measure 1 cup. In small saucepan, simmer juice and slivers over low heat 5 minutes. In small bowl, combine sugar and cornstarch; blend into hot mixture. Cook and stir over medium heat until mixture boils and thickens. Add lemon juice; cool. Add walnuts just before serving. Makes about 3/4 cup sauce.

Holiday Creme Chantilly

Easy Chocolate Cheesecake

Easy Chocolate Cheesecake

Makes 8 servings

> 2 packages (4 oz. each) BAKER'S®
> GERMAN'S® Sweet Chocolate
> 1/3 cup heavy cream
> 2 eggs
> 2/3 cup corn syrup
> 1 1/2 teaspoons vanilla
> 2 packages (8 oz. each) cream cheese, cut into
> cubes
> Crumb Crust (recipe follows)

Microwave 1 1/2 packages (6 oz.) of the chocolate and the cream in microwavable bowl at HIGH 2 minutes. *Stir until chocolate is completely melted.* Blend eggs, corn syrup and vanilla in blender until smooth. With blender running, gradually add cream cheese; blend until smooth. Add chocolate mixture; blend. Pour into crust. Bake at 325°F for 45 minutes or until set. Cool on rack. Cover; chill. Melt remaining chocolate; drizzle over top.

Crumb Crust: In 9-inch pie plate or 9×3-inch springform pan, combine 1 3/4 cups chocolate cookie or graham cracker crumbs, 2 tablespoons sugar and 1/3 cup butter or margarine, melted, until well mixed. Press evenly in pie plate or on bottom and 1 1/4 inches up side of springform pan.

Range Top: Heat chocolate and cream in saucepan over very low heat, stirring until chocolate is melted. Continue as above.

Butterscotch Apple Squares

Makes 12 servings

> 1/4 cup margarine or butter
> 1 1/2 cups graham cracker crumbs
> 2 small all-purpose apples, pared and chopped
> (about 1 1/4 cups)
> 1 (6-ounce) package butterscotch flavored chips
> 1 (14-ounce) can EAGLE® Brand Sweetened
> Condensed Milk (NOT evaporated milk)
> 1 (3 1/2-ounce) can flaked coconut (1 1/3 cups)
> 1 cup chopped nuts

Preheat oven to 350°F (325° for glass dish). In 13×9-inch baking pan, melt margarine in oven. Sprinkle crumbs evenly over margarine; top with apples. In heavy saucepan, over medium heat, melt chips with sweetened condensed milk. Pour butterscotch mixture evenly over apples. Top with coconut and nuts; press down firmly. Bake 25 to 30 minutes or until lightly browned. Cool. Garnish as desired. Refrigerate leftovers.

Microwave: In 12×7-inch baking dish, melt margarine on 100% power (high) 1 minute. Sprinkle crumbs evenly over margarine; top with apples. In 1-quart glass measure, cook chips with sweetened condensed milk on 75% power (medium-high) 2 to 3 minutes. Mix well. Pour butterscotch mixture evenly over apples. Top with coconut and nuts. Press down firmly. Cook on 100% power (high) 8 to 9 minutes. Proceed as above.

Creamy Macaroon Indulgence

Makes 4 servings

> 1 1/2 cups cold milk
> 1 cup (1/2 pint) sour cream
> 2 tablespoons almond liqueur*
> 1 package (4-serving size) JELL-O® Instant
> Pudding and Pie Filling, any flavor
> 1/2 cup crumbled macaroon cookies

Mix milk, sour cream and liqueur in small bowl until smooth. Add pudding mix. Beat with wire whisk until well blended, 1 to 2 minutes. Spoon 1/2 the pudding mixture into dessert dishes. Sprinkle crumbled macaroons evenly over pudding. Top with remaining pudding mixture. Chill. Garnish with additional cookies, if desired.

Preparation time: 15 minutes

*1/4 teaspoon almond extract may be substituted for the almond liqueur.

Christmas Tree Poke Cake

Makes 24 servings

2 packages (2-layer size each) white cake mix
1 package (4-serving size) JELL-O® Brand
    Gelatin, Strawberry Flavor
1 package (4-serving size) JELL-O® Brand
    Gelatin, Lime Flavor
2 cups boiling water
2²/₃ cups (7 oz.) BAKER'S® ANGEL FLAKE®
    Coconut
    Green food coloring
5¹/₄ cups (12 oz.) COOL WHIP® Whipped
    Topping, thawed
    Assorted gumdrops (optional)
    Peppermint candies (optional)
    Red string licorice (optional)

Prepare 1 cake mix as directed on package. Pour batter into greased and floured 9-inch square pan. Bake at 325°F for 50 to 55 minutes or until cake tester inserted in center comes out clean. Cool 10 minutes. Remove from pan; finish cooling on rack. Repeat with remaining cake mix.

Place cake layers, top sides up, in 2 clean 9-inch square cake pans. Pierce cakes with large fork at ¹/₂-inch intervals. Dissolve each flavor of gelatin separately in 1 cup of the boiling water. Carefully pour strawberry flavor gelatin over 1 cake layer and lime flavor gelatin over second cake layer. Chill 3 hours.

Toast ¹/₃ cup of the coconut; set aside. Tint remaining coconut with green food coloring. Dip 1 cake pan in warm water 10 seconds; unmold. Place right side up on large serving plate or cutting board. Cut cake as shown in Diagram 1. Arrange pieces as shown in Christmas tree shape (Diagram 2), using small amount of whipped topping to hold pieces together. Top with about 1¹/₂ cups of the whipped topping. Unmold second cake layer; cut into pieces as shown in Diagram 1. Place pieces on first layer. Use remaining whipped topping to frost entire cake.

Sprinkle trunk of tree with toasted coconut. Sprinkle remaining cake with green coconut. Decorate with gumdrops, peppermint candies and string licorice, if desired. Chill until ready to serve.

Preparation time: 30 minutes
Chill time: 3 hours

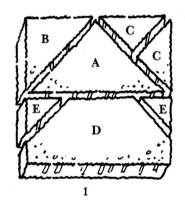

1

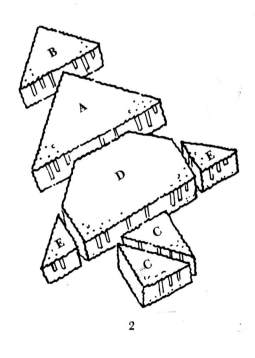

2

Christmas Tree Poke Cake

Fruitcake Bars (left), Fruitcake-in-a-Can (center), Chocolate Fruitcake (right)

Ever-so-Easy Fruitcake

Makes one 10-inch cake

2 1/2 cups unsifted flour
  1 teaspoon baking soda
  2 eggs, slightly beaten
  1 jar NONE SUCH® Ready-to-Use Mincemeat
    (Regular *or* Brandy & Rum)
  1 (14-ounce) can EAGLE® Brand Sweetened
    Condensed Milk (NOT evaporated milk)
  2 cups (1 pound) mixed candied fruit
  1 cup coarsely chopped nuts

Preheat oven to 300°F. Grease and flour 10-inch fluted tube pan. Combine flour and baking soda; set aside. In large bowl, combine remaining ingredients; blend in dry ingredients. Pour batter into prepared pan. Bake 1 hour and 45 to 50 minutes or until wooden pick comes out clean. Cool 15 minutes. Turn out of pan. Garnish as desired.

Tip: To substitute condensed mincemeat for ready-to-use mincemeat, crumble 2 (9-ounce) packages NONE SUCH® Condensed Mincemeat into small saucepan; add 1 1/2 cups water. Boil briskly 1 minute. Cool. Proceed as above.

Chocolate Fruitcake: Prepare fruitcake batter as above, adding 3 (1-ounce) squares unsweetened chocolate, melted. For glaze, melt 3 (1-ounce) squares semi-sweet chocolate with 2 tablespoons margarine or butter. Spoon over fruitcake.

Fruitcake-in-a-Can: Grease three 1-pound coffee cans; fill each can with about 2 2/3 cups batter. Bake 1 hour and 20 to 25 minutes.

Fruitcake Bars: Grease 15×10-inch jellyroll pan; spread batter evenly in pan. Bake 40 to 45 minutes. Cool. Glaze if desired. Makes about 4 dozen bars.

Lemon Cheesecake Squares

Makes 18 servings

1 1/4 cups (18 to 19) shortbread cookie crumbs
  1/3 cup ground almonds
  3 tablespoons PARKAY® Margarine, melted
  2 tablespoons sugar
  1 6-oz. container frozen lemonade concentrate,
    thawed
  3 8-oz. pkgs. PHILADELPHIA BRAND®
    Cream Cheese, softened
  1 cup sour cream
  1 3 1/2-oz. pkg. JELL-O® Brand Lemon Flavor
    Instant Pudding and Pie Filling
  2 cups COOL WHIP® Whipped Topping,
    thawed

Preheat oven to 350°F. Stir together crumbs, almonds, margarine and sugar in small bowl; press onto bottom of 13×9-inch baking pan. Bake 10 minutes. Cool. Gradually add lemonade concentrate to cream cheese in large mixing bowl, mixing at low speed with electric mixer until well blended. Add sour cream and pudding mix; beat 1 minute. Fold in whipped topping; pour over crust. Freeze until firm. Cut into squares. Garnish with fresh berries and mint, if desired.

Preparation time: 15 minutes plus freezing

Festive Eggnog Cake

Makes 16 servings

Cake
1¹/₃ cups sugar
  ¹/₂ cup **LAND O LAKES®** Sweet Cream
      Butter
  2 eggs
2¹/₂ cups all-purpose flour
  ¹/₂ cup chopped blanched almonds
1¹/₄ cups milk
  1 tablespoon baking powder
  1 teaspoon nutmeg
  ¹/₂ teaspoon rum extract

Glaze
  1 cup powdered sugar
  2 tablespoons **LAND O LAKES®** Sweet Cream
      Butter
  4 to 5 teaspoons milk
  ¹/₄ teaspoon rum extract

    Whole almonds
    Candied cherries

Heat oven to 350°F. For cake, in large mixer bowl combine sugar and butter. Beat at medium speed, scraping bowl often, until well mixed (2 to 3 minutes). Add eggs; continue beating until light and fluffy (3 to 5 minutes). Add remaining cake ingredients. Reduce to low speed; continue beating, scraping bowl often, until well mixed (2 to 3 minutes). Pour into greased and floured 10-inch fluted tube pan. Bake for 45 to 55 minutes or until wooden pick inserted near center comes out clean. Cool in pan 10 minutes. Loosen edge; remove from pan and cool completely. In small bowl combine all glaze ingredients until smooth. Drizzle over cake; garnish with whole almonds and candied cherry halves. Store tightly covered.

Heath® Bar Cheesecake

Makes 10 to 12 servings

Crust
1³/₄ cups vanilla wafer crumbs
  2 tablespoons sugar
  ¹/₃ cup margarine, melted

Filling
  3 (8 oz.) packages cream cheese, softened
  1 cup sugar
  3 eggs
  1 cup sour cream
1¹/₂ teaspoons vanilla
  5 (1.2-oz.) **HEATH®** Bars, crushed

Preheat oven to 350°F. Combine crust ingredients; press into bottom and 1¹/₂ inches up side of 9-inch springform pan. Refrigerate.

In large mixer bowl, beat cream cheese with sugar at medium speed until fluffy. Add eggs, 1 at a time, beating well after each addition. Beat in sour cream and vanilla; blend until smooth. Spoon half of the filling over prepared crust. Sprinkle half of the **HEATH®** Bars over the filling; cover with remaining filling. Bake 1 hour or until cheesecake is just firm when pan is tapped gently. Cool completely in pan on wire rack. Sprinkle remaining **HEATH®** Bars over the top. Refrigerate until chilled.

Pumpkin Jingle Bars

Makes about 3 dozen

³/₄ cup **MIRACLE WHIP®** Salad Dressing
  1 two-layer spice cake mix
  1 16-oz. can pumpkin
  3 eggs
    Confectioners' sugar
    Vanilla frosting
    Red and green gum drops, sliced

Mix first 4 ingredients in large bowl at medium speed of electric mixer until well blended. Pour into greased 15¹/₂×10¹/₂×1-inch jelly roll pan. Bake at 350°F, 18 to 20 minutes or until edges pull away from sides of pan. Cool. Sprinkle with sugar. Cut into bars. Decorate with frosting and gum drops.

Preparation time: 5 minutes
Cooking time: 20 minutes

Pumpkin Jingle Bars

Cranmallow Cheesecake

Makes 10 to 12 servings

¾ cup graham cracker crumbs
½ cup finely chopped macadamia nuts
¼ cup PARKAY® Margarine, melted
2 tablespoons sugar
1 envelope unflavored gelatin
¼ cup cold water
2 8-oz. pkgs. PHILADELPHIA BRAND®
   Cream Cheese, softened
1 7-oz. jar KRAFT® Marshmallow Creme
1 16-oz. can whole berry cranberry sauce
1 cup whipping cream, whipped

Combine crumbs, nuts, margarine and sugar; press onto bottom of 9-inch springform pan. Bake at 350°F, 10 minutes; cool. In small saucepan, soften gelatin in water; stir over low heat until dissolved. Mix cream cheese and marshmallow creme at medium speed with electric mixer until well blended. Gradually add gelatin mixture and cranberry sauce, mixing until well blended. Fold in whipped cream; pour over crust. Chill until firm. Garnish with fresh cranberries and mint sprigs, if desired.

Variation: Substitute ½ cup finely chopped walnuts for macadamia nuts.

Cranmallow Cheesecake

Gingerbread Upside-Down Cake

Makes 8 to 10 servings

1 can (20 oz.) DOLE® Pineapple Slices
½ cup margarine, softened
1 cup brown sugar, packed
10 maraschino cherries
1 egg
½ cup dark molasses
1½ cups all-purpose flour
1 teaspoon baking soda
1 teaspoon ground ginger
½ teaspoon ground cinnamon
½ teaspoon salt

Preheat oven to 350°F. Drain pineapple; reserve ½ cup syrup. In 10-inch cast iron skillet, melt ¼ cup margarine. Remove from heat. Add ½ cup brown sugar and stir until blended. Arrange pineapple slices in skillet. Place 1 cherry in center of each slice. In large mixer bowl, beat remaining ¼ cup margarine and ½ cup brown sugar until light and fluffy. Beat in egg and molasses. In small bowl, combine flour, baking soda, ginger, cinnamon and salt.

In small saucepan, bring reserved pineapple syrup to boil. Add dry ingredients to creamed mixture alternately with hot syrup. Spread evenly over pineapple in skillet. Bake in preheated oven 30 to 40 minutes or until wooden pick inserted into center comes out clean. Let stand in skillet on wire rack 5 minutes. Invert onto serving plate.

Mocha Walnut Tart

Makes one 9-inch pie

1 (9-inch) unbaked pastry shell
2 (1-ounce) squares unsweetened chocolate
¼ cup margarine or butter
1 (14-ounce) can EAGLE® Brand Sweetened
   Condensed Milk (NOT evaporated milk)
¼ cup water
2 eggs, well beaten
¼ cup coffee-flavored liqueur
1 teaspoon vanilla extract
⅛ teaspoon salt
1 cup walnuts, toasted and chopped

Preheat oven to 350°F. In medium saucepan, over low heat, melt chocolate and margarine. Stir in sweetened condensed milk, water and eggs; *mix well.* Remove from heat; stir in liqueur, vanilla and salt. Pour into pastry shell; top with walnuts. Bake 40 to 45 minutes or until center is set. Cool. Serve warm or chilled. Garnish as desired. Refrigerate leftovers.

Creole Lemon Cake

Creole Lemon Cake

Makes one 10-inch cake

2 cups butter or margarine, softened
2 cups granulated sugar
6 eggs
1/2 cup lemon juice
3 tablespoons grated lemon peel
3 3/4 cups all-purpose flour
2 teaspoons baking powder
4 cups coarsely chopped DIAMOND® Walnuts
2 1/2 cups SUN-MAID® Raisins or Golden Raisins
   Powdered sugar, for garnish

In large bowl, cream butter and granulated sugar. Add eggs, one at a time, beating well after each addition. Stir in lemon juice and peel. In another large bowl, combine remaining ingredients, except powdered sugar; gradually stir into butter mixture, mixing just until blended. Spoon batter into well-greased and floured 10-inch tube pan; let stand 10 minutes. Bake in preheated 325°F oven 1 hour and 45 minutes or until browned and pick inserted near center comes out clean. Let cool in pan on wire rack 15 minutes. Loosen edges and remove from pan. Cool completely on wire rack. Wrap; let stand a day before slicing. Before serving, dust with powdered sugar, if desired.

Note: Cake can be wrapped in brandy-soaked cheesecloth and stored in covered container in cool, dry place 1 to 2 weeks.

Chocolate Applesauce Cake

Makes about 12 servings

2 1/2 cups all-purpose flour
1/3 cup unsweetened cocoa
2 teaspoons baking soda
3/4 teaspoon salt
3/4 cup shortening
1 3/4 cups sugar
2 eggs
1 1/2 teaspoons vanilla
1 1/2 cups sweetened applesauce
1/2 cup buttermilk

In small bowl, combine flour, cocoa, baking soda and salt. In large bowl, cream shortening and sugar. Beat in eggs and vanilla. In small bowl, combine applesauce and buttermilk; mix well. Add dry ingredients to creamed mixture alternately with applesauce mixture; mix until well blended. Pour batter into greased 13×9×2-inch pan. Bake in preheated 350°F oven 35 to 40 minutes or until toothpick inserted into center comes out clean. Cool completely in pan on wire rack. Serve plain or top with your favorite frosting.

Favorite recipe from **Western New York Apple Growers Association, Inc.**

Traditional Pumpkin Pie

Traditional Pumpkin Pie

Makes one 9-inch pie

1 (9-inch) unbaked pastry shell
1 (16-ounce) can pumpkin (2 cups)
1 (14-ounce) can **EAGLE®** Brand Sweetened
     Condensed Milk (**NOT** evaporated milk)
2 eggs
1 teaspoon ground cinnamon
1/2 teaspoon ground ginger
1/2 teaspoon ground nutmeg
1/2 teaspoon salt

Place rack in lowest position in oven; preheat oven to 425°F. In large mixer bowl, combine all ingredients except pastry shell; mix well. Pour into pastry shell. Bake 15 minutes. *Reduce oven temperature to 350°F;* bake 35 to 40 minutes longer or until knife inserted near edge comes out clean. Cool. Garnish as desired. Refrigerate leftovers.

Optional Toppings

Sour Cream Topping: In medium bowl, combine 1 1/2 cups BORDEN® or MEADOW GOLD® Sour Cream, 2 tablespoons sugar and 1 teaspoon vanilla extract. After 30 minutes of baking, spread evenly over top of pie; bake 10 minutes longer. Garnish as desired.

Streusel Topping: In medium bowl, combine 1/2 cup firmly packed light brown sugar and 1/2 cup unsifted flour; cut in 1/4 cup cold margarine or butter until crumbly. Stir in 1/4 cup chopped nuts. After 30 minutes of baking, sprinkle on top of pie; bake 10 minutes longer.

Cinnamon Crisp Plum Pudding

Makes 8 to 10 servings

2 cups **KEEBLER®** Cinnamon Crisp Graham
     Cracker Crumbs (about 15 large crackers)
1 1/4 teaspoons baking soda
1/2 teaspoon salt
1/4 teaspoon ground ginger
1/4 teaspoon ground cloves
1/2 cup shortening
1/2 cup packed brown sugar
2 eggs
1/2 cup water
1 can (16 ounces) purple plums in heavy syrup,
     drained, pitted and chopped (syrup
     reserved)
1 cup golden raisins
1/2 cup chopped walnuts
  Plum Sauce (recipe follows)

Stir together Cinnamon Crisp Cracker Crumbs, baking soda, salt, ginger and cloves; set aside. Cream shortening with brown sugar until fluffy. Beat in eggs 1 at a time. Add crumb mixture alternately with water to sugar mixture, beating well after each addition. Stir in chopped plums, raisins, and walnuts. If mixture is dry, stir in more water 1 tablespoon at at time. Pour batter into well-greased 5- or 6-cup kugelhopf or Bundt® pan. Bake in preheated 375°F oven 40 to 50 minutes or until wooden pick inserted near center comes out clean. Loosen edges of plum pudding; immediately turn out of pan onto serving platter. Spoon Plum Sauce over slices of pudding.

Plum Sauce: Combine plum syrup (about 1 cup), 1/4 cup granulated sugar and 2 tablespoons cornstarch in small saucepan. Cook over medium heat, stirring constantly, until thickened, about 5 minutes. Stir in 1 tablespoon lemon juice or brandy.

Raspberry Pear Cheesecake

Makes 6 to 8 servings

1 (6½- to 8-inch diameter) prepared plain
cheesecake
1 (10-ounce) package frozen raspberries in
syrup, thawed
2 teaspoons cornstarch
3 to 4 canned pear halves, well drained
Fresh raspberries, if desired
½ ounce semi-sweet chocolate
½ teaspoon solid shortening

Combine frozen raspberries in syrup and cornstarch
in a small saucepan. Stir to dissolve cornstarch. Over
medium heat, bring to a boil and cook just until
clear and thickened, stirring constantly. Cool for 10
minutes. Spoon ⅓ cup raspberry sauce on top of
cheesecake. Cut pear halves in half lengthwise.
Arrange pears spoke-fashion on top of sauce. Garnish
with fresh raspberries, if desired. Melt chocolate with
shortening. Drizzle over pears. Cut into wedges and
serve with remaining raspberry sauce.

Canned Pears

4 pounds pears
3½ cups water
1¾ cups sugar
3 tablespoons bottled lemon juice
6 KERR® pint jars *or* 3 KERR® quart jars (with
bands and lids)

Peel, core and halve pears lengthwise. In 6- to 8-
quart saucepan, combine water, sugar and lemon
juice. Over medium-high heat, bring to a boil. Add
pears and return to a boil. Remove from heat.
Immediately fill jars with pears and syrup, leaving
½-inch headspace. Carefully run a non-metallic
utensil down inside of jars to remove trapped air
bubbles. Wipe jar tops and threads clean. Place hot
lids on jars and screw bands on firmly. Process in
Boiling Water Canner 20 minutes for pint jars, 25
minutes for quart jars. Makes 6 pints or 3 quarts.

*Notes: For smaller yield, halve ingredients. Processing times
and other directions remain the same.*

*Processing times must be increased for altitudes higher than
1000 feet. For altitudes between 1001-3000 feet add 5
minutes; 3001-6000 feet add 10 minutes; 6001-8000 feet add
15 minutes; 8001-10,000 feet add 20 minutes.*

Raspberry Pear Cheesecake

French Silk Mint Pie

Makes 1 pie

1 KEEBLER® Chocolate-flavored Ready Crust
    pie crust
2 cups powdered sugar, sifted
1/2 lb. unsalted butter, softened
4 eggs*
4 (1-ounce) squares unsweetened chocolate,
    melted and cooled
1/4 teaspoon mint extract
1/4 teaspoon vanilla extract
    Fresh mint and maraschino cherries, for
    garnish

Beat sugar with butter in large bowl until smooth.
Add eggs, 1 at a time, beating well after each
addition. Add melted chocolate; stir in extracts. Mix
well; pour into crumb crust. Refrigerate until firm.
Just before serving, garnish with mint and cherries.
Cut into small pieces.

Use clean, uncracked eggs.

French Silk Mint Pie

Winterfruit Cobbler

Makes 6 servings

Filling
  2 cups SUN-MAID® Raisins
  2 cups fresh or frozen cranberries
3/4 cup sugar
  2 teaspoons cornstarch
1/2 teaspoon ground allspice
  1 cup orange juice

Topping
  1 cup all-purpose flour
  2 tablespoons sugar
  2 teaspoons baking powder
1/4 teaspoon salt
1/4 cup butter or margarine
1/2 cup milk
    Sugar
    Ground cinnamon

To prepare Filling: In medium saucepan, combine
raisins, cranberries, sugar, cornstarch and allspice.
Gradually stir in orange juice. Bring to boil over high
heat; reduce heat to low and simmer, stirring until
cranberries begin to pop and mixture thickens
slightly. Pour into shallow 1 1/2-quart baking dish.

To prepare Topping: In small bowl, combine flour,
sugar, baking powder and salt. Cut in butter until
mixture resembles coarse meal. Mix in milk lightly
with fork. Drop spoonfuls of batter over filling;
sprinkle lightly with additional sugar mixed with a
little cinnamon. Bake in preheated 400°F oven about
25 minutes or until golden. Serve warm with ice
cream or whipping cream.

Pumpkin Orange Cheesecake

Makes one 9-inch cheesecake

1 1/2 cups gingersnap cookie crumbs (32 cookies)
1/4 cup margarine or butter, melted
  3 (8-ounce) packages cream cheese, softened
  1 (14-ounce) can EAGLE® Brand Sweetened
    Condensed Milk (NOT evaporated milk)
  1 (16-ounce) can pumpkin (2 cups)
  2 eggs
  3 tablespoons orange-flavored liqueur *or* orange
    juice
  1 teaspoon pumpkin pie spice
1/4 teaspoon salt
    Whipped topping or whipped cream

Preheat oven to 300°F. Combine crumbs and margarine. Press firmly on bottom and halfway up side of 9-inch springform pan. In large mixer bowl, beat cheese until fluffy. Gradually beat in sweetened condensed milk until smooth. Add remaining ingredients except whipped topping; mix well. Pour into prepared pan. Bake 1 hour and 15 minutes or until cake springs back when lightly touched (center will be slightly soft). Cool to room temperature. Chill. Serve with whipped topping. Garnish as desired. Refrigerate leftovers.

Plum Pudding Pie (top), Pumpkin & Cream Cheese Tart with Cranberry-Orange Topping (bottom)

Pumpkin & Cream Cheese Tart with Cranberry-Orange Topping

Makes 10 to 12 servings

   Pie crust mix for single 9-inch crust
   4 packages (3 ounces each) cream cheese, softened
³/₄ cup packed brown sugar
   2 eggs
   1 teaspoon ground cinnamon
¹/₄ teaspoon ground nutmeg
   1 teaspoon grated orange peel
   1 can (16 ounces) solid pack pumpkin
   1 can (16 ounces) OCEAN SPRAY® Whole Berry Cranberry Sauce
   Glazed Orange Slices (recipe follows)

Prepare pie crust mix according to package directions. Press dough onto bottom and 1¹/₂ inches up side of ungreased 9-inch springform pan; set aside. In large bowl, beat cream cheese and sugar until light and fluffy. Beat in eggs, 1 at a time. Stir in cinnamon, nutmeg, orange peel and pumpkin until smooth and well blended. Pour into pastry-lined pan; spread evenly. Place in preheated 425°F oven; *immediately reduce oven temperature to 350°F.* Bake 35 minutes or until center is almost set. Cool completely in pan on wire rack. Spread whole berry cranberry sauce on top. Arrange Glazed Orange Slices in overlapping ring on top of cranberry sauce. Refrigerate until serving time. Remove side of springform pan before serving.

Glazed Orange Slices: In medium skillet, combine 1 cup granulated sugar and ¹/₄ cup water. Bring to a boil over medium heat; boil 1 minute. Add 12 thin orange slices. Cook over low heat, turning frequently, 5 minutes or until slices are almost translucent.

Plum Pudding Pie

Makes 8 servings

¹/₃ cup plus 2 tablespoons KAHLÚA®
¹/₂ cup golden raisins
¹/₂ cup chopped pitted dates
¹/₃ cup chopped candied cherries
¹/₂ cup chopped walnuts
¹/₃ cup dark corn syrup
¹/₂ teaspoon pumpkin pie spice
¹/₄ cup butter or margarine, softened
¹/₄ cup packed brown sugar
   2 tablespoons all-purpose flour
¹/₄ teaspoon salt
   2 eggs, slightly beaten
   1 (9-inch) unbaked pie shell
   1 cup whipping cream
   Maraschino cherries (optional)

In medium bowl, combine ¹/₃ cup of the KAHLÚA®, the raisins, dates and cherries; mix well. Cover; let stand 1 to 4 hours. Stir in walnuts, corn syrup and spice. In large bowl, cream butter, sugar, flour and salt. Stir in eggs. Add fruit mixture; blend well. Pour into unbaked pie shell. Bake in preheated 350°F oven 35 minutes or until filling is firm and crust is golden. Cool completely on wire rack. When ready to serve, in small bowl, beat whipping cream with remaining 2 tablespoons KAHLÚA® just until soft peaks form. Spoon cream into pastry bag fitted with large star tip and pipe decoratively on top. If desired, garnish with maraschino cherries.

Acknowledgments

*The publishers would like to thank the companies
and organizations listed below for the use
of their recipes in this book.*

American Egg Board
Blue Diamond Growers
Borden, Inc.
Campbell Soup Company
Checkerboard Kitchens, Ralston Purina
   Company
Chef Paul Prudhomme's Magic Seasoning
   Blends™
Del Monte Corporation
Dole Packaged Foods Company
Domino® Sugars
Durkee-French Foods, A Division of Reckitt
   & Colman Inc.
Heinz U.S.A.
Hellmann's® Mayonnaise
The J. M. Smucker Company
Keebler Company
Kellogg Company
Kerr Corporation
Kikkoman International Inc.

Knorr® Soup and Recipe Mix
Kraft General Foods, Inc.
Land O' Lakes, Inc.
Lawry's Foods, Inc.
Maidstone Wine & Spirits, Inc.
McIlhenny Company
National Pork Producers Council
National Turkey Federation
Norseland Foods, Inc.
Ocean Spray Cranberries, Inc.
The Procter & Gamble Company, Inc.
The Quaker Oats Company
Refined Sugars Incorporated
StarKist Seafood Company
Sun-Diamond Growers of California
Swift-Eckrich, Inc.
Thomas J. Lipton, Inc.
Western New York Apple Growers
   Association, Inc.
Wisconsin Milk Marketing Board

Photo Credits

*The publishers would like to thank the companies
and organizations listed below for the use
of their photographs in this book.*

Blue Diamond Growers
Borden, Inc.
Campbell Soup Company
Checkerboard Kitchens, Ralston Purina
   Company
Del Monte Corporation
Dole Packaged Foods Company
Heinz U.S.A.
Hellmann's® Mayonnaise
Keebler Company
Kellogg Company
Kerr Corporation

Kikkoman International Inc.
Knorr® Soup and Recipe Mix
Kraft General Foods, Inc.
Land O' Lakes, Inc.
Lawry's Foods, Inc.
Maidstone Wine & Spirits, Inc.
The Procter & Gamble Company, Inc.
StarKist Seafood Company
Sun-Diamond Growers of California
Swift-Eckrich, Inc.
Thomas J. Lipton, Inc.

Index

Treasury of Christmas Recipes

From Your Favorite Brand Name Companies

ALL NEW

PUBLICATIONS INTERNATIONAL, LTD.

Cover photography by Sacco Productions, Ltd./Chicago
Photography: Laurie Proffitt
Photo Stylist: Betty Karslake
Food Stylist: Lois Hlavac, Assistant: Moisette Sintov-McNerney

8   7   6   5   4   3   2   1
ISBN: 1-56173-302-4
Library of Congress Catalog Card Number: 91-61593

Pictured on the front cover (*clockwise from bottom left*): Warm Vegetable Seafood Dip (*page 15*), Eggnog Cheesecake (*page 76*), Peppermint Stick Punch (*page 11*), Honey Glazed Ham (*page 56*), Fudge Rum Balls (*page 70*), Stained Glass Cookies (*page 68*) and Gingerbread Men (*page 67*).

Pictured on the back cover (*from top to bottom*): Christmas Tree Cake (*page 84*), Turkey Breast with Southwestern Corn Bread Dressing (*page 59*), Decorator White Icing (*page 73*) and Hot 'n' Honeyed Chicken Wings (*page 4*).

Microwave ovens vary in wattage and power output; cooking times given with microwave directions in this book may need to be adjusted.

Contents

Hot 'n' Honeyed Chicken Wings

Makes about 34 appetizers

　3 pounds chicken wings
　¾ cup PACE® Picante Sauce
　⅔ cup honey
　⅓ cup soy sauce
　¼ cup Dijon-style mustard
　3 tablespoons vegetable oil
　2 tablespoons grated fresh ginger
　½ teaspoon grated orange peel
　　Additional PACE® Picante Sauce

Cut off and discard wing tips; cut each wing in half at joint. Place in 13×9-inch baking dish. Combine ¾ cup picante sauce, honey, soy sauce, mustard, oil, ginger and orange peel in small bowl; mix well. Pour over chicken wings. Cover and refrigerate at least 6 hours or overnight.

Preheat oven to 400°F. Place chicken wings and sauce in single layer on foil-lined 15×10-inch jelly-roll pan. Bake 40 to 45 minutes or until brown. Serve warm with additional picante sauce. Garnish as desired.

Citrus Berry Frost

Makes about 8 servings

　4 scoops or ¾ cup WYLER'S® Sugar
　　Sweetened Lemonade Flavor Crystals
　4 cups cranberry juice cocktail, chilled
　4 cups water
　1 cup chilled orange juice

In large pitcher, combine all ingredients. Serve over ice and garnish, if desired, with cranberries and orange slices.

Gingered Turkey Meatballs

Makes about 34 appetizers

　1 pound ground raw turkey
　½ cup gingersnap crumbs
　¼ cup finely chopped onion
　2 tablespoons soy sauce, divided
　½ teaspoon curry powder
　⅛ teaspoon pepper
　2 tablespoons vegetable oil
　1 can (10½ ounces) FRANCO-AMERICAN®
　　chicken gravy
　1 tablespoon brown sugar
　½ teaspoon grated fresh ginger

1. In medium bowl, thoroughly mix turkey, gingersnap crumbs, onion, *1 tablespoon* of the soy sauce, the curry and pepper. Shape into 1-inch meatballs.

2. In 10-inch skillet over medium heat, heat oil until hot. Cook meatballs, a few at a time, until browned on all sides. Remove meatballs as they brown. Spoon off fat. Return all meatballs to skillet.

3. Stir in gravy, sugar, ginger and remaining soy sauce. Heat to boiling. Reduce heat to low. Cover; simmer 20 minutes or until meatballs are done, stirring occasionally. Pour into serving bowl; serve with decorative toothpicks.

Hot 'n' Honeyed Chicken Wings

Hot Spiced Cider

Hot and Sweet Pepper Relish

Makes 3 cups

> 4 cups chopped red peppers (about 3 large)
> 1/3 cup seeded, chopped jalapeño peppers, fresh or pickled*
> 2 teaspoons salt
> 1 1/3 cups cider vinegar
> 1 cup finely chopped onion
> 1 cup sugar
> 2/3 cup KARO® Light Corn Syrup

In large glass or stainless steel bowl combine peppers and salt. Let stand 3 hours, stirring occasionally. In medium saucepan combine pepper mixture and any liquid with vinegar, onion, sugar and corn syrup. Bring to boil over medium-high heat. Reduce heat to maintain moderate boil. Cook uncovered, stirring occasionally, until peppers are translucent and syrup thickens, about 1 hour. Cover; refrigerate.

Preparation Time: 1 hour, 15 minutes, plus standing

Wear rubber gloves when working with hot peppers or wash hands in warm soapy water after handling. Avoid touching face or eyes.

Bloody Mary Mix

Makes about 1 quart

> 1 quart vegetable juice cocktail
> 2 tablespoons HEINZ Worcestershire Sauce
> 1 tablespoon fresh lime or lemon juice
> 1/4 teaspoon granulated sugar
> 1/4 teaspoon pepper
> 1/4 teaspoon hot pepper sauce
> 1/8 teaspoon garlic powder

In pitcher, thoroughly combine vegetable juice, Worcestershire sauce, lime juice, sugar, pepper, hot pepper sauce and garlic powder; cover and chill. Serve over ice. Garnish with celery stalks and lime wedges, if desired.

Note: To prepare Bloody Mary Cocktail, add 3 or 4 parts Bloody Mary Mix to 1 part vodka.

Hot Spiced Cider

Makes about 10 servings

> 2 quarts apple cider
> 2/3 cup KARO® Light or Dark Corn Syrup
> 3 cinnamon sticks
> 1/2 teaspoon whole cloves
> 1 lemon, sliced
> Cinnamon sticks and lemon slices (optional)

In medium saucepan combine cider, corn syrup, cinnamon sticks, cloves and lemon slices. Bring to boil over medium-high heat. Reduce heat; simmer 15 minutes. Remove spices. If desired, garnish each serving with a cinnamon stick and lemon slice.

Preparation Time: 20 minutes

Bacon and Two Onion Cheesecake

Makes 10 appetizer servings

- 6 slices bacon, diced
- 1 large sweet onion, chopped
- 1 clove garlic, minced
- 1 container (15 oz.) SARGENTO® Light Ricotta Cheese
- 1/2 cup half-and-half
- 2 tablespoons flour
- 1/2 teaspoon salt
- 1/4 teaspoon cayenne pepper
- 2 eggs
- 1/2 cup thinly sliced green onions

In 10-inch skillet, cook bacon until crisp; remove to paper towels with slotted spoon. Cook onion and garlic in drippings until tender, about 6 minutes. Drain in strainer; discard bacon drippings. In bowl of electric mixer, combine ricotta cheese, half-and-half, flour, salt and pepper; blend until smooth. Add eggs, one at a time; blend until smooth. Reserve 3 tablespoons of the bacon for garnish. Stir remaining bacon, cooked onion mixture and green onions into ricotta mixture. Lightly grease sides of 8- or 9-inch springform pan; pour batter into pan. Bake at 350°F 40 minutes or until center is just set. Remove to wire cooling rack; cool to room temperature. Garnish with reserved bacon; serve with assorted crackers.

Savory Pepper-Herb Cheesecake

Makes 10 appetizer servings

CRUST:
- 1 1/4 cups fresh dark rye or pumpernickel breadcrumbs (about 2 slices, processed in blender or food processor)
- 3 tablespoons melted margarine

FILLING:
- 1 container (15 oz.) SARGENTO® Light Ricotta Cheese
- 1/2 cup half-and-half
- 2 tablespoons flour
- 2 eggs
- 1/3 cup chopped mixed fresh herbs (such as parsley, basil, mint, tarragon, rosemary, thyme and oregano)
- 1/4 cup chopped fresh chives or green onion tops
- 1 1/2 teaspoons finely grated lemon peel
- 1/2 teaspoon cracked black pepper
- 3/4 teaspoon salt

Lightly grease sides of 8- or 9-inch springform pan. Combine crust ingredients; press evenly over bottom of pan. Chill while preparing filling. In bowl of electric mixer, combine ricotta cheese, half-and-half and flour; blend until smooth. Add eggs, one at a time; blend until smooth. Blend in fresh herbs, chives, lemon peel, pepper and salt. Pour into crust; bake at 350°F 30 to 35 minutes or until center is just set. Remove to wire cooling rack; cool to room temperature.

Bacon and Two Onion Cheesecake (left) and Savory Pepper-Herb Cheesecake (right)

Beef with Walnuts and Kiwi

Beef with Walnuts and Kiwi

Makes 12 appetizer servings

  4 ounces sliced rare roast beef, cut into
     12 uniform pieces
  ¼ cup finely chopped walnuts, toasted
  1 tablespoon *each* fresh lemon juice, olive
     oil, wine vinegar and snipped dill
  1 small clove garlic, crushed
  ¼ teaspoon freshly ground black pepper
     Dash salt
  12 slices French bread, ¼ inch thick
  2 kiwi, peeled, cut into 12 slices
     Pimiento

Place roast beef slices in glass dish; sprinkle with walnuts. Combine lemon juice, oil, vinegar, dill, garlic, pepper and salt. Pour over beef and walnuts, lifting meat to coat. Cover and marinate 30 minutes. Drain marinade. To assemble, arrange one piece beef with walnuts onto bread round. Top with kiwi slice; garnish with pimiento.

Preparation/Marinating time: 40 minutes

Assembling time: 10 minutes

Favorite recipe from **National Live Stock and Meat Board**

Wisconsin Spicy Apple Eggnog

Makes 12 servings

  2 beaten eggs
  3 cups milk
  2 cups light cream or half-and-half
  ⅓ cup sugar
  ½ teaspoon ground cinnamon
     Dash salt
  ¾ cup apple brandy
     Ground nutmeg

In a large saucepan combine beaten eggs, milk, light cream or half-and-half, sugar, cinnamon and salt. Cook and stir over medium heat till mixture is slightly thickened and heated through, but *do not boil.* Remove from heat; stir in apple brandy. To serve, ladle mixture into 12 heat-proof glasses or cups. Sprinkle each serving with nutmeg. Serve warm.

Preparation Time: 25 minutes

Favorite recipe from **Wisconsin Milk Marketing Board** ©1991

Holiday Crab Spread

Makes 12 appetizer servings

  1 envelope plain gelatin
  ¼ cup cold water
  1 cup clam juice, heated to boiling
  1 cup mayonnaise
  2 tablespoons Dijon-style mustard
  ½ teaspoon salt
  ½ teaspoon TABASCO® Pepper Sauce
  1 can (6½ ounces) white crabmeat, drained
  ½ cup pared, seeded and chopped
     cucumber
  ½ cup chopped red pepper
  ½ cup chopped yellow pepper
  ½ cup chopped scallions
  ¾ cup heavy cream, whipped

In medium bowl mix gelatin with water; let stand 1 minute. Pour boiling clam juice over gelatin and stir until completely dissolved. In small bowl mix mayonnaise, mustard, salt and TABASCO® sauce; stir into gelatin mixture. Chill until the consistency of unbeaten egg whites. Stir in crabmeat, cucumber, red and yellow peppers and scallions. Fold in whipped cream. Turn mixture into a lightly oiled 4-cup mold. Chill until firm, at least 4 hours. Flavors will blend if refrigerated overnight. Unmold and serve with crackers.

Hot Artichoke Spread

Hot Artichoke Spread

Makes 2 cups

1 cup MIRACLE WHIP® Salad Dressing
**1 cup (4 oz.) KRAFT® 100% Grated
   Parmesan Cheese**
**1 (14 oz.) can artichoke hearts, drained,
   chopped**
**1 (4 oz.) can chopped green chilies,
   drained**
1 garlic clove, minced
2 tablespoons green onion slices
2 tablespoons chopped tomato

• Preheat oven to 350°F.

• Mix together all ingredients except onions and tomatoes until well blended.

• Spoon into shallow ovenproof dish or 9-inch pie plate.

• Bake 20 to 25 minutes or until lightly browned. Sprinkle with onions and tomatoes. Serve with toasted bread cutouts.

Prep time: 10 minutes

Cooking time: 20 minutes

Chili Go Rounds

Makes about 4 dozen appetizers

**1 cup finely chopped fully-cooked smoked
   sausage**
2 tablespoons HEINZ Chili Sauce
1 tablespoon grated Parmesan cheese
1/4 teaspoon ground cinnamon
1/4 teaspoon dried thyme leaves, crushed
**1 package (8 ounces) refrigerated crescent
   dinner rolls**

In small bowl, combine sausage, chili sauce, Parmesan cheese, cinnamon and thyme. Remove half of dough from container; unroll. Place dough between 2 pieces of waxed paper and roll into 13×5×1/8-inch rectangle. Spread 1/2 of sausage mixture over dough. Roll, jelly-roll fashion, starting at longest side. Cut into 1/2-inch slices with sharp knife; place cut-side down on baking sheet. Repeat with remaining dough and sausage mixture. Bake in preheated 375°F oven, 12 to 14 minutes or until golden brown.

Smoked Turkey Roll-Ups

Smoked Turkey Roll-Ups

Makes 56 appetizer servings

> 2 packages (4 ounces *each*) herb-flavored soft spreadable cheese
> 4 flour (8-inch diameter) tortillas*
> 2 packages (6 ounces *each*) smoked turkey breast slices
> 2 green onions, sliced lengthwise into quarters
> Whole, pickled red cherry peppers (optional)

1. Divide one package of cheese equally and spread over each tortilla. Divide turkey slices equally and layer over cheese, overlapping turkey slices slightly to cover tortilla. Divide remaining package of cheese equally and spread over the turkey slices.

2. At one edge of each tortilla, place 2 quarters of green onion. Roll up tortillas, jelly-roll style. Place turkey tortilla rolls, seam-side down, in self-closing plastic bag; refrigerate several hours or overnight.

3. To serve, cut each turkey tortilla roll-up crosswise into ¹/₂-inch slices to form pinwheels. If desired, arrange pinwheels on serving plate and garnish with cherry peppers in center.

To keep flour tortillas soft while preparing the turkey rolls, cover with a slightly damp cloth.

Favorite recipe from **National Turkey Federation**

Sausage-Stuffed Mushrooms

Makes 24 appetizer servings

> 1 pound bulk pork sausage
> 1 pound fresh mushrooms
> 1 clove garlic, minced
> 2 tablespoons chopped parsley
> 1¹/₂ cups (6 ounces) shredded Cheddar cheese
> Chopped pimiento (optional)
> Fresh snipped parsley (optional)

Rinse mushrooms and pat dry; remove and chop stems. Combine stems, sausage, garlic and chopped parsley in a medium skillet; cook until sausage is browned, stirring often. Drain pan drippings. Stir in cheese, mixing well.

Fill mushroom caps with sausage mixture. Place in a 13×9×2-inch baking dish. Bake at 350°F for 20 minutes. Garnish with pimiento and snipped parsley, if desired.

Preparation Time: 20 minutes

Cooking Time: 20 minutes

Favorite recipe from **National Pork Producers Council**

Herb Cheesecake

Makes 16 appetizer servings

3 packages (8 ounces *each*) cream cheese, softened
2 cups sour cream, divided
1 can (10¾ ounces) CAMPBELL'S® condensed cream of celery or cream of asparagus soup
3 eggs
½ cup grated Romano or Asiago cheese
2 cloves garlic, minced
1 tablespoon cornstarch
2 tablespoons finely chopped fresh basil leaves *or* 2 teaspoons dried basil leaves, crushed
1 tablespoon finely chopped thyme leaves *or* 1 teaspoon dried thyme leaves, crushed
1 teaspoon finely chopped fresh tarragon leaves *or* ¼ teaspoon dried tarragon leaves, crushed
½ teaspoon cracked pepper
Sweet red pepper strips, lemon peel twists and assorted fresh herbs for garnish
Crackers, melba toast *or* fresh cut-up vegetables

1. Preheat oven to 350°F. Grease side and bottom of 9-inch springform pan.

2. In covered food processor* or large mixer bowl, combine cream cheese, *1 cup* of the sour cream and the soup. Blend in food processor or beat with mixer at medium speed until smooth. Add eggs, Romano cheese, garlic, cornstarch, basil, thyme, tarragon and pepper. Blend or beat until smooth. Turn into prepared springform pan; place on jelly-roll pan.

3. Bake 1 hour or until light brown (top may crack). Turn off oven; let stand in oven 30 minutes more. Cool in pan on wire rack. Cover; refrigerate until serving time, at least 4 hours or overnight.

4. Carefully remove from pan. Spread remaining sour cream over cheesecake. Garnish with red pepper strips, lemon peel twists and fresh herbs, if desired. Serve with crackers.

*Quantity of mixture requires an 8-cup capacity food processor.

Peppermint Stick Punch

Makes about 2½ quarts

1½ cups sugar
1½ cups REALIME® Lime Juice from Concentrate
1 cup vodka or water
2 tablespoons white creme de menthe *or* ⅛ teaspoon peppermint extract
2 (32-ounce) bottles club soda, chilled
Candy canes

In punch bowl, combine all ingredients except club soda and candy canes; stir until sugar dissolves. Just before serving, add club soda. Hang candy canes on edge of punch bowl or place in each punch cup for stirrer.

Peppermint Stick Punch

Polenta Triangles

Polenta Triangles

Makes about 30 appetizers

- 1 cup coarse yellow cornmeal
- 1 envelope LIPTON® Onion or Golden Onion Recipe Soup Mix
- 3 cups cold water
- 1 can (4 oz.) mild chopped green chilies, drained
- ½ cup whole kernel corn
- ⅓ cup finely chopped roasted red peppers
- ½ cup shredded sharp Cheddar cheese (about 2 oz.)

In 3-quart microwave-safe casserole, combine cornmeal, onion recipe soup mix and water. Microwave covered at HIGH (Full Power) 20 minutes, stirring every 5 minutes (mixture will be thick). Stir in chilies, corn and roasted red peppers. Spread into lightly greased 9-inch square baking pan; sprinkle with cheese. Let stand 20 minutes or until firm; cut into triangles. Serve at room temperature or microwave at HIGH 30 seconds or until warm.

Conventional Directions: In 3-quart saucepan, bring 3 cups water to a boil. With wire whisk, stir in cornmeal, then onion recipe soup mix. Simmer uncovered, stirring constantly, 25 minutes or until thickened. Stir in chilies, corn and roasted red peppers. Spread into pan and proceed as above. Serve at room temperature or heat in oven at 350°F for 5 minutes or until warm.

Taco Dip

Makes 10 appetizer servings

- 12 ounces cream cheese, softened
- ½ cup dairy sour cream
- 2 teaspoons chili powder
- 1½ teaspoons ground cumin
- ⅛ teaspoon ground red pepper
- ½ cup salsa
- 2 cups shredded lettuce or lettuce leaves
- 1 cup (4 ounces) shredded Wisconsin Cheddar cheese
- 1 cup (4 ounces) shredded Wisconsin Monterey Jack cheese
- ½ cup diced plum tomatoes
- ⅓ cup sliced green onions
- ¼ cup sliced ripe olives
- ¼ cup pimiento-stuffed green olives
  Tortilla chips and blue corn chips

Combine cream cheese, sour cream, chili powder, cumin and red pepper in large bowl; mix until well blended. Stir in salsa. Spread onto 10-inch serving platter lined with lettuce. Top with cheeses, tomatoes, green onions and olives. Serve with chips.

Favorite recipe from **Wisconsin Milk Marketing Board** ©1991

Hot "White Chocolate"

Makes four 1-cup servings

- 1 quart milk
- 1 cup NESTLÉ® Toll House® Treasures® Premier White deluxe baking pieces, chopped and divided
- ¼ cup almond-flavored liqueur
- ½ cup heavy or whipping cream, whipped
- 4 cinnamon sticks, for garnish

In 2-quart saucepan, combine milk and ⅔ cup Treasures® Premier White deluxe baking pieces. Stir over medium heat until baking pieces are melted and mixture is hot but *not boiling*. Remove from heat; stir in liqueur.

Pour into 4 heatproof mugs. Top with whipped cream and sprinkle with remaining chopped baking pieces. Garnish with cinnamon sticks.

Taco Dip

Cranberry Orange Punch

Cranberry Orange Punch

Makes about 3 1/2 quarts

  2 (32-ounce) bottles cranberry juice
    cocktail, chilled
1 1/2 cups REALEMON® Lemon Juice from
    Concentrate
  2/3 cup sugar
  2 (12-ounce) cans orange soda, chilled
    Ice

In large punch bowl, combine cranberry juice,
REALEMON® brand and sugar; stir until sugar
dissolves. Just before serving, add orange soda and
ice. Garnish as desired.

Hot Buttered
Pineapple Smoothie

Makes 1 1/2 quarts

5 1/2 cups DOLE® Pineapple Juice
  1/4 cup brown sugar, packed
  2 tablespoons butter or margarine
 10 whole cloves
  3 cinnamon sticks
  1 DOLE® Lemon, sliced

In large saucepan, combine pineapple juice, brown
sugar, butter, cloves and cinnamon sticks. Bring to
a boil; simmer 5 minutes. Remove spices. Add
lemon slices. Serve hot in mugs.

Hot Apple 'N Spice Lemonade

Makes about 6 servings

  4 scoops or 3/4 cup WYLER'S® Sugar
    Sweetened Lemonade Flavor Crystals
  3 cups apple juice
  3 cups water
  3 cinnamon sticks
  6 whole cloves

In 2-quart saucepan, combine all ingredients.
Simmer 10 minutes or until heated through.
Remove spices. Serve in mugs and garnish, if
desired, with apple slices.

Cheesy Sun Crisps

Makes 4 to 5 dozen crackers

  2 cups (8 ounces) shredded Cheddar cheese
  1/2 cup grated Parmesan cheese
  1/2 cup sunflower oil margarine, softened
  3 tablespoons water
  1 cup all-purpose flour
  1/4 teaspoon salt (optional)
  1 cup uncooked quick oats
  2/3 cup roasted, salted sunflower kernels

Beat cheeses, margarine and water in large bowl
until well blended. Add flour and salt; mix well.
Stir in oats and sunflower kernels; mix until well
combined. Shape dough into 12-inch-long roll;
wrap securely. Refrigerate about 4 hours (dough
may be stored up to 1 week in refrigerator).

Preheat oven to 400°F. Lightly grease cookie
sheets. Cut roll into 1/8- to 1/4-inch slices; flatten
each slice slightly. Place on prepared cookie
sheets. Bake 8 to 10 minutes or until edges are
light golden brown. Remove immediately; cool on
wire rack.

Favorite recipe from **National Sunflower Association**

Cheesy Sun Crisps

Warm Vegetable Seafood Dip (left) and Holiday Chestnut Spread (right)

Warm Vegetable Seafood Dip

Makes about 2 cups

- **1 envelope LIPTON® Vegetable Recipe Soup Mix**
- **1 container (15 oz.) ricotta cheese**
- **6 ounces imitation crabmeat, cooked shrimp or frozen crabmeat, thawed**
- **1 package (3 oz.) cream cheese, softened**
- **1 teaspoon lemon juice**
- **Suggested Dippers***

Preheat oven to 325°F.

In 1-quart casserole, thoroughly combine all ingredients. Bake 20 minutes or until heated through. Serve with Suggested Dippers.

*Suggested Dippers: Use assorted crackers, vegetables, bread sticks, pita bread or chips.

Microwave Directions: In 1-quart microwave-safe casserole, thoroughly combine vegetable recipe soup mix, ricotta cheese, cream cheese and lemon juice. Microwave uncovered at MEDIUM (50% Power) 3 minutes, stirring twice. Stir in crabmeat. Microwave uncovered at MEDIUM 3 minutes or until heated through, stirring once. Serve as above.

Holiday Chestnut Spread

Makes about 2 cups

- **1 envelope LIPTON® Vegetable Recipe Soup Mix**
- **1 container (15 oz.) ricotta cheese**
- **1 package (3 oz.) cream cheese, softened**
- **1 tablespoon light rum (optional)**
- **1 cup jarred or canned roasted whole chestnuts**
- **Suggested Dippers***

Preheat oven to 325°F.

In food processor, combine vegetable recipe soup mix, cheeses and rum until smooth. Add chestnuts and process until just blended, about 10 seconds. (Do not overprocess chestnuts.) Turn into 1-quart casserole and bake 20 minutes or until warm. Serve with Suggested Dippers.

*Suggested Dippers: Use breadsticks, sliced apples or assorted crackers.

Microwave Directions: In food processor, process as above. Turn into 1-quart microwave-safe casserole. Microwave uncovered at MEDIUM (50% Power) 6 minutes or until heated through, stirring every 2 minutes. Serve as above.

Zesty Shrimp Dip (top left), Layered Crab Spread (top right) and Deviled Clam Mushrooms (bottom)

Zesty Shrimp Dip

Makes about 2 cups

- ¼ cup mayonnaise or salad dressing
- 1 (8-ounce) container BORDEN® or MEADOW GOLD® Sour Cream
- ¼ cup BENNETT'S® Cocktail Sauce
- 1 (4¼-ounce) can ORLEANS® Shrimp, drained and soaked as label directs
- 2 tablespoons sliced green onion
- 1 teaspoon REALEMON® Lemon Juice from Concentrate

In small bowl, combine ingredients; mix well. Chill. Serve with assorted fresh vegetables or potato chips. Refrigerate leftovers.

Layered Crab Spread

Makes 12 appetizer servings

- 2 (8-ounce) packages cream cheese, softened
- 2 tablespoons REALEMON® Lemon Juice from Concentrate
- 1 teaspoon Worcestershire sauce
- ¼ teaspoon garlic powder
- 2 tablespoons finely chopped green onion
- ¾ cup BENNETT'S® Chili Sauce
- 1 (6-ounce) can HARRIS® Crab Meat, drained

In large mixer bowl, beat cheese, REALEMON® brand, Worcestershire and garlic powder until fluffy; stir in onion. On serving plate, spread cheese mixture into 6-inch circle. Top with chili sauce then crabmeat. Cover; chill. Serve with crackers. Refrigerate leftovers.

Deviled Clam Mushrooms

Makes 12 appetizers

- 12 **large mushrooms**
  Melted margarine or butter
- 1 **clove garlic, finely chopped**
- 2 **tablespoons margarine or butter**
- 1 **tablespoon flour**
- 1 **(6½-ounce) can SNOW'S® or DOXSEE®**
  Minced Clams, drained, reserving
  2 tablespoons liquid
- 1 **cup fresh bread crumbs (2 slices)**
- 1 **tablespoon chopped parsley**
- 2 **teaspoons Worcestershire sauce**
- ½ **teaspoon dry mustard**

Preheat oven to 400°F. Remove and finely chop mushroom stems; set aside. Brush caps with melted margarine. In medium skillet, cook garlic in *2 tablespoons* margarine until tender. Stir in flour. Add chopped mushroom stems and remaining ingredients except mushroom caps; mix well. Mound into mushroom caps; place in shallow baking pan. Bake 8 to 10 minutes or until hot. Refrigerate leftovers.

Microwave: In 1-quart glass measure, combine garlic and margarine. Cook on 100% power (high) 1 to 1½ minutes or until garlic is tender. Stir in flour then chopped mushroom stems and remaining ingredients except mushroom caps; mix well. Mound into mushroom caps; arrange on microwave-safe plate. Cook on 100% power (high) 5 to 6 minutes, rotating plate once.

Greek-Style Sausage Roll

Makes 16 appetizer servings

- 1 **pound bulk sausage**
- ¼ **cup finely chopped onion**
- 1 **10-ounce package frozen chopped**
  spinach, thawed and drained
- ¼ **pound feta cheese, crumbled**
- ¼ **cup finely chopped parsley**
- ⅛ **teaspoon white pepper**
- 1 **egg, beaten**
- 10 **sheets frozen phyllo dough**
  (17×13-inch rectangles), thawed
- ½ **cup butter or margarine, melted**

In a large skillet, cook sausage and onion over medium-high heat till sausage is done and onion is tender, stirring occasionally. Drain. Stir in spinach, feta cheese, parsley, white pepper and egg. Set aside.

Preheat oven to 350°F. Unfold the phyllo dough. Spread 1 sheet flat; top with another sheet of phyllo. Gently brush with some of the melted butter. Top with the remaining sheets of phyllo, brushing each with butter. Reserve 1 tablespoon butter for top of pastry.

Spread sausage-spinach mixture lengthwise over bottom third of layered phyllo dough to within 2 inches of ends. Fold ends over. Carefully roll up the phyllo. Place the roll, seam-side down, on a lightly greased baking sheet; brush with the 1 tablespoon butter. Bake in a 350°F oven for 30 to 35 minutes or till golden.

Preparation Time: 30 minutes

Cooking Time: 30 minutes

Favorite recipe from **National Pork Producers Council**

Lemon Fruit Splash

Makes about 2 quarts

- 4 **scoops or ¾ cup WYLER'S® Sugar**
  Sweetened Lemonade Flavor Crystals
- 1 **orange, sliced**
- 1 **quart cold water**
- 2 **tablespoons grenadine syrup**
- 1 **liter club soda, chilled**
- 1 **apple, sliced**

In large punch bowl or pitcher, combine lemonade flavor crystals with orange slices. Stir in cold water and grenadine; chill at least 2 hours. To serve, add remaining ingredients and, if desired, pour over ice.

Lemon Fruit Splash

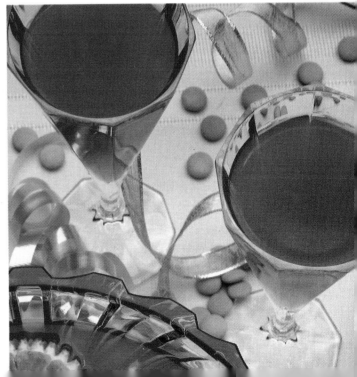

Breads, Muffins & Coffee Cakes

Wholesome Wheat Bread

Makes 2 loaves

5 1/2 to 6 cups whole wheat flour
  2 packages active dry yeast
  1 teaspoon salt
  1 teaspoon ground cinnamon
  1 cup KARO® Dark Corn Syrup
  1 cup water
  1/2 cup HELLMANN'S® or BEST FOODS®
    Real Mayonnaise
  2 eggs

In large mixer bowl, combine 2 cups of the flour, the yeast, salt and cinnamon. In medium saucepan, combine corn syrup, water and real mayonnaise; heat mixture over medium heat, stirring occasionally, until very warm (120° to 130°F). Pour hot mixture into flour mixture; beat at medium speed 2 minutes. Reduce speed to low; beat in 2 more cups of the flour and the eggs until well mixed. Beat at medium speed 2 minutes. By hand, stir in enough of the remaining flour to make dough easy to handle. Turn out onto lightly floured surface. Knead 10 minutes or until dough is smooth and elastic, adding as much remaining flour as needed to prevent sticking. Shape dough into a ball. Place in large, greased bowl; turn dough once to grease surface. Cover with towel; let rise in warm place (85°F) until doubled, about 1 hour.

Punch dough down; divide in half. Cover; let rest 10 minutes. Shape each half into 8×4-inch oval. Place on large, greased and floured baking sheet. Cut 3 slashes, 1/4 inch deep, in top of each loaf. Cover; let rise in warm place until doubled, about 1 1/2 hours. Bake in preheated 350°F oven 30 to 40 minutes or until loaves are browned and sound hollow when tapped. Immediately remove from baking sheet to wire racks to cool.

Apple-Cranberry Muffins

Makes 1 dozen muffins

1 3/4 cups *plus* 2 tablespoons all-purpose flour
  1/2 cup sugar
1 1/2 teaspoons baking powder
  1/2 teaspoon baking soda
  1/2 teaspoon salt
  1 egg
  3/4 cup milk
  3/4 cup sweetened applesauce
  1/4 cup butter or margarine, melted
  1 cup fresh cranberries, coarsely chopped
  1/2 teaspoon ground cinnamon

In medium bowl, combine 1 3/4 cups of the flour, 1/4 cup of the sugar, the baking powder, baking soda and salt. In small bowl, combine egg, milk, applesauce and butter; mix well. Add egg mixture to flour mixture; stir just until moistened. Batter will be lumpy; do not overmix. In small bowl, toss cranberries with remaining 2 tablespoons flour; fold into batter. Spoon batter evenly into 12 greased 2 3/4-inch muffin cups. In measuring cup, combine remaining 1/4 cup sugar and the cinnamon. Sprinkle over tops of muffins. Bake in preheated 400°F oven 20 to 25 minutes or until golden brown. Remove to wire rack to cool.

Favorite recipe from **Western New York Apple Growers Association, Inc.**

Clockwise from top left: Apple-Cranberry Muffins, Nut-Filled Christmas Wreath (page 20) and Wholesome Wheat Bread

Nut-Filled Christmas Wreath

Makes 1 coffee cake

2 tablespoons warm water (105° to 115°F)
1 package active dry yeast
3 tablespoons sugar, divided
2 eggs
¼ cup butter or margarine, melted, cooled
3 tablespoons milk
¾ teaspoon salt
½ teaspoon ground cardamom
2½ to 3 cups all-purpose flour
  Cherry-Nut Filling (recipe follows)
  Almond Icing (recipe follows)

In large bowl, combine water, yeast and 1 tablespoon of the sugar; stir to dissolve yeast. Let stand until bubbly, about 5 minutes. Add remaining 2 tablespoons sugar, the eggs, butter, milk, salt and cardamom; mix well. Stir in 1½ cups of the flour until smooth. Stir in enough of the remaining flour to make dough easy to handle. Turn out onto lightly floured surface. Knead 10 minutes or until dough is smooth and elastic, adding as much remaining flour as needed to prevent sticking. Shape dough into ball. Place in large, lightly greased bowl; turn dough once to grease surface. Cover with waxed paper; let rise in warm place (85°F) until doubled, about 1 hour. Meanwhile, prepare Cherry-Nut Filling.

Punch dough down. Roll out dough on floured surface into 24×9-inch rectangle. Sprinkle Cherry-Nut Filling over dough to within 1 inch from edges. Roll up dough, jelly-roll style, beginning on 24-inch side; pinch seam to seal. Using sharp knife, cut roll in half lengthwise; turn each half cut-side up. Carefully twist halves together, keeping cut sides up to expose filling. Place dough on greased cookie sheet; shape into a ring. Pinch ends together to seal. Cover; let stand in warm place until almost doubled, about 45 minutes. Bake in preheated 375°F oven 20 minutes or until evenly browned. Remove bread from cookie sheet to wire rack; cool slightly. Prepare Almond Icing; drizzle over warm bread. Serve warm or at room temperature.

Cherry-Nut Filling: In medium bowl, combine ¾ cup chopped nuts (hazelnuts, almonds, walnuts or pecans), ¼ cup *each* all-purpose flour, chopped candied red cherries, chopped candied green cherries and softened butter or margarine, 2 tablespoons brown sugar and ½ teaspoon almond extract; mix well.

Almond Icing: In small bowl, combine 1 cup sifted powdered sugar, 1 to 2 tablespoons milk and ¼ teaspoon almond extract; blend until smooth.

Fruited Scones

Makes about 1½ dozen

2 cups unsifted flour
¼ cup sugar
1 tablespoon baking powder
½ teaspoon salt
½ cup cold margarine or butter
1 egg
⅓ cup BORDEN® or MEADOW GOLD® Milk
1 (9-ounce) package NONE SUCH®
  Condensed Mincemeat, crumbled
1 egg, beaten, optional

Preheat oven to 400°F. In large bowl, combine flour, sugar, baking powder and salt; cut in margarine until crumbly. Stir in *1 egg*, milk and mincemeat; mix well. On floured surface, knead dough lightly 10 times. Roll out to ½-inch thickness; cut into 2-inch circles. Place 1 inch apart on ungreased baking sheets. For a more golden color, brush with beaten egg if desired. Bake 10 to 12 minutes or until golden. Serve warm.

Pumpkin Apple Streusel Muffins

Makes 18 muffins

2½ cups all-purpose flour
2 cups granulated sugar
1 tablespoon pumpkin pie spice
1 teaspoon baking soda
½ teaspoon salt
2 eggs, lightly beaten
1 cup LIBBY'S® Solid Pack Pumpkin
½ cup vegetable oil
2 cups peeled, finely chopped apples
  Streusel Topping (recipe follows)

In large bowl, combine flour, sugar, pumpkin pie spice, baking soda and salt; set aside. In medium bowl, combine eggs, pumpkin and oil. Add liquid ingredients to dry ingredients; stir just until moistened. Stir in apples. Spoon batter into greased or paper-lined muffin cups, filling ¾ full. Sprinkle Streusel Topping over batter. Bake in preheated 350°F oven for 35 to 40 minutes, or until toothpick comes out clean.

Streusel Topping: In small bowl, combine 2 tablespoons all-purpose flour, ¼ cup sugar and ½ teaspoon ground cinnamon. Cut in 4 teaspoons butter, until mixture is crumbly.

Peachy Cinnamon Coffeecake

Makes 9 servings

> 1 package DUNCAN HINES® Bakery Style Cinnamon Swirl with Crumb Topping Muffin Mix
> 1 can (8¼ ounces) juice pack sliced yellow cling peaches
> 1 egg

1. Preheat oven to 400°F. Grease 8-inch square or 9-inch round pan.

2. Drain peaches, reserving juice. Add water to reserved juice to equal ¾ cup liquid. Chop peaches.

3. Combine muffin mix, egg and ¾ cup peach liquid in medium bowl; fold in peaches. Pour batter into pan. Knead swirl packet 10 seconds before opening. Squeeze contents on top of batter and swirl with knife. Sprinkle topping over batter. Bake at 400°F for 28 to 33 minutes for 8-inch pan (or 20 to 25 minutes for 9-inch pan) or until golden. Serve warm.

Banana Scotch Muffins

Makes 12 muffins

> 1 ripe, large DOLE® Banana, peeled
> 1 egg, beaten
> ½ cup sugar
> ¼ cup milk
> ¼ cup vegetable oil
> 1 teaspoon vanilla
> 1 cup all-purpose flour
> 1 cup quick-cooking rolled oats
> 1 teaspoon baking powder
> ½ teaspoon baking soda
> ½ teaspoon salt
> ½ cup butterscotch chips

Preheat oven to 400°F. Puree banana in blender (⅔ cup). In medium bowl, combine pureed banana, egg, sugar, milk, oil and vanilla. In large bowl, combine flour, oats, baking powder, baking soda and salt. Stir banana mixture into dry ingredients with butterscotch chips until just blended. Spoon into well greased 2½-inch muffin cups. Bake 12 to 15 minutes. Remove from pan.

Peachy Cinnamon Coffeecake

Clockwise from bottom right: Cheddar 'n Pecan Swirls, Healthy Pecan Bread, Banana Pecan Braid and 60-Minute Oatmeal Nut Loaf

Banana Pecan Braid

Makes 2 loaves

    6 cups all-purpose flour, divided
 ¹/₂ cup sugar
    1 cup pecan halves, chopped
    1 teaspoon salt
    2 pkgs. FLEISCHMANN'S® RapidRise Yeast
 ¹/₃ cup undiluted evaporated milk
 ¹/₃ cup water
 ¹/₃ cup magarine or butter
    2 eggs, at room temperature
    1 cup mashed banana
    2 tablespoons margarine or butter, melted
       Cinnamon Sugar (recipe follows)

Set aside 1 cup flour. In large bowl, mix remaining 5 cups flour, sugar, pecans, salt and yeast. In saucepan over low heat, heat evaporated milk, water and ¹/₃ cup margarine until very warm (125° to 130°F); stir into dry mixture. Mix in eggs, banana and enough reserved flour to make soft dough. On lightly floured surface, knead until smooth and elastic, about 8 to 10 minutes. Cover; let rest 10 minutes.

Divide dough into 6 equal pieces; shape each piece into a 15-inch rope. Braid 3 ropes together for each loaf; seal ends. Place on greased baking sheet. Cover; let rise in warm (80° to 85°F) draft-free place until double in size, about 1 hour.

Preheat oven to 375°F. Brush loaves with melted margarine; sprinkle with Cinnamon Sugar. Bake 30 to 35 minutes or until golden brown. Remove from pans; cool on wire racks.

Cinnamon Sugar: Combine 2 tablespoons sugar and 1 teaspoon ground cinnamon.

Favorite recipe from **National Pecan Marketing Council**

22

60-Minute Oatmeal Nut Loaf

Makes 1 loaf

3 1/4 cups all-purpose flour, divided
  1 cup rolled oats
1/2 cup pecan pieces
  2 teaspoons grated orange peel
1/2 teaspoon salt
  1 pkg. FLEISCHMANN'S® RapidRise Yeast
  1 cup milk
1/4 cup water
  2 tablespoons honey
  1 tablespoon margarine or butter
  1 egg, beaten
1/2 cup powdered sugar
  1 to 1 1/2 teaspoons milk
  Pecan halves

Set aside 1 cup flour. In large bowl, mix remaining 2 1/4 cups flour, oats, pecan pieces, orange peel, salt and yeast. In saucepan, over low heat, heat 1 cup milk, water, honey and margarine until very warm (125° to 130°F); stir into dry mixture. Mix in only enough reserved flour to make soft dough. On lightly floured surface, knead 4 minutes.

Roll dough in 13×9-inch rectangle. Roll up from short side as for jelly roll; seal seam and ends. Place on greased baking sheet; flatten slightly to form oval. Cover; let rise in warm (80° to 85°F) draft-free place 20 minutes.

Preheat oven to 375°F. Make 3 diagonal slashes on top of loaf; brush with egg. Bake 20 to 25 minutes or until golden. Remove from baking sheet; cool on wire rack. In small bowl, mix powdered sugar and 1 teaspoon milk. Add additional milk, if necessary, to make desired consistency. Drizzle over loaf; garnish with pecan halves.

Favorite recipe from **National Pecan Marketing Council**

Cheddar 'n Pecan Swirls

Makes 1 dozen

3/4 cup chopped onion
  3 tablespoons margarine, softened and divided
  3 cups all-purpose flour, divided
  1 tablespoon sugar
1/2 teaspoon salt
  1 pkg. FLEISCHMANN'S® RapidRise Yeast
3/4 cup water
1/4 cup milk
  1 cup (4 oz.) shredded Cheddar cheese
1/2 cup pecan halves, chopped
  Paprika

In medium skillet over medium heat, cook onion in 2 tablespoons margarine until tender; set aside.

Set aside 1 cup flour. In large bowl, mix remaining 2 cups flour, sugar, salt and yeast. In saucepan, over low heat, heat water, milk and remaining 1 tablespoon margarine until very warm (125° to 130°F); stir into dry mixture. Mix in only enough reserved flour to make soft dough. On lightly floured surface, knead 4 minutes. Roll dough into 14×8-inch rectangle. Spread onion mixture evenly over dough; sprinkle with cheese and pecans. Roll up from long side as for jelly roll; seal seam. Cut roll into 12 equal pieces. Arrange cut-side up in greased 8-inch round cake pan; cover. Let rise in warm (80° to 85°F) draft-free place 20 minutes.

Preheat oven to 375°F. Sprinkle with paprika. Bake 25 to 30 minutes or until golden brown. Remove from pan; cool slightly on wire rack. Serve warm.

Favorite recipe from **National Pecan Marketing Council**

Healthy Pecan Bread

Makes 2 loaves

5 cups all-purpose flour, divided
  2 cups whole wheat flour
1/2 cup wheat germ
  1 cup pecan halves, chopped
  2 teaspoons salt
  2 pkgs. FLEISCHMANN'S® RapidRise Yeast
  1 cup water
  1 cup plain yogurt
1/3 cup honey
1/4 cup margarine or butter
  2 eggs, at room temperature

Set aside 1 cup all-purpose flour. In large bowl, mix remaining 4 cups all-purpose flour, whole wheat flour, wheat germ, pecans, salt and yeast. In saucepan, over low heat, heat water, yogurt, honey and margarine until very warm (125° to 130°F); stir into dry mixture. Mix in eggs and only enough reserved flour to make soft dough. On lightly floured surface, knead until smooth and elastic, about 8 to 10 minutes. Cover; let rest 10 minutes.

Divide dough in half; shape each half into smooth ball. Place in two greased 8-inch round cake pans. Cover; let rise in warm (80° to 85°F) place until doubled in size, about 1 hour and 15 minutes.

Preheat oven to 375°F. Bake 35 to 40 minutes or until golden brown. Remove from pans; cool on wire racks.

Favorite recipe from **National Pecan Marketing Council**

Holiday Cranberry Bread

Makes 1 loaf

 2 cups all-purpose flour
 1/2 cup granulated sugar
 1 1/2 teaspoons baking powder
 1/2 teaspoon baking soda
 1/2 teaspoon salt
 3/4 cup milk
 1/3 cup vegetable oil
 2 teaspoons white vinegar
 1 teaspoon grated orange rind
 1 egg
 One 6-oz. pkg. (1 cup) NESTLÉ® Toll House®
 Semi-Sweet Chocolate Morsels
 1/2 cup walnuts, chopped
 2 cups cranberries, chopped
 Confectioners' sugar, optional

Preheat oven to 350°F. Grease 9×5×3-inch loaf pan. In large bowl, combine flour, granulated sugar, baking powder, baking soda and salt. In small bowl, blend milk, oil, vinegar, orange rind and egg. Stir milk mixture, semi-sweet chocolate morsels and nuts into flour mixture just until flour mixture is moistened and ingredients are evenly mixed. Fold in cranberries. Spoon into prepared pan.

Bake 55 to 60 minutes until skewer inserted into center comes out clean. Cool 10 minutes; remove from pan. Cool completely. Sprinkle confectioners' sugar on top.

Holiday Cranberry Bread

Chocolate Streusel 'n Spice Coffeecake

Makes 9 servings

 1 package (10 to 13 ounces) fruit,
 cinnamon, spice or bran muffin mix
 1/2 cup HERSHEY'S Semi-Sweet Chocolate
 Chips
 3/4 cup powdered sugar
 1/2 cup chopped nuts
 1/4 cup HERSHEY'S Cocoa
 3 tablespoons butter or margarine, melted

Preheat oven to 350°F. Grease *bottom only* of 9-inch square baking pan. Prepare muffin mix as directed for coffeecake; stir in chocolate chips. Pour batter into prepared pan. In small bowl, stir together powdered sugar, nuts and cocoa; with fork, stir in butter until crumbly. Sprinkle over batter.

Bake 25 to 30 minutes or until wooden pick inserted in center comes out clean. Cool in pan on wire rack.

Bishop's Bread

Makes 1 loaf

 3 cups packaged biscuit mix
 1/2 cup sugar
 1 egg
 1 tablespoon grated orange peel
 1 1/4 cups Florida orange juice
 3 tablespoons vegetable oil
 1/2 cup wheat germ
 1 6-ounce package (1 cup) semi-sweet
 chocolate morsels, divided
 1/4 cup seedless raisins
 1/4 cup candied cherries, halved
 1/4 cup chopped nuts

Preheat oven to 350°F.

Combine biscuit mix and sugar in large mixing bowl.

In a separate bowl, combine egg, orange peel, orange juice and oil. Add to biscuit mix and beat with wooden spoon until mixture is smooth. Stir in wheat germ, 2/3 cup of chocolate morsels, raisins, cherries and nuts.

Turn into greased 9×5×3-inch loaf pan. Sprinkle remaining chocolate morsels on top of batter. Bake in 350°F oven 55 to 60 minutes, until wooden pick inserted in center comes out clean. Let cool in pan 10 minutes. Turn out of pan. Cool completely on wire rack.

Favorite recipe from **Florida Department of Citrus**

Pear Cream Breakfast Cake

Pear Cream Breakfast Cake

Makes 8 to 10 servings

> 1 29-oz. can pear halves in heavy syrup, undrained
> 1 8-oz. pkg. PHILADELPHIA BRAND® Cream Cheese, softened
> ¼ cup KRAFT® Apricot Preserves
> 2 tablespoons PARKAY® Margarine
> 1 9-oz. pkg. yellow cake mix
> 2 tablespoons oil
> 1 egg
> 1 teaspoon ground ginger

• Preheat oven to 350°F.

• Drain pears, reserving ½ cup syrup. Slice pears; place on bottom of 8-inch square baking pan.

• Beat cream cheese, preserves and margarine in small mixing bowl at medium speed with electric mixer until well blended; pour over pears.

• Beat cake mix, reserved syrup, oil, egg and ginger in large mixing bowl at low speed with electric mixer until well blended; pour over cream cheese mixture.

• Bake 35 to 40 minutes or until golden brown. Serve warm with half and half.

Prep time: 15 minutes

Cooking time: 40 minutes

Apple Whole Wheat Muffins

Makes 12 muffins

> 1¼ cups all-purpose flour
> ¾ cup whole wheat flour
> ⅓ cup granulated sugar
> 1 tablespoon baking powder
> 1 teaspoon ground cinnamon
> ½ teaspoon ground ginger
> ⅔ cup *undiluted* CARNATION® Evaporated Lowfat Milk
> ⅓ cup apple juice
> ¼ cup vegetable oil
> 1 egg
> 1¼ cups (1 large) peeled, finely diced apple Cinnamon-Sugar Topping (recipe follows)

In medium bowl, combine flours, sugar, baking powder, cinnamon and ginger. In small bowl, combine milk, apple juice, oil and egg; beat to blend in egg. Add liquid ingredients to dry ingredients; stir just until moistened. Fold in apple. Spoon batter into 12 paper-lined muffin cups. Sprinkle with Cinnamon-Sugar Topping. Bake in preheated 400°F oven for 15 minutes or until toothpick inserted in center comes out clean. Remove from muffin cups to cool.

Cinnamon-Sugar Topping: Combine 1 tablespoon granulated sugar and ½ teaspoon ground cinnamon.

Oven-Baked French Toast with Cranberry Maple Sauce

Makes 10 to 12 servings

> 1 (8 oz.) pkg. PHILADELPHIA BRAND® Cream Cheese, softened
> ³/₄ cup sugar
> ¹/₄ cup PARKAY® Margarine
> 2 teaspoons vanilla
> 1 teaspoon ground cinnamon
> 4 eggs
> 2¹/₂ cups milk
> 1 (1 lb.) French bread loaf, cut into 1¹/₂-inch slices
> 1 cup cranberries
> Cranberry Maple Sauce (recipe follows)

• Preheat oven to 350°F.

• Beat cream cheese, sugar, margarine, vanilla and cinnamon in large mixing bowl at medium speed with electric mixer until well blended. Add eggs, one at a time, mixing well after each addition. Stir in milk.

• Pour cream cheese mixture over combined bread and cranberries in large bowl; toss lightly. Let stand 15 minutes, rearranging bread in bowl occasionally to moisten evenly.

• Arrange bread in rows in greased 13×9-inch baking pan. Pour remaining cream cheese mixture over bread.

• Bake 40 to 45 minutes or until golden brown. Serve with Cranberry Maple Sauce.

Cranberry Maple Sauce

> 1 cup LOG CABIN® Syrup
> 2 cups cranberries
> 2 tablespoons sugar

• Bring syrup to boil in medium saucepan. Add cranberries and sugar.

• Cook over low heat 10 minutes, stirring occasionally. Cool slightly.

Prep time: 25 minutes plus standing

Cooking time: 45 minutes

Pumpkin Cheese Bread

Makes 2 loaves

> 2¹/₂ cups sugar
> 1 (8 oz.) pkg. PHILADELPHIA BRAND® Cream Cheese, softened
> ¹/₂ cup PARKAY® Margarine
> 4 eggs
> 1 (16 oz.) can pumpkin
> 3¹/₂ cups flour
> 2 teaspoons baking soda
> 1 teaspoon salt
> 1 teaspoon cinnamon
> ¹/₂ teaspoon CALUMET® Baking Powder
> ¹/₄ teaspoon ground cloves
> 1 cup chopped nuts
> Icing (recipe follows)

• Preheat oven to 350°F.

• Beat sugar, cream cheese and margarine in large mixing bowl at medium speed with electric mixer until well blended.

• Add eggs, one at a time, mixing well after each addition. Blend in pumpkin.

• Add combined dry ingredients, mixing just until moistened. Fold in nuts. Pour into two greased and floured 9×5-inch loaf pans.

• Bake 1 hour or until wooden pick inserted in center comes out clean. Cool 5 minutes; remove from pans. Drizzle with Icing. Garnish with pecan halves and red maraschino cherry halves, if desired.

Icing

> 2 cups powdered sugar
> 3 tablespoons milk

• Stir ingredients together in small bowl until smooth.

Prep Time: 20 minutes

Cooking Time: 1 hour plus cooling

Oven-Baked French Toast with Cranberry Maple Sauce

Pepper-Cheese Bread

Pepper-Cheese Bread

Makes 2 braids

5 1/2 to 6 cups all-purpose flour
  2 packages active dry yeast
  1 cup milk
2/3 cup butter, cut up
  1 tablespoon sugar
  1 to 2 teaspoons coarse black pepper
  1 teaspoon salt
  4 eggs
  2 cups (8 ounces) shredded sharp
     Wisconsin Cheddar cheese
1 1/4 cups unseasoned mashed potatoes

In large mixer bowl combine *2 cups* of the flour and the yeast. In small saucepan combine the milk, butter, sugar, pepper and salt. Cook and stir until warm (115° to 120°F) and butter is almost melted. Add to flour mixture. Add eggs. Beat with an electric mixer on low speed for 30 seconds, scraping sides of bowl. Beat on high speed for 3 minutes. Stir in Cheddar cheese, mashed potatoes and as much remaining flour as can be mixed in with a spoon.

Turn out onto a lightly floured surface. Knead 6 to 8 minutes or until dough is smooth and elastic, adding as much remaining flour as needed to make a moderately stiff dough. Shape into a ball. Place in greased bowl; turn once to grease surface. Cover; let rise in warm place (80° to 85°F) until double (about 1 hour).

Punch down dough; turn out onto lightly floured surface. Divide dough into 6 pieces. Cover; let rest 10 minutes. Roll each piece into 16-inch-long rope. On greased baking sheet braid 3 ropes together. Repeat on second greased baking sheet with remaining ropes. Cover; let rise in warm place until nearly doubled (about 30 minutes).

Preheat oven to 375°F. Bake 35 to 40 minutes or until golden brown, covering with foil the last 15 minutes of baking to prevent overbrowning. Remove from pans; cool.

Preparation time: 50 minutes plus rising

Favorite recipe from **Wisconsin Milk Marketing Board**© 1991

Breakfast Raisin Ring

Makes 8 to 10 servings

 1 8-oz. pkg. PHILADELPHIA BRAND®
    Cream Cheese, cubed
 1 cup cold water
 1 16-oz. pkg. hot roll mix
 1 egg
 1 teaspoon vanilla
 ½ cup packed brown sugar
 ⅓ cup PARKAY® Margarine
 ¼ cup granulated sugar
 1½ teaspoons cinnamon
 1½ teaspoons vanilla
 ½ cup golden raisins
    Vanilla Drizzle (recipe follows)

• Preheat oven to 350°F.

• Blend 6 ounces cream cheese and water in small saucepan. Cook over low heat until mixture reaches 115° to 120°F, stirring occasionally.

• Stir together hot roll mix and yeast packet in large bowl. Add cream cheese mixture, egg and 1 teaspoon vanilla, mixing until dough pulls away from sides of bowl.

• Knead dough on lightly floured surface 5 minutes or until smooth and elastic. Cover; let rise in warm place 20 minutes.

• Beat remaining cream cheese, brown sugar, margarine, granulated sugar, cinnamon and 1½ teaspoons vanilla in small mixing bowl at medium speed with electric mixer until well blended.

• Roll out dough to 20×12-inch rectangle; spread cream cheese mixture over dough to within 1½ inches from outer edges of dough. Sprinkle with raisins.

• Roll up from long end, sealing edges. Place, seam-side down, on greased cookie sheet; shape into ring, pressing ends together to seal. Make 1 inch cuts through ring from outer edge at 2 inch intervals. Cover; let rise in warm place 30 minutes.

• Bake 30 to 40 minutes or until golden brown. Cool slightly. Drizzle with Vanilla Drizzle.

Prep time: 30 minutes plus rising

Cooking time: 40 minutes

Vanilla Drizzle

 1 cup powdered sugar
 1 to 2 tablespoons milk
 1 teaspoon vanilla
 ½ teaspoon cinnamon (optional)

• Stir ingredients together in small bowl until smooth.

Breakfast Raisin Ring

Bacon Cheese Muffins

Makes 12 muffins

- ¹/₂ pound bacon (10 to 12 slices)
  Vegetable oil
- 1 egg, beaten
- ³/₄ cup milk
- 1³/₄ cups all-purpose flour
- ¹/₄ cup sugar
- 1 tablespoon baking powder
- 1 cup (4 ounces) shredded Wisconsin
  Cheddar cheese
- ¹/₂ cup crunchy nugget-like cereal

Preheat oven to 400°F. In large skillet, cook bacon over medium-high heat until crisp. Drain, reserving drippings. If necessary, add oil to drippings to measure ¹/₃ cup. In small bowl, combine dripping mixture, egg and milk; set aside. Crumble bacon; set aside.

In large bowl, combine flour, sugar and baking powder. Make well in center. Add dripping-egg mixture all at once to flour mixture, stirring just until moistened. Batter should be lumpy. Fold in bacon, cheese and cereal. Spoon into buttered or paper-lined 2¹/₂-inch muffin cups, filling about ³/₄ full. Bake 15 to 20 minutes or until golden. Remove from pan. Cool on wire rack.

Favorite recipe from **Wisconsin Milk Marketing Board**© 1991

Bacon Cheese Muffins

Cranberry Streusel Coffee Cake

Makes about 9 servings

CAKE BATTER:
- 1¹/₂ cups flour
- 1¹/₂ teaspoons baking powder
- ¹/₂ teaspoon salt
- 6 tablespoons (³/₄ stick) unsalted butter,
  softened
- ³/₄ cup sugar
- 2 teaspoons grated orange peel
- 2 eggs
- ¹/₂ cup milk

STREUSEL:
- ¹/₂ cup light brown sugar
- ¹/₄ cup flour
- ¹/₂ teaspoon cinnamon
- 2 tablespoons butter, softened
- ¹/₂ cup chopped walnuts

CRANBERRY FILLING:
- 1¹/₂ cups OCEAN SPRAY® fresh or frozen
  cranberries
- ¹/₄ cup sugar
- 2 tablespoons orange juice

1. Preheat oven to 350°F. Grease and flour 8-inch square cake pan. Stir together flour, baking powder and salt on piece of wax paper until well mixed.

2. Cream together butter, sugar and orange peel in large bowl. Add eggs, one at a time, beating well after each addition. Stir in flour mixture alternately with milk, beginning and ending with flour. Set batter aside.

3. For streusel, combine all streusel ingredients in small mixing bowl. Mix together with fork until crumbly. Set mixture aside.

4. For cranberry filling, place all filling ingredients in a small saucepan. Cook over medium heat, stirring constantly, until berries start to pop. Remove from heat; cool to room temperature.

5. Spread half of the coffee cake batter over bottom of prepared pan. Sprinkle with half of the streusel mixture; spoon on half the cranberry filling. Cover with remaining batter; top with remaining filling and streusel.

6. Bake 50 to 60 minutes until toothpick inserted in center comes out clean. Cool on wire rack. Serve warm or at room temperature.

Preparation time: 20 minutes

Quicky Sticky Buns

Quicky Sticky Buns

Makes 9 buns

3 tablespoons packed brown sugar, divided
¹⁄₄ cup KARO® Light or Dark Corn Syrup
¹⁄₄ cup coarsely chopped pecans
2 tablespoons softened MAZOLA®
    Margarine, divided
1 can (8 ounces) refrigerated crescent
    dinner rolls
1 teaspoon cinnamon

Preheat oven to 350°F. In small bowl combine
2 tablespoons of the brown sugar, the corn syrup,
pecans and 1 tablespoon of the margarine. Spoon
about 2 teaspoons mixture into each of 9 (2¹⁄₂-
inch) muffin pan cups. Unroll entire crescent roll
dough; pinch seams together to form 1 rectangle.
Combine remaining 1 tablespoon brown sugar and
the cinnamon. Spread dough with remaining
1 tablespoon margarine; sprinkle with cinnamon
mixture. Roll up from short end. Cut into 9 slices.
Place one slice in each prepared muffin pan cup.
Bake 25 minutes or until golden brown.
Immediately invert pan onto cookie sheet or tray;
cool 10 minutes.

Preparation Time: 15 minutes

Bake Time: 25 minutes, plus cooling

Streusel Raspberry Muffins

Makes 12 muffins

Pecan Streusel Topping (recipe follows)
1¹⁄₂ cups all-purpose flour
¹⁄₂ cup sugar
2 teaspoons baking powder
¹⁄₂ cup milk
¹⁄₂ cup butter or margarine, melted
1 egg, beaten
1 cup fresh or individually frozen, whole
    unsugared raspberries

Preheat oven to 375°F. Grease or paper-line
12 (2¹⁄₂-inch) muffin cups. Prepare Pecan Streusel
Topping; set aside.

In large bowl, combine flour, sugar and baking
powder. In small bowl, combine milk, butter and
egg until blended. Stir into flour mixture just until
moistened. Spoon ¹⁄₂ of the batter into muffin
cups. Divide raspberries among cups, then top
with remaining batter. Sprinkle Pecan Streusel
Topping over tops. Bake 25 to 30 minutes or until
golden and wooden pick inserted in center comes
out clean. Remove from pan.

Pecan Streusel Topping: In small bowl,
combine ¹⁄₄ cup *each* chopped pecans, packed
brown sugar and all-purpose flour. Stir in 2
tablespoons melted butter or margarine until
mixture resembles moist crumbs.

Soups, Salads & Side Dishes

Strawberry Miracle Mold

Makes 4 to 6 servings

> **2 packages (4-serving size) JELL-O® Brand Strawberry Flavor Gelatin**
> **1¹/₂ cups boiling water**
> **1³/₄ cups cold water**
> **¹/₂ cup MIRACLE WHIP® Salad Dressing**
> **Assorted Fruit**

• Dissolve gelatin in boiling water; add cold water. Gradually add to salad dressing, mixing until blended.

• Pour into lightly oiled 1-quart mold or glass serving bowl; chill until firm. Unmold onto serving plate; serve with fruit.

Prep time: 10 minutes plus chilling

Twice-Baked Potatoes

Makes 12 servings

> **3 pounds baking potatoes (about 6 large)**
> **Vegetable oil**
> **¹/₄ cup sour cream**
> **1 can (11 ounces) CAMPBELL'S® condensed Cheddar cheese soup/sauce**
> **2 tablespoons chopped green onion**
> **Generous dash pepper**
> **Paprika**

1. Wash and dry potatoes; rub lightly with oil. Prick potatoes with tines of fork. Bake at 400°F for 1 hour or until potatoes are fork-tender. Remove potatoes from oven.

2. Cut potatoes in half lengthwise. Carefully scoop out pulp from each half, leaving a thin shell.

3. In medium bowl with mixer on medium speed, beat together potato pulp and sour cream. Gradually add soup, green onion and pepper; beat until light and fluffy. Spoon potato mixture into shells.

4. Place on baking sheet. Sprinkle with paprika. Bake 15 minutes until hot.

To assemble ahead: Prepare potatoes as directed through step 3. Arrange in 13×9-inch baking dish. Cover; refrigerate up to 6 hours. Sprinkle with paprika. Bake at 350°F for 35 minutes or until hot.

To Microwave: *Omit* vegetable oil. Prick potatoes with tines of fork in several places. Arrange potatoes on large microwave-safe plate. Microwave, uncovered, on HIGH 18 minutes or until tender, rearranging potatoes twice during cooking. Continue as directed in steps 2 and 3. Arrange potatoes on large microwave-safe plate. Sprinkle with paprika. Microwave, uncovered, on HIGH 8 minutes or until hot, rotating plate once during heating.

Strawberry Miracle Mold

Sweet and Sour Chicken Salad

Makes 4 servings

- ½ cup HEINZ Chili Sauce
- ⅓ cup apple juice
- 1 tablespoon HEINZ Distilled White Vinegar
- 2 teaspoons cornstarch
- 2 teaspoons granulated sugar
- 2 cups cubed cooked chicken
- 1 can (8 ounces) sliced water chestnuts, drained
- 1 small zucchini, halved lengthwise, sliced (about 1 cup)
- 1 medium-size red apple, cut into chunks
- ¾ cup sliced celery
  Leaf lettuce
  Apple wedges
- 1 cup chow mein noodles

In 1-quart saucepan, combine chili sauce, apple juice, vinegar, cornstarch and sugar. Bring to a boil over medium heat, stirring constantly. Boil 1 minute or until thickened and clear; cool slightly. In medium bowl, combine chicken, water chestnuts, zucchini, apple chunks and celery. Pour warm dressing over chicken mixture; mix well. Line individual plates with lettuce; arrange apple wedges on lettuce. Spoon chicken mixture on top. Sprinkle with chow mein noodles.

Sweet and Sour Chicken Salad

Wild Rice Apple Dressing

Makes about 2 quarts

- ⅔ cup wild rice, rinsed and drained
- 2 tablespoons WYLER'S® or STEERO® Chicken-Flavor Instant Bouillon *or* 6 Chicken-Flavor Bouillon Cubes
- 3 cups water
- ½ cup uncooked long grain rice
- ½ cup chopped celery
- ⅓ cup chopped onion
- ⅓ cup margarine or butter
- 1 cup chopped apple
- 1½ cups dry bread cubes
- ½ cup chopped pecans
- ½ cup raisins
- 1 egg, beaten
- 1 teaspoon poultry seasoning
- ¼ teaspoon rubbed sage

In medium saucepan, combine wild rice and bouillon in water; bring to boil. Reduce heat; cover and simmer 20 minutes. Add long grain rice; cover and simmer 25 minutes longer or until water is absorbed. In skillet, cook celery and onion in margarine until tender. In large bowl, combine rice mixture, celery mixture and remaining ingredients; mix well. Spoon into 2-quart baking dish. Cover; bake in preheated 325°F oven 35 minutes. Uncover; bake 15 minutes longer or until hot. Refrigerate leftovers.

Turkey Gravy Dijon

Makes about 1 cup

- 1 can (10½ ounces) FRANCO-AMERICAN® turkey gravy
- 2 tablespoons milk
- 2 teaspoons Dijon-style mustard
- ¼ cup shredded Swiss cheese (1 ounce)

In 1½-quart saucepan, stir together gravy, milk and mustard. Over medium heat, heat until warm, stirring often. Add cheese; cook until cheese melts, stirring constantly. *Do not boil.* Serve with turkey or rice.

To Microwave: In 4-cup glass measure or 1-quart microwave-safe casserole, stir together gravy, milk and mustard. Microwave, uncovered, on HIGH 4 minutes or until heated through, stirring once during cooking. Stir in cheese. Microwave on MEDIUM (50% power) 2 to 3 minutes or until cheese melts, stirring twice during cooking. *Do not boil.* Serve as directed above.

Quick Garden Cheese Soup (left) and Italian-Style Chili (right)

Quick Garden Cheese Soup

Makes about 2 quarts

1 cup sliced celery
1 cup chopped onion
2 tablespoons margarine or butter
²/₃ cup unsifted flour
4 cups water
2 tablespoons WYLER'S® or STEERO®
   Chicken-Flavor Instant Bouillon
   or 6 Chicken-Flavor Bouillon Cubes
¼ teaspoon pepper
2 cups frozen broccoli, cauliflower and
   carrot combination
1 cup frozen hash brown potatoes
3 cups BORDEN® or MEADOW GOLD® Milk
   or Half-and-Half
2½ cups (10 ounces) shredded Cheddar
   cheese

In large kettle or Dutch oven, cook celery and
onion in margarine until tender; stir in flour until
smooth. Gradually add water then bouillon,
pepper and vegetables; bring to a boil. Reduce
heat; cover and simmer 15 minutes. Add milk and
cheese. Cook and stir until cheese melts and soup
is hot *(do not boil)*. Garnish as desired. Refrigerate
leftovers.

Italian-Style Chili

Makes about 2 quarts

1 pound lean ground beef
³/₄ cup chopped onion
1 (26-ounce) jar CLASSICO® Di Napoli
   (Tomato & Basil) Pasta Sauce
1½ cups water
1 (14½-ounce) can whole tomatoes,
   undrained and broken up
1 (4-ounce) can sliced mushrooms, drained
2 ounces sliced pepperoni (¹/₃ cup)
1 tablespoon WYLER'S® or STEERO® Beef-
   Flavor Instant Bouillon *or* 3 Beef-
   Flavor Bouillon Cubes
1 tablespoon chili powder
2 teaspoons sugar

In large kettle or Dutch oven, brown meat with
onion; pour off fat. Add remaining ingredients;
bring to a boil. Reduce heat; simmer uncovered
30 minutes, stirring occasionally. Garnish as
desired. Refrigerate leftovers.

Turkey Waldorf Salad

Makes about 4 to 6 servings

2/3 cup HELLMANN'S® or BEST FOODS® Real, Light or Cholesterol Free Reduced Calorie Mayonnaise
2 tablespoons lemon juice
1/2 teaspoon salt
1/4 teaspoon freshly ground pepper
2 cups diced cooked turkey or chicken
2 red apples, cored and diced
2/3 cup sliced celery
1/2 cup chopped walnuts

In large bowl combine mayonnaise, lemon juice, salt and pepper. Add turkey, apples and celery; toss to coat well. Cover; chill. Just before serving, sprinkle with walnuts.

Turkey Waldorf Salad

Apricot and Walnut Brown Rice Stuffing

Makes 6 servings

1/2 cup chopped onion
1/2 cup chopped celery
1 teaspoon margarine
3 cups cooked brown rice
2/3 cup coarsely chopped dried apricots
1/4 cup coarsely chopped walnuts
1/4 cup raisins, plumped
2 tablespoons snipped parsley
1/2 teaspoon dried thyme leaves
1/4 teaspoon salt
1/4 teaspoon rubbed sage
1/4 teaspoon ground black pepper
1/2 cup chicken broth

Cook onion and celery in margarine in large skillet over medium-high heat until tender crisp. Add rice, apricots, walnuts, raisins, parsley, thyme, salt, sage, pepper and broth; transfer to 2-quart baking dish. Bake in covered baking dish at 375°F for 15 to 20 minutes. (Stuffing may be baked inside poultry.)

Tip: To plump raisins, cover with 1 cup boiling water. Let stand 1 to 2 minutes; drain.

Favorite recipe from **USA Rice Council**

Vegetables in Two Cheese Beer Sauce

Makes 6 servings

2 cups broccoli flowerets
2 cups cauliflowerets
1 can (11 ounces) CAMPBELL'S® condensed Cheddar cheese soup/sauce
1/3 cup beer
1 1/2 cups shredded Swiss cheese (6 ounces)
Dash ground nutmeg

1. In covered 4-quart saucepan over medium heat, in 1 inch boiling water, cook broccoli and cauliflower 6 minutes or until tender. Drain in colander.

2. Meanwhile, in 2-quart saucepan, combine soup, beer, cheese and nutmeg. Over medium heat, heat through, stirring frequently.

3. On serving platter, arrange vegetables alternating broccoli and cauliflower to resemble a head of cauliflower. Pour sauce over vegetables. Makes 2 cups sauce for vegetables.

Clockwise from bottom left: Kahlúa® Savory Stuffing, Turkey with Kahlúa® Glaze and Kahlúa® Candied Yams

Kahlúa® Savory Stuffing

Makes about 3 quarts stuffing, enough for a 12 to 14 pound turkey

3 quarts coarse day old bread crumbs
³/₄ cup butter
2 cups chopped onions
2 cups chopped celery
1 cup chopped mushrooms
2 cups raisins
1 cup browned crumbled sausage
¹/₂ to ³/₄ cup broth
¹/₂ cup chopped pecans
¹/₃ cup KAHLÚA®
¹/₄ cup chopped fresh parsley
2 teaspoons dried thyme, crushed
2 teaspoons grated orange peel
1 teaspoon salt
¹/₂ teaspoon dried sage
¹/₂ teaspoon pepper

Preheat oven 350°F. Bake bread crumbs for 5 minutes in shallow baking pan. Stir. Continue baking 5 minutes longer until lightly toasted. Remove from oven. Place in large bowl. In large skillet, melt butter. Add vegetables; saute lightly. Remove from heat; add balance of ingredients. Pour over bread crumbs. Toss to moisten evenly, adding additional broth if necessary. Stuff turkey.

Kahlúa® Candied Yams

Makes 4 to 6 servings

4 medium-sized yams, cooked* *or* 1 can
    (1 lb. 3 oz.) yams
¹/₄ cup butter
¹/₃ cup brown sugar
¹/₄ cup KAHLÚA®

Cut yams in serving size pieces. In heavy skillet, melt butter with sugar. Add KAHLÚA®; cook 1 minute. Add yams; turn until brown on all sides. Cover. Reduce heat; cook about 15 minutes. Turn yams once more before serving.

In large saucepan, boil yams until tender but still firm. Remove from pan; let cool slightly. Peel.

Kahlúa® Glaze

Makes enough to glaze a 12 to 14 pound turkey

¹/₃ cup apricot jam
¹/₃ cup KAHLÚA®

Strain jam through a sieve or smooth it in a blender. Add KAHLÚA® and mix well. Use to baste turkey throughout roasting period.

Tip: Also superb with goose, duck or any other poultry.

Marinated Vegetable Spinach Salad (left) and Hearty Minestrone Gratiné (right)

Marinated Vegetable Spinach Salad

Makes 4 servings

> **Mustard Tarragon Marinade (recipe follows)**
> **8 ounces fresh mushrooms, quartered**
> **2 slices purple onion, separated into rings**
> **16 cherry tomatoes, halved**
> **4 cups fresh spinach leaves, washed and stems removed**
> **3 slices (3 oz.) SARGENTO® Preferred Light™ Sliced Mozzarella Cheese, cut into julienne strips**
> **Fresh ground black pepper**

Prepare marinade. Place mushrooms, onion and tomatoes in bowl. Toss with marinade and let stand 15 minutes. Meanwhile, wash and dry spinach leaves. Arrange on 4 individual serving plates. Divide marinated vegetables between plates and top each salad with ¼ of the cheese. Serve with fresh ground pepper, if desired.

Mustard Tarragon Marinade

> **3 tablespoons red wine vinegar**
> **1 tablespoon Dijon mustard**
> **½ tablespoon dried tarragon**
> **2 tablespoons olive oil**

Combine first three ingredients. Slowly whisk oil into mixture until slightly thickened.

Hearty Minestrone Gratiné

Makes 4 servings

> **1 cup diced celery**
> **1 cup diced zucchini**
> **1 can (28 oz.) tomatoes with liquid, chopped**
> **2 cups water**
> **2 teaspoons sugar**
> **1 teaspoon dried Italian herb seasoning**
> **1 can (15 oz.) garbanzo beans, drained**
> **4 (3 × ½-inch) slices French bread, toasted**
> **1 cup (4 oz.) SARGENTO® Preferred Light™ Fancy Shredded Mozzarella Cheese**
> **2 tablespoons SARGENTO® Preferred Light™ Grated Gourmet Parm**
> **Freshly chopped parsley**

Spray a large saucepan or Dutch oven with nonstick cooking spray. Over medium heat, sauté celery and zucchini until tender. Add tomatoes, water, sugar and herb seasoning. Simmer, uncovered, 15 to 20 minutes. Add garbanzo beans and heat an additional 10 minutes. Meanwhile, heat broiler. Place toasted French bread on broiler pan. Divide Mozzarella on bread slices. Broil until cheese melts. Ladle soup into bowls and top with Mozzarella French bread. Sprinkle Gourmet Parm cheese over each bowl and garnish with parsley. Serve immediately.

Fruity Apple Yam Puffs

Makes 36 to 40 puffs

> 2 cans (16 ounces *each*) yams or sweet potatoes, well drained
> 1 can SOLO® or 1 jar BAKER® Apple or Pineapple Filling
> 1/4 cup all-purpose flour
> 1 teaspoon cinnamon
> 1/4 teaspoon nutmeg
> 1/8 teaspoon ground cloves
> 4 cups corn flakes, crushed

Preheat oven to 375°F. Grease 2 baking sheets and set aside.

Place yams in container of food processor and process until puréed, or mash in bowl with potato masher. Spoon puréed yams into medium-size bowl. Add apple filling and stir until combined. Stir flour, cinnamon, nutmeg and cloves; fold into yam mixture.

Place corn flake crumbs in shallow bowl. Drop yam mixture into crumbs, 1 tablespoonful at a time, and turn to coat all sides. Shape into balls and place on prepared baking sheets.

Bake 20 to 25 minutes or until deep golden brown. Remove from baking sheets and place on serving plate. Serve warm with baked ham, roast pork or turkey.

Quick and Zesty Vegetable Soup

Makes 8 servings

> 1 lb. lean ground beef
> 1/2 cup chopped onion
> 2 cans (14 1/2 oz. *each*) DEL MONTE® Italian Style Stewed Tomatoes
> 2 cans (13 3/4 fl. oz. *each*) beef broth
> 1 can (17 oz.) DEL MONTE® Mixed Vegetables
> 1/2 cup uncooked medium egg noodles
> 1/2 teaspoon oregano

In large pot, brown meat with onion. Cook until onion is tender; drain. Salt and pepper to taste. Stir in remaining ingredients. Bring to boil; reduce heat. Cover and simmer 15 minutes or until noodles are tender.

Prep Time: 5 minutes

Cook Time: 15 minutes

Muffin Pan Snacks

Makes 6 servings

> 1 package (4-serving size) JELL-O® Brand Gelatin, any flavor
> 3/4 cup boiling water
> 1/2 cup cold water
> Ice cubes
> 1 1/2 cups diced fresh fruit or vegetables

Dissolve gelatin in boiling water. Combine cold water and ice cubes to make 1 cup. Add to gelatin, stirring until slightly thickened. Remove any unmelted ice. Add fruit. Chill until thickened, about 10 minutes.

Place foil baking cups in muffin pans, or use small individual molds. Spoon gelatin mixture into cups or molds, filling each about 2/3 full. Chill until firm, about 2 hours.

Peel away foil cups carefully or dip molds in warm water for about 5 seconds to unmold.

Prep time: 15 minutes

Chill time: 2 hours

Muffin Pan Snacks

Italian Vegetable Soup (left) and Broccoli Cheese Soup (right)

Italian Vegetable Soup

Makes about 2¹/₂ quarts

  1 pound bulk Italian sausage
  2 cups chopped onion
  2 cloves garlic, finely chopped
  7 cups water
  4 medium carrots, pared and sliced
  1 (28-ounce) can whole tomatoes,
    undrained and broken up
  2 tablespoons WYLER'S® or STEERO® Beef-
    Flavor Instant Bouillon *or* 6 Beef-
    Flavor Bouillon Cubes
  1 teaspoon Italian seasoning
  ¹/₄ teaspoon pepper
1¹/₂ cups coarsely chopped zucchini
  1 (15-ounce) can garbanzo beans, drained
  1 cup uncooked CREAMETTE® Rotini or
    Elbow Macaroni

In large kettle or Dutch oven, brown sausage, onion and garlic; pour off fat. Add water, carrots, tomatoes, bouillon, Italian seasoning and pepper; bring to a boil. Reduce heat; cover and simmer 30 minutes. Add zucchini, beans and rotini. Cook 15 to 20 minutes or until rotini is tender, stirring occasionally. Refrigerate leftovers.

Broccoli Cheese Soup

Makes about 2 quarts

¹/₂ cup chopped onion
¹/₄ cup margarine or butter
¹/₄ cup unsifted flour
  3 cups water
  2 (10-ounce) packages frozen chopped
    broccoli, thawed and well drained
  4 teaspoons WYLER'S® or STEERO®
    Chicken-Flavor Instant Bouillon
    or 4 Chicken-Flavor Bouillon Cubes
  1 teaspoon Worcestershire sauce
  3 cups (12 ounces) shredded Cheddar
    cheese
  2 cups (1 pint) BORDEN® or MEADOW
    GOLD® Coffee Cream *or* Half-and-Half

In large kettle or Dutch oven, cook onion in margarine until tender; stir in flour until smooth. Gradually add water then broccoli, bouillon and Worcestershire. Over medium heat, cook and stir until thickened and broccoli is tender, about 10 minutes. Add cheese and cream. Cook and stir until cheese melts and soup is hot *(do not boil)*. Refrigerate leftovers.

Tip: 6 cups (about 1¹/₄ pounds) chopped fresh broccoli can be substituted for frozen broccoli.

Microwave: In 3- to 4-quart round baking dish, combine onion and margarine; cook covered on 100% power (high) 2 to 3 minutes or until onion is tender. Stir in flour. Gradually stir in water then broccoli, bouillon and Worcestershire. Cook covered on 100% power (high) 10 to 12 minutes or until thickened and broccoli is tender. Add cheese and cream; mix well. Cook covered on 100% power (high) 2 to 4 minutes or until heated through.

Thai Chicken Fettucine Salad

Makes 4 servings

- 1 cup PACE® Picante Sauce
- 1/4 cup chunk-style peanut butter
- 2 tablespoons honey
- 2 tablespoons orange juice
- 1 teaspoon soy sauce
- 1/2 teaspoon ground ginger
- 6 ounces dry fettucine, cooked according to package directions, well drained
- 3 chicken breast halves, boned, skinned and cut into 1-inch pieces (about 12 ounces)
- 2 tablespoons vegetable oil
  Lettuce or savoy cabbage leaves (optional)
- 1/4 cup coarsely chopped cilantro
- 1/4 cup peanut halves
- 1/4 cup thin red bell pepper strips

Combine PACE® Picante Sauce, peanut butter, honey, orange juice, soy sauce and ginger in small saucepan. Cook and stir over low heat until blended and smooth. Reserve 1/4 cup picante sauce mixture; toss remaining mixture with hot cooked fettucine. Cook chicken in oil in large skillet until browned and cooked through, about 5 minutes. Add reserved picante sauce mixture; mix well. Line large platter with lettuce leaves, if desired. Arrange fettucine mixture over lettuce; top with chicken mixture. Sprinkle with cilantro, peanut halves and pepper strips. Cool to room temperature before serving. Serve with additional PACE® Picante Sauce.

Thai Chicken Fettucine Salad

Ribbon Squares

Ribbon Squares

Makes 12 servings

- 1 package (4-serving size) JELL-O® Brand Gelatin, Lemon Flavor
- 1 package (4-serving size) JELL-O® Brand Gelatin, Cherry, Raspberry or Strawberry Flavor
- 1 package (4-serving size) JELL-O® Brand Gelatin, Lime Flavor
- 3 cups boiling water
- 1 package (8 ounces) PHILADELPHIA BRAND® Cream Cheese, softened
- 1 can (8¼ ounces) crushed pineapple in syrup, undrained
- 1 cup thawed COOL WHIP® Whipped Topping
- ½ cup MIRACLE WHIP® Salad Dressing
- 1½ cups cold water
  Canned pineapple slices, drained (optional)
  Celery leaves (optional)

Dissolve each flavor of gelatin in separate bowls, using 1 cup of the boiling water for each.

Blend lemon gelatin into cream cheese, beating until smooth. Add pineapple with syrup. Chill until slightly thickened. Stir in whipped topping and salad dressing. Chill until thickened. Stir ¾ cup of the cold water into cherry gelatin; pour into 9-inch square pan. Chill until set but not firm.

Stir remaining ¾ cup cold water into lime gelatin; chill until slightly thickened. Spoon lemon gelatin mixture over cherry gelatin layer in pan. Chill until set but not firm. Top with lime gelatin. Chill until firm, about 4 hours or overnight. Unmold; cut into squares. Garnish with pineapple slices and celery leaves, if desired.

Prep time: 1 hour

Chill time: 6 hours

Sweet Potato Crisp

Makes 8 servings

- 1 (8 oz.) pkg. PHILADELPHIA BRAND® Cream Cheese, softened
- 1 (40 oz.) can cut sweet potatoes, drained
- ¼ cup packed brown sugar
- ¼ teaspoon ground cinnamon
- 1 cup chopped apples
- ⅔ cup chopped cranberries
- ½ cup flour
- ½ cup old fashioned or quick oats, uncooked
- ½ cup packed brown sugar
- ⅓ cup PARKAY® Margarine
- ¼ cup chopped pecans

- Preheat oven to 350°F.

- Beat cream cheese, potatoes, ¼ cup sugar and cinnamon in large mixing bowl at medium speed with electric mixer until well blended.

- Spoon into 1½-quart casserole or 10×6-inch baking dish. Top with apples and cranberries.

- Stir together flour, oats and ½ cup sugar in medium bowl; cut in margarine until mixture resembles coarse crumbs. Stir in pecans. Sprinkle over fruit.

- Bake 35 to 40 minutes or until thoroughly heated.

Prep time: 20 minutes

Cooking time: 40 minutes

Variation: Substitute four cooked, peeled medium sweet potatoes, cubed, for canned sweet potatoes.

Cobb Salad

Cobb Salad

Makes 4 servings

4 skinless boneless chicken breast halves, cooked, cooled
²/₃ cup vegetable oil
¹/₃ cup HEINZ Distilled White or Apple Cider Vinegar
1 clove garlic, minced
2 teaspoons dried dill weed
1¹/₂ teaspoons granulated sugar
¹/₂ teaspoon salt
¹/₄ teaspoon pepper
8 cups torn salad greens, chilled
1 large tomato, diced
1 medium green bell pepper, diced
1 small red onion, chopped
³/₄ cup crumbled blue cheese
6 slices bacon, cooked, crumbled
1 hard-cooked egg, chopped

Shred chicken into bite-size pieces. For dressing, in jar, combine oil, vinegar, garlic, dill, sugar, salt and pepper; cover and shake vigorously. Pour ¹/₂ cup dressing over chicken; toss well to coat. Toss greens with remaining dressing. Line each of 4 large individual salad bowls with greens; mound chicken mixture in center. Arrange mounds of tomato, green pepper, onion, cheese, bacon and egg around chicken.

Easy Turkey Salad

Easy Turkey Salad

Makes about 8 servings

    1 can (10¾ ounces) CAMPBELL'S®
       condensed cream of celery soup
½ cup mayonnaise
    4 cups chopped cooked turkey
    1 cup finely chopped celery
½ cup chopped sweet red pepper
½ cup sliced green onions
    2 tablespoons chopped fresh parsley
⅛ teaspoon pepper
    Leaf lettuce

In large bowl, stir together soup and mayonnaise until smooth. Fold in turkey, celery, red pepper, onions, parsley and pepper. Serve mixture on leaf lettuce. Cover and refrigerate any remaining salad mixture.

Asparagus Dijonnaise

Makes 4 servings

    1 can (15 oz.) DEL MONTE® Tender Green™
       Asparagus Spears, drained
¼ cup mayonnaise
    1 teaspoon Dijon-style mustard
    2 teaspoons chopped parsley
    Dash garlic powder

Arrange asparagus in a row, about 2 deep, in 8×8-inch broiler-proof dish. Combine mayonnaise, mustard, parsley and garlic powder. Spread mixture across center of asparagus. Broil 6 inches from heat 3 minutes or until topping browns and asparagus are warm.

Prep & Cook Time: 7 minutes

Cranberry and Red Pepper Relish

Makes 1 1/2 cups

2 medium red bell peppers, roasted, peeled, seeded and cut into 1-inch pieces*
1 cup fresh cranberries, rinsed and drained
1 green onion, cut into 1-inch pieces
3 tablespoons fresh cilantro leaves
2 tablespoons fresh orange juice
1/2 teaspoon grated lime peel
1/2 cup sugar
1/8 teaspoon salt

1. In food processor bowl fitted with steel blade, process peppers, cranberries, onion, cilantro, orange juice and lime peel until coarsely chopped.

2. In medium-size bowl combine cranberry mixture, sugar and salt. Cover and refrigerate 1 or more hours to allow flavors to mix.

To roast bell peppers, place peppers under broiler, turning frequently, until slightly scorched on all sides. Place broiled peppers in a paper bag; close bag and set aside five minutes. Remove blistered skins from peppers.

Favorite recipe from **National Turkey Federation**

Cheddar Sesame Garden Vegetables

Makes 2 servings

1/2 cup *undiluted* CARNATION® Evaporated Skimmed Milk
1 tablespoon plus 2 teaspoons all-purpose flour
1/4 cup water
1 teaspoon country Dijon-style mustard
1/2 cup (2 ounces) shredded reduced-fat Cheddar cheese
3 to 4 cups cooked fresh vegetables,* drained
1 tablespoon toasted sesame seeds

In small saucepan, whisk small amount of milk into flour. Stir in remaining milk with water and mustard. Cook over medium heat, stirring constantly, until mixture comes to a boil and thickens. Add cheese; stir until melted. Serve over vegetables. Sprinkle with sesame seeds.

Your choice of carrots, summer squash, broccoli, cauliflower or asparagus.

Maple Glazed Sweet Potatoes

Makes 6 to 8 servings

1 1/2 pounds sweet potatoes or yams, cooked, peeled and quartered
1/2 cup CARY'S®, VERMONT MAPLE ORCHARDS® or MACDONALD'S® Pure Maple Syrup
1/2 cup orange juice
3 tablespoons margarine or butter, melted
1 tablespoon cornstarch
1 teaspoon grated orange peel

Preheat oven to 350°F. Arrange sweet potatoes in 1 1/2-quart shallow baking dish. Combine remaining ingredients; pour over potatoes. Bake 40 minutes or until hot and sauce is thickened, basting frequently. Refrigerate leftovers.

Salmon Platter Salad

Makes 4 to 6 servings

1 can (15 1/2 oz.) salmon
1 pound asparagus
2 tablespoons oil
2 tablespoons lemon juice
1/4 teaspoon dry mustard
1/4 teaspoon salt
Dash pepper
Salad greens
Tomato wedges
Cucumber slices
Pimiento strips
Radish roses
1/2 cup dairy sour cream
1 teaspoon dried dill weed

Chill can of salmon. Cook asparagus in boiling salted water until just tender. Drain and place in shallow glass container. Combine oil, lemon juice, mustard, salt and pepper. Pour over asparagus. Marinate for 1 hour. Drain, reserving marinade. Drain salmon and remove from can in one piece. Place salmon and asparagus on platter lined with greens. Garnish with tomato wedges, cucumber slices, pimiento strips and radish roses. Combine reserved marinade with sour cream. Blend in dill weed. Season with additional salt and pepper to taste. Pass with salad.

Favorite recipe from **Alaska Seafood Marketing Institute**

Main Dishes

Apple & Herb Stuffing

Makes about 2 1/2 quarts

   2 cups sliced celery
1 1/2 cups chopped onion
   1/2 cup margarine or butter
1 3/4 cups hot water
   1 tablespoon WYLER'S® or STEERO®
      Chicken-Flavor Instant Bouillon
      or 3 Chicken-Flavor Bouillon Cubes
  12 cups dry bread cubes (about 16 slices
      bread)
   3 cups coarsely chopped apple
   1 cup toasted slivered almonds
   1 tablespoon chopped parsley
   2 teaspoons poultry seasoning
   1/4 teaspoon rubbed sage
      Rich Turkey Gravy (recipe follows)

In large skillet, cook celery and onion in margarine until tender. Add water and bouillon; cook until bouillon dissolves. In large bowl, combine remaining ingredients except Rich Turkey Gravy; add bouillon mixture. Mix well. Loosely stuff turkey just before roasting. Place remaining stuffing in greased baking dish. Bake at 350°F for 30 minutes or until hot. Serve with Rich Turkey Gravy, if desired. Refrigerate leftovers.

Rich Turkey Gravy: In medium skillet, stir 1/4 to 1/3 cup flour into 1/4 cup pan drippings; cook and stir until dark brown. Stir in 2 cups hot water and 2 teaspoons WYLER'S® or STEERO® Chicken-Flavor Instant Bouillon *or* 2 Chicken-Flavor Bouillon Cubes; cook and stir until thickened and bouillon is dissolved. Refrigerate leftovers.

Makes about 1 1/2 cups

Tortellini with Mushrooms and Ham

Makes 4 servings

   1 tablespoon olive oil
   1/2 cup cooked ham, cut into strips
   1/4 cup chopped onion
   1 clove garlic, minced
   1/2 teaspoon dried basil leaves, crushed
   1 can (10 3/4 ounces) CAMPBELL'S®
      condensed cream of mushroom soup
   1 cup frozen peas
   1 soup can milk
   2 tablespoons chopped fresh parsley
   1/8 teaspoon pepper
   3 cups hot cooked cheese tortellini
      (2 1/2 cups uncooked)
      Grated Parmesan cheese
      Cherry tomatoes, curly endive, sweet red
      pepper rings and Italian parsley for
      garnish

1. In 2-quart saucepan over medium heat, in hot oil, cook ham, onion, garlic and basil 2 minutes, stirring often.

2. Stir in soup and peas; heat to boiling. Reduce heat to low. Cover; simmer 5 minutes or until peas are tender.

3. Stir in milk, parsley and pepper; heat through. In large bowl, pour soup mixture over tortellini; toss lightly to coat. Serve with Parmesan. Garnish with cherry tomatoes, endive, red pepper and parsley, if desired.

Apple & Herb Stuffing

Chicken-Broccoli Divan

Chicken-Broccoli Divan

Makes 4 servings

  1 pound fresh broccoli, cut into spears
    or 1 package (10 ounces) frozen
    broccoli spears, cooked and drained
1½ cups cubed cooked chicken or turkey
  1 can (10¾ ounces) CAMPBELL'S®
    condensed cream of broccoli or cream
    of chicken soup
⅓ cup milk
½ cup shredded Cheddar cheese (2 ounces)
  2 tablespoons fine dry bread crumbs
  1 tablespoon margarine or butter, melted

1. Preheat oven to 450°F.

2. In 10×6-inch baking dish, arrange broccoli; top with chicken. In small bowl, combine soup and milk; pour over chicken. Sprinkle with cheese. In cup, combine bread crumbs and margarine; sprinkle over cheese.

3. Bake 15 minutes or until hot and bubbling.

To microwave: *Do not cook* broccoli. In 10×6-inch microwave-safe baking dish, arrange broccoli. Cover with vented plastic wrap; microwave on HIGH 6 minutes, rearranging broccoli halfway through cooking. Drain. Top with chicken. In small bowl, combine soup and milk; pour over chicken. Sprinkle with cheese. In cup, combine bread crumbs and margarine; sprinkle over cheese. Cover with waxed paper; microwave on HIGH 6 minutes or until heated through, rotating dish halfway through heating.

Spicy Chicken Cacciatore

Makes 6 servings

  2 pounds chicken breasts and thighs,
    skinned
¼ cup flour
  1 teaspoon salt
½ teaspoon freshly ground black pepper
  2 tablespoons olive oil
¾ cup PACE® Picante Sauce
  1 can (8 ounces) tomato sauce
¼ cup dry red wine
  8 ounces mushrooms, halved or quartered,
    as desired
  2 cloves garlic, minced
  1 teaspoon basil leaves, crushed
  1 teaspoon oregano leaves, crushed
  1 small green bell pepper, cut into short,
    thin strips

Coat chicken in combined flour, salt and pepper. Cook chicken in oil in large, deep skillet or Dutch oven until lightly browned on both sides, about 8 minutes; drain. Add remaining ingredients except pepper strips. Cover and simmer 20 minutes. Stir in pepper strips; simmer uncovered about 10 minutes or until chicken is tender and sauce has thickened. Serve with additional PACE® Picante Sauce.

Almondine Fish

Makes 4 servings

½ cup margarine or butter, melted
  3 tablespoons REALEMON® Lemon Juice
    from Concentrate
  3 tablespoons sliced almonds, toasted
  1 pound fish fillets, fresh or frozen,
    thawed

Combine margarine and REALEMON® brand; reserve ¼ cup. Add almonds to remaining margarine mixture; set aside. Broil or grill fish as desired, basting frequently with reserved margarine mixture. Serve with almond sauce. Refrigerate leftovers.

Herb Fish: Omit almonds. Add 1 teaspoon dill weed.

Garlic Fish: Omit almonds. Add ½ teaspoon garlic powder.

Holiday Beef Steaks with Vegetable Saute and Hot Mustard Sauce

Makes 6 servings

  Boneless beef top loin steaks, cut 1 inch thick
½ cup plain yogurt
1 teaspoon cornstarch
¼ cup condensed beef broth
2 teaspoons coarse-grained mustard
1 teaspoon *each* prepared grated horseradish and Dijon-style mustard
¼ teaspoon sugar
½ teaspoon lemon-pepper
1 package (16 ounces) frozen whole green beans
1 cup quartered large mushrooms
1 tablespoon butter
¼ cup water

Place yogurt and cornstarch in medium saucepan and stir until blended. Stir in beef broth, coarse-grained mustard, horseradish, Dijon-style mustard and sugar; reserve. Press an equal amount of lemon-pepper into surface of boneless beef top loin steaks. Place steaks on rack in broiler pan so surface of steaks is 3 to 4 inches from heat. Broil steaks about 15 minutes for rare; 20 minutes for medium, turning once. Meanwhile cook beans and mushrooms in butter in large frying pan over medium heat 6 minutes, stirring occasionally. Add water; cover and continue cooking 6 to 8 minutes, stirring occasionally until beans are tender. Cook reserved sauce over medium-low heat 5 minutes, stirring until sauce is slightly thickened. Serve steaks and vegetables with sauce.

Preparation time: 15 minutes

Cooking time: 15 minutes

Note: A boneless beef top loin steak will yield four 3-ounce cooked servings per pound.

Favorite recipe from **National Live Stock and Meat Board**

Holiday Beef Steaks with Vegetable Saute and Hot Mustard Sauce

Sweet & Sour Meatballs

Makes 6 to 8 servings

1½ pounds lean ground beef
1 (8-ounce) can water chestnuts, drained
   and chopped
2 eggs, slightly beaten
⅓ cup plain dry bread crumbs
4 teaspoons WYLER'S® or STEERO®
   Beef-Flavor Instant Bouillon
1 tablespoon Worcestershire sauce
1 cup water
½ cup firmly packed light brown sugar
½ cup REALEMON® Lemon Juice from
   Concentrate
¼ cup ketchup
2 tablespoons cornstarch
¼ teaspoon salt
1 cup coarsely chopped red and green
   bell peppers
Hot cooked rice

In large bowl, combine meat, water chestnuts, eggs, crumbs, bouillon and Worcestershire; mix well. Shape into 1¼-inch meatballs. In large skillet, brown meatballs. Remove from pan; pour off fat. In same skillet, combine remaining ingredients except peppers and rice; mix well. Over medium heat, cook and stir until sauce thickens. Reduce heat. Add meatballs; simmer uncovered 10 minutes. Add peppers; heat through. Serve with rice. Garnish with parsley if desired. Refrigerate leftovers.

Pork Tenderloin Waldorf

Makes 4 to 6 servings

2 pork tenderloins (about 1½ pounds)
¾ cup BAMA® Apple Jelly
¼ cup REALEMON® Lemon Juice from
   Concentrate
¼ cup soy sauce
¼ cup vegetable oil
1 tablespoon finely chopped fresh
   ginger root
1 cup chopped apple
1 cup fresh bread crumbs (2 slices)
¼ cup finely chopped celery
¼ cup chopped pecans

Partially slit tenderloins lengthwise, being careful not to cut all the way through; arrange in shallow dish. In small saucepan, combine jelly, REALEMON® brand, soy sauce, oil and ginger; cook and stir until jelly melts. Reserving *3 tablespoons* jelly mixture, pour remainder over meat. Cover; refrigerate 4 hours or overnight. Place meat in shallow baking pan. Combine apple, crumbs, celery, nuts and reserved jelly mixture. Spread slits open; fill with apple mixture. Bake 30 minutes in preheated 375°F oven. Loosely cover meat; bake 10 minutes longer or until meat thermometer reaches 160°F. Refrigerate leftovers.

Seafood Royale

Makes 6 servings

4 tablespoons butter or margarine, divided
2 tablespoons all-purpose flour
½ teaspoon dried dill weed
¼ teaspoon seasoned salt
1½ cups (12-ounce can) *undiluted*
   CARNATION® Evaporated Milk
½ cup dry white wine
½ cup shredded Swiss cheese
1½ cups sliced mushrooms
½ cup finely sliced green onions
1 pound salmon, cooked, bones and skin
   removed
6 rolls or puff pastry shells

In medium saucepan, melt *2 tablespoons* butter. Whisk in flour, dill and salt; heat until bubbling. Add evaporated milk; stir constantly over medium heat until well thickened. Add wine and cheese; stir until blended. Keep warm. In small skillet, sauté mushrooms and green onions in *remaining 2 tablespoons* butter. Combine sauce, mushrooms, onions and salmon over low heat; stir gently to blend. Serve in hollowed out rolls or puff pastry shells.

*Sweet & Sour Meatballs (top) and
Pork Tenderloin Waldorf (bottom)*

Roast Turkey with Herb Gravy

Roast Turkey with Herb Gravy

Makes 10 to 12 servings

  2 small tart apples, cored and cut into
    eighths
  2 leeks, quartered lengthwise and cut into
    2-inch pieces
  ¹/₃ cup coarsely chopped fresh sage,
    optional
  2 bay leaves
  1 tablespoon rubbed sage
  1 tablespoon dried thyme leaves
  12- to 14-pound SWIFT BUTTERBALL®
    Turkey, thawed if frozen
    Vegetable oil
    Herb Gravy (recipe follows)

Preheat oven to 325°F. In large bowl, combine all
ingredients except turkey, oil and Herb Gravy.
Remove neck and giblets from turkey cavities.
Rinse turkey; drain well. Stuff neck and body
cavities with apple mixture.* Turn wings back to
hold neck skin in place. Place turkey lifter on flat
rack in shallow roasting pan. Place turkey on lifter,
breast-side up. Bring loops of lifter up over turkey.

Insert meat thermometer deep into thickest part of
thigh next to body, not touching bone. Brush skin
with oil. Roast 3¹/₂ to 4 hours. When skin is
golden brown, shield breast loosely with
aluminum foil to prevent overbrowning. Check for
doneness; thigh temperature should be 180° to
185°F. Let turkey stand 15 to 20 minutes before
carving.

Herb Gravy: Remove turkey from pan; pour
drippings from roasting pan into 1-quart measure.
Remove ¹/₄ cup fat from drippings; return to
roasting pan. Skim off and discard remaining fat
from drippings. Add water to drippings to make
3 cups. Gradually stir ¹/₃ cup all-purpose flour into
fat until smooth. Then add drippings, 2 teaspoons
WYLER'S® or STEERO® Chicken-Flavor Instant
Bouillon and dash ground pepper. Over medium
heat, cook and stir until gravy comes to a boil and
thickens.   *Makes about 3 cups*

**The apple mixture placed in the turkey is not a
stuffing to be eaten. Rather it flavors the pan
drippings to make the Herb Gravy.*

Savory Corn Bread Stuffing

Makes about 3 quarts

1 pound fresh mushrooms, sliced (about 4 cups)
1 cup chopped celery
3/4 cup chopped onion
1/2 cup margarine or butter
4 teaspoons WYLER'S® or STEERO® Chicken-Flavor Instant Bouillon *or* 4 Chicken-Flavor Bouillon Cubes
1 2/3 cups boiling water
1 pound bulk sausage, browned and drained
1 (16-ounce) package corn bread stuffing mix
1 1/2 teaspoons poultry seasoning

In large skillet, cook mushrooms, celery and onion in margarine until tender. In large bowl, dissolve bouillon in water. Add sausage, mushroom mixture and remaining ingredients; mix well. Loosely stuff turkey just before roasting. Place remaining stuffing in greased baking dish. Bake at 350°F for 30 minutes or until hot. Refrigerate leftovers.

Broiled Rainbow Trout with Herb Mayonnaise

Makes 2 to 4 servings

6 tablespoons regular or light mayonnaise
1 clove garlic, minced
1 tablespoon lemon juice
Herbs to taste
Dash of pepper
4 CLEAR SPRINGS BRAND® Idaho Rainbow Trout fillets (4 ounces *each*)

Combine mayonnaise, garlic, lemon juice, herbs and pepper in bowl; mix well. Cover flesh side of each trout fillet with 1/4 of mayonnaise mixture. Broil 4 inches from heat source for about 3 to 5 minutes, or until fish flakes with a fork and topping is bubbly.

Double Onion Quiche

Makes 8 servings

3 cups thinly sliced yellow onions
3 tablespoons butter or margarine
1 cup thinly sliced green onions
3 eggs
1 cup heavy cream
1/2 cup grated Parmesan cheese
1/4 teaspoon hot pepper sauce
1 package (1 ounce) HIDDEN VALLEY RANCH® Milk Recipe Original Ranch® Salad Dressing Mix
1 9-inch deep-dish pastry shell, baked and cooled
Sprig fresh oregano

Preheat oven to 350°F. In medium skillet, saute yellow onions in butter, stirring occasionally, about 10 minutes. Add green onions and cook 5 minutes longer. Remove from heat and let cool.

In large bowl, whisk eggs until frothy. Whisk in cream, cheese, pepper sauce and salad dressing mix. Stir in onion mixture. Pour egg and onion mixture into baked and cooled pastry shell. Bake until top is browned and knife inserted in center comes out clean, 35 to 40 minutes. Cool on wire rack 10 minutes before slicing. Garnish with oregano.

Double Onion Quiche

Dressed Chicken Breasts with Angel Hair Pasta

Makes 8 servings

> 1 cup prepared **HIDDEN VALLEY RANCH®**
>   **Original Ranch® Salad Dressing**
> 1/3 cup Dijon-style mustard
> 4 whole chicken breasts, halved, skinned,
>   boned and pounded thin
> 1/2 cup butter or margarine
> 1/3 cup dry white wine
> 10 ounces angel hair pasta, cooked and
>   drained
>   Chopped parsley

In small bowl, whisk together salad dressing and mustard; set aside. In medium skillet, saute chicken in butter until browned; transfer to dish. Keep warm. Pour wine into skillet; cook over medium-high heat, scraping up any browned bits from bottom of skillet, about 5 minutes. Whisk in dressing mixture; blend well. Serve chicken with sauce over pasta; sprinkle with parsley.

Cajun Cornish Hens

Makes 4 servings

> 4 oz. hot smoked sausage, chopped
> 1/2 cup long grain white rice
> 1 can (14 1/2 oz.) **DEL MONTE®** Cajun Style
>   Stewed Tomatoes
> 1/2 cup sliced green onion
> 1/4 cup chopped green pepper
> 1 clove garlic, minced
> 1/4 teaspoon thyme
> 4 (20 oz. *each*) Rock Cornish Hens, thawed
> 1 tablespoon butter, melted

Brown sausage in saucepan. Stir in rice; cook 2 minutes. Add tomatoes, onion, pepper, garlic and thyme. Bring to boil. Cover; simmer 20 minutes (rice will be firm). Remove giblet package from hens and set aside for another use. Rinse hens; drain well. Stuff with rice mixture. Tie legs together with string. Place breast-side up on rack in shallow pan. Brush with butter. Bake at 375°F 1 hour or until done. Remove string from legs and serve.

Dressed Chicken Breasts with Angel Hair Pasta

Beef Tenderloin en Croute

Beef Tenderloin en Croute

Makes 8 to 10 servings

   1 (3 to 4 lb.) beef tenderloin
   1/2 lb. mushrooms, finely chopped
   2 tablespoons PARKAY® Margarine
   1 (8 oz.) container PHILADELPHIA
      BRAND® Soft Cream Cheese with
      Herb & Garlic
   1/4 cup seasoned dry bread crumbs
   2 tablespoons Madeira wine
   1 tablespoon chopped fresh chives
   1/4 teaspoon salt
   1 (17 1/4 oz.) pkg. frozen ready-to-bake
      puff pastry sheets
   1 egg, beaten
   1 tablespoon cold water

• Preheat oven to 425°F.

• Tie meat with string at 1-inch intervals, if
necessary. Place meat on rack in baking pan.

• Roast 45 to 50 minutes or until meat
thermometer registers 135°F. Remove from oven;
cool 30 minutes in refrigerator. Remove string.

• Saute mushrooms in margarine in large skillet
10 minutes or until liquid evaporates, stirring
occasionally.

• Add cream cheese, bread crumbs, wine, chives
and salt; mix well. Cool.

• Thaw puff pastry sheets according to package
directions.

• On lightly floured surface, overlap pastry sheets
1/2 inch to form 14×12-inch rectangle; press edges
firmly together to seal. Trim length of pastry 2 1/2
inches longer than length of meat.

• Spread mushroom mixture over top and sides of
meat. Place meat in center of pastry.

• Fold pastry over meat; press edges together to
seal. Decorate top with pastry trimmings, if
desired.

• Brush pastry with combined egg and water.
Place meat in greased 15×10×1-inch jelly roll pan.

• Bake 20 to 25 minutes or until pastry is golden
brown. Let stand 10 minutes before slicing.

Prep time: 25 minutes plus chilling

Cooking time: 1 hour and 15 minutes

Honey Glazed Ham

Honey Glazed Ham

Makes enough to glaze a 4-pound ham

**¼ cup VERMONT MAPLE ORCHARDS® Pure
  Honey
3 tablespoons light brown sugar
2 teaspoons prepared mustard**

Combine ingredients. Use to baste ham frequently
during last hour of baking.

Caraway Turkey-Noodle Bake

Makes 8 servings

**6 cups wide egg noodles, uncooked
    (8 ounces)
2 cups coarsely chopped cabbage
½ cup diced carrots
3 cups diced cooked turkey or chicken
1 can (10½ ounces) FRANCO-AMERICAN®
    chicken gravy
½ cup sour cream
3 slices bacon, cooked and crumbled
4 teaspoons spicy brown mustard
½ teaspoon caraway seed
½ cup shredded Swiss cheese (2 ounces)**

1. Preheat oven to 400°F. Cook noodles with
cabbage and carrots according to noodle package
directions; drain.

2. Meanwhile, in bowl, combine turkey, gravy,
sour cream, bacon, mustard and caraway. Add
noodle mixture; toss. Spoon into 2-quart casserole.
Bake 20 minutes or until heated through. Top with
cheese. Bake 5 minutes more or until cheese is
melted.

To Microwave: Prepare noodles, cabbage and
carrots as directed in step 1. In 3-quart microwave-
safe casserole, combine turkey, gravy, sour cream,
bacon, mustard and caraway. Cover with lid;
microwave on HIGH 2 minutes. Stir in noodle
mixture. Cover; microwave on HIGH 7 minutes or
until heated through, stirring once during cooking.
Top with cheese. Microwave, uncovered, on HIGH
2 minutes or until cheese is melted.

Broccoli-Stuffed Shells

Makes 4 servings

> 1 tablespoon butter or margarine
> ¼ cup chopped onion
> 1 cup ricotta cheese
> 1 egg
> 2 cups chopped cooked broccoli *or* 1 package (10 ounces) frozen chopped broccoli, thawed and well-drained
> 1 cup (4 ounces) shredded Monterey Jack cheese
> 20 jumbo pasta shells
> 1 can (28 ounces) crushed tomatoes with added puree
> 1 package (1 ounce) HIDDEN VALLEY RANCH® Milk Recipe Original Ranch® Salad Dressing Mix
> ¼ cup grated Parmesan cheese

Preheat oven to 350°F. In small skillet, melt butter over medium heat. Add onion; cook until onion is tender but not browned. Remove from heat; cool. In large bowl, stir ricotta cheese and egg until well-blended. Add broccoli and Jack cheese; mix well. In large pot of boiling water, cook pasta shells 8 to 10 minutes or just until tender; drain. Rinse under cold running water; drain again. Stuff each shell with about 2 tablespoons broccoli-cheese mixture.

In medium bowl, combine tomatoes, sauteed onion and salad dressing mix; mix well. Pour one-third of the tomato mixture into 13×9-inch baking dish. Arrange filled shells in dish. Spoon remaining tomato mixture over top. Sprinkle with Parmesan cheese. Bake, covered, until hot and bubbly, about 30 minutes.

Bayou Jambalaya

Makes 4 to 6 servings

> 1 medium onion, sliced
> ½ cup chopped green bell pepper
> 1 clove garlic, minced
> 1 cup uncooked white rice
> 2 tablespoons butter or margarine
> 1 cup HEINZ Tomato Ketchup
> 2¼ cups water
> 1 tablespoon HEINZ Vinegar
> ⅛ teaspoon black pepper
> ⅛ teaspoon ground red pepper
> 1 medium tomato, coarsely chopped
> 1 cup cubed cooked ham
> ½ pound deveined shelled raw medium-size shrimp

In large skillet, sauté onion, green pepper, garlic and rice in butter until onion is tender. Stir in ketchup, water, vinegar, black pepper, red pepper, tomato and ham. Cover; simmer 20 to 25 minutes or until rice is tender. Add shrimp; simmer, uncovered, 3 to 5 minutes or until shrimp turn pink, stirring occasionally.

Microwave Directions: Place onion, green pepper, garlic and butter in 3-quart microwave-safe casserole. Cover dish with lid or vented plastic wrap; microwave at HIGH (100%) 3 to 4 minutes, stirring once. Stir in rice, ketchup, water, vinegar, black pepper, red pepper, tomato and ham. Cover and microwave at HIGH 10 to 12 minutes or until mixture comes to a boil. Microwave at MEDIUM (50%) 18 to 20 minutes until rice is cooked, stirring once. Stir in shrimp; cover and microwave at HIGH 2 to 3 minutes or until shrimp turn pink. Let stand, covered, 5 minutes before serving.

Bayou Jambalaya

Cheesy Mushroom Frittata

Makes 5 servings

1 can (10¾ ounces) CAMPBELL'S®
   condensed cream of mushroom soup
6 eggs, slightly beaten
1½ cups shredded mozzarella cheese
   (6 ounces), divided
¼ teaspoon dried basil leaves, crushed
⅛ teaspoon pepper
2 tablespoons margarine or butter
1 cup sliced fresh mushrooms
1 medium onion, chopped
   Chopped fresh parsley for garnish
   Tomato wedges for garnish
   Fresh basil leaves for garnish

1. In medium bowl with wire whisk, beat soup until smooth. Gradually blend in eggs, *1 cup* of the cheese, the basil and pepper.

2. In 10-inch *oven-safe* omelet pan or skillet over medium heat, in hot margarine, cook mushrooms and onion until mushrooms are tender and liquid is evaporated, stirring occasionally.

3. Pour soup mixture into skillet. Reduce heat to low. Cook 6 minutes or until eggs are set 1 inch from edge. *Do not stir.* Remove from heat.

4. Broil 6 inches from heat 5 minutes or until frittata is puffy and lightly browned. Top with remaining cheese. Cover; let stand 2 minutes or until cheese melts. Garnish with parsley, tomato wedges and fresh basil.

Cheesy Mushroom Frittata

Herbed Chicken and Broccoli

Makes 4 servings

10 ounces boneless, skinless chicken
   breasts, sliced into ½-inch strips
1 teaspoon Italian herb seasoning
1 cup *undiluted* CARNATION® Evaporated
   Skimmed Milk
2 tablespoons all-purpose flour
1 clove garlic, crushed
¼ teaspoon salt (optional)
⅛ teaspoon white pepper
½ cup (2 ounces) shredded, reduced-fat
   Swiss cheese
1 package (10 ounces) frozen broccoli
   spears, thawed, drained and cut into
   bite-size pieces
   Paprika

Sprinkle chicken with Italian seasoning. Pound between sheets of wax paper. Remove paper. Spray nonstick skillet with nonstick cooking spray. Sauté chicken strips just until no longer pink. Keep warm. In small saucepan, whisk small amount of evaporated skimmed milk into flour. Stir in remaining milk with garlic, salt and pepper. Cook over medium heat, stirring constantly, until mixture just comes to a boil and thickens. Add cheese; stir until melted. Spray 10×6×2-inch baking dish with nonstick cooking spray. Spread about *¼ cup* sauce in bottom of dish. Arrange broccoli over sauce, then chicken pieces. Pour *remaining* sauce over top. Sprinkle with paprika. Cover. Bake in preheated 350°F oven for 20 to 25 minutes or until heated through.

Ham Glaze

Makes about 1 cup

1 cup KARO® Light or Dark Corn Syrup
½ cup packed brown sugar
3 tablespoons prepared mustard
½ teaspoon ground ginger
   Dash ground cloves

In medium saucepan combine corn syrup, brown sugar, mustard, ginger and cloves. Bring to boil over medium heat; boil 5 minutes, stirring constantly. Brush on ham frequently during last 30 minutes of baking.

Preparation Time: 10 minutes

Microwave Directions: In 1½-quart microwavable bowl combine all ingredients. Microwave on HIGH (100%), 6 minutes. Glaze ham as above.

Turkey Breast with Southwestern Corn Bread Dressing and Cranberry and Red Pepper Relish (page 45)

Turkey Breast with Southwestern Corn Bread Dressing

Makes 12 servings

    5 cups corn bread, coarsely crumbled
    4 English muffins, coarsely crumbled
    3 mild green chilies, roasted, peeled,
       seeded and chopped
    1 red bell pepper, roasted, peeled, seeded
       and chopped
 ³/₄ cup pine nuts, toasted
    1 tablespoon fresh cilantro, chopped
    1 tablespoon fresh parsley, chopped
 1¹/₂ teaspoons *each* fresh basil, thyme and
       oregano, chopped, *or* 1 teaspoon *each*
       dried basil, thyme and oregano
    1 pound bulk turkey sausage
    3 cups chopped celery
    1 cup chopped onions
    2 to 4 tablespoons turkey broth or water
    1 bone-in turkey breast (5 to 6 pounds)
    2 tablespoons chopped garlic
 ¹/₂ cup fresh cilantro, chopped

1. Preheat oven to 325°F.

2. In large bowl combine corn bread, muffins, chilies, red pepper, pine nuts, 1 tablespoon cilantro, parsley, basil, thyme and oregano.

3. In large skillet, over medium-high heat, saute sausage, celery and onions 8 to 10 minutes or until sausage is no longer pink and vegetables are tender. Combine with corn bread mixture. Add broth if mixture is too dry. Set aside.

4. Loosen skin on both sides of turkey breast, being careful not to tear skin and leaving it connected at breast bone. Spread 1 tablespoon garlic under loosened skin over each breast half. Repeat procedure with ¹/₄ cup cilantro on each side.

5. In lightly greased 13×9×2-inch roasting pan, place turkey breast. Spoon half of stuffing mixture under breast cavity. Spoon remaining stuffing into a lightly greased 2-quart casserole; set aside. Roast turkey breast, uncovered, 2 to 2¹/₂ hours or until meat thermometer registers 170°F in deepest portion of breast. Bake remaining stuffing, uncovered, along with turkey breast during last 45 minutes.

Favorite recipe from **National Turkey Federation**

Cookies & Candies

Chocolate Raspberry Linzer Cookies

Makes about 3 dozen cookies

2¹/₃ cups all-purpose flour
  1 teaspoon baking powder
  ¹/₂ teaspoon salt
  ¹/₂ teaspoon cinnamon
  1 cup granulated sugar
  ³/₄ cup (1¹/₂ sticks) butter, softened
  2 eggs
  ¹/₂ teaspoon almond extract
One 12-oz. pkg. (2 cups) NESTLÉ® Toll House®
  Semi-Sweet Chocolate Morsels
  6 tablespoons raspberry jam or preserves
  Confectioners' sugar

In small bowl, combine flour, baking powder, salt and cinnamon; set aside. In large mixer bowl, beat granulated sugar and butter until creamy. Beat in eggs and almond extract. Gradually beat in flour mixture. Divide dough in half. Wrap in plastic wrap; refrigerate until firm.

Preheat oven to 350°F. On lightly floured board, roll half of dough ¹/₈ inch thick. Cut with 2¹/₂-inch fluted round cookie cutter. Repeat with remaining dough. Cut 1-inch round centers from half of unbaked cookies. Place cookies on ungreased cookie sheets. Reroll dough trimmings.

Bake 8 to 10 minutes. Let stand on cookie sheets 2 minutes. Remove from cookie sheets; cool completely.

Melt semi-sweet chocolate morsels. Spread 1 measuring teaspoonful chocolate on flat side of each whole cookie. Top with ¹/₂ measuring teaspoonful raspberry jam. Sprinkle confectioners' sugar on cookies with center holes; place sugar-side up on top of chocolate-jam cookies to form sandwiches.

Chocolate Mint Pinwheels

Makes about 3¹/₂ dozen cookies

One 10-oz. pkg. (1¹/₂ cups) NESTLÉ® Toll
  House® Mint Flavored Semi-Sweet
  Chocolate Morsels, divided
  ³/₄ cup (1¹/₂ sticks) butter, softened
  ¹/₃ cup sugar
  ¹/₂ teaspoon salt
  1 egg
  1 teaspoon vanilla extract
2¹/₄ cups all-purpose flour

Melt ¹/₂ cup mint chocolate morsels; cool to room temperature. Set aside. In large mixer bowl, beat butter, sugar and salt until creamy. Beat in egg and vanilla extract (mixture may appear curdled). Gradually beat in flour. Place 1 cup dough in bowl; blend in melted chocolate. Shape each dough into a ball; flatten and wrap with plastic wrap. Refrigerate about 1¹/₂ hours.

Preheat oven to 375°F. Between sheets of waxed paper, roll each ball of dough into a 13×9-inch rectangle. Remove top layers of waxed paper. Invert chocolate dough onto plain dough. Peel off waxed paper. Starting at 13-inch side, roll up jelly-roll style. Cut into ¹/₄-inch thick slices. Place slices on ungreased cookie sheets. Bake 7 to 10 minutes. Let stand on cookie sheets 2 minutes. Remove from cookie sheets; cool completely.

Melt remaining 1 cup mint chocolate morsels. Spread slightly rounded ¹/₂ teaspoonful chocolate on flat side of each cookie. Refrigerate to set chocolate.

Clockwise from top right: Chocolate Mint Pinwheels, Chocolate Raspberry Linzer Cookies and New Wave Chocolate Spritz Cookies (page 62)

New Wave Chocolate Spritz Cookies

Makes about 7 1/2 dozen cookies

**One 6-oz. pkg. (1 cup) NESTLÉ® Toll House®
  Semi-Sweet Chocolate Morsels
  1 cup (2 sticks) butter, softened
  2/3 cup sugar
  1 teaspoon vanilla extract
  2 eggs
2 1/2 cups all-purpose flour
One 4-oz. jar cinnamon candies**

Melt semi-sweet chocolate morsels; set aside. In large mixer bowl, beat butter, sugar and vanilla extract until creamy. Beat in eggs. Stir in melted chocolate. Gradually beat in flour. Cover dough; refrigerate until firm.

Preheat oven to 400°F. Place dough in cookie press. Using star tip, press into 2-inch circles onto ungreased cookie sheets. Decorate with candies. Bake 5 minutes or just until set. Let stand on cookie sheets 2 minutes. Remove from cookie sheets; cool.

Holiday Wreaths

Makes 16 wreaths

**1/2 cup margarine or butter
  1 pkg. (10 oz., about 40) regular
    marshmallows
  1 teaspoon green food coloring
  6 cups KELLOGG'S® CORN FLAKES® cereal
    Red cinnamon candies**

1. Melt margarine in large saucepan over low heat. Add marshmallows and cook, stirring constantly, until marshmallows melt and mixture is syrupy. Remove from heat. Stir in food coloring.

2. Add KELLOGG'S® CORN FLAKES® cereal. Stir until well coated.

3. Portion warm cereal mixture using 1/4 cup dry measure. Using buttered fingers, quickly shape into individual wreaths. Dot with red cinnamon candies.

Variation: Press warm cereal mixture into buttered 5 1/2-cup ring mold or shape into ring on serving plate. Remove from mold and dot with red candies. Slice to serve.

Cherry Chewbilees

Makes 36 bars

**CRUST
  1 cup walnut pieces, divided
1 1/4 cups all-purpose flour
  1/2 cup firmly packed brown sugar
  1/2 cup BUTTER FLAVOR CRISCO®
  1/2 cup flake coconut**

**FILLING
  2 packages (8 ounces *each*) cream cheese,
    softened
  2/3 cup granulated sugar
  2 eggs
  2 teaspoons vanilla
  1 can (21 ounces) cherry pie filling**

Heat oven to 350°F. Grease 13×9×2-inch pan with BUTTER FLAVOR CRISCO®. Set aside. Chop 1/2 cup nuts coarsely for topping. Set aside. Chop remaining 1/2 cup nuts finely. For crust, combine flour and brown sugar. Cut in BUTTER FLAVOR CRISCO® until fine crumbs form. Add 1/2 cup finely chopped nuts and coconut. Mix well. Remove 1/2 cup. Set aside. Press remaining crumbs in bottom of pan. Bake at 350°F for 12 to 15 minutes, until edges are lightly browned.

For filling, beat cream cheese, granulated sugar, eggs and vanilla in small bowl at medium speed of electric mixer until smooth. Spread over hot baked crust. Return to oven. Bake 15 minutes longer or until set. Spread cherry pie filling over cheese layer. Combine reserved coarsely chopped nuts and reserved crumbs. Sprinkle evenly over cherries. Return to oven. Bake 15 minutes longer. Chill. Refrigerate several hours. Cut into bars, about 2×1 1/2 inches.

Preparation time: 15 minutes

Bake time: 45 minutes

Cherry Chewbilees

Butter Almond Crunch

Butter Almond Crunch

Makes about 2 pounds candy

1½ cups HERSHEY'S Semi-Sweet Chocolate
   Chips, divided
1¾ cups chopped almonds, divided
1½ cups butter or margarine
1¾ cups sugar
   3 tablespoons light corn syrup
   3 tablespoons water

Heat oven to 350°F. Line 13×9×2-inch pan with
foil; butter foil. Sprinkle 1 cup chocolate chips
into pan; set aside. In shallow baking pan spread
chopped almonds. Bake about 7 minutes or until
golden brown; set aside. In heavy 3-quart
saucepan melt butter; blend in sugar, corn syrup
and water. Cook over medium heat, stirring
constantly, to 300°F on a candy thermometer
(hard-crack stage) or until mixture, when dropped
into very cold water, separates into threads that are
hard and brittle. Bulb of candy thermometer
should not rest on bottom of saucepan. Remove
from heat; stir in 1½ cups toasted almonds.
Immediately spread mixture evenly over chocolate
chips in prepared pan; *do not disturb chips.*
Sprinkle with remaining ¼ cup toasted almonds
and remaining ½ cup chocolate chips; cool
slightly. With sharp knife score into 1½-inch
squares, wiping knife blade after drawing through
candy. Cool completely; remove from pan.
Remove foil; break into pieces. Store in airtight
container in cool, dry place.

Apple Cinnamon Bars

Makes 36 bars

¾ cup ROMAN MEAL® Apple Cinnamon
   Multi-Bran Cereal
1 cup applesauce (or finely chopped
   apples)
⅔ cup raisins, plumped
½ teaspoon freshly grated orange peel
½ cup margarine
¾ cup brown sugar, packed
2 eggs or 4 egg whites
1½ cups flour
1 teaspoon baking powder
½ teaspoon baking soda
½ teaspoon salt
½ teaspoon cinnamon
½ teaspoon nutmeg
½ cup chopped walnuts

Heat oven to 375°F. In a medium bowl combine
cereal, applesauce, raisins and orange peel. Set
aside. In a large bowl, cream margarine and sugar.
Add eggs and beat well. Stir in the combined dry
ingredients. Blend in applesauce mixture and nuts.
Spread evenly in a well-greased 13×9×2-inch
baking pan. Bake 18 to 22 minutes or until lightly
browned. Cool and cut into 36 bars.

Rich Chocolate Pumpkin Truffles (left) and Holiday Almond Treats (right)

Rich Chocolate Pumpkin Truffles

Makes 4 dozen candies

2¹/₂ cups crushed vanilla wafers
  1 cup toasted ground almonds
  ³/₄ cup sifted powdered sugar, divided
  2 teaspoons ground cinnamon
  1 cup (6 ounces) chocolate pieces, melted
  ¹/₂ cup LIBBY'S® Solid Pack Pumpkin
  ¹/₃ cup coffee liqueur or apple juice

In medium bowl, combine vanilla wafer crumbs, ground almonds, *¹/₂ cup* powdered sugar and cinnamon. Blend in melted chocolate, pumpkin and coffee liqueur. Form into 1-inch balls. Refrigerate. Dust with *remaining ¹/₄ cup* powdered sugar just before serving.

Holiday Almond Treats

Makes 4 dozen

2¹/₂ cups crushed vanilla wafers
1³/₄ cups toasted ground almonds, divided
  ¹/₂ cup sifted powdered sugar
  ¹/₂ teaspoon ground cinnamon
  1 cup LIBBY'S® Pumpkin Pie Mix
  ¹/₃ cup almond liqueur or apple juice

In medium bowl, blend vanilla wafer crumbs, *1 cup* ground almonds, powdered sugar and cinnamon. Stir in pumpkin pie mix and almond liqueur. Form into 1-inch balls. Roll in *remaining ³/₄ cup* ground almonds. Refrigerate.

Oatmeal Cranberry-Nut Cookies

Makes about 4 dozen cookies

  ³/₄ cup BUTTER FLAVOR CRISCO®
  1 cup firmly packed dark brown sugar
  ¹/₄ cup dark molasses
  1 egg
  2 tablespoons milk
1¹/₂ teaspoons vanilla
  1 cup all-purpose flour
1¹/₄ teaspoons cinnamon
  ¹/₂ teaspoon baking soda
  ¹/₂ teaspoon salt
  ¹/₄ teaspoon allspice
  1 cup crushed whole-berry cranberry
    sauce
  ¹/₂ cup sliced almonds, broken
  3 cups quick oats (not instant or old
    fashioned)

1. Heat oven to 375°F. Grease baking sheet with BUTTER FLAVOR CRISCO®.

2. Combine BUTTER FLAVOR CRISCO® and sugar in large bowl. Beat at medium speed of electric mixer until well blended. Beat in molasses, egg, milk and vanilla.

3. Combine flour, cinnamon, baking soda, salt and allspice. Mix into creamed mixture at low speed until just blended. Stir in cranberry sauce and nuts. Stir in oats with spoon.

4. Drop tablespoonfuls of dough 2 inches apart onto baking sheet.

5. Bake at 375°F 12 minutes, or until set. Cool 2 minutes on baking sheet. Remove to cooling rack.

Peanut Butter Bears

Makes about 3 dozen bears

> 1 cup SKIPPY® Creamy Peanut Butter
> 1 cup MAZOLA® Margarine, softened
> 1 cup packed brown sugar
> ²/₃ cup KARO® Light or Dark Corn Syrup
> 2 eggs
> 4 cups flour, divided
> 1 tablespoon baking powder
> 1 teaspoon cinnamon (optional)
> ¼ teaspoon salt

In large bowl with mixer at medium speed, beat peanut butter, margarine, brown sugar, corn syrup and eggs until smooth. Reduce speed; beat in 2 cups of the flour, the baking powder, cinnamon and salt. With spoon stir in remaining 2 cups flour. Wrap dough in plastic wrap; refrigerate 2 hours. Preheat oven to 325°F. Divide dough in half; set aside half. On floured surface roll out half the dough to ¹/₈-inch thickness. Cut with floured bear cookie cutter. Repeat with remaining dough. Bake on ungreased cookie sheets 10 minutes or until lightly browned. Remove from cookie sheets; cool completely on wire rack. Decorate as desired.

Preparation Time: 35 minutes, plus chilling

Bake Time: 10 minutes, plus cooling

Note: Use scraps of dough to make bear faces. Make one small ball of dough for muzzle. Form 3 smaller balls of dough and press gently to create eyes and nose; bake as directed. If desired, use frosting to create paws, ears and bow ties.

Cappucino Bon Bons

Peanut Butter Bears

Cappucino Bon Bons

Makes 40 bon bons

> 1 package DUNCAN HINES® Fudge Brownie Mix, Family Size
> 2 eggs
> ¹/₃ cup water
> ¹/₃ cup CRISCO® Oil or PURITAN® Oil
> 1¹/₂ tablespoons FOLGERS® Instant Coffee
> 1 teaspoon ground cinnamon
> Whipped topping
> Cinnamon

1. Preheat oven to 350°F. Place 40 (2-inch) foil cupcake liners on cookie sheet.

2. Combine brownie mix, eggs, water, oil, instant coffee and cinnamon. Stir with spoon until well blended, about 50 strokes. Fill each cupcake liner with 1 measuring tablespoon batter. Bake at 350°F for 12 to 15 minutes or until toothpick inserted in center comes out clean. Cool completely. Garnish with whipped topping and a dash of cinnamon. Refrigerate until ready to serve.

Angel Pillows

Angel Pillows

Makes 1½ dozen cookies

½ cup BUTTER FLAVOR CRISCO®
1 package (3 ounces) cream cheese, softened
1 tablespoon milk
¼ cup firmly packed brown sugar
½ cup apricot preserves
1¼ cups all-purpose flour
1½ teaspoons baking powder
1½ teaspoons cinnamon
¼ teaspoon salt
½ cup coarsely chopped pecans or flake coconut

FROSTING
1 cup confectioners' sugar
¼ cup apricot preserves
1 tablespoon BUTTER FLAVOR CRISCO®
Flake coconut or finely chopped pecans (optional)

Heat oven to 350°F. Grease baking sheets with BUTTER FLAVOR CRISCO®. Set aside. Cream ½ cup BUTTER FLAVOR CRISCO®, cream cheese and milk at medium speed of electric mixer until well blended. Beat in brown sugar. Beat in ½ cup preserves. Combine flour, baking powder, cinnamon and salt. Mix into creamed mixture. Stir in ½ cup nuts. Drop 2 level measuring tablespoons of dough into a mound to form each cookie. Place 2 inches apart on baking sheet.

Bake at 350°F for 14 minutes. Cool on baking sheet one minute. Remove to cooling rack. Cool completely before frosting.

For frosting, combine confectioners' sugar, ¼ cup preserves and 1 tablespoon BUTTER FLAVOR CRISCO® in small mixing bowl. Beat with electric mixer until well blended. Frost cooled cookies. Sprinkle coconut over frosting, if desired.

Tip: Try peach or pineapple preserves in place of apricot.

Preparation time: 25 minutes

Bake time: 14 minutes

Peppermint Patties

Makes about 8 dozen

1 (14-ounce) can EAGLE® Brand Sweetened Condensed Milk (NOT evaporated milk)
1 tablespoon peppermint extract
Green or red food coloring, optional
6 cups confectioners' sugar
Additional confectioners' sugar
1½ pounds EAGLE™ Brand Chocolate-Flavored Candy Coating, melted

In large mixer bowl, combine sweetened condensed milk, extract and food coloring if desired. Add 6 cups sugar; beat on low speed until smooth and well blended. Turn mixture onto surface sprinkled with confectioners' sugar. Knead lightly to form smooth ball. Shape into 1-inch balls. Place 2 inches apart on wax paper-lined baking sheets. Flatten each ball into a 1½-inch patty. Let dry 1 hour or longer; turn over and let dry at least 1 hour. With fork, dip each patty into warm candy coating (draw fork lightly across rim of pan to remove excess coating). Invert onto wax paper-lined baking sheets; let stand until firm. Store covered at room temperature or in refrigerator.

Marzipan Fruits

Makes 2 to 3 dozen confections

1¾ cups BAKER'S® ANGEL FLAKE® Coconut, finely chopped
1 package (4-serving size) JELL-O® Brand Gelatin, any flavor
1 cup ground blanched almonds
⅔ cup sweetened condensed milk
1½ teaspoons sugar
1 teaspoon almond extract
Food coloring (optional)
Whole cloves (optional)
Citron (optional)

Mix together coconut, gelatin, almonds, milk, sugar and extract. Shape by hand into small fruits, or use small candy molds. If desired, use food coloring to paint details on fruit; add whole cloves and citron for stems and blossom ends. Chill until dry. Store in covered container at room temperature up to 1 week.

Prep time: 30 minutes

Nutcracker Sweets

Makes 36 squares

BASE
- ⅓ cup BUTTER FLAVOR CRISCO®
- ½ cup creamy peanut butter
- 1½ cups firmly packed brown sugar
- 2 eggs
- 1½ cups all-purpose flour
- 1½ teaspoons baking powder
- ½ teaspoon salt
- ¼ cup milk
- 1 teaspoon vanilla

FROSTING and DRIZZLE
- ¼ cup BUTTER FLAVOR CRISCO®
- ⅔ cup creamy peanut butter
- 4 cups (1 pound) confectioners' sugar
- ½ cup milk
- ½ cup semi-sweet chocolate pieces

Heat oven to 350°F. Grease 15×10-inch baking pan with BUTTER FLAVOR CRISCO®. Set aside. For base, cream BUTTER FLAVOR CRISCO® and peanut butter in large bowl at medium speed of electric mixer. Blend in brown sugar. Beat in eggs one at a time. Beat until creamy. Combine flour, baking powder and salt in small bowl. Set aside. Combine milk and vanilla in measuring cup. Add dry ingredients and milk alternately to creamed mixture. Mix at low speed of electric mixer. Scrape sides of bowl frequently. Beat until blended. Spread batter into prepared pan. Bake at 350°F for 18 to 20 minutes. Cool.

For frosting, cream BUTTER FLAVOR CRISCO® and peanut butter in large bowl at medium speed of electric mixer. Add sugar and milk. Beat until fluffy. Spread on cooled cookie base. For drizzle, melt chocolate pieces on *very* low heat in small saucepan. Drizzle chocolate from end of spoon back and forth over frosting. Cut into 2-inch squares. Refrigerate 15 to 20 minutes until chocolate is firm.

Preparation time: 45 minutes

Chill time: 15 to 20 minutes

Bake time: 18 to 20 minutes

Nutcracker Sweets

Gingerbread Men

Gingerbread Men

Makes 12 to 14 six-inch tall gingerbread men

- 1 package DUNCAN HINES® Moist Deluxe Spice Cake Mix
- ½ cup all-purpose flour
- 2 eggs
- ⅓ cup CRISCO® Oil or PURITAN® Oil
- ⅓ cup dark molasses
- 2 teaspoons ground ginger
- Raisins for decorations

1. Combine cake mix, flour, eggs, oil, molasses and ginger in large bowl (mixture will be soft). Refrigerate 2 hours.

2. Preheat oven to 375°F.

3. Roll dough to ¼-inch thickness on lightly floured surface. Cut with gingerbread man cookie cutter. Place on ungreased baking sheet 3 inches apart. Decorate with raisins.

4. Bake at 375°F for 8 to 10 minutes or until edges start to brown. Remove immediately to cooling rack.

Tip: You may also decorate baked and cooled cookies with DUNCAN HINES® Vanilla Layer Cake Frosting and assorted candies.

Versatile Cut-Out Cookies

Makes about 6½ dozen cookies

**3½ cups unsifted flour
1 tablespoon baking powder
½ teaspoon salt
1 (14-ounce) can EAGLE® Brand Sweetened
      Condensed Milk (NOT evaporated milk)
¾ cup margarine or butter, softened
2 eggs
1 tablespoon vanilla *or* 2 teaspoons
      almond or lemon extract**

Combine flour, baking powder and salt. In large mixer bowl, beat sweetened condensed milk, margarine, eggs and vanilla until well blended. Add dry ingredients; mix well. Chill 2 hours. On floured surface, knead dough to form a smooth ball. Divide into thirds. On well-floured surface, roll out each portion to ⅛-inch thickness. Cut with floured cookie cutter. Reroll as necessary to use all dough. Place 1 inch apart on greased baking sheets. Bake in preheated 350°F oven 7 to 9 minutes or until lightly browned around edges *(do not overbake)*. Cool. Frost and decorate as desired. Store loosely covered at room temperature.

Chocolate Cookies: Decrease flour to 3 cups. Add ½ cup unsweetened cocoa. Proceed as above.   *Makes about 6½ dozen*

Mincemeat Peek-a-Boo Cookies: Prepare and roll dough as above. Cut into 3-inch rounds. Using sharp knife, cut "X" in center of half the rounds. Place 1 teaspoon mincemeat in center of remaining rounds. Top with cut rounds; press edges to seal. Bake 8 to 10 minutes. Cool. Sprinkle with confectioners' sugar if desired.
                    Makes about 4 dozen

Stained Glass Cookies: Prepare and roll dough as above. Using 3-inch cookie cutters, cut into desired shapes. Cut out holes for "stained glass" in each cookie with small cutters or knife. Place on aluminum foil-lined baking sheets. Fill holes with crushed hard candies. (If planning to hang cookies, make hole in each cookie in dough near edge with straw.) Bake 6 to 8 minutes or until candy has melted. Cool 10 minutes; remove from foil.   *Makes about 8 dozen*

Cinnamon Pinwheel Cookies: Decrease baking powder to 2 teaspoons. Prepare and chill dough as above. Divide into quarters. Roll each quarter of dough into a 16×8-inch rectangle. Brush with melted margarine or butter. Top each with 2 tablespoons sugar combined with ½ teaspoon ground cinnamon. Roll up tightly beginning at 8-inch side. Wrap tightly; freeze until firm, about 20 minutes. Cut into ¼-inch slices. Place on ungreased baking sheets. Bake 12 to 14 minutes or until lightly browned.   *Makes about 6½ dozen*

Mocha Mint Crisps

Makes about 4 dozen cookies

**1 cup butter or margarine, softened
1 cup sugar
1 egg
¼ cup light corn syrup
¼ teaspoon peppermint extract
1 teaspoon powdered instant coffee
1 teaspoon hot water
2 cups all-purpose flour
6 tablespoons HERSHEY'S Cocoa
2 teaspoons baking soda
¼ teaspoon salt
      Mocha Mint Sugar (recipe follows)**

Heat oven to 350°F. In large mixer bowl beat butter and sugar until light and fluffy. Add egg, corn syrup and peppermint extract; mix thoroughly. Dissolve instant coffee in water; stir into butter mixture. Stir together flour, cocoa, baking soda and salt; gradually add to butter mixture, blending thoroughly. Shape dough into 1-inch balls. (Dough may be refrigerated for a short time for easier handling.) Prepare Mocha Mint Sugar. Roll dough balls in sugar mixture. Place on ungreased cookie sheet about 2 inches apart. Bake 8 to 10 minutes or until no imprint remains when touched lightly. Cool slightly; remove from cookie sheet to wire rack. Cool completely.

Mocha Mint Sugar: In small bowl stir together ¼ cup powdered sugar, 2 tablespoons crushed hard peppermint candies (about 6 candies) and 1½ teaspoons powdered instant coffee.

Clockwise from top: Versatile Cut-Out Cookies, Mincemeat Peek-a-Boo Cookies, Chocolate Cookies, Stained Glass Cookies and Cinnamon Pinwheel Cookies

Fudge Rum Balls

Fudge Rum Balls

Makes 6 dozen

    1 package DUNCAN HINES® Moist Deluxe
        Butter Recipe Fudge Cake Mix
    1 cup finely chopped pecans or walnuts
    1 tablespoon rum extract
    2 cups sifted confectioners sugar
  ¼ cup unsweetened cocoa
      Pecans or walnuts, finely chopped

1. Preheat oven to 375°F. Grease and flour
13×9×2-inch pan. Prepare, bake and cool cake
following package directions.

2. Crumble cake into large bowl. Stir with fork
until crumbs are fine and uniform in size. Add
1 cup nuts, rum extract, confectioners sugar and
cocoa. Stir until well blended.

3. Shape heaping tablespoonfuls mixture into balls.
Garnish by rolling balls in finely chopped nuts.
Press firmly to adhere nuts to balls.

Tip: Substitute real rum for rum extract.

Butter Drop-Ins

Makes 1½ to 2 dozen cookies

  ½ cup BUTTER FLAVOR CRISCO®
  ¾ cup granulated sugar
    1 tablespoon milk
    1 egg
  ½ teaspoon vanilla
  1¼ cups all-purpose flour
  ¼ teaspoon salt
  ¼ teaspoon baking powder

FROSTING
  ½ cup BUTTER FLAVOR CRISCO®
    1 pound (4 cups) confectioners' sugar
  ⅓ cup milk
    1 teaspoon vanilla

Heat oven to 375°F. Grease baking sheets with
BUTTER FLAVOR CRISCO®. Set aside. Cream
½ cup BUTTER FLAVOR CRISCO®, granulated
sugar and 1 tablespoon milk in medium bowl at
medium speed of electric mixer until well
blended. Beat in egg and ½ teaspoon vanilla.
Combine flour, salt and baking powder. Mix into
creamed mixture. Drop level measuring
tablespoons 2 inches apart onto baking sheet. Bake
at 375°F for 7 to 9 minutes. Remove to cooling
rack. Cool completely before frosting.

For frosting, combine ½ cup BUTTER FLAVOR
CRISCO®, confectioners' sugar, ⅓ cup milk and 1
teaspoon vanilla in small mixing bowl. Beat at low
speed of electric mixer for 15 seconds. Scrape
bowl. Beat at high speed for 2 minutes, or until
smooth and creamy.

Preparation time: 20 minutes

Bake time: 7 to 9 minutes

Butter Drop-Ins

Cookie Cutouts

Cookie Cutouts

Makes about 4¹/₂ dozen cookies

   1 cup margarine, softened
¹/₂ cup granulated sugar
¹/₂ cup light brown sugar
   1 egg
   1 teaspoon vanilla extract
   3 cups all-purpose flour
   1 teaspoon baking soda
      Assorted SUNKIST® Fun Fruits®

In large bowl, with electric mixer, beat margarine with sugars until light and fluffy. Beat in egg and vanilla until smooth. Combine flour with baking soda. Gradually add to margarine mixture, blending well after each addition. Chill at least 2 hours.

Preheat oven to 375°F. On lightly floured board, roll dough ¹/₈ inch thick; cut into assorted shapes. Decorate with fun fruit snacks. Place on lightly greased cookie sheets and bake 8 to 9 minutes. On wire rack, cool completely. Decorate, if desired, with decorative icing.

Spicy Cookie Cutouts: Increase brown sugar to ³/₄ cup and add 1¹/₂ teaspoons ground cinnamon and 1 teaspoon ground ginger to flour mixture.

Chocolate Cookie Cutouts: Decrease flour to 2³/₄ cups, increase granulated sugar to 1 cup and add ¹/₂ cup unsweetened cocoa powder to flour mixture.

Mincemeat Oatmeal Chewies

Makes about 5 dozen cookies

¹/₂ cup BUTTER FLAVOR CRISCO®
   1 cup firmly packed brown sugar
   1 egg
1¹/₃ cups prepared mincemeat
1¹/₂ cups all-purpose flour
   1 teaspoon baking soda
¹/₂ teaspoon salt
   1 cup quick oats (not instant or old fashioned)
¹/₂ cup coarsely chopped walnuts

1. Heat oven to 350°F. Grease baking sheet with BUTTER FLAVOR CRISCO®.

2. Combine BUTTER FLAVOR CRISCO®, sugar and egg in large bowl. Beat at medium speed of electric mixer until well blended. Beat in mincemeat.

3. Combine flour, baking soda and salt. Mix into creamed mixture at low speed until blended. Stir in oats and nuts with spoon.

4. Drop rounded tablespoonfuls of dough 2 inches apart onto baking sheet.

5. Bake at 350°F for 10 to 12 minutes, or until set and lightly browned around edges. Cool 1 minute on baking sheet. Remove carefully to cooling rack.

Easy Rocky Road (top) and Fast Chocolate-Pecan Fudge (bottom)

Easy Rocky Road

Makes 16 squares

>   2 cups (12-ounce package) HERSHEY'S
>   Semi-Sweet Chocolate Chips
>   ¼ cup butter or margarine
>   2 tablespoons shortening
>   3 cups miniature marshmallows
>   ½ cup coarsely chopped nuts

Butter 8-inch square pan. In large microwave-safe bowl, place chocolate chips, butter and shortening. Microwave at HIGH (100%) 1 to 1½ minutes or just until chocolate chips are melted and mixture is smooth when stirred. Add marshmallows and nuts; blend well. Spread evenly in prepared pan. Cover; refrigerate until firm. Cut into 2-inch squares.

Fast Chocolate-Pecan Fudge

Makes about 4 dozen squares

>   ½ cup butter or margarine
>   ¾ cup HERSHEY'S Cocoa
>   4 cups powdered sugar
>   1 teaspoon vanilla extract
>   ½ cup evaporated milk
>   1 cup pecan pieces

Line 8-inch square pan with foil; set aside. In 2-quart microwave-safe bowl, place butter. Microwave at HIGH (100%) ½ to 1 minute or until melted. Add cocoa; stir until smooth. Stir in powdered sugar and vanilla; blend well (mixture will be dry and crumbly). Stir in evaporated milk. Microwave at HIGH 1 minute; stir. Microwave additional 1 minute or until mixture is hot. Beat with wooden spoon until smooth; add pecans. Pour into prepared pan. Cool. Cover; refrigerate until firm. Cut into 1-inch squares. Garnish as desired. Cover; store in refrigerator.

Conventional Directions: Prepare pan as above. In medium saucepan, melt butter. Remove from heat; stir in cocoa. Stir in powdered sugar and vanilla; add evaporated milk. Stir constantly over low heat until warm and smooth; add pecans. Pour into prepared pan; refrigerate and store as above.

Rice Krispies Treats®

Makes 24 squares

>   ¼ cup margarine or butter
>   1 pkg. (10 oz., about 40) regular
>   marshmallows *or* 4 cups miniature
>   marshmallows
>   6 cups KELLOGG'S® RICE KRISPIES® cereal

1. Melt margarine in large saucepan over low heat. Add marshmallows and stir until completely melted. Remove from heat.

2. Add RICE KRISPIES® cereal, stirring until well coated.

3. Using buttered spatula or waxed paper, press mixture evenly into buttered 13×9×2-inch pan. Cut into squares when cool.

Microwave Directions: Microwave margarine and marshmallows on HIGH in large glass mixing bowl for 2 minutes. Stir to combine. Microwave on HIGH 1½ to 2 minutes longer. Stir until smooth. Add cereal. Stir until well coated. Press into pan as directed in Step 3.

Christmas Wreaths: Add green food color to hot marshmallow mixture before adding RICE KRISPIES® cereal. Portion mixture, using buttered ½ cup measure. Quickly shape into wreaths. Decorate with small cinnamon candies.

Gifts: Use fruit leather, rolled gum drops and other candies to wrap and decorate each "gift."

Note: Use fresh marshmallows for best results.

Decorator White Icing

Makes about 1¼ cups icing

One 6-oz. pkg. (3 foil-wrapped bars) NESTLÉ®
    Premier White baking bars, broken up
  3 tablespoons heavy or whipping cream
 ¾ cup confectioners' sugar, sifted
  3 tablespoons butter, softened
 ¼ teaspoon almond, orange or mint extract
    Paste food colorings, optional*

Melt over hot (not boiling) water, Premier White baking bars with heavy cream, stirring until smooth. Transfer to small mixer bowl. Beat in confectioners' sugar, butter and extract until smooth.

To color icing, use paste food colorings rather than liquid food colorings. Spread or pipe icing onto cookies; let stand until set. Store decorated cookies in single layer in refrigerator.

*Paste food colorings can be purchased where cake decorating supplies are sold.

Champagne Cocoa Truffles

Makes about 2½ dozen candies

 ¾ cup unsalted butter
 ¾ cup HERSHEY'S Cocoa
  1 can (14 ounces) sweetened condensed
    milk
  1 teaspoon vanilla extract
  2 to 3 tablespoons champagne
    Cocoa or powdered sugar

In heavy medium-size saucepan over low heat, melt butter. Add cocoa; stir until smooth. Blend in sweetened condensed milk; stir constantly until mixture is thick, smooth and glossy, about 4 minutes. Remove from heat; stir in vanilla. Pour mixture into medium-size bowl; cool to room temperature. Stir in champagne. Cover and refrigerate until firm, 4 to 5 hours. Taking small amount of mixture at a time, form into 1¼-inch balls; roll in cocoa or powdered sugar. Place balls on wax paper-lined tray; refrigerate until firm, 1 to 2 hours. Store, covered, in refrigerator.

Decorator White Icing

Left to right: Marzipan Truffles and shaped Marzipan (page 75)

Marzipan Truffles

Makes about 56 truffles

> 1 recipe Marzipan (page 75)
> About 3 cups confectioners sugar
> 2 tablespoons unsweetened cocoa powder
> 2 teaspoons brandy extract
> 1 teaspoon vegetable shortening
> 1 pound top-quality milk or semi-sweet chocolate, coarsely chopped
> 1 can SOLO® Crunch Topping (any kind), crushed

Divide marzipan in half. Wrap 1 piece in plastic wrap and refrigerate. Sprinkle work surface and hands with confectioners sugar. Knead remaining marzipan on sugared surface until pliable. Shape into 12×1-inch log. Dust with confectioners sugar, wrap in plastic wrap, and refrigerate overnight.

Break remaining marzipan into small pieces and place on work surface or in food processor. Add cocoa and brandy extract and knead or process until thoroughly blended. Sugar work surface and knead 1 cup confectioners sugar into mixture. Divide chocolate marzipan in half. Shape each piece into 8×¾-inch log. Dust with confectioners sugar and wrap in plastic wrap. Refrigerate overnight.

Line 2 baking sheets with waxed paper and set aside.

Unwrap plain marzipan and place on sugared surface. Cut log into about ½-inch-thick slices. Roll between sugared palms to make balls; place on prepared baking sheet and refrigerate. Repeat with chocolate marzipan.

Melt shortening and half of chopped chocolate in top of double boiler set over pan of barely simmering water, stirring constantly. Add remaining chopped chocolate and stir until chocolate is completely melted and mixture is smooth. Remove top of double boiler from pan and set aside to cool slightly.

Dip balls, 1 at a time, into melted chocolate and shake off excess chocolate. Dipped truffles may be rolled immediately in crunch topping or let stand at room temperature until chocolate is set. Store in refrigerator.

Note: Chocolate may be reheated over simmering water if it hardens during dipping.

Marzipan

Makes about 1¼ pounds

1 can (8 ounces) SOLO® Almond Paste
1 egg white
About 2 to 2½ cups confectioners sugar

Break almond paste into small pieces and place in medium-size bowl. Add egg white and 1 cup confectioners sugar. Knead in bowl until mixture binds together and is no longer crumbly. Sprinkle clean work surface with confectioners sugar. Place marzipan on sugared surface and knead in 1 to 1½ cups confectioners sugar. Continue kneading until marzipan is smooth and pliable. If desired, marzipan can be colored and shaped into fruit.

Coconut Macaroons

Makes about 4 dozen cookies

2 (7-ounce) packages flaked coconut
(5⅓ cups)
1 (14-ounce) can EAGLE® Brand Sweetened Condensed Milk (NOT evaporated milk)
2 teaspoons vanilla extract
1½ teaspoons almond extract

Preheat oven to 350°F. In large bowl, combine coconut, sweetened condensed milk and extracts; mix well. Drop by rounded teaspoonfuls onto aluminum foil-lined and *generously greased* baking sheets. Bake 8 to 10 minutes or until lightly browned around edges. *Immediately* remove from baking sheets (macaroons will stick if allowed to cool). Store loosely covered at room temperature.

Macaroon Kisses: Prepare and bake as above. Press solid milk chocolate candy star or drop in center of each macaroon immediately after baking.

Old-Fashioned Molasses Cookies

Makes about 3 dozen cookies

4 cups sifted all-purpose flour
2 teaspoons ARM & HAMMER® Pure Baking Soda
1½ teaspoons ground ginger
½ teaspoon ground cinnamon
⅛ teaspoon salt
1½ cups molasses
½ cup lard or shortening, melted
¼ cup butter or margarine, melted
⅓ cup boiling water

Sift together flour, baking soda, spices and salt. Combine molasses, lard, butter and water in large bowl. Add dry ingredients to liquid and blend well. Cover and chill several hours or overnight.

Turn onto well-floured board. Using floured rolling pin, roll to ¼-inch thickness. Cut with 3½-inch floured cookie cutter. Sprinkle with sugar and place on ungreased baking sheets. Bake in 375°F oven 12 minutes. Cool on racks.

Chocolate-Dipped Dried Apricots

Makes 4 dozen candies

1 cup sugar
⅔ cup water
48 dried California apricot halves (about 10 ounces)
6 ounces semi-sweet chocolate, divided
1 tablespoon shortening
2 tablespoons apricot brandy

Combine sugar and water in saucepan; bring to a boil and cook for 5 minutes. Reduce heat and add apricots. Gently simmer for about 2 minutes. Remove apricots; cool on waxed paper. In double boiler over simmering water, combine 2 ounces chocolate, shortening and brandy, stirring constantly until smooth. Add remaining 4 ounces chocolate and stir until melted. Do not heat chocolate over 96°F. Dip apricots halfway into chocolate. Remove and cool on waxed paper. Store covered in refrigerator.

Favorite recipe from **California Apricot Advisory Board**

Macaroon Kisses

Desserts

Eggnog Cheesecake

Makes 12 servings

  2 packages (5½ ounces each) chocolate-
    laced pirouette cookies
⅓ cup graham cracker crumbs
  3 tablespoons PARKAY® Margarine, melted
  2 packages (8 ounces each) PHILADELPHIA
    BRAND® Cream Cheese, softened
  2 cups cold prepared eggnog
1¾ cups cold milk
  2 packages (4-serving size each) JELL-O®
    Instant Pudding and Pie Filling, French
    Vanilla or Vanilla Flavor
  1 tablespoon rum
⅛ teaspoon ground nutmeg
    COOL WHIP® Whipped Topping, thawed
    (optional)
    Ribbon (optional)

Reserve 1 cookie for garnish, if desired. Cut 1-inch
piece off 1 end of each of the remaining cookies.
Crush 1-inch pieces into crumbs; set aside
remaining cookies for sides of cake. Combine
cookie crumbs, graham cracker crumbs and
margarine until well mixed. Press crumb mixture
firmly onto bottom of 9-inch springform pan.

Beat cream cheese at low speed of electric mixer
until smooth. Gradually add 1 cup of eggnog,
blending until mixture is very smooth. Add
remaining eggnog, milk, pudding mix, rum and
nutmeg. Beat until well blended, about 1 minute.
Pour cream cheese mixture carefully into pan.
Chill until firm, about 3 hours. Run hot metal
spatula or knife around edges of pan before
removing sides of pan.

Press remaining cookies, cut-sides down, into sides
of cake. Garnish with whipped topping and
reserved cookie, if desired. Tie ribbon around
cake, if desired.

Prep time: 45 minutes

Chill time: 3 hours

Holiday Fruitcake

Makes 12 servings

  1 cup chopped candied fruit
⅔ cup pitted dates, chopped
½ cup chopped walnuts
¼ cup brandy or orange juice
  1 package (6-serving size) JELL-O® Instant
    Pudding and Pie Filling, Vanilla Flavor
  1 package (2-layer size) yellow cake mix
  4 eggs
  1 cup (½ pint) sour cream
⅓ cup vegetable oil
  1 tablespoon grated orange rind
⅔ cup cold milk
    Marzipan Fruits (page 66) (optional)

Mix together candied fruit, dates, walnuts and
brandy.

Reserve ⅓ cup pudding mix; set aside. Combine
cake mix, remaining pudding mix, eggs, sour
cream, oil and orange rind in large bowl. Beat at
low speed of electric mixer just to moisten,
scraping sides of bowl often. Beat at medium
speed 4 minutes. Stir in fruit mixture.

Pour batter into well-greased and floured 10-inch
fluted tube pan. Bake at 350°F for 45 minutes or
until cake tester inserted in center comes out
clean. Cool in pan 15 minutes. Remove from pan;
finish cooling on wire rack.

Beat reserved pudding mix and milk in small bowl
until smooth. Spoon over top of cake to glaze.
Garnish with Marzipan Fruits, if desired.

Prep time: 30 minutes

Baking time: 45 minutes

*Top to bottom: Eggnog Cheesecake, Holiday
Fruitcake, Marzipan Fruits (page 66) and
Raspberry Gift Box (page 78)*

Raspberry Gift Box

Makes 8 servings

> 2 packages (4-serving size each) or 1 package (8-serving size) JELL-O® Brand Gelatin, Raspberry Flavor
> 1½ cups boiling water
> ¾ cup cran-raspberry juice
> Ice cubes
> 3½ cups (8 ounces) COOL WHIP® Whipped Topping, thawed
> Raspberry Sauce (recipe follows)
> Gumdrop Ribbon* (optional)
> Frosted Cranberries** (optional)

Dissolve gelatin in boiling water. Combine cran-raspberry juice and ice cubes to make 1¾ cups. Add to gelatin, stirring until ice is melted. Chill until slightly thickened. Fold in whipped topping. Pour into 9 × 5-inch loaf pan. Chill until firm, about 4 hours.

Prepare Raspberry Sauce, Gumdrop Ribbon and Frosted Cranberries, if desired.

Unmold gelatin mixture onto serving plate. Cut Gumdrop Ribbon into 2 (10 × 1-inch) strips and 1 (5 × 1-inch) strip. Place strips on raspberry loaf, piecing strips together as necessary, to resemble ribbon. Cut 7 (3 × 1-inch) strips; form into bow. Place on gumdrop ribbon. Decorate with Frosted Cranberries. Serve with Raspberry Sauce.

Raspberry Sauce

Makes 2 cups

> 2 packages (10 ounces each) BIRDS EYE® Quick Thaw Red Raspberries, thawed
> 2 teaspoons cornstarch

Place raspberries in food processor or blender; cover. Process until smooth; strain to remove seeds. Combine cornstarch with small amount of the raspberries in medium saucepan; add remaining raspberries. Bring to boil over medium heat, stirring constantly; boil 1 minute. Chill.

Prep time: 30 minutes

Chill time: 4 hours

*To make ribbon, place gumdrops, small ends up, on surface lightly sprinkled with sugar. Flatten into strips with rolling pin. Cut with sharp knife into 1-inch-wide strips. Use to decorate as desired.

**To frost cranberries, dip cranberries into beaten egg white. Roll in sugar; let stand on waxed paper until dry.

Chocolate Truffle Loaf with Sweet Raspberry Sauce

Makes 12 servings

> 2 cups heavy cream, divided
> 3 egg yolks
> 16 squares (1 ounce *each*) semisweet chocolate
> ½ cup KARO® Light or Dark Corn Syrup
> ½ cup MAZOLA® Margarine
> ¼ cup confectioners sugar
> 1 teaspoon vanilla
> Sweet Raspberry Sauce (recipe follows)

Line 9¼ × 5¼ × 2¾-inch loaf pan with plastic wrap. In small bowl mix ½ cup of the cream with the egg yolks. In large saucepan combine chocolate, corn syrup and margarine; stir over medium heat until melted. Add egg mixture. Cook 3 minutes over medium heat, stirring constantly. Cool to room temperature. In small bowl with mixer at medium speed, beat remaining 1½ cups cream, the sugar and vanilla until soft peaks form. Gently fold into chocolate mixture just until combined. Pour into prepared pan; cover with plastic wrap. Refrigerate overnight or chill in freezer 3 hours. Slice and serve with Sweet Raspberry Sauce.

Sweet Raspberry Sauce: In blender or food processor puree 1 package (10 ounces) frozen raspberries, thawed; strain to remove seeds. Stir in ⅓ cup KARO® Light Corn Syrup.

Preparation Time: 30 minutes, plus chilling

Microwave Directions: Prepare pan and egg mixture as above. In 3-quart microwavable bowl mix chocolate, corn syrup and margarine. Microwave on HIGH (100%), 2 to 2½ minutes or until melted, stirring twice. Stir in egg mixture. Microwave 3 minutes, stirring twice. Continue as above.

Chocolate Truffle Loaf with Sweet Raspberry Sauce

Classic Pecan Pie

Classic Pecan Pie

Makes 8 servings

3 eggs
1 cup sugar
1 cup KARO® Light or Dark Corn Syrup
2 tablespoons MAZOLA® Margarine, melted
1 teaspoon vanilla
1½ cups pecan halves
Easy-As-Pie Crust (recipe follows)

Preheat oven to 350°F. In medium bowl beat eggs slightly. Add sugar, corn syrup, margarine and vanilla; stir until well blended. Stir in pecans. Pour into pie crust. Bake 50 to 55 minutes or until knife inserted halfway between center and edge comes out clean. Cool on wire rack.

Preparation Time: 10 minutes

Bake Time: 55 minutes, plus cooling

California Pecan Pie: Stir ¼ cup sour cream into eggs until blended.

Kentucky Bourbon Pecan Pie: Add up to 2 tablespoons bourbon to filling.

Chocolate Pecan Pie: Reduce sugar to ⅓ cup. Melt 4 squares (1 ounce each) semisweet chocolate with margarine.

Easy-As-Pie Crust

Makes 1 (9-inch) pie crust

1¼ cups flour
⅛ teaspoon salt
½ cup MAZOLA® Margarine
2 tablespoons cold water

In medium bowl mix flour and salt. With pastry blender or 2 knives, cut in margarine until mixture resembles fine crumbs. Sprinkle water over flour mixture while tossing with fork to blend well. Press dough firmly into ball. On lightly floured surface roll out to 12-inch circle. Fit loosely into 9-inch pie plate. Trim and flute edge. Fill and bake according to recipe.

Preparation Time: 15 minutes

Chilled Raspberry Cheesecake

Chilled Raspberry Cheesecake

Makes 10 to 12 servings

1½ cups vanilla wafer crumbs (about
    45 wafers, crushed)
⅓ cup HERSHEY'S Cocoa
⅓ cup powdered sugar
⅓ cup butter or margarine, melted
1 package (10 ounces) frozen raspberries,
   thawed
1 envelope unflavored gelatin
½ cup cold water
½ cup boiling water
2 packages (8 ounces *each*) cream cheese,
   softened
½ cup granulated sugar
1 teaspoon vanilla extract
3 tablespoons seedless red raspberry
   preserves
  Chocolate Whipped Cream (recipe
   follows)

Heat oven to 350°F. In medium bowl stir together crumbs, cocoa and powdered sugar; stir in melted butter. Press mixture onto bottom and 1½ inches up side of 9-inch springform pan. Bake 10 minutes; cool completely. Puree and strain raspberries; set aside. In small bowl sprinkle gelatin over cold water; let stand several minutes to soften. Add boiling water; stir until gelatin dissolves completely and mixture is clear. In large mixer bowl beat cream cheese, granulated sugar and vanilla, blending well. Gradually add raspberry puree and gelatin, mixing thoroughly; pour into prepared crust. Refrigerate several hours or overnight; remove rim of pan. Spread raspberry preserves over top. Garnish with Chocolate Whipped Cream. Cover; refrigerate leftovers.

Chocolate Whipped Cream: In small mixer bowl stir together ½ cup powdered sugar and ¼ cup HERSHEY'S Cocoa. Add 1 cup chilled whipping cream and 1 teaspoon vanilla extract; beat until stiff.

Cranberry Nut Roll

Makes 10 to 12 servings

 4 eggs, separated
 ½ cup granulated sugar, divided
 1 cup cranberries, chopped
 ½ cup walnuts, finely chopped
 ⅓ cup sifted cake flour
 2 tablespoons cornstarch
 1 teaspoon cinnamon
 2 tablespoons (¼ stick) butter, melted
   Confectioners' sugar
   Premier White Whipped Cream
     (recipe follows)
   White Buttercream (recipe follows)

Preheat oven to 350°F. Grease 15½×10½×1-inch jelly-roll pan. Line with waxed paper; grease paper. In large mixer bowl, beat egg whites until foamy. Gradually add ¼ cup granulated sugar, beating until stiff peaks form; set aside.

In small mixer bowl, beat egg yolks and remaining ¼ cup granulated sugar until light and fluffy, about 3 minutes. Fold in cranberries, walnuts, flour, cornstarch and cinnamon; gently fold into egg white mixture. Fold in melted butter. Spread in prepared pan. Bake 20 minutes or until top springs back when lightly pressed. Loosen cake from sides of pan; cool 10 minutes. Sprinkle cloth towel with confectioners' sugar; invert cake onto towel. Peel off waxed paper. Starting at 10-inch side, roll up warm cake with towel inside. Cool cake completely, seam-side down, on wire rack.

Prepare Premier White Whipped Cream. Unroll cooled cake. Spread whipped cream mixture to within ½ inch of edges; roll up cake. Pipe or spread White Buttercream over cake. Store in refrigerator.

Premier White Whipped Cream

Makes about 2 cups whipped cream

 2 foil-wrapped bars (4 oz.) NESTLÉ®
   Premier White baking bars
 1 cup heavy or whipping cream, divided

Melt over hot (not boiling) water, Premier White baking bars with 2 tablespoons heavy cream, stirring until smooth. Stir in remaining cream; refrigerate until well chilled. In small mixer bowl, beat cream mixture *just* until soft peaks form. Use as cake filling, frosting or dessert topping.

Cranberry Nut Roll

White Buttercream

Makes about 3 cups frosting

 One 6-oz. pkg. (3 foil-wrapped bars)
   NESTLÉ® Premier White baking bars,
   broken up
 ¼ cup heavy or whipping cream
 1 cup (2 sticks) cold butter, cut into pieces
 1 cup confectioners' sugar

Melt over hot (not boiling) water, Premier White baking bars with heavy cream, stirring until smooth. Transfer to large mixer bowl; cool to room temperature.

Gradually beat in cold butter and confectioners' sugar; continue beating until light and fluffy. Buttercream may be made 1 to 2 days ahead of time and refrigerated; beat until light and fluffy before using.

Fudge Ribbon Cake

Makes one 10-inch cake

> 1 (18¼- or 18½-ounce) package chocolate cake mix
> 1 (8-ounce) package cream cheese, softened
> 2 tablespoons margarine or butter, softened
> 1 tablespoon cornstarch
> 1 (14-ounce) can EAGLE® Brand Sweetened Condensed Milk (NOT evaporated milk)
> 1 egg
> 1 teaspoon vanilla extract
> Confectioners' sugar or Chocolate Drizzle (recipe follows)

Preheat oven to 350°F. Prepare cake mix as package directs. Pour batter into *well-greased* and floured 10-inch fluted tube pan. In small mixer bowl, beat cheese, margarine and cornstarch until fluffy. Gradually beat in sweetened condensed milk, then egg and vanilla until smooth. Pour evenly over cake batter. Bake 50 to 55 minutes or until wooden pick inserted near center comes out clean. Cool 15 minutes; remove from pan. Cool. Sprinkle with confectioners' sugar or drizzle with Chocolate Drizzle.

Chocolate Drizzle: In small saucepan, over low heat, melt 1 (1-ounce) square unsweetened or semi-sweet chocolate and 1 tablespoon margarine or butter with 2 tablespoons water. Remove from heat. Stir in ¾ cup confectioners' sugar and ½ teaspoon vanilla extract. Stir until smooth and well blended. *Makes about ⅓ cup*

Fudge Ribbon Sheet Cake: Prepare cake mix as package directs. Pour batter into *well-greased* and floured 15×10-inch jellyroll pan. Prepare cream cheese topping as above; spoon evenly over batter. Bake 20 minutes or until wooden pick inserted near center comes out clean. Cool. Frost with 1 (16-ounce) can ready-to-spread chocolate frosting.

Fudge Ribbon Sheet Cake (left) and Fudge Ribbon Cake (right)

Cranberry-Apple Tart

Makes 9 servings

CRUST
  3 cups RALSTON® brand Fruit & Nut Muesli
     with Cranberries, crushed to 2 cups
  ¼ cup (½ stick) margarine or butter, melted
  ¼ cup packed brown sugar

FILLING
  2 cups cranberries, fresh or frozen
  ½ cup sugar
  ½ cup water
  1 tablespoon lemon juice
  1 can (20 oz.) apple pie filling
     Shredded cheese and mint leaves,
     optional

To prepare crust, preheat oven to 350°F. In
medium bowl combine cereal, margarine and
brown sugar. Press cereal mixture firmly into
9-inch fluted tart pan or 9-inch pie plate. Bake
7 to 8 minutes or until lightly browned. Cool
completely.

To prepare filling, in medium saucepan over
medium heat combine cranberries, sugar, water
and lemon juice. Cook, stirring frequently, until
mixture comes to a boil; reduce heat and simmer
15 to 18 minutes, stirring frequently. Remove from
heat and cool completely. Pour apple pie filling
into cooled crust; top with cooled cranberry
mixture. Garnish with cheese and mint if desired.

Chocolate Mousse

Makes four ½-cup servings

  1 teaspoon unflavored gelatin
  1 tablespoon cold water
  2 tablespoons boiling water
  ½ cup sugar
  ¼ cup HERSHEY'S Cocoa
  1 cup chilled whipping cream
  1 teaspoon vanilla extract

In small bowl sprinkle gelatin over cold water; let
stand 1 minute to soften. Add boiling water; stir
until gelatin is completely dissolved and mixture is
clear. Cool slightly. In small mixer bowl stir
together sugar and cocoa; add whipping cream
and vanilla. Beat at medium speed, scraping
bottom of bowl occasionally, until mixture is stiff;
pour in gelatin mixture and beat until well
blended. Spoon into serving dishes. Refrigerate
about 30 minutes.

Apple Pumpkin Dessert

Apple Pumpkin Desserts

Makes 8 to 10 servings

  1 (21-ounce) can COMSTOCK® Brand Apple
     Filling or Topping
  1 (16-ounce) can COMSTOCK® Brand
     Pumpkin (about 2 cups)
  1 (14-ounce) can EAGLE® Brand Sweetened
     Condensed Milk (NOT evaporated milk)
  2 eggs
  1 teaspoon ground cinnamon
  ½ teaspoon ground nutmeg
  ½ teaspoon salt
  1 cup gingersnap crumbs (about
     18 cookies)
  2 tablespoons margarine or butter, melted

Heat oven to 400°F. Spoon apple filling into 8 to
10 custard cups. In large mixer bowl, beat
pumpkin, sweetened condensed milk, eggs,
cinnamon, nutmeg and salt; spoon over apple
filling. Combine crumbs and margarine. Sprinkle
over pumpkin. Place cups on 15×10-inch baking
pan. Bake 10 minutes. *Reduce heat to 350°F;* bake
15 minutes or until set. Cool. Refrigerate leftovers.

Preparation time: 20 minutes

Total time: 1 hour

Triple Chocolate & Vanilla Cheesecake

Triple Chocolate & Vanilla Cheesecake

Makes one 9-inch cheesecake

1½ cups finely crushed creme-filled
    chocolate sandwich cookies (about
    18 cookies)
3 tablespoons margarine or butter, melted
4 (8-ounce) packages cream cheese,
    softened
1 (14-ounce) can EAGLE® Brand Sweetened
    Condensed Milk (NOT evaporated milk)
4 eggs
⅓ cup unsifted flour
1 tablespoon vanilla extract
2 (1-ounce) squares semi-sweet chocolate,
    melted
    Chocolate Glaze (recipe follows)

Preheat oven to 350°F. Combine crumbs and
margarine; press firmly on bottom of 9-inch
springform pan. In large mixer bowl, beat cheese
until fluffy. Gradually beat in sweetened
condensed milk until smooth. Add eggs, flour and
vanilla; mix well. Divide batter in half. Add
chocolate to one half of batter; mix well. Pour
into prepared pan. Top evenly with vanilla batter.
Bake 50 to 55 minutes or until center springs back
when lightly touched. Cool. Top with Chocolate
Glaze. Chill. Refrigerate leftovers.

Chocolate Glaze: In small saucepan, over low
heat, melt 2 (1-ounce) squares semi-sweet
chocolate with ¼ cup BORDEN® or MEADOW
GOLD® Whipping Cream. Cook and stir until
thickened and smooth. Remove from heat; spread
over cheesecake.   *Makes about ⅓ cup*

Christmas Tree Cake

Makes 16 to 20 servings

1 package DUNCAN HINES® Moist Deluxe
    Cake Mix (any flavor)
5 cups confectioners sugar
¾ cup CRISCO® Shortening
½ cup water
⅓ cup non-dairy creamer
2 teaspoons vanilla extract
½ teaspoon salt
1 tablespoon green food coloring
    Peppermint candies
    Pretzel rods
    Large gumdrops

1. Preheat oven to 350°F. Grease and flour
13×9×2-inch pan. Prepare, bake and cool cake
following package directions.

2. For decorator frosting, combine confectioners
sugar, shortening, water, non-dairy creamer, vanilla
extract and salt in large bowl. Beat at medium
speed with electric mixer for 3 minutes. Beat at
high speed for 5 minutes. Add more confectioners
sugar to thicken or more water to thin as needed.
Reserve 1 cup frosting. Tint remaining frosting
with green food coloring.

3. Cut cooled cake and arrange as shown. Spread
green frosting over cake. Decorate tree with
reserved white frosting and peppermint candies.
Make tree trunk of pretzel rods. Roll out large
gumdrops and cut with star cookie cutters. Top
tree with gumdrop star.

Tip: To make the garland, pipe frosting using a
pastry bag fitted with a star tip, or use red rope
licorice.

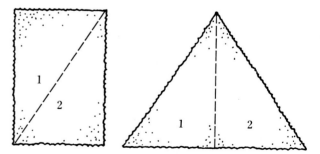

Christmas Tree Cake

Almond Pumpkin Pie

Almond Pumpkin Pie

Makes one 9-inch pie

- 1 (9-inch) unbaked pastry shell
- 1 (16-ounce) can pumpkin (2 cups)
- 1 (14-ounce) can EAGLE® Brand Sweetened Condensed Milk (NOT evaporated milk)
- 2 eggs
- 1 teaspoon almond extract
- 1/2 teaspoon ground cinnamon
- 1 (6-ounce) package almond brickle chips *or* 1 cup almonds, toasted and finely chopped

Preheat oven to 425°F. In large mixer bowl, combine all ingredients except pastry shell and brickle chips; mix well. Stir in *1/2 cup* brickle chips. Pour into pastry shell. Top with remaining brickle chips. Bake 15 minutes. *Reduce oven temperature to 350°F;* bake 30 minutes longer or until knife inserted near center comes out clean. Cool. Garnish as desired. Refrigerate leftovers.

Dessert Gingerbread

Makes one 8-inch square cake

- 1 1/2 cups sifted all-purpose flour
- 1 teaspoon ARM & HAMMER® Pure Baking Soda
- 1 teaspoon ground ginger
- 1/4 teaspoon salt
- 1/3 cup vegetable shortening
- 1/2 cup sugar
- 1 egg
- 1/2 cup light molasses
- 3/4 cup boiling water

Sift together flour, baking soda, ginger and salt. Using an electric mixer, cream shortening until light and fluffy in large bowl. Add sugar gradually, beating after each addition. Beat in egg thoroughly; blend in molasses.

Gradually stir dry ingredients into creamed mixture. Beat thoroughly. Stir in water. Turn into greased and floured 8-inch square baking pan. Bake in 350°F oven 40 minutes or until toothpick inserted in center of cake comes out clean. Cool in pan 10 minutes; remove from pan and cool on rack.

Creamy Eggnog Dessert

Makes 12 to 16 servings

CRUST
- 1 package DUNCAN HINES® Moist Deluxe Swiss Chocolate Cake Mix
- 1/2 cup butter or margarine, melted
- 1/2 cup chopped pecans

FILLING
- 1 package (8 ounces) cream cheese, softened
- 1 cup sugar
- 1 container (12 ounces) frozen whipped topping, thawed and divided
- 2 packages (4-serving size *each*) French vanilla instant pudding and pie filling mix
- 3 cups cold milk
- 1/4 teaspoon rum extract
- 1/4 teaspoon ground nutmeg

1. Preheat oven to 350°F.

2. **For crust,** combine cake mix, butter and pecans. Reserve 1/2 cup mixture. Press remaining mixture into bottom of 13×9×2-inch pan. Bake at 350°F for 15 to 20 minutes or until surface is firm. Cool. Toast reserved 1/2 cup mixture on cookie sheet at 350°F for 3 to 4 minutes, stirring once. Cool completely. Break lumps with fork to make small crumbs.

3. **For filling,** beat cream cheese and sugar until smooth in large bowl. Stir in 1 cup whipped topping. Spread over cooled crust. Refrigerate. Combine pudding mix and milk; beat 1 minute. Add rum extract and nutmeg. Spread over cheese layer. Spread remaining whipped topping over pudding layer. Sprinkle with reserved toasted mixture. Refrigerate at least 2 hours.

Premier White Fruit Tart

Makes 6 to 8 servings

> **Pastry for one 9-inch pie shell**
> ¼ **cup apricot jam, melted**
> ⅓ **cup sugar**
> ⅓ **cup all-purpose flour**
> 1 **cup milk**
> 3 **egg yolks**
> One 6-oz. pkg. (3 foil-wrapped bars)
> **NESTLÉ® Premier White baking bars,**
> **broken up**
> 1 **teaspoon vanilla extract**
> 2 **kiwifruit, peeled and sliced**
> **Premier White Leaves (recipe follows),**
> **optional**
> 1 **cup raspberries**

Preheat oven to 425°F. On lightly floured board, roll pastry into 11-inch circle. Line 9-inch removable bottom tart pan with pastry; trim edges. With fork, prick pastry in several places. Bake 10 to 12 minutes until crust is lightly browned. Cool. Brush tart shell with apricot jam; set aside.

In medium saucepan, combine sugar and flour; gradually whisk in milk and egg yolks. *Bring to a boil* over medium heat, whisking constantly. Reduce heat; cook, *whisking constantly*, for 3 minutes or until thickened and smooth. Remove from heat; stir in Premier White baking bars and vanilla extract until smooth. Pour into tart shell; press plastic wrap directly on surface. Refrigerate until chilled, about 30 minutes.

Remove tart from pan. Arrange kiwifruit slices in slightly overlapping circle around edge of tart. Arrange Premier White Leaves and raspberries in center. Store in refrigerator.

Premier White Leaves

Makes about 6 large leaves

Wash and *dry very well* about 6 non-toxic leaves, such as lemon leaves, grape leaves, rose leaves, violet leaves or nasturtium leaves;* set aside.

Melt 4 ounces NESTLÉ® Premier White baking bars or NESTLÉ® Toll House® Treasures® Premier White deluxe baking pieces.

Onto the back side of each leaf, spoon or brush melted Premier White mixture about ¹⁄₁₆ inch thick. If Premier White mixture runs over edge of leaf, wipe off edge of leaf with fingertip. Place coated leaves on plate or cookie sheet; refrigerate about 30 minutes or until firm.

Gently peel leaf from firm Premier White mixture.

Arrange leaves on dessert.

These non-toxic leaves are available in florist shops.

Premier White Fruit Tart

Chocolate Mini Cheesecake (top) and Mini Cheesecake (bottom)

Mini Cheesecakes

Makes about 2 dozen

1½ cups graham cracker or chocolate wafer
    crumbs
¼ cup sugar
¼ cup margarine or butter, melted
3 (8-ounce) packages cream cheese,
    softened
1 (14-ounce) can EAGLE® Brand Sweetened
    Condensed Milk (NOT evaporated milk)
3 eggs
2 teaspoons vanilla extract

Preheat oven to 300°F. Combine crumbs, sugar
and margarine; press equal portions onto bottoms
of 24 lightly greased* or paper-lined muffin cups.
In large mixer bowl, beat cheese until fluffy.
Gradually beat in sweetened condensed milk until
smooth. Add eggs and vanilla; mix well. Spoon
equal amounts of mixture (about 3 tablespoons)
into prepared cups. Bake 20 minutes or until cakes
spring back when lightly touched. Cool. Chill.
Garnish as desired. Refrigerate leftovers.

Chocolate Mini Cheesecakes: Add 1 (6-ounce)
package semi-sweet chocolate chips (1 cup),
melted, to batter; mix well. Proceed as above.
Bake 20 to 25 minutes.

**If greased muffin cups are used, cool baked
cheesecakes. Freeze 15 minutes; remove from
pans. Proceed as above.*

Kahlúa® Marbled Pumpkin Cheesecake

Makes about 12 servings

¾ cup gingersnap crumbs
¾ cup graham cracker crumbs
¼ cup powdered sugar
¼ cup (4 tablespoons) melted unsalted
    butter
2 (8-ounce) packages cream cheese,
    softened
1 cup granulated sugar
4 eggs
1 (1-pound) can pumpkin
½ teaspoon ground cinnamon
¼ teaspoon ground ginger
¼ teaspoon ground nutmeg
½ cup KAHLÚA®

In bowl, combine gingersnap and graham cracker
crumbs with powdered sugar and butter. Toss to
combine. Press evenly onto bottom of 8-inch
springform pan. Bake at 350°F 5 minutes. Cool.

In mixer bowl, beat cream cheese until smooth.
Gradually add granulated sugar and beat until
light. Add eggs, one at a time, beating well after
each addition. Transfer 1 cup mixture to separate
bowl and blend in pumpkin, cinnamon, ginger,
nutmeg and KAHLÚA®. Pour half of pumpkin
mixture into prepared crust. Top with half of
cream cheese mixture. Repeat layers using
remaining pumpkin and cream cheese mixtures.
Using table knife, cut through layers with uplifting
motion in four to five places to create marbled
effect. Place on baking sheet and bake at 350°F
for 45 minutes. Without opening oven door, let
cake stand in turned-off oven 1 hour. Remove
from oven and cool, then chill. Remove from pan.

Kahlúa® Marbled Pumpkin Cheesecake

Top to bottom: Viennese Poppy Cake (page 90) and Cherry Cream Nut Roll

Cherry Cream Nut Roll

Makes 8 to 10 servings

- 5 eggs, separated
- 1/2 cup granulated sugar
- 1 teaspoon brandy extract or rum extract
- 1 can SOLO® *or* 1 jar BAKER® Nut Filling
- 1/2 cup all-purpose flour
- 1/2 teaspoon baking powder
- 1/4 teaspoon salt
  Confectioners sugar

FILLING:

- 2 cups heavy cream
- 3 to 4 tablespoons confectioners sugar
- 1 1/2 teaspoons brandy extract or rum extract
- 1 can SOLO® *or* 1 jar BAKER® Cherry Filling

Preheat oven to 350°F. Grease 15×10-inch jelly-roll pan. Line pan with waxed paper. Grease paper and set aside.

Beat egg yolks and granulated sugar about 5 minutes in large bowl with electric mixer until thick and pale yellow. Beat in brandy extract and nut filling until well blended.

Beat egg whites in separate bowl with electric mixer until stiff peaks form. Stir 3 heaping tablespoons egg whites into nut mixture to lighten. Fold in remaining egg whites. Sift flour, baking powder and salt over nut mixture and fold in. Spread batter evenly in prepared pan.

Bake 20 to 22 minutes or until center springs back when lightly pressed.

Sprinkle towel with confectioners sugar. Invert cake onto sugared towel and remove pan. Peel off lining paper and trim off any crusty edges. Roll up cake and towel, jelly-roll style, starting from short side. Place on wire rack and cool completely.

To fill cake, unroll cooled cake on flat surface. Whip cream in large bowl with electric mixer until soft peaks form. Add confectioners sugar and brandy extract and whip until firm. Fold whipped cream into cherry filling. Spread half of cherry cream over cake. Reroll cake without towel and place, seam-side down, on serving plate. Spread remaining cherry cream over side and top of cake. Refrigerate until ready to serve.

Two Great Tastes Pudding Parfaits

Makes about 4 to 6 servings

    1 package (4³/₄ ounces) vanilla pudding and
        pie filling
  3¹/₂ cups milk
    1 cup REESE'S Peanut Butter Chips
    1 cup HERSHEY'S Semi-Sweet Chocolate
        Chips
        Whipped topping (optional)

In large, heavy saucepan combine pudding mix and 3¹/₂ cups milk (rather than amount listed in package directions). Cook over medium heat, stirring constantly, until mixture comes to full boil. Remove from heat; divide hot mixture between 2 heatproof medium bowls. Immediately stir peanut butter chips into mixture in one bowl and chocolate chips into mixture in second bowl. Stir both mixtures until melted and smooth. Cool slightly, stirring occasionally. Alternately spoon peanut butter and chocolate mixtures into parfait glasses, champagne glasses or dessert dishes. Place plastic wrap directly onto surface of each dessert; refrigerate several hours or overnight. Top with whipped topping and garnish as desired.

Two Great Tastes Pudding Parfaits

Viennese Poppy Cake

Makes 10 to 12 servings

   ³/₄ cup cake flour
   ¹/₂ teaspoon baking powder
   ¹/₂ teaspoon salt
   ¹/₂ cup raisins, finely chopped
   ¹/₂ cup butter or margarine, softened
   ³/₄ cup granulated sugar, divided
    6 eggs, separated
    1 can SOLO® *or* 1 jar BAKER® Poppy Filling
   ¹/₄ cup dark rum

CHOCOLATE GLAZE:
    2 squares (2 ounces) unsweetened
        chocolate, chopped
    2 tablespoons unsalted butter
    1 tablespoon light corn syrup
    2 tablespoons dark rum
    1 tablespoon warm water
    1 cup confectioners sugar

Preheat oven to 350°F. Grease 9-inch springform pan and line bottom of pan with parchment paper or waxed paper. Grease paper and set aside.

Sift flour, baking powder and salt into small bowl. Add raisins and toss to coat. Set aside.

Beat butter and ¹/₂ cup granulated sugar in large bowl with electric mixer until light and fluffy. Add egg yolks, 2 at a time, beating well after each addition. Add poppy filling and rum and beat until blended. Fold in flour-raisin mixture.

Beat egg whites in separate bowl with electric mixer until soft peaks form. Add remaining ¹/₄ cup granulated sugar gradually and beat until stiff peaks form. Stir one-third of beaten egg whites into poppy seed mixture to lighten. Fold in remaining egg whites. Spread batter evenly in prepared pan.

Bake 40 to 45 minutes or until wooden pick inserted in center comes out clean. Cool in pan on wire rack 10 minutes. Remove from pan; peel off lining paper and cool completely on rack.

To make glaze, melt chocolate, butter and corn syrup in small saucepan over low heat, stirring constantly until smooth. Cook 1 minute and remove from heat. Add rum, water and confectioners sugar. Beat vigorously until glaze is smooth and glossy. Line edge of serving plate with strips of waxed paper. Place cake on serving plate and pour glaze over. Spread evenly over top and around side of cake. Remove waxed paper carefully and let stand until glaze is set.

Note: Flavor of cake will be enhanced if cake is wrapped and set aside overnight before it is glazed.

Glazed Cranberry Mini-Cakes

Glazed Cranberry Mini-Cakes

Makes about 3 dozen mini-cakes

- ¼ cup butter or margarine, softened
- ¼ cup packed light brown sugar
- ¼ cup granulated sugar
- 1 egg
- 1 teaspoon vanilla extract
- 1 cup all-purpose flour
- ½ teaspoon baking powder
- ¼ teaspoon baking soda
- ¼ teaspoon salt
- 1 cup coarsely chopped fresh cranberries
- ½ cup coarsely chopped walnuts
- ⅓ cup HERSHEY'S Vanilla Milk Chips
  Vanilla Glaze (recipe follows)
  Additional cranberries (optional)

Heat oven to 350°F. Lightly grease or paper-line 36 small muffin cups (1¾ inches in diameter). In small mixer bowl beat butter, brown sugar, granulated sugar, egg and vanilla extract until light and fluffy. Stir together flour, baking powder, baking soda and salt; gradually blend into butter mixture. Stir in cranberries, walnuts and vanilla milk chips. Fill muffin cups ¾ full with batter. Bake 12 to 14 minutes or until wooden pick inserted in center comes out clean. Cool in pans on wire rack 5 minutes; invert onto rack. Cool completely. Prepare Vanilla Glaze; dip rounded portion of each muffin into glaze (or spread glaze over tops). Place on wax-paper-covered tray; refrigerate 10 minutes to set glaze. Garnish with additional cranberries, if desired.

Vanilla Glaze: In small microwave-safe bowl stir together 1 cup HERSHEY'S Vanilla Milk Chips and 2 tablespoons vegetable oil. Microwave at HIGH (100%) 30 seconds; stir until smooth. If necessary, microwave at HIGH additional 30 seconds or just until chips are melted and smooth when stirred.

Acknowledgments

The publishers would like to thank the companies and organizations listed below for the use of their recipes in this book.

Alaska Seafood Marketing Institute
Arm & Hammer Division, Church & Dwight Co., Inc.
Borden, Inc.
California Apricot Advisory Board
Campbell Soup Company
Carnation Company
Clear Springs Idaho Rainbow Trout
Curtice Burns, Inc.
Del Monte Corporation
Dole Food Company
Florida Department of Citrus
Heinz U.S.A.
Hellmann's Mayonnaise
Hershey Chocolate U.S.A.
The HVR Company
Karo Corn Syrup
Kellogg Company
Kraft General Foods, Inc.
Libby's Pumpkin, Division of Carnation Company

Maidstone Wine & Spirits, Inc. (Kahlúa)
McIlhenny Company
National Live Stock and Meat Board
National Pecan Marketing Council
National Pork Producers Council
National Sunflower Association
National Turkey Federation
Nestlé Chocolate and Confection Company
Ocean Spray Cranberries, Inc.
Pace Foods, Inc.
The Procter & Gamble Company, Inc.
Ralston Purina Company
Roman Meal Hot Cereals
Sargento Cheese Company, Inc.
Sokol and Company
Thomas J. Lipton, Co.
U.S.A. Rice Council
Western New York Apple Growers Association, Inc.
Wisconsin Milk Marketing Board

Photo Credits

The publishers would like to thank the companies and organizations listed below for the use of their photographs in this book.

Borden, Inc.
Campbell Soup Company
Heinz U.S.A.
Hellmann's Mayonnaise
Hershey Chocolate U.S.A.
The HVR Company
Karo Corn Syrup
Kellogg Company
Kraft General Foods, Inc.
Libby's Pumpkin, Division of Carnation Company

Maidstone Wine & Spirits, Inc. (Kahlúa)
National Live Stock and Meat Board
National Pecan Marketing Council
National Turkey Federation
Nestlé Chocolate and Confection Company
The Procter & Gamble Company, Inc.
Sargento Cheese Company, Inc.
Sokol and Company
Thomas J. Lipton, Co.
Wisconsin Milk Marketing Board

Index